LEARNING FROM SIX PHIL

Jonathan Bennett engages with the thought of six great thi[nkers] [of the early m]odern period: Descartes, Spinoza, Leibniz, Locke, Berkeley, Hume. Wh... not neglecting the historical setting of each, his chief focus is on the words they wrote. What problem is being tackled? How exactly is the solution meant to work? Does it succeed? If not, why not? What can we learn from its success or its failure? These questions reflect Bennett's dedication to engaging with philosophy as philosophy, not as museum exhibit, and they require a close and demanding attention to textual details; these being two features that characterize all Bennett's work on early modern philosophy.

For newcomers to the early modern scene, this clearly written work is an excellent introduction to it. Those already in the know can learn how to argue with the great philosophers of the past, treating them as colleagues, antagonists, students, teachers.

In this volume Jonathan Bennett examines the views of Locke, Berkeley, and Hume on thought and sensation, meaning, language, classification, innate ideas and knowledge, our knowledge of necessary truths (bringing in Descartes and Leibniz as well), the basis for our belief that we live in a world of material things, causation, the fundamental difference between colours and shapes, the passage of time and our ability to live through it. While finding much to criticize, Bennett shows that we can learn much about these and other topics under the guidance and inspiration of the energy, courage, and insight of the three great British philosophers.

Learning from Six Philosophers

Descartes, Spinoza, Leibniz, Locke, Berkeley, Hume

JONATHAN BENNETT

VOLUME 2

CLARENDON PRESS · OXFORD

*This book has been printed digitally and produced in a standard specification
in order to ensure its continuing availability*

OXFORD
UNIVERSITY PRESS

Great Clarendon Street, Oxford OX2 6DP

Oxford University Press is a department of the University of Oxford.
It furthers the University's objective of excellence in research, scholarship,
and education by publishing worldwide in

Oxford New York

Auckland Cape Town Dar es Salaam Hong Kong Karachi
Kuala Lumpur Madrid Melbourne Mexico City Nairobi
New Delhi Shanghai Taipei Toronto
With offices in
Argentina Austria Brazil Chile Czech Republic France Greece
Guatemala Hungary Italy Japan South Korea Poland Portugal
Singapore Switzerland Thailand Turkey Ukraine Vietnam

Oxford is a registered trade mark of Oxford University Press
in the UK and in certain other countries

Published in the United States
by Oxford University Press Inc., New York

© Jonathan Bennett 2001

The moral rights of the author have been asserted

Database right Oxford University Press (maker)

Reprinted 2007

ISBN 978-0-19-926629-6

Preface to Volume 2

This second half of my two-volume work is mainly concerned with themes in the philosophies of Locke, Berkeley, and Hume, though Leibniz will appear as a commentator on Locke and (in Chapters 23 and 40) in other ways as well. Chapter 24 expounds a theory of Descartes's which I prefer to treat only after presenting related work by Locke and Leibniz.

Fifteen of the chapters in this volume (the exceptions being 23, 24, and 38–40) overlap my *Locke, Berkeley, Hume: Central Themes* (1971) in the topics covered and, to a considerable extent, in what I have to say about them. Except in Chapter 37, however, hardly a sentence has been carried over intact from the earlier book, and what I now offer reflects the intervening three decades of further reading and reflection and of growth as a philosopher.

I respond to some criticisms of my earlier work, where it seems profitable to do so. But my main concern is to present what I now have to say in as clear and uncluttered a manner as possible.

Each volume contains the Contents and Abbreviations for the entire work. The Bibliography and Indexes have been divided, with each volume containing only what is relevant to it. Each Index of Topics includes references to the 'six philosophers'; all other personal references are in the Index of Persons.

A comprehensive treatment of my six philosophers, even on the topics within their work which I discuss, could not be achieved by one person or presented in a mere forty chapters. I have chosen topics which I find interesting and nourishing to wrestle with. A reader who stays with me will at the end have some sense of the overall shape of each of the six, though providing this has not been my chief aim.

The title *Learning from Six Philosophers* declares my attitude in this work: I want to learn from these men, which I do by arguing with them. I explain and defend this approach in the Introduction to Volume 1.

This work arises out of teaching across forty years at several universities— Cambridge, Cornell, Michigan, Princeton, British Columbia, Syracuse. My intellectual debts to colleagues and students at those institutions are too numerous, and not clearly enough remembered, for me to acknowledge them in detail; but I place on record my gratitude for the doctoral programme at Syracuse University, and for my eighteen happy years of contact with its students and faculty.

I was also helped by sabbatical leaves in which I was supported by Syracuse University and (in two) by the National Endowment for the Humanities and (in a third) by the John Simon Guggenheim Foundation. To all three organizations I am grateful.

At a late stage in its life, the entire manuscript was read for the Oxford University Press by Don Garrett, who provided several dozen comments and suggestions for its improvement. I have availed myself of many of these, and thank Garrett for the generosity and thoughtfulness of his help.

Readers who have comments, suggestions, or corrections to offer are invited to send them to me at jfb@mail.com.

J.F.B.

Bowen Island, BC
May 2000

Contents

VOLUME 2

Abbreviations and Other Conventions used in Text and Bibliography

The symbol '§' refers only to sections of this book. Unadorned occurrences of the form '§n' mean '[Some aspect of] this was discussed in §n above' or '. . . will be more fully discussed in §n below'.

An asterisk after a reference to a translation means that the translation contains a significant error which I have corrected in quoting.

All references are by page number unless otherwise indicated here.

In quotations from Descartes, material in ⟨angle brackets⟩ is not in the original, and comes from a later translation which Descartes is thought to have approved.

Individual works by the 'six philosophers' that are listed here are characterized more fully in the Bibliography.

A	German Academy of Science, ed., *Gottfried Wilhelm Leibniz: Sämtliche Schriften und Briefe* (Darmstadt and Berlin: Akademie Verlag, 1926–); reference by series, volume, and page.
Abstract	Abstract of Hume's *Treatise of Human Nature*; reference by paragraph.
AG	R. Ariew and D. Garber (eds.), *G. W. Leibniz: Philosophical Essays* (Indianapolis: Hackett, 1989).
Alexander	*The Leibniz–Clarke Correspondence*, ed. H. G. Alexander (Manchester University Press, 1956).
AT	C. Adam and P. Tannery (eds.), *Œuvres de Descartes*, nouvelle présentation (Paris: Vrin, 1964–76); reference by volume and page.
Comments	Leibniz, Comments on Spinoza's Philosophy (1707).
Couturat	Louis Couturat (ed.), *Opuscules et fragments inédits de Leibniz* (Hildesheim: Olms, 1988).
Critique	Immanuel Kant, *Critique of Pure Reason* (1781); reference by A and B numbers given in the margin of the Kemp Smith (Macmillan) edition.
CS	E. Curley (ed.), *The Collected Works of Spinoza*, vol. 1 (Princeton University Press, 1985).
CSM	J. Cottingham, R. Stoothoff, and D. Murdoch (eds.), *The Philosophical Writings of Descartes*, vols. 1 and 2 (Cambridge University Press, 1984–5); reference by volume and page.
CSMK	J. Cottingham, R. Stoothoff, D. Murdoch, and A. Kenny (eds.), *The Philosophical Writings of Descartes*, vol. 3 (Cambridge University Press, 1991).

CT	Leibniz, Critical Thoughts on the General Part of the *Principles* of Descartes (1692).
Dia 1	The first of Berkeley's *Three Dialogues between Hylas and Philonous* (1713); similarly 'Dia 2' and 'Dia 3'; reference by page in LJ 3.
DM	Leibniz, *Discourse on Metaphysics* (1686a); reference by section.
DP	Spinoza, *Parts I and II of Descartes's 'Principles of Philosophy'* (1663).
Enquiry	Hume, *Enquiry Concerning the Human Understanding* (1748); reference by section and part, and by marginal number in the Selby-Bigge (OUP) edition.
Essay	Locke, *An Essay Concerning Human Understanding* (1690); reference by book, chapter, section, or by page and line in the Nidditch (OUP) edition.
Ethics	Spinoza, *Ethics Demonstrated in Geometrical Order* (1675?); reference by part and axiom (a), definition (d), proposition (p), corollary (c), demonstration (d), and scholium (s) (thus 1d4 is the fourth definition in part 1, and '2p13,d' refers to part 2's 13th proposition *and* its demonstration), or by page in *CS*.
F. de C.	Foucher de Careil (ed.), *Nouvelles lettres et opuscules inédits de Leibniz* (Paris, 1857).
FW	G. W. Leibniz, *Philosophical Texts*, trans. and ed. R. S. Woolhouse and R. Francks (Oxford University Press, 1998).
G	C. I. Gerhardt (ed.), *Die philosophischen Schriften von Gottfried Wilhelm Leibniz* (Berlin, 1875–90); reference by volume and page.
GH	R. Gennaro and C. Huenemann (eds.), *New Essays on the Rationalists* (Oxford University Press, 1999).
GM	C. I. Gerhardt (ed.), *Leibnizens mathematische Schriften* (Berlin, 1875–90); reference by volume and page.
Grua	G. W. Leibniz, *Textes inédits*, ed. Gaston Grua (New York: Garland, 1985).
LBH	Jonathan Bennett, *Locke, Berkeley, Hume: Central Themes* (Oxford University Press, 1971).
L	Gottfried Wilhelm Leibniz, *Philosophical Papers and Letters*, ed. L. E. Loemker (Dordrecht: Reidel, 1969).
LJ	A. A. Luce and T. E. Jessop (eds.), *The Works of George Berkeley* (London: Nelson, 1949); reference by volume and page.
Mason	H. T. Mason (ed.), *The Leibniz–Arnauld Correspondence* (Manchester University Press, 1967).
Med 1	The first of Descartes's *Meditations on First Philosophy* (1641); similarly 'Med 2', etc.
Method	Descartes, *Discourse on the Method of Rightly Conducting One's Reason and Seeking the Truth in the Sciences* (1637a).
MM	Descartes, *Principles of Philosophy*, ed. V. R. Miller and R. P. Miller (Dordrecht: Reidel, 1983).
Mon	Leibniz, 'Monadology' (1714a); reference by section.

NE	G. W. Leibniz, *New Essays on Human Understanding* (1705); reference by book, chapter, section, or by page in the Remnant–Bennett edition (which has the same pagination as the French text in A 6:6).
NI	Leibniz, 'On Nature Itself' (1698); reference by section.
NS	Leibniz, 'New System of Nature' (1695).
NT	Berkeley, *An Essay Towards a New Theory of Vision*, reference by section.
Obj 1	The first set of Objections to Descartes's Meditations; similarly 'Obj 2', etc.
OED	*Oxford English Dictionary*.
PAB	Leibniz, 'A Physicist against Barbarism' (1716).
Passions	Descartes, *Passions of the Soul* (1649); reference by section.
PC	Berkeley, *Philosophical Commentaries* (1708); reference by number of entry.
PHK	Berkeley, *A Treatise Concerning the Principles of Human Knowledge* (1710); reference by section.
PHKI	Ibid., introduction; reference by section.
PM	G. W. Leibniz, *Philosophical Writings*, ed. M. Morris and G. H. R. Parkinson (London: Dent, 1973).
PNG	Leibniz, 'Principles of Nature and of Grace' (1714).
PP	Descartes, *Principles of Philosophy* (1644); reference by part and section.
PT	Leibniz, 'Primary Truths' (1686).
Rep 1	The first set of Descartes's Replies to Objections to the Meditations; similarly 'Rep 2', etc.
Rules	Descartes, *Rules for the Direction of the Mind* (1628).
SD	Leibniz, 'Specimen of Dynamics' (1695b).
Study	Jonathan Bennett, *A Study of Spinoza's Ethics* (Indianapolis: Hackett, 1984).
Treatise	Hume, *A Treatise of Human Nature* (1739); reference by part and section (always of book I except where otherwise noted), and by pages in the Selby-Bigge (OUP) edition.
UO	Leibniz, 'On the Ultimate Origin of Things' (1697b).
W	Descartes, *The World* (1633).
Wolf	A. Wolf (ed.), *The Correspondence of Spinoza* (London: Allen & Unwin, 1928).

Chapter 21

Lockean Ideas, Overview and Foundations

154. Locke's explanation of the term 'idea'

About two-thirds of the sections of Locke's *Essay* contain the word 'idea'. Apologizing for his frequent use of this word, he explains it in two ways, both indirect. In one he equates it with certain technical terms—'phantasm', 'notion', and 'species'—from late medieval philosophy. Set this aside for now (§156). Before that he introduces 'idea' in a relative or functional way, saying that it stands for items that have a certain role in our lives—namely, 'whatsoever is the object of the understanding when a man thinks . . . or whatever it is which the mind can be employed about in thinking' (I.i.8). This is like an early geneticist's explaining 'gene' as standing for whatever it is that controls heredity in accordance with Mendelian laws. For several decades geneticists believed in genes, but knew nothing of their intrinsic nature. Locke's repeated use of 'what[so]ever' sounds like that. He thought that each individual idea has an intrinsic nature which is very well known to its owner, but he did not think he could capture this nature in public language which would help to explain what ideas are and how they do whatever they do. Hence the functional definition.

Like Descartes with *cogitare* and *penser*, Locke uses 'think' to cover the entire range of mental events, sensory as well as intellectual. Despite the use of 'think' in his definition, he views ideas as first and foremost items belonging on the sensory side of our nature. We can best understand the roles he gives to 'ideas' by starting with ideas as something like sense-data or sensory qualia. The sensory use of 'idea' is ubiquitous throughout the *Essay*—see, for example, II.ix, where Locke describes sense perception as the receiving of 'ideas' from objects in one's environment. Locke makes room for ideas not only of 'sensation', but also of 'reflection': these are the ideas the mind acquires 'when it turns its view inward upon itself, and observes its own actions about those ideas it has' (II.vi.1). These pose some tricky problems of philosophy and of exegesis; throughout most of my discussions of Locke I shall silently set them aside.

The 'object' of a thought or perception might seem to be the item that is thought about or perceived. That is indeed how Locke sees sense perception. If you see a tree, for example, you do so by immediately perceiving a tree-betokening idea: 'Whatsoever the mind perceives in itself, or is the immediate object of perception, thought or understanding, that I call idea' (II.viii.8). Notice the word 'immediate': in sense perception we immediately perceive our own ideas, and through them—mediately or indirectly—we perceive outer things. (Sometimes Locke writes as though ideas were themselves perceptions. This reflects a wavering in his use not of 'idea' but rather of 'perception', as Chappell points out (1994: 33). There is no need to linger on it.)

However, when Locke's topic is thinking as you and I understand it—namely, as an intellectual activity—he does not take ideas to be 'objects of thought' in the sense of what the thought is about. In using the phrase 'object of', as also in writing that ideas are what a mind 'employed about when thinking' or 'applied about whilst thinking', he means only that ideas are involved in all our thought—we think *with* them. For confirmation, see *OED*, 'employ', sense 4.

For Locke, I have said, ideas have sensory as well as intellectual roles; the latter are many and various; he makes the word 'idea' sprawl across a lot of disparate territory. If this were mere sloppiness in word usage—a set of careless, unrecognized ambiguities—we could tag the different meanings with subscripts, cleaning up his verbal act for him, and then move comfortably on. In fact, things stand otherwise. Locke's various ways of using 'idea' are connected in his thought, usually by a philosophical belief or assumption, though in one case by something else. To sort them out, we must explore those connections—the philosophical underlay of his uses of 'idea'. This is harder and more worthwhile than merely tagging ambiguities.

155. The roles played by Lockean Ideas

I shall now sketch five chief uses to which Locke puts the term 'idea', the first being a closely linked pair. So we can have a six-letter acronym: PITMAC, for (1) perceiving and imagining, (2) thinking, (3) meaning, (4) a priori knowledge, and (5) classifying.

We have just glanced at the role of ideas in sense perception, which we can link with their involvement in imagining. So:

   (1) When I see something circular, or when I imagine something circular, I
       have a circle-type idea.

Ideas in this role are sense-data—what we are immediately given in sense perception, the sheer, raw sense-contents which confront our minds in seeing, feeling, etc. and also in imagining and dreaming. I am not endorsing any of this—merely pointing to one role that Locke gives to his term 'idea'.

He also uses 'idea' to stand for concepts—understanding these as personal possessions, not as eternal abstract objects. To be able to think about horses, one needs an idea of *horse*. Thus:

   (2) In thinking about circles—as when I wonder whether there are any circu-
       lar objects on Mars—I make use of my idea of *circle*.

What links 1 with 2 is Locke's concept-empiricism, according to which all the materials of our thinking are derived from sensory experience. As he says, 'Perception [is] the first step and degree towards knowledge, and the inlet of all the materials of it' (II.ix.15). The 'materials' of knowledge are not only the propositions that are known, but also the concepts out of which they are built.

Almost all writers on Locke have attributed this view to him:

> (3) When I understand or meaningfully use the word 'circle', I give it meaning by associating it with my idea of *circle*.[1]

He gets from 2 to 3 by assuming, plausibly, that what you mean by an expression depends on what thought or concept you take it to convey. That also takes him from concept-empiricism to meaning-empiricism, as here:

He that has not before received into his mind by the proper inlet the simple idea which any word stands for can never come to know the signification of that word by any other words or sounds whatsoever, put together according to any rules of definition. The only way is by applying to his senses the proper object, and so producing that idea in him, for which he has learned the name already. (III.iv.11)

Notice the word 'simple'. Locke holds that ideas (= meanings) which are *complex* can be explained and learned through verbal definitions which exhibit the complexity; but that the ultimate elements of those complexes are *simple* ideas. Because these have no structure, Locke holds, they cannot be explained or learned verbally, and so must be acquired through the outer senses ('sensation') or from introspection, inner sense ('reflection').

Locke holds that our 'ideas' are also the basis for our a priori knowledge: we acquire the latter by attending to relations among concepts (as we might say); but for him concepts are 'ideas', which even in this role are items that come before the mind in an immediate way. Leibniz sometimes held that we discover truths about what is necessary or impossible by finding them inscribed on our minds by God: to know them we have only to look in and find them written there (§176). Locke also thought that to discover such truths you have to look inwards—but not to find ready-made truths in your mind; rather, to find certain data upon which a priori knowledge can be based (§173). In this intricate story, all that matters now is this:

> (4) I learn that all circles are closed plane figures by inspecting my idea of *circle*.

Fifthly, Locke has a theory about how ideas enable us to classify things, recognizing them as belonging to kinds or—via the 2–3 link—as falling under this or that general term.

---

[1] Hacking (1975: ch. 5) is an exception, though he does not defend his denial against the textual evidence that has convinced the rest of us. Locke's name for meaning is 'common acceptation', he contends, quoting from the only sentence in the *Essay* containing that phrase (III.ii.4). In what Hacking quotes—and even more in what he omits—Locke openly equates sameness of 'acceptation' with sameness of idea.

(5) When I classify something as circular, or when I judge that 'circular' applies to a thing, I do this by seeing how it compares with my idea of circle.

Here is Locke's statement of this theory:

Ideas taken from particular beings become general representatives of all of the same kind, and their names general names, applicable to whatever exists conformable to such . . . ideas. Such precise naked appearances in the mind, without considering how, whence, or with what others they came there, the understanding lays up (with names commonly annexed to them) as the standards to rank real existences into sorts, as they agree with these patterns, and to denominate them accordingly. (II.xi.9; see also III.iii.12)

In many places Locke seems to reject real universals, implying that so-called sameness of kind is purely an upshot of our classificatory activities. 'All things that exist are only particulars' (III.iii.6), he writes, and then: 'What are the essences of those species, set out and marked by names, but those . . . ideas in the mind, which are as it were the bonds between particular things that exist and the names they are to be ranked under?' (III.iii.13). This may not be his message in the passage displayed above, however, for he writes there that an idea taken from a particular can represent 'all of the same kind', apparently assuming that things *do* fall into kinds independently of how we classify them (§202).

If this theory of Locke's purports to provide *an all-purpose technique for ranking things into kinds*, it cannot succeed. There cannot be such a thing, because you cannot implement any technique unless you can already do some classification. Example: to implement Locke's technique, you must already be able to classify your ideas.

This point—which I expound more fully in *LBH* 11–20—is memorably dramatized by Wittgenstein (1958: 3, 12). You might think that in order to obey the order 'Fetch me a red patch', you must first imagine something red and then look for an object that matches the image; but, Wittgenstein continues: 'Consider the order "*imagine* a red patch". You are not tempted in this case to think that *before* obeying you must have imagined a red patch to serve you as a pattern for the red patch you were ordered to imagine.'

In *LBH* I remarked that if Locke means to be offering only a technique for classifying outer things, with the classification of ideas taken for granted, then he should explain why we need a technique to help us to classify one kind of item but not the other. Two decades later, Ayers (1991: i. 248–9) pushed Locke along this path of escape I had sceptically suggested for him: Wittgenstein's point does not count against Locke, he writes, because Locke was offering a technique for classifying non-ideas only, not items of all kinds. Ayers allows his Locke free access to the notion of 'distinct tokens of the same precise [idea-]type', with this taken as unproblematic; but he does not explain why, if the recognition of ideas is so easy, we should need help in classifying other things.

156. How ideas represent: two theories

Of the roles that Locke assigns to ideas, embodied in the acronym PITMAC, all but P = perceiving require that ideas be able to represent items other than themselves. We have to explore how they could do this.

The topic is not the representation of particulars, such as my having an idea or image of my house; but rather the representation of kinds or properties, such as my having an of-a-house idea—an idea or image of a house, but not of any house in particular. That is what is needed for ideas to have any chance of doing their work in imagining, thinking, meaning, a priori knowledge, and classifying. Try out the difference on physical pictures: no actual building is depicted in Bruegel's glowing picture of a house; my sketch of my home is so clumsy that it hardly qualifies as being of the of-a-house kind.

To find out what, if any, particular thing an idea represents, you must attend not only to the idea, but also to something else—namely, a suitably related cause of it. We do not attend to the rest of the world in that way in order to determine what kind an idea represents; to know that an idea of yours is of the of-a-tiger kind, you do not have to inspect the jungle.

Still, perhaps you have to relate the idea to something, namely yourself. It may be that for an idea of yours to represent the kind K, you must use it as, take it to be, intend it for, a representative of K. Unpublished work by William Alston has satisfied me that Locke often and variously commits himself to this 'owner's intent' view of mental representation, especially in *Essay* II.xxx–xxxii. According to this view, an idea represents tigers in the way that the word 'tiger' means tigers—through somebody's stipulating that it do so.

Although Locke is committed to this 'owner's intent' view, it is not comfortably available to him. His theory of ideas is supposed to cover our entire intellectual lives; all our thinkings are to consist in operations on ideas. That being so, you cannot think 'I stipulate that the idea I am having right now is to stand for tigers' unless you already, without that stipulation, have some way of thinking about tigers. If Locke has a way out of this difficulty, I cannot see it.

Anyway, even on the 'owner's intent' view of it, mental representation differs from the linguistic variety in one important way. The meanings of words are purely conventional; except for onomatopoeic words, which are negligible, no physical feature of any word makes it suitable to bear one meaning rather than any other. In contrast, even if Locke held the 'owner's intent' view of mental representation, he certainly thought that a given idea can be more suitable for one significance than for any other—that is, that the 'meanings' of our ideas are natural rather than conventional. So we still have the question of what, for Locke, relates a given idea to a given kind. In the light of the 'owner's intent' view, we should understand this to be the question of what enables an idea to *be suitable for its owner to intend as representing* a given kind; but from now on I shall for brevity's sake simplify that to: what enables an idea to *represent* a given kind.

It is plausible to suppose that an idea's representing a given kind is an intrinsic property of it—a fact about it that could be discovered just by examining the idea itself. How could this be? Only two answers seem possible; they are the only two that have ever been proposed.

According to one, an idea of the of-an-F kind is an idea that is itself F. An idea represents circles or circularity by being circular. This is the property-possession theory of how kinds or properties are represented: it says that an idea represents a property by having it.

Many philosophers have committed themselves to something like this. Broad once argued (1923: 240) that if a field looks square to me I must have a sense-datum that is itself square, because nothing else could explain how 'square' comes to play a part in how the field looks. Locke implies that some ideas represent in this manner, though not all. Berkeley argues extensively on the assumption that ideas can represent only things that they resemble (§213).

The friends of this view must avoid implying that a thing can look cheap or fake only to someone who has a cheap or fake idea of it. They do so by mainly confining themselves to visual 'ideas', thinking of these as (in John Wisdom's phrase) 'extremely thin coloured pictures', and supposing that they represent shapes and colours and little else. That avoids some trouble, but does not rescue the theory, which is rotten at the core. My idea of triangle is not triangular; on any even barely tolerable theory of what it is to be triangular, no idea could possibly be so.

In §35 I sketched the theory that sense perception involves the transfer of a trope from the perceived object to the perceiver. That was presumably encouraged by the theory of mental representation nested within it: anybody attracted by the view that when I see a coin, a roundness trope passes from the coin to my mind must be drawn partly by the thought that the trope would represent roundness in my mind. That is the second theory about the representation of kinds as an intrinsic feature of ideas: an idea represents F-ness not by being F, but by being an instance of F-ness. It will have to be an unowned trope—an instance of roundness, perhaps, that does not consist in any item's being round. Otherwise we are led straight back to the incredible thesis that an idea represents F-ness by itself being F.

No early modern philosopher that I know of explicitly held that ideas are unowned tropes. But some of the main things they said about ideas could be true if they were tropes and perhaps not otherwise. Consider this from Berkeley:

It may perhaps be objected that if extension and figure exist only in the mind, it follows that the mind is extended and figured . . . I answer, Those qualities are in the mind only as they are perceived by it, that is, not by way of mode or attribute but only by way of idea; and it [does not] follow that the soul or mind is extended because extension exists in it [in that way]. (PHK 49)

This is more like the unowned-trope theory than like anything else I can make sense of. But Berkeley did not openly accept this account of mental representation, or indeed any other. After the quoted passage he launches into a filibuster-ing attack on 'what philosophers say of subject and mode', instead of soberly explaining what it is for a quality to be 'in' a mind 'by way of idea'.

Anyway, it is intelligible that Donald Williams (1953) should have asserted without argument that Lockean ideas are tropes. Alston has argued for this in detail, in work that is still unpublished, his main support being the one I have been discussing (which I learned from him): namely, Locke's need for some intrinsic and immediately given kind of representativeness. That includes a need for abstractness. Locke needs there to be ideas of (say) isosceles triangles and ideas that are of the of-a-triangle type, though not of the of-an-F-triangle type for any F. Tropes provide neatly for this: there is the property of triangularity and the property of isosceles-triangularity, and each can spawn its own array of tropes.

Although Locke did not consciously and explicitly hold that ideas are unowned tropes, I agree with Williams and Alston that the roles he assigns to them are better performed by tropes than by anything else. It is worth adding that when he equates his 'ideas' with medieval 'species', he commits himself to their being tropes (§§154, 35).

157. A third theory

Probably nobody today believes that mental representation is performed by unowned tropes, so we need some other account of what it is, because it does exist. Without giving to 'ideas' the protean role that most early modern philoso-phers assign them on the mental stage, we must admit that there are mental items—including images—which are *of* various kinds or properties. When you see an F in your mind's eye, and when it seems to you, going by your sensory state, that you are confronted by an F thing though really you are not—in these situations there is something F-indicating about your sensory or imaginative state, and this does not come from its being caused by an external F item.

The account of this that Locke seems to have accepted for the representation of colours, tastes, and smells, and that most philosophers today accept across the board, denies that an idea's representation of a kind is an intrinsic feature of it. Granted that my present of-a-house image need not be of any particular house, still, it counts as an image of a house because of its resemblance to many other sensory states that are of particular houses. This kind of representativeness does not (dyadically) relate an idea to a unique other particular; but it does (polyadi-cally) relate it to many other actual and/or possible particulars. So we can repre-sent roundness without having a mental image that is an internal circle or an unowned instance of circularity.

What 'other sensory states'? The simplest answer is that an idea is an of-F idea if it is significantly like ideas that typically occur in sensory encounters with *things that are F*. So I now have a sensory idea of a circle if some aspect of my present sensory state is sufficiently like the state that people are typically in when they see or feel circular things.

This polyadic account of the representation of kinds is awkward in a couple of ways that should be acknowledged.

The account allows me to think: 'I have an of-a-golden-mountain idea, but I wonder if I am actually perceiving a golden mountain'; and even to think: 'I have an of-a-golden-mountain idea, but I wonder if there is or ever was a golden mountain'. The latter is possible because I might have views about what people typically would experience if they did perceive a golden mountain. But the polyadic account does not provide for anyone's thinking: 'I have an of-a-golden-mountain idea, but I wonder if there are or ever have been any material things.' Descartes in his First Base position believes that his own mental contents are *as though* he occupied a world of bodies, but questions whether there really is such a world (§144). According to the polyadic account of the representation of kinds, that starting-point is impossible. This is awkward from the standpoint of those of us who think it is possible.

Also, the polyadic account implies that each representing idea has an intrinsic nature through which it resembles others, and thus has a representative content. I accept that, but it is embarrassing to believe in these intrinsic natures about which we apparently cannot say or even think anything. I can describe my present intrinsic visual state to you only in representational or relational terms, comparing it with the states people are in when they see red square things in sunlight. That would not be so bad if it arose merely from the need for publicness, but it does not: I cannot tell *myself* any more than that about my present visual state. I do still believe in it; but this aspect of the view is troubling.

158. Against reification

In the past three sections I have mainly been thinking of ideas as sensory items— something in the nature of images. In my next chapter we shall look at how those relate to the other guises in which 'ideas' appear in Locke and some of our other philosophers; but for this section the topic will be, quite explicitly, images.

We all agree that there are mental images. They are presented to us—are subjects of our awareness, come before our minds—in sense perception and also in hallucinations and the like. But that is not to say that there are such *things* as images. I shall explain.

When we say that *Harry has an image in which circularity is represented*, is this a monadic predication on Harry, or a dyadic statement relating him to something else? The sentence contains two noun phrases, which makes it look dyadic, but that can be misleading. When we say that *Harry is in a bad mood*, nobody would think that this relates Harry to a distinct item, a mood; we all know that really the statement is a monadic predication on Harry, saying that he is irritable, depressed, or the like.

The statement that Harry has an image representing circularity might be like that too. Perhaps it is best understood as meaning that *Harry is F* (logically like *Harry is suffering*), where F is the predicate that applies to all and only people who are in a state typical of perceiving something circular. This amounts to a refusal to reify mental images—a refusal to treat them as things. Here are two reasons for going along with this, holding that mental images are best regarded not as things, but rather as states of people, ways people temporarily are.

What is the point of representing a state of affairs in the relational form R(x,y) rather than in the form F(x)? Most, and perhaps all, of what makes the former appropriate is that we might have occasion to refer to x or to y in contexts where it is not R-related to the other. I propose this:

> When it is fully legitimate to treat a state of affairs as involving a relation between two distinct things x and y, it is at least conceptually possible that x and y should both exist without being thus related.

She is *in* the forest, but both she and the forest could exist while she was *out* of it. We say that he *has* a pain, but we have no notion of that pain's existing without being had by him; and so by my principle we should not regard 'He has a pain' as a relating of one thing to another. So 'He has (perceives) an image of kind K' is not genuinely relational, because that particular image could not have existed without being had or perceived by that person.

Secondly, in conformity with Occam's razor we should not postulate that there are any such things as images if we do not need to. We do not need to, because all the things that are said with substantival references to images can be said in other ways in which images are not reified. These 'other ways' fall into three groups.

(1) Some statements about images are equivalent, in obvious ways, to ones about people's sensory states. We speak about who has an image, when it occurred, and how long it lasted, and how it compared and contrasted with other images—all these routinely go over into statements about which person is F, when he became F, and how long he remained so, how his condition compared with how other people were at other times. This pain is more severe than the one I had three hours ago; I am suffering more severely now than I was an hour ago.

(2) Other statements about images can also be rescued in a non-reifying form, but only through a paraphrase. People sometimes describe images as having colours, shapes, volumes (for auditory images), and so on. That seems to be an irreducibly reifying way of talking, and, understood as such, it is indefensible. It would be worrying, however, if we had to write it off altogether, because when someone says 'I had a brilliant orange visual image', we do attach some meaning to this. What lets us recognize the kind of experience he is reporting is our having a non-reifying paraphrase of what he has said. What we get from the statement 'I had a brilliant orange visual image' is that he was sensorily affected in a manner typical of seeing something orange in brilliant illumination; and similarly with all the apparent attributions to images of shapes, sizes, colours, and so

on. This form of paraphrase is desirable for reasons of economy, and also because the original statements are incredible when taken literally. We do not believe that the person had an image which was itself orange; for we think that a thing's being orange has to do with how it looks in white light, and we know that a mental image cannot be put under any light.

(3) Some things philosophers have said about images cannot be preserved in a non-reifying format. These are well lost. They used to plague the philosophical literature in the guise of problems about 'sense-data', as they were called. 'Can there be an unapprehended sense-datum?'; 'Are sense-data perceived in the same way, or in the same sense of "perceive", as are physical things?'; 'Do apprehended sense-data exist in the same sense of "exist" as do unobserved things?'; 'Is the visual sense-datum I have just after blinking the very same one that I had just before?'; 'How do visual sense-data relate to the surfaces of physical objects?' (See e.g. Moore 1922: 189 ff.; 1953: 34; 1962: 119–20.) Even before one has grasped the reification issue, these questions look empty, pointless, arising not out of real phenomena but out of bad theories. That the anti-reification thesis cannot rescue them is a virtue in it.

Frank Jackson (1975) has argued that certain valid arguments cannot be sustained unless we reify images. 'He had a square, orange visual image'—so Jackson's argument goes—entails 'He had a square visual image'. But 'He was in a state typical of people who are seeing square orange things' does not entail 'He was in a state typical of people who are seeing square things', because it might be that a certain sensory state is typical of seeing square things except in the special case when they are orange, when the percipient's state is utterly different. Although this argument has been soberly debated, it collapses at a touch. The second entailment does indeed not hold, and accordingly the first doesn't either. If you think it obvious that someone who has a square orange image has a square image, you are reifying the image; and you should justify that. This argument will not help you.

159. Locke and the reification of ideas

Although Locke speaks of ideas as 'objects of thoughts', he does not confront the reification issue. Indeed, the ontological status of ideas is not a topic that engaged his attention in any serious way (for support and discussion see Winkler 1991: 217–18). Of the many things Locke says about ideas, some go one way, and some the other.

He commits himself to reifying ideas when he says that some of them resemble outer things. This comes to a boil in his treatment of ideas as pictures:

'... which idea is in our minds, as one picture, though an aggregate of diverse parts' (II.xxv.6).

'. . . our ideas which are as it were pictures of things . . . mental drafts . . .'
(II.xxix.8).

'If [ideas] be not sometimes renewed by repeated exercise of the senses, . . . the
print wears out, and at last there remains nothing to be seen' (II.x.5).[2]

However, Locke seems to have no further explanation of—no metaphysical
underlay for—the view that an unextended mind can have a picture in it.

Much of what he says about memory in II.x.2,7 sounds reifying:

'as it were the store-house of our ideas';
'It was necessary to have a repository to lay up those ideas which at another
time [the mind] might have use of';
'Ideas lodged in the memory and upon occasion revived by the mind . . . are
. . . (as the word 'revive' imports) none of them new ones';
'Ideas that are lodged in the memory [are] dormant pictures';
'[They] are roused and tumbled out of their dark cells into open daylight.'

We cannot accept these just as they stand. They imply that an idea stored in
memory is in the mind but out of its awareness, which conflicts with the thesis,
which Locke took over unquestioningly from Descartes, that a mind must be
aware at every moment of all its contents (§26).

It is not surprising, then, that immediately after the bit about 'laying up' ideas
in the memory Locke writes:

But our ideas being nothing but actual perceptions in the mind, which cease to be anything when there is no perception of them, this laying up of our ideas in the repository of
the memory signifies no more but this, that the mind has a power in many cases to revive
perceptions which it has once had . . . (II.x.2)

That opens the door to anti-reifying paraphrases. 'Harry received an idea
through the senses, stored it in memory, then revived it again' turns into 'Harry's
senses caused him to be F (a certain sensory state), then he stopped being F but
retained a disposition to become F again under certain stimuli, then he became
F again under those stimuli'.

However, Locke does not ever officially take a stand against reification. His
only published discussion of the ontology of ideas is in his 'Examination of
Malebranche'. Corresponding to Locke's term 'idea', Malebranche had two: *sen-*
timent and *idée*, the former corresponding to Lockean ideas in their role as sensory images, the latter to Lockean ideas as they serve in intellectual thought.
Locke purports to be bewildered by this distinction, but he is willing to discuss
the nature of a *sentiment*, which Malebranche describes as 'a modification of our
soul'—that is, a state of the mind. Locke opens his comments on this with a blus-
tery suggestion that the word 'modification' is idle in this context; but a few sentences later he gives it work to do, clearly seeing that he is up against the view

---

[2] R. B. Braithwaite once examined a doctoral dissertation whose author (he told me) argued that Locke
regarded ideas as pictures, giving as one reason his saying that we 'frame' them.

that for someone to have or perceive an image is for the person to be in a certain monadic state:

Different sentiments are different modifications of the mind [according to Malebranche]. The mind or soul that perceives is one immaterial indivisible substance. Now I see the white and black on this paper, I hear one singing in the next room, I feel the warmth of the fire I sit by, and I taste an apple I am eating, and all this at the same time. Now I ask, take 'modification' for what you please, can the same unextended indivisible substance have different, nay inconsistent and opposite (as these of black and white must be), modifications at the same time? Or must we suppose distinct parts in an indivisible substance, one for black, another for white, another for red ideas, and so of the rest of those infinite sensations which we have in sorts and degrees? (1706: 234–5 = section 39)

This argument starts from a firm grasp that the anti-reifying view of images says that 'x has an image of something white and of something black' has the form 'Fx & Gx'. In rejecting this, Locke assumes that in this case the values of F and G must be inconsistent with one another, just as 'white' is with 'black'. That is wrong. The value of F must be a predicate applicable only to people when they are seeing (perhaps among other things) something white, and the value of G only to people when they are seeing (perhaps among other things) something black; there is no clash here. Perhaps Locke is assuming that the predicates in question are 'white' and 'black': to have an image of something white is to be white, and so on. That is not an essential part of the anti-reifying proposal.

In rejecting the latter, Locke is not standing up for any rival to it. Samuel Alexander was right about this (1908: 31): 'The word "idea" . . . contains for Locke no theory; it means simply an object of the understanding when we think. Unfortunately he also did not inquire what was involved in assigning to ideas a twilight existence between the things they represent and the mind which understands them.' Nor, we might add, did he inquire what was involved in saying that when someone 'perceives' an idea, this is a relation between a mind and another object.

If Locke had openly held that ideas are tropes, that would have given him an ontology for them. Whether it would have been a reifying one depends on a detail. Someone who holds that ideas are tropes and that a single trope can exist in a given mind or out of it (whether or not in another mind) is committed to allowing that 'Idea I is in mind M' is genuinely relational; and so he reifies tropes. We saw in §36 that Descartes objected against tropes that they are *things* pretending to belong on the right of the thing/property line. But a trope theorist might, for various reasons, maintain that a given trope essentially belongs only to one substance; in that case a trope-possession statement would fail my test for relationalness, and so tropes would not count as things—that is, as reified.

Chapter 22

Lockean Ideas, Some Details

160. Are all Lockean ideas images?

It is widely alleged that Locke's uses of the term 'idea' have a great split through them: he takes an 'idea' sometimes to be an image, a sensory content, a sense-datum, and sometimes to be a concept or meaning. In his hands, that is, 'idea' has a sensory use and an intellectual use; the two can be seen in his text to be quite different, yet Locke shows no awareness of the difference. The thesis is not the patently false one that in Locke's usage the term 'idea' is ambiguous, but rather that he uses 'idea' sometimes to refer to images and sometimes to other items—concepts, perhaps. This thesis is mainly correct, but I shall examine some objections to it.

(Two warnings: Never mind the reification issue now; I suppress it by using the term 'item', which is general and empty enough to straddle states and things. Also, I always use 'image' in your and my sense of the word, not in the sense that was common in the early modern period, in which 'x is an image of y' means that x resembles y.)

Locke starts with a view of ideas as images, and then develops a theory to the effect that, after being processed, they become the entire raw material of the intellect. Two processes may be involved: abstraction, in which detail is omitted from an idea, and composition, in which simple ideas are assembled to make complex ones. Thinking, according to Locke, consists in operating variously on these processed ideas—meaning, classifying, inferring, modal inquiry, and so on.

Does he really think that sensory-type images are involved in all those intellectual activities? Well, it could be his view that when an image is processed—made more abstract or more complex—the end-product is no longer an image. That possibility has been put to me by Alston, and is favoured by Peter Alexander (1974: 74):

[Locke] wants to show 'whence the understanding may get all the ideas it has'; that it is in experience that 'all our knowledge is *founded*, and from that it *ultimately* derives itself'; and that sensation and reflection together supply 'our understandings with all the *materials* of thinking'. This implies that the understanding is able to work on these materials. He nowhere appears to be committed to the slogan 'Nothing in the mind which was not first in the senses'. At most he is committed to some such more moderate slogan as 'Nothing in the mind that is not somehow connected with the senses'.

Indeed, Locke does not say enough about how we make complex ideas to commit himself to their being images. Some of his turns of phrase suggest it, however, as when he speaks of complex ideas as 'made up of collections' of simple
ideas (II.xxix.13). And in II.xiii and elsewhere he strongly suggests that certain
complex ideas (unhelpfully called 'simple modes') are formed by mentally juxta-
posing simple ideas; in which case the complex idea does, after all, retain the
nature of an image.

Mere juxtaposition is indeed plausible for so-called simple modes (read II.xiii.5
to see why), but although Locke writes as though all complex ideas were made
merely by 'repeating and joining together' simple ones, he cannot be right about
that. To see why, consider his point in II.xxix.13–14 that it is hard to distinguish
the idea of a chiliagon, a 1,000-sided figure, from that of a 999-sided figure.
Leibniz rightly responds that the ideas (= concepts) of those two figures are as
easy to distinguish as are the ideas (= concepts) of the numbers 1,000 and 999. I
cannot easily tell whether I am seeing (or imagining) a 1,000-sided figure or one
with one fewer sides than that, but it is easy for me to know whether I am thinking about a 1,000-sided figure or rather one with 999 sides. A more likely muddle
would involve my not being sure whether my subject of thought has 100 sides or
10,000 sides.

Now see what Locke says about someone trying to separate his idea of a 1,000-
sided piece of gold from his idea of a 999-sided one:

> He will, I doubt not, be able to distinguish these two ideas from one another by the num-
> ber of sides, and reason and argue distinctly about them while he keeps his thoughts and
> reasoning to that part only of these ideas which is contained in their numbers, as [for
> instance] that the sides of the one could be divided into two equal numbers, and of the
> other not, etc. But when he goes about to distinguish them by their figure, he will there
> be presently at a loss, and not be able, I think, to frame in his mind two ideas, one of them
> distinct from the other, by the bare figure of these two pieces of gold, as he could if the
> same parcels of gold were made one into a cube, the other a figure of five sides.
> (II.xxix.14)

Locke is trying here to cope with the very facts that Leibniz uses against him, but
I do not think he succeeds. He says that it is hard to distinguish the two ideas if
one attends only to their shapes and does not attend to 'that part' of them which
'is contained in their numbers'; and I cannot make any sense of this. The phrase
'by their figure' seems to require the ideas to be images; but never mind that.
Whether or not the idea of a chiliagon is an image, its properties cannot be captured by a characterization in terms of what 'parts' it has: there is also the question of how the parts are put together. On any reasonable understanding of
'part', the parts of

the idea of a figure with 1,000 sides

are just exactly the parts of

the idea of 1,000 figures with sides.

We need a basis upon which complex ideas can relate to their 'parts' as a sentence does to its constituent words. That is, we need a *syntax* for complex ideas, analogous to the syntax that lets us distinguish 'The dog bit the man' from 'The man bit the dog'. The same need makes itself felt all through the *Essay*. For example, in Locke's account of one of the causes of confusion: 'Another default which makes our ideas confused is when, though the particulars that make up any idea are in number enough, yet they are so jumbled together that it is not easily discernible whether . . . etc.' (II.xxix.8). What is it for the elements in a complex idea to be, or not be, 'jumbled'? To answer this, Locke would have to tackle the syntax of complex ideas.

Locke evidently senses this need. There is evidence of his doing so in his doctrine that in sense perception we passively receive *simple* ideas; all complex ideas, he says, are the result of intellectual activity—specifically composition—on our part:

> The mind, in respect of its simple ideas, is wholly passive, and receives them all from the existence and operations of things, such as sensation or reflection offers them . . . [But the mind] being once furnished with simple ideas, it can put them together in several compositions, and so make variety of complex ideas. (II.xxii.2)

This is typical. Immediately after introducing the concept of composition, Locke writes about non-human animals: 'Though they take in and retain together several combinations of simple ideas, as possibly the shape, smell and voice of his master make up the complex idea a dog has of him—or rather are so many distinct marks whereby he knows him—yet I do not think they do of themselves ever compound them and make complex ideas' (II.xi.7). Having seemed to imply that the dog has a complex idea not made by itself, Locke immediately retracts that, in favour (it seems) of the statement that the dog merely has the simple ideas that would be ingredients in such a complex idea. He must hold, then, that passively receiving several simple ideas at once is not the same as receiving a complex idea.

Some of his turns of phrase also strongly suggest that a complex idea has a logical structure given to it by its owner; as when he writes of the mind's power to 'consider several [simple ideas] united together as one idea; and that not only as they are united in external objects, but as itself has joined them' (II.xii.1), and of 'having combined into one idea several loose ones' (III.v.11). Locke ought to, but does not, tell us what the process of composition consists in—that is, how one combines 'several loose ones'—but he does believe that there is some such procedure.

What is less certain is his having inferred from this that complex ideas are not images. The fact is that we cannot get far with the *Essay* on the assumption that its 'ideas' are not all images, because Locke has no rival account of what they may be, and nobody has provided one for him.

161. Locke's two accounts of abstract ideas

Locke confronts a problem that arises for the use of ideas in TMAC—(2) thinking, (3) meaning, (4) a priori knowledge, and (5) classifying (§155). If for some intellectual purpose I want an idea of *horse*, and accordingly bring one into my mind, it will be an idea of an F horse for some fairly specific value of F—one that partly determines colour, shape, size, etc. But no such idea will serve (2) to enable me to think about horses in general, or (3) as my meaning for the single word 'horse', or (4) as my basis for necessary truths about horses (if I have in mind an idea of a brown horse, I shall give the wrong truth-value to 'Horses can be white'), or (5) as my basis for classifying things into horses and non-horses. All these needs were supposed to be met by 'abstract ideas'.

An abstract idea is a qualitatively thinned-out one; it lacks or omits detail. Locke thought I could have an idea of *horse* which was, so to speak, silent with respect to colour, size, and aspects of shape other than those that are required to make a thing a horse; this would be an abstract idea of *horse* that simply did not have any details that pinned it down to any specific kind of horse. He did not invent this view: it is to be found in Descartes and some Cartesians, and goes back to at least the thirteenth century, when Bonaventure developed a theory about how the 'active intellect' abstracts from the contents received by the 'passive intellect'—that is, the senses; and the seeds of it are even earlier than that. (I rely here on Copleston 1950: 283–4.) Our concern is with Locke's form of the theory.

When he first introduces abstract ideas in the *Essay*, they do not fit the sketch I have just given:

The mind makes the particular ideas received from particular objects to become general; which is done by considering them as they are in the mind, such appearances, separate from all other existences and the circumstances of real existence, as time, place, or any other concomitant ideas. This is called abstraction, whereby ideas taken from particular beings become general representatives of all of the same kind, and their names general names, applicable to whatever exists conformable to such abstract ideas. (II.xi.9)

This is not about the omission of qualitative detail. I could start with my fully detailed sensory idea of a horse that I see galloping in the meadow and peel off from it any representation of the 'circumstances'—the coolness of the wind, the drumming of the hooves, the scent of the heather, the feel of my grandson's hand in mine—while still retaining a fully detailed idea of the horse itself. The result of that kind of abstraction, then, does not meet the needs I have described.

Those needs are catered to in Locke's only other account of what abstraction is:

The ideas of the persons children converse with . . . are, like the persons themselves, only particular. The ideas of the nurse and the mother are well framed in their minds, and . . . represent only those individuals. The names they first give to them are confined to these individuals . . . Afterwards, when [they] observe that there are a great many other things in the world that in some common agreements of shape and several other qualities resemble . . . those persons they have been used to, they frame an idea which they find those many particulars do partake in; and to that they give, with others, the name *man* for example. And thus they come to have a general name and a general idea. Wherein they make nothing new, but only leave out of the complex idea they had of Peter and James, Mary and Jane, that which is peculiar to each, and retain only what is common to them all. (III.iii.7)

Usually when Locke writes about abstraction, it is in conformity with this second account. He nearly always takes abstract ideas to be lacking in intrinsic detail, which means that he takes abstraction to be a procedure of omitting not the *circumstances surrounding* but rather some *detail in* something received through the senses.

Ayers (1991: 1. 251) does not agree. According to his Locke, an abstract idea, rather than being incomplete or unsaturated or short on detail, is an ordinary perception or image 'partially considered' and given a certain function in thought. He appeals to II.xiii.13, which contains the sole occurrence of 'partial consideration' in the *Essay*. He does not say why he thinks that Locke is here explaining what 'abstract ideas' are; the passage is in the middle of a fourteen-page stretch (166:17 to 180:19) in which 'abstract[ion]' does not occur once.

The book III passage which I have quoted also seems decisive against Ayers's view, as does the fact that in several places where Locke does discuss abstract ideas by name, he explicitly calls them 'partial ideas', not partial considerations of complete ones. Also, 'Let any one reflect, and then tell me, wherein does his idea of man differ from that of Peter and Paul . . . but in the leaving out something that is peculiar to each individual' (III.iii.9).

A word of caution. In contexts where he is writing about abstraction, Locke is apt to speak of unabstract ideas as 'particular' and of abstract ones as 'general'. He is talking about what ideas are fit to represent, not about what their metaphysical nature is. In his view of things, the process whereby an idea 'becomes general' in this sense does not stop it from being a particular mental item occurring at one time in one mind. Locke is forthright about this: 'All things that exist are only particulars' (III.iii.6); 'Universality belongs not to things themselves, which are all of them particular in their existence; even those words and ideas which in their signification are general' (11).

162. Berkeley's first attack on abstract ideas

Berkeley rejects Locke's theory of abstraction totally, on the strength of two claims: nothing could answer to Locke's description of abstract ideas; and losing them is no loss, because the work they are supposed to do can be done without them. Let us examine these in turn.

What would an abstract idea of *triangle* be like? Locke holds that some ideas, including those of shapes, represent properties by having them; so he ought to hold that an idea of *isosceles triangle* will itself have the form of an isosceles triangle, and that an idea of *triangle*—one that is abstract enough not to represent any special kind of triangle—will itself be triangular but not F for any other geometrical value of F. Sometimes he seems to accept this commitment, as in the notorious passage in which he exclaims that the forming of abstract ideas, although adults become nimble at it, is a considerable feat:

Does it not require some pains and skill to form the general idea of a *triangle*, . . . for it must be neither oblique, nor rectangle, neither equilateral, equicrural, nor scalenon; but all and none of these at once. In effect, it is something imperfect, that cannot exist; an idea wherein some parts of several different and inconsistent ideas are put together. (596:4)

The phrase 'all . . . of these at once' is not implied or invited by the theory, and Locke should not have used it. He has no reason to admit that an abstract idea breaks the law of non-contradiction. The last clause does not make that admission, because it speaks only of putting together 'some parts' of mutually inconsistent ideas, and that need not involve inconsistency.

Berkeley in quoting that passage italicizes 'all and none', and in his next section he writes that a Lockean abstract idea cannot be formed until one has 'first tacked together numberless inconsistencies' (*PHKI* 13–14). Perhaps this shows Berkeley making capital out of 'all . . . of these at once'; but he does not do so elsewhere, and he does not think he needs to. In his view, the 'none of these' aspect of abstract ideas condemns them.

Sometimes Berkeley writes as though his grounds were empirical: 'If any man has the faculty of framing in his mind such an idea of a triangle as is here described, it is in vain to pretend to dispute him out of it, nor would I go about it. All I desire is, that the reader would fully and certainly inform himself whether he has such an idea or no' (*PHKI* 13). His real position, however, is that Lockean abstract ideas are impossible. Although he does not say so clearly and explicitly in the Introduction to his *Principles of Human Knowledge*, the makings of an argument for this are there in his work. The key to it is his frequently stressing that an idea must 'copy' or 'resemble' its object, or, more accurately, that an idea must possess the property which it represents.

From this he infers that an abstract idea of *triangle* must itself be triangular without being F, for any value of F which applies only to some triangles. Adopting an example from Locke: the idea is triangular, but it is not equilateral, equicrural or scalene; that is, it does not have all its sides of equal length, nor just two the same, nor all different. This infringes the law of *saturation*, which says that any particular thing falls under one or another of each complementary set of predicates. That is at the root of Berkeley's rejection of abstract ideas.

Winkler (1989: 34) tells a different story: 'Berkeley's central objection to abstract ideas . . . is that they claim to represent what cannot possibly exist.' There is little of this in Berkeley's writings, which is just as well because the objection is a bad one. Here is one of the rare passages that go Winkler's way:

Euphranor [= Berkeley]: Pray, Alciphron, which are those things you would call absolutely impossible?

Alciphron: Such as include a contradiction.

Eu: Can you frame an idea of what includes a contradiction?

Al: I cannot.

Eu: Consequently, whatever is absolutely impossible you cannot form an idea of?

Al: This I grant.

Eu: But can a colour or triangle, such as you describe their abstract general ideas, really exist?

Al: It is absolutely impossible such things should exist in Nature.

Eu: Should it not follow, then, that they cannot exist in your mind, or, in other words, that you cannot conceive or frame an idea of them?

(1732, LJ 3:333–4)

This, which was dropped from the third edition of *Alciphron*, is wholly mistaken. An abstract idea of *triangle* is not a representation of a triangle that is not equilateral, equicrural, or scalene, and is therefore impossible. Rather, it is a representation of a triangle, and is (so to speak) *silent* about whether the triangle is equilateral, equicrural or scalene. Similarly, *Macbeth* is a not an impossible story about a woman who has no particular number of children; it is a coherent story about a woman, and is silent about how many children she has. In the above argument Berkeley is caught in a shallow muddle, from which there is little to learn. More nourishing is his argument against abstract ideas from the premise that what represents F-ness must itself be F—a premiss which we shall find all through the texts. It constitutes, among other things, a stern warning to Locke that he had better not combine his book III account of abstraction with that view of mental representation.

163. Can images be abstract?

If we set aside the thesis that an idea of an F or of F-ness must itself be F, we can revive the question of whether any idea can be in any degree abstract. Let us approach the idea of a triangle through polyadic representation (§157):

> For an idea to represent triangularity is, approximately, for it to have some feature F such that: F ideas usually occur when people sensorily confront something triangular and seldom occur otherwise.

Such an idea would be abstract: it would represent triangularity, but not (for instance) scalene triangularity. For an idea to represent scalene triangularity, on this account, it must have some feature F such that F ideas usually occur when people sensorily confront something scalene-triangular and seldom occur otherwise.

This makes it easy for ideas to be abstract. The abstractness of an idea would be like—and perhaps even a case of—the partial uninformativeness of a clue or bit of evidence. 'From what you heard, could you tell what mood the crowd was in?' 'No. I could hear that they were worked up about something, but not whether they were cheerful, angry, afraid, or what.' That would be an 'abstract hearing', so to speak; its way of telling only part of the story would be comparable to that of an abstract idea on the polyadic account.

Berkeley had another arrow in his quiver: an argument that does not openly rely on the thesis that an F-representing idea must itself be F. Reasonably taking Lockean ideas to be sensory images, he inferred from that alone that they could not be abstract. In *PHKI* 10 and elsewhere he writes as though every image is saturated with detail, so that you cannot hear a tune in your mind's ear except as played in some absolutely specific manner.

This is wrong, for images can be to some degree abstract. I can imagine or see someone's face while not imagining or seeing it as smiling or as not smiling; I can hear a tune, either acoustically or imaginatively in my mind's ear, hearing it as orchestrated but not as orchestrated with woodwinds or without woodwinds. Indeed, I think that all images are somewhat 'abstract'—they never tell the whole tellable story. The exact shape of an imaged triangle can be logically on a par with the exact number of Lady Macbeth's children.

To see how, start with a part of the polyadic theory of representation: to have an image of an F is to be in a state which is significantly like that of perceiving an F—by which I mean that it is somewhat like perceiving an F, and is more like that than like perceiving anything else. This gives us a handhold on such expressions as 'see in the mind's eye, as from the main entrance' and 'hear in the mind's ear, as played by a brass band'. The phrase 'significantly like' should be replaced by something more precise; but probably not by anything much more specific, because people differ in how, and how closely, their imaging resembles sensing.

What detail can be omitted from an image of an F? I suggest that one can omit from an induced image any details that one could fail to notice when actually perceiving an F and noticing that it was an F. Combine that with the 'significantly like' story and you will see how to analyse:

I have an image of a yacht.
I have an image of a yacht tacking into the wind.
I have an image of a yacht, but not one of a yacht tacking into the wind or of one not doing so.

Supply the analyses for yourself. Or, for more about the topics of this section, consult *LBH* 39–43.

We know, then, how an image can be abstract. This enables Locke to meet this latest objection to his theory of abstract ideas, while still regarding the latter as images. Still, he would be in trouble. We have no mental contents that are, as one of his theories requires, as abstract as the meanings of our most general words. There is no such thing as (for example) a visual field of a kind such that people

would usually have that kind of visual field when seeing a mammal, and would seldom have it otherwise. One could not be in a position to say: 'I saw that it was a
mammal, but wasn't able to pin it down any further.' To take in enough to rule out
'It was a reptile', one must at least take in whether it was more like an elephant
than like a marmoset. Moving higher up the scale to the ideas that are needed to
correspond to 'shaped', 'moving', 'coloured', and so on, the difficulty grows.

This may cause us to reconsider whether Locke really thinks of all ideas as
images. He knew he had trouble over the meanings of some general terms—most
notably the word 'thing' or the equivalent 'substance' (§203)—but the trouble is
acute even with more humdrum terms such as 'animal', 'valley', 'building', 'hour'.
'inch', 'problem', 'obstacle', 'celebration'. The implausibility of the associated-
image theory of meaning is some reason to think that Locke did not hold it, in which
case he did not after all hold that the ideas which define meanings are all images.

164. Berkeley's second attack

So much for Berkeley's contention that Lockean abstract ideas are impossible.
We now come to the second prong of his attack: namely, the claim that the theory of abstract ideas is wrongly motivated. Locke's view about what they can do
for us, Berkeley argues, is wrong:

[Locke asks:] 'Since all things that exist are only particulars, how come we by general
terms?' His answer is, 'Words become general by being made the signs of general ideas'
(*Essay* III.iii.6). But it seems that a word becomes general by being made the sign, not of
an abstract general idea, but of several particular ideas, any one of which it indifferently
suggests to the mind. . . . An idea which, considered in itself, is particular becomes general by being made to represent or stand for all other particular ideas of the same sort.
(*PHKI* 11, 12)

Some enthusiasts have taken this to herald the shift in meaning-theory that
Wittgenstein later popularized, from *the mental content associated with a word* to
the use of a word. A word is general if it is used generally: what a breath of fresh
air this is, after the choking Lockean assumption that the semantic properties of
words are dictated by what ideas they are associated with! So it has been said, but
this is too kind to Berkeley, and—more important—it gets the philosophy
wrong.

Berkeley is firmly committed to holding that this can happen:

At time T_1 I am thinking about triangles in general, using for this purpose an
idea of an isosceles triangle. At time T_2 I am thinking about isosceles triangles,
using an idea that is exactly like the one I used at T_1.

Let us ask him: (1) What feature of me differs from T_1 to T_2, making it the case
that I am thinking first about triangles generally and then specifically about

isosceles ones? (2) How do I know at each time which class of triangles I am thinking about? Locke can answer each question: that I am thinking about triangles generally at T_1 is a fact about my mental content at that time; and I can know this because I can introspect that content. Berkeley, however, holds that the mental content may be the same each time.

Still, there are answers that Berkeley can give. He may respond: '(1) There is a difference in what intellectual behaviour you are disposed to engage in on the two occasions; and (2) you know what you are thinking about on each occasion because you know how you are disposed to behave.' Those are pretty good answers. The truth about what one is up to on the intellectual front consists largely in facts about what one would do if . . . Furthermore, the answers fit Berkeley's thesis that language often does its work without any associated ideas. In explaining how, he seems to picture us as having dispositions of certain kinds—to act or think or feel in a certain way upon hearing a certain sound sequence; which moves him close to the two answers I have proposed for him.

Locke, however, was trying to answer a third question—not (1) 'What makes it the case that I am . . .', or (2) 'How can I know that I am . . . ?', but (3) 'What enables me to . . . ?' What enables me to bring one word or idea to bear on many particulars? How do I steer? What guides me in sorting out the items to which the word or idea does apply from the ones to which it does not? Locke thinks that any kind of generalizing—any bringing of a 'many' under a 'one'—is an intellectual feat that requires a guiding rule or procedure; and the only guide he can find is *abstract ideas*. Berkeley evidently did not see the place of question 3 in Locke's thinking. He certainly had no answer to it.

The question is brave and deep. Of something that is so intimately woven into every aspect of the life of the mind as to be almost invisible to us, Locke dares to ask, 'How is the trick worked?' Yet there can be no answer, or so I have argued in §155 (item 5), following Wittgenstein. Should we then congratulate Berkeley for not answering it, and take him to have seen that no answer can be given? No.

I base this especially on some passages in his first draft of the Introduction. For example:

Suppose I have the idea of some one particular dog to which I give the name Melampus and then frame this proposition Melampus is an animal, where it is evident the name Melampus denotes one particular idea. And as for the other name [in] the proposition . . . [some philosophers hold that] I must make the name animal stand for an abstract, generical idea which agrees to and corresponds with the particular idea marked by the name Melampus. But . . . I do declare that in my thoughts the word animal [does not] in that proposition stand for any idea at all. All that I intend to signify thereby being only this, that the particular thing I call Melampus has a right to be called by the name animal. (LJ 2:136; see also 127)

In this passage Berkeley presents a Platonist answer to the question (not quoted), the Lockean answer, and then one of his own which exposes his failure to understand the question. The words 'has a right to be called by the name animal' shows that Berkeley has not grasped Locke's problem. For something to 'have a right' to be described as an animal is for it to be an animal—that is, to be properly co-classifiable with other animals or with other things called 'animal'. Having sorted out Berkeley's obscure phrase thus far, we have reached the end of what he offers us and the place where the Lockean and Platonist theories start. Berkeley may have taken over the notion of having a right to a name from Locke (see *Essay* III.iii.12); but Locke uses it to set a problem, whereas Berkeley parades it as a solution.

165. Hume's variant on it

Hume credits Berkeley with 'one of the greatest and most valuable discoveries that has been made of late years in the republic of letters': namely, the falsity of 'the received opinion' that there are abstract ideas. Hume says he will 'confirm' Berkeley's view 'by some arguments which I hope will put it beyond all doubt and controversy' (*Treatise* 17). In arguing against abstract ideas, Hume mainly retraces Berkeley's steps, though he rightly claims also to bring in something new. I shall not go into this material here; of his three arguments, the third (on 19–20) is the most interesting but also the most puzzling. My present concern is with Hume's way of arguing that the work which abstract ideas are supposed to do can be done without them, and in particular on his response to question 3.

He writes: 'The image in the mind is only that of a particular object, though the application of it in our reasoning be the same as if it were universal' (20). How can we do this? Berkeley ignored this question, but Hume faces it squarely, which makes his treatment of abstract ideas the superior one.

In Hume's answer, words come to the rescue. I have a fully detailed triangle-type idea in my mind, I associate it with the word 'triangle', and the latter is linked with a certain range of other ideas, all resembling my present one in some respects and most being unlike it in other respects. My awareness of the word does not bring all those ideas crowding into my mind, which is not capacious enough for that, but it is dispositionally linked to them in a certain way:

When we have found a resemblance among several objects that often occur to us, we apply the same name to all of them . . . After we have acquired a custom of this kind, the hearing of that name revives the idea of one of these objects, and makes the imagination conceive it with all its particular circumstances and proportions. But as the same word is supposed to have been frequently applied to other individuals that are different in many respects from that idea which is immediately present to the mind, the word—not being able to revive the idea of all these individuals—only touches the soul, . . . so to speak, and revives that custom which we have acquired by surveying them. [We] keep ourselves in a readiness to survey any of them . . . The word raises up an individual idea, along with a certain custom, and that custom produces any other individual one for which we may have occasion. (*Treatise* 20–1)

This involves something that is rarer than it should be in Hume's account of the human mind: namely, an intellectual happening in which there is a change not in mental content, but in disposition—a change in what the person would do if the trigger were pulled.

But now consider what this trigger is—that is, what Hume uses to fill the gap in Berkeley's account. The disposition, he says, is created by hearing or seeing (or thinking of?) the word. It is the word that touches the soul, raising up the disposition to bring to mind other ideas of a certain kind.

This fills the gap, at the price of implying that only a creature with a language can have propositional thoughts, and (even more strongly) that every instance of such thought involves a use of language. It is a pretty high price. Various people have contended that only creatures endowed with language can have general thoughts—that is, ones that could be expressed with quantifiers (Bennett 1964). But Hume goes further by implying that only language-users can have thoughts that could be expressed using general words. Not only can a dog not think *cats always climb trees when chased*, but it cannot even think *that's a cat over there*. It was careless of Hume to commit himself to this, because he flat-out disbelieves it, and ardently maintains that in most intellectual respects humans differ little from other animals (§285).

That specific matter aside, it is worth attending to what Hume says in defence of his thesis that you acquire a certain 'custom' whereby the presence in your mind of a particular word readies you for having a certain range of ideas. Without knowing what the 'ultimate causes' are of this phenomenon, he says, he can 'produce other instances which are analogous to it, and other principles which facilitate its operation' (*Treatise* 22). The fourth and last of these, though obscurely presented, is of great interest. It concerns our ability to actualize potential ideas at need. This is required for Hume's theory of general thought, but also for other goings-on, as when I remark to you that nobody would eat fish caught in a certain shipping channel, and you immediately reply that you have seen many people fishing there, apparently not for pleasure. To do that, you must bring (the meaning of) my remark hard up against a memory of yours that contradicts it. But you had that memory only dispositionally: you were not thinking back on those fishermen when I spoke; you had to *find* that memory, to bring it up out of the ocean of potential mental contents that you have at your disposal. This familiar aspect of our lives involves a real skill of ours; and Hume has the insight to be impressed by it:

Nothing is more admirable than the readiness with which the imagination suggests its ideas, and presents them at the very instant in which they become necessary or useful. . . . One would think the whole intellectual world of ideas was at once subjected to our view, and that we did nothing but pick out such as were most proper for our purpose. There may not, however, be any present beside those very ideas that are thus collected by a kind of magical faculty in the soul which . . . is inexplicable by the utmost efforts of human understanding. (*Treatise* 24)

This offers too rosy a view of our skill at retrieving relevant knowledge. Leibniz would agree. This is something we do rather badly, he thought, and what we need is not a 'magical faculty' but a disciplined technique: 'Sometimes when a person needs to think of something which he knows, and which he would call to mind if he had perfect control of his memory, it does not occur to him to do so. . . . If someone discovered the art of bringing to mind at the right time the things that one knows, it would be of prime importance' (*NE* 206). Still, even if it glows less brightly than Hume suggests, the phenomenon is real, and poses a challenge.

In all of this material—including other examples of dispositions to run through ideas in certain ways—Hume is playing with fire. In most of what he says about the life of the mind, we shall see, he is committed to holding that thoughts are mental contents—that is, ideas. Yet here we have him cleaning up after Berkeley in a manner which implies that ideas are often not at the centre of the stage, prompting the question of why they should have any part in the drama. The danger appears again when Hume writes that it is 'usual, after the frequent use of terms which are really significant and intelligible, to omit the idea which we would express by them, and to preserve only the custom by which we recall the idea at pleasure' (*Treatise* 224). If it is all right frequently to use a word without associating it with an idea, why is it not all right to do so always? If it is, then what is wrong with using a word which one cannot associate with an idea?

Berkeley in his Introduction also says that words are not always used to convey ideas, and he gives examples. But the very passages in which he says this imply that general words are meaningful only if they can be, and perhaps only if they sometimes are, associated with appropriate ideas:

Whoever therefore designs to read the following sheets, I entreat him to make my words the occasion of his own thinking, and endeavour to attain the same train of thoughts in reading that I had in writing them. By this means it will be easy for him to discover the truth or falsity of what I say. He will be out of all danger of being deceived by my words, and I do not see how he can be led into an error by considering his own naked, undisguised ideas. (*PHKI* 25)

Berkeley's attacks on Lockean materialism utterly depend on the view that meaning is ultimately and centrally a matter of associated ideas. Neither in his work nor in Hume's do we cleanly escape from the 'associated mental content' view of meaning.

166. Abstract ideas and complex ideas

On the detail-omitting account of it, abstraction seems to be the converse of composition. If x can be reached from y, z, w by composition, then it seems that y or z or w could be reached from x by abstraction. I base this primarily on what Locke says about what each procedure is: composition is building, abstraction is dismantling; how can they not be converses?

It follows that if I_2 is formed by abstraction from I_1, then I_2 will be simpler than I_1 is. Locke often writes of 'abstract complex ideas', but that is all right: the idea corresponding to the word 'horse' is abstract because it omits detail, yet complex because it still includes a lot of detailed qualitative variety.

Locke never says outright that 'more abstract' goes with 'more simple' or 'less complex', however, and sometimes he goes the other way, with phrases such as 'more abstract and compounded' (433:29) and 'more simple and less abstract' (597:21). He seems mainly to assume that the simple / complex scale lies along a different dimension from the abstract / concrete one. He is mistaken in this, I submit, because he is committed to the view that abstractness is the opposite of complexity. In one place he indicates this himself, writing of 'abstract and partial ideas of more complex ones' (412.9). That is how Berkeley saw the situation. He describes Lockean *abstract* ideas as supposedly achieved by resolving a 'compound idea . . . into its simple constituent parts' (*PHKI* 7). This was brought to my attention by Winkler (1989: 66–7).

The view that abstractness is simplicity, as well as not being explicitly adopted by Locke and being in conflict with some of his turns of phrase, also faces one solid theoretical obstacle. He often writes that in sensory experience we passively receive simple ideas which we then actively assemble into complex ones. If abstraction is just the reverse of this process, one would expect it to be a smooth glide back to the disassembled simples which we passively received in the first place; and one might think that we could reach the same result even more easily by receiving some simple ideas and not building them into compounds in the first place. Locke, however, firmly holds that we can have abstract ideas only if we engage in abstraction, a special task which 'require[s] some pains and skill'.

I do not know how he can, or would, resolve this matter. How he *ought* to resolve it, I believe, is by invoking the doctrine that Kant came up with a century later: namely, that there is no pure, sheer, unconceptualized sensory intake, and even our initial sensory intake must be logically structured in some manner. This would involve denying that in our sensory intake we are purely passive; it would be a radical change in Locke's view of the human condition; there is no point in following it out further here.

167. Ideas and concepts

Locke is often said to have smudged the line between sense and intellect, and there is something in this. To the extent that he does so, it is in an asymmetric fashion. The *Essay* contains no passages in which he mishandles some aspect of sensory intake because he thinks of these 'ideas' as having a role in the life of the intellect; but he often seems to get intellectual matters wrong through tying them too closely to sensory ideas.

Leibniz noticed this tendency in Locke, and protested his use of 'idea' to cover what Leibniz thought to be two kinds of item, intellectual and sensory, which he called 'ideas' and 'images' respectively. In one place, Locke says that it is hard to make a certain distinction between two ideas, and in another that a certain kind of idea is easy to have; and Leibniz remarks each time that what Locke says depends on his using 'idea' to refer to images (§160). If he were talking about the items that Leibniz calls 'ideas'—thoughts or contents of thoughts—he would be wrong about the former difficulty and the latter easiness (*Essay* and *NE* II.xxix.13 and IV.ii.15).

Despite insisting on this distinction, Leibniz does a little smudging of his own, though from the opposite direction: 'This *clear image* that one may have of a regular ten-sided figure or of a 99-pound weight—this accurate sense that one may have of them—consists merely in a *confused idea*' (*NE* 262; see also 487). There is, then, truth in both halves of Kant's famous charge: 'Leibniz intellectualized appearances, just as Locke . . . sensualized all the concepts of the understanding' (*Critique* B 327); though for reservations about this see Parkinson 1981.

Whatever Kant's exact meaning was, *we* need to be careful in saying that Locke sensualized concepts, or used the word 'idea' to cover not only sensory images but also concepts. We have two main uses for the word 'concept', neither of which serves to express accurately the undoubted truth that Locke gave the output of the senses too large a role in his account of the intellect. (1) We speak of concepts as human possessions, in saying things like this: 'Her judgements on the conduct of others tell us a lot about her concept of responsibility'; 'One's concept of causation is exercised in statements using verbs such as "cook" and "destroy"'. (2) We also speak of 'concepts' as objective, interpersonal items which we may know about a priori. In this we follow the lead of Frege's famous 1918 paper 'The Thought'. A Fregean 'thought' is what we call a 'proposition'. It is not an intellectual episode—a thinking—but rather an item which can be thought, a possible object or accusative of a thinking as a football can be the object of a kicking. These, Frege argued, cannot be mental items such as thinkings, or physical ones such as sentences, and so 'a third realm must be recognized'—a realm of items that are objective, interpersonal, timeless, necessarily existing, the sort of things that these days are called 'abstract' without this term being given any precise meaning. And the constituents of these abstract propositions, Frege held, are concepts. Now let us see how these two uses of 'concept' relate to Locke's work.

(1) Every philosopher today would agree that for someone to have a certain concept is for her to have a certain disposition or skill or intellectual power. What concept of causation she has, for instance, is determined by how she is disposed to handle causal judgements, what inferences she is inclined to think valid, what evidence she is disposed to regard as supporting what causal conclusions, and so on. In this we follow Kant, who derived a list of 'categories'—concepts which a person must have and use—from a list of basic kinds of judgement. This derivation relied on the seminal view that a concept is a judgement-making skill, an ability to proceed in a certain way in forming opinions of a certain kind. For this way of seeing Kant's categories I am indebted to Ryle (1938–9). A helpful treatment of concepts as skills is in Geach 1957.

Kant, however, was not the first to think of concepts as skills. When Leibniz distinguishes 'ideas' from 'images', accusing Locke of using 'idea' to sprawl across both, his 'ideas' are our concepts; and he mainly thinks of them as intellectual skills or dispositions (§178).

Such dispositions also have a vital role in Locke's picture of the life of the mind. They come to the surface when he writes about the mind's 'faculties', which are dispositions it exercises in its 'operations'. These two terms occur frequently throughout the work, sometimes in combination, as in these bits from II.xi.14:

These, I think, are the first faculties and operations of the mind, which it makes use of in understanding: And though they are exercised about all its ideas in general . . . etc.

Observing the faculties of the mind, how they operate about simple ideas, which are usually in most men's minds much more clear, precise, and distinct than complex ones, we may the better examine and learn how the mind abstracts, denominates, compares, and exercises its other operations about those which are complex . . . etc.

Although there are dozens of such passages, Locke denies these faculties and operations the prominence they deserve, allowing them to create a background hum but not bringing them forward for detailed analysis.

His treatment of meaning is an example. He holds that what someone means by a word is fixed by the idea that she customarily associates with it. Thus he describes a definition as 'the explaining of one word by several others, so that the meaning or idea it stands for may be certainly known' (413:30). About interpersonal misunderstandings he writes: 'A man may use what words he pleases to signify his own ideas to himself: and there will be no imperfection in them if he constantly use the same sign for the same idea, for then he cannot fail of having his meaning understood' (III.ix.2). These passages and others suggest that to have a meaning for a word is just to associate it with a specific kind of idea. That would be a poor account of what meaning is. The meaningful use of language involves a grasp of these four things, at least:

what can be achieved by this utterance in this situation,
how to put words together to make meaningful sentences,
how linguistic expressions relate to extra-linguistic reality,
how sentences should be related to other sentences.

Of these, the first is required for conversational coherence, the second for syntactic propriety, the next for truth or at least plausibility, and the last for cogency of inference. If Locke's theory of meaning excluded all of these, as I once believed, it was a dismal affair indeed.

Now, however, I question whether he intended to offer a comprehensive account of what meaning is. He does not positively exclude any of those four aspects of meaning, and he might agree with me about them. He could justify his emphasis on associated ideas on two grounds. One is that the four aspects are involved in all meaning, in meaning as such, whereas he is concerned with the differences between the meaning of one word and that of another. Those differences, he thinks, are determined purely by differences between the associated ideas. Also, Locke was concerned with misuses of language—about two-fifths of Book III treats the causes and cures of linguistic pathology—and he traced most of that to troubles in how words relate to ideas.

Now, competence in the four listed aspects of meaning is a skill or disposition or faculty; Locke's relative silence about it is a notable aspect of his reticence about faculties and operations generally. We are entitled to hold this against him, but notice that, in doing so, we are not touching on his tendency to smudge the line between sense and intellect. When Leibniz complained that Locke did not properly distinguish images from ideas, he meant to be making a point about sense/intellect; but now that seems to have been diverted by a quite different point about episodes versus dispositions. We need to get clear about this matter if we are to move deeper into Lockean territory without stumbling.

The proper way to describe Locke's sense/intellect trouble is to say that he wrongly gave sensory images too large a role in intellectual *episodes*, individual bits of thinking, meaning, understanding, and the like. Or we can say that he smudged a certain line, and did not properly distinguish having an image from engaging in an intellectual act. Either way, the issue concerns sensory episodes in relation to intellectual episodes, not in relation to *concepts*, which are dispositional rather than episodic.

(2) Concepts of the Fregean kind—belonging to a 'third realm' lying outside time and contingency—have played a part in theories of modal truth. We think that some propositions are absolutely and eternally necessary, such as the proposition that if a necessary condition for P's truth suffices for its falsity, then P is false. Two questions arise: what makes this necessarily true? how can we know that it is necessarily true? I shall consider these questions more fully in Chapter 23. At present I merely remark that one pair of answers says that the truth-makers for necessary propositions are relations amongst concepts, and that we can know them because we can know intuitively how concepts are related. This involves intuitive access to Frege's 'third realm', because the concepts in question are the eternal, 'abstract' ones that he postulated, not the concepts that you and I *have*.

Now, Locke's only account of modal knowledge says that we learn modal truths—he is fond of instancing the truths of geometry, which he thought were knowable a priori—by attending to properties of and relations amongst *our* ideas. In this he laid himself open to the charge, which Leibniz energetically brought, of trying to derive necessary conclusions from contingent psychological premisses.[1] How true this is, how free Leibniz is of the same charge, and whether it is possible to have a modal epistemology that is not open to the charge of psychologizing, are topics for Chapter 23. What matters just now is that Locke does try to base modal knowledge on 'ideas' understood psychologically; we could

---

[1] Others had similar complaints, notably Malebranche against Descartes. For an instructive account of this, see Jolley 1990.

describe this as his allowing the term 'idea' to sprawl over concepts; but this is not a matter of smudging the line between the sensory and the intellectual; rather, it concerns the line separating what is contingent and psychological from what is eternal and abstract.

168. Ideas and qualities

A peculiar quirk in Locke's thinking affects how he uses the term 'idea', and I had better deal with it now. (In Chapter 29 we shall see it running amok in the philosophy of Berkeley.) Most Locke scholars seem to have taken it calmly, if indeed they have noticed it; but to anyone who reads the *Essay* carefully and philosophically, it sticks out like a sore thumb. For more about it, see my 1996.

One aspect of it is Locke's tendency to use the word 'idea' to mean 'quality'. He is not expressing the theory that ideas are quality-instances, however. He tells us how to understand him when he calls qualities 'ideas', and his explanation has nothing to do with the trope theory of ideas. It occurs in the part of this I have italicized:

Whatsoever the mind perceives in itself . . . that I call idea; and the power to produce any idea in our mind I call quality of the subject wherein that power is. Thus a snowball having the power to produce in us the ideas of white, cold and round, the powers to produce those ideas in us, as they are in the snowball, I call qualities; and as they are sensations or perceptions in our understandings, I call them ideas; *which ideas if I speak of sometimes as in the things themselves, I would be understood to mean those qualities in the objects which produce them in us.* (II.viii.8)

So, our minds contain ideas, and external objects have powers to cause ideas in our minds; and if Locke sometimes speaks of ideas as being in the object, he is using 'ideas' to mean:

> powers to cause ideas,
> qualities that cause ideas,
> qualities by virtue of which the object causes ideas,

or the like. Because the word 'ideas' occurs in each phrase, Locke is abbreviating when he replaces any of them by that one word; this usage merely cuts long stories short. Thus his explanation.

It fits some of the idea/quality occurrences well enough—this, for example: 'We cannot observe any alteration to be made in . . . any thing but by the observable change of its sensible ideas, nor conceive any alteration to be made but by conceiving a change of some of its ideas' (II.xxi.1). That can be unpacked according to Locke's instructions: when he writes of 'a change of some of its *ideas*', we can take him to mean 'a change of some of the *qualities by virtue of which it causes ideas in us*', and all is well.

Many passages cannot be unpacked in this way, however, including one in the very sentence in which the unpacking instructions occur. Look carefully at this: 'the powers to produce those ideas in us, as *they* are in the snowball, I call qualities; and as *they* are sensations or perceptions in our understandings, I call them ideas.' Are there any items that Locke could soberly mean as the referents of both occurrences of 'they'? Clearly not. This sentence employs two tokens of that pronoun in a manner that makes sense only if one refers to qualities and the other to ideas; and that is not made legitimate by having a single ambiguous word ('idea') that can refer to either.

If Locke were using 'idea' in two senses, one involving the other, the overall effect of those occurrences of 'they' would be ludicrous. Nurses sometimes used to refer to patients through the parts of their bodies that were diseased: in 'the prostate in the third bed on the left' the word 'prostate' would mean 'man who is being treated for a prostate condition'. Imagine a nurse saying: 'My whole morning has been occupied with prostates. First I assisted at operations in which two of them were removed, and then I had to spend nearly an hour trying to help another of them out of a panic attack.' This is perfectly absurd; one cannot use 'them' in that way. The very same absurdity would infect Locke's use of 'they' in the quoted passage, if it were understood as involving a mere ambiguity in 'idea'.

Plenty of other occurrences of the idea/quality mix-up also resist being explained in Locke's official way. The most striking is an aspect of his use of the term 'mode'. He introduces this as part of a trio—*mode, substance, relation*, meaning roughly *quality, thing, relation*. Strictly speaking, he says he is introducing his three grand categories of 'complex ideas' (II.xii.3), but he means that they are categories of items *of* which we have ideas, not that these items are themselves ideas. Where substances are concerned, Locke makes this explicit by always writing of our ideas *of* them. He often alludes in similar fashion to ideas *of* modes, implying that modes are not themselves ideas (see e.g. 291:34, 383:35, 430:5). In many other places, though, he proceeds differently. Here, for example: 'Modes I call such complex ideas which, however compounded, contain not in them the supposition of subsisting by themselves', etc. (II.xii.4; for other examples, see xii.5, xiii.6, xviii.5–6, xxii.5, III.xi.15). In short, whereas he is always careful to distinguish substances from ideas of them, Locke often collapses 'ideas of modes' into 'modes'. Far from using 'idea' to mean 'quality (causing the idea)', this is close to using 'quality' to mean 'idea (of the quality)'.

Do not say: 'Granted, Locke sometimes says "mode" meaning "idea of mode", but why all the fuss? This is just another of his bits of shorthand, with no deep significance.' It would be shallow and unphilosophical to settle for that, without asking why Locke frequently shortens 'idea of mode' to 'mode' but almost never shortens 'idea of substance' to 'substance', and without picking up a scent from the fact that as well as abbreviating a mental-item phrase into a quality word he also abbreviates a quality phrase into a mental-item word.

It is not believable that all this is mere shorthand. I submit that Locke runs ideas together with qualities as a matter of a substantive conflation.

169. Explaining the idea/quality conflation

Sometimes a dense network of isomorphisms between two related areas of our conceptual scheme can create a magnetic field, pulling a philosopher across from one towards the other, so that he ends up unwittingly thinking about both at once. One may be shielded against this by being conceptually insensitive, so that the isomorphisms do not register on one's mind. Or one may be protected in a different way: one can be helped to identify and then avoid a tempting conflation by studying the work of someone who has been thoroughly, powerfully, intelligently guilty of it. That is not the least of the services that Locke can render us, if we will attend in detail to what he wrote. In this section I shall outline three isomorphisms which, severally or jointly, might produce the idea/quality conflation in a philosopher's mind.

(1) Lockean 'ideas', when they are items that are 'in' or 'before' the mind, are sometimes sensory inputs from the outer world, or simulacra of these in imagination or memory, and are sometimes intellectual items—*thoughts* out of which propositions can be constructed. Either way, they can be, as Locke says, 'abstract'; that is, they can be less than fully saturated with detail. This is obviously true of thoughts, for no one would dispute that I can think about the fact that she smiled at me, without having any thought about how in detail she smiled. Similarly, I have argued, with images: I can picture her in my mind's eye as smiling without picturing her as smiling in any specific manner.

Now, ideas share their ability to be abstract with qualities and not with concrete substances. My thought of her as smiling abstracts from the concrete (= unabstract) reality of her face, but it exactly matches one quality of her face, namely its smilingness. This is a crucial similarity between qualities and ideas as Locke understands the latter, and I conjecture that it encouraged him to conflate the two.

(2) When Locke uses 'idea' to refer to mental items, he is often thinking of them as sensory, as something in the nature of sense-data. There are strong temptations to assimilate these to qualities. When Locke writes, 'We cannot observe any alteration to be made in . . . any thing but by the observable change of its sensible ideas', he could be saying either (a) that we observe things to alter only by noting changes in our sensory states, or (b) that we observe things to alter only by observing their qualities.

On each interpretation he would be denying something that he certainly does deny—that we have direct knowledge of (a) an extra-mental reality, or of (b) the substratum that supports the qualities of the observed thing. In §218 we shall see Berkeley being led by his idea/quality conflation into muddling *a* with *b*.

(3) Platonist philosophers say that reality contains universal things—properties or qualities—and that what makes two items co-describable is their having some universal thing in common. Locke disagrees: 'All things that exist are only particulars' (III.iii.6). This should mean that he will not include properties or

qualities in his inventory of the basic contents of reality, but in fact he uses 'quality', etc. lavishly throughout the *Essay*. In defence of that he might say that his anti-universalism does not forbid him to use 'quality', but only commits him to its being dispensable. If he tried to eliminate it, he would have to lean heavily on his theory that the principal role classically assigned to qualities—namely, helping to explain how we can bring many particulars under a single description—is really played by ideas. This theory has the following as a consequence:

> Words are general . . . when used for signs of general ideas, . . . and ideas are general when they are set up as the representatives of many particular things. But universality belongs not to things themselves, which are all of them particular in their existence . . . When therefore we quit particulars, the generals that rest are only creatures of our own making, their general nature being nothing but the capacity they are put into by the understanding of signifying or representing many particulars. (III.iii.11)

So Locke has the co-classifying work of qualities being done by ideas, though he still avails himself liberally of the word 'quality' and of its near equivalent 'mode'. It would not be surprising if he tended to assume that wherever 'quality' is used, it could be dispensed with in favour of 'idea'. In the event, he is by no means faithful to his anti-universalism; but it is visibly there as a strand in his thought.

Chapter 23

Knowledge of Necessity

170. Innate knowledge: Introduction

After the Introduction to the *Essay*, Locke plunges into an attack on the view that some of our knowledge is innate: 'It is an established opinion amongst some men that there are in the understanding certain innate principles, . . . characters, as it were stamped upon the mind of man, which the soul receives in its very first being and brings into the world with it' (I.ii.1). Some commentators think he was attacking a version of the doctrine of innate knowledge that nobody had ever accepted, but we need not settle that issue in order to learn from his attack and from Leibniz's replies to it.

Innatism tries to explain how we come to know certain things. In recent decades, largely through Chomsky's influence, innatism has been invoked to explain how we know certain things so easily, so quickly, so young, or with so little evidence. The grasp that young children have of the grammar of their native language cannot (it is argued) come simply from their applying general intelligence to the linguistic data they confront; so Chomsky postulated that we have something like an abstract grammar built into us as part of our biological birthright. Nobody thinks that grammar could not be known otherwise; general intelligence could do the job, given enough time and opportunity, but the evidence indicates that it does not.

The innatism that exercised Locke and Leibniz was meant to explain how we know certain things *at all*. There is no obvious and earthy source for knowledge that:

> For any proposition P, if (if P then not-P) then not-P.
> We ought not to lie, cheat, or betray our friends.
> There is an almighty and omniscient God who loves us.

Logic, ethics, theology—three areas with famous epistemological problems which some have tried to solve by supposing that the relevant knowledge is built into us, not acquired by learning. Locke sees no need to suppose this, because:

A man, by the right use of his natural abilities, may without any innate principles attain a knowledge of a God and other things that concern him. God having endued man with those faculties of knowledge which he hath, was no more obliged by his goodness to plant those innate notions in his mind, than that having given him reason, hands, and materials, he should build him bridges or houses. (I.iv.12)

Arguing like that, he owes us some account of how these discoveries can be made. He deals with theology in IV.x, where he offers an alternative to an innatist theology. Nobody today could think that he succeeds in showing 'the necessary existence of an eternal mind' whose 'omniscience, power, and providence' can be learned from the excellences of the world he has made. Locke's God chapter contains fine things (§118), but they are not epistemological; he is not stimulating or challenging on the issue of how we know theological truths. My personal conviction that no theology is true encourages me to drop that topic now.

Unlike many of us, Locke held that the fundamental principles of morality are propositions with truth-values, so that for him there was a question about how they are known. He drew his answer from theology:

I think it a very good argument to say the infinitely wise God hath made it so and therefore it is best. But it seems to me a little too much confidence of our own wisdom to say I think it best and therefore God hath made it so. (I.iv.12)

This might be written by someone who holds that we must first know some moral truths about God, such as that he is good or always acts for the best; which would raise once again the question of moral epistemology. For Locke, however, the truths about God's will *determine* what is right and good, rather than merely being infallible guides to it: 'The true ground of morality . . . can only be the will and law of a God, who sees men in the dark, has in his hand rewards and punishments, and power enough to call to account the proudest offender' (I.iii.6). Later he gives ethics a twofold basis, in God's will and human nature:

The idea of a supreme being, infinite in power, goodness, and wisdom, whose workmanship we are and on whom we depend; and the idea of ourselves as understanding rational beings . . . would . . . afford such foundations of our duty and rules of action as might place morality amongst the sciences capable of demonstration. (IV.iii.18)

Although he refers to 'the idea of' God and of ourselves, I think Locke really means morality to be demonstrable from true non-analytic premisses about God's will and our nature.

So he escapes from the impiety (as Descartes saw it) of believing in moral standards that exist and are valid independently of God's will. This pushes him to the conclusion, which Leibniz thought impious, that God's always willing what is right or for the best, far from being a reason to praise him, is true by definition (§72). Locke placidly impales himself on one horn of this dilemma.

There remains modal knowledge, concerning what is and what is not absolutely necessary or absolutely impossible. (I have meant 'logic' to cover this whole area.) That is a continuing problem, and there is much to be learned from attending to what Locke and Leibniz had to say about it (§§173–8).

Before doing so, we should glance at the other half of Locke's attack on the thesis that we know some things innately. Whether or not there is work for the thesis to do, he argues, there is decisive empirical evidence against it. If we knew innately that P, then every human being would know that P—not just cultivated, thoughtful folk, but also 'children, idiots, savages, and illiterate people'. Thus Locke; and he asserts that no values of P are like that. Few people reach the level of abstract reflectiveness at which one becomes conscious that it is impossible for any thing both to be and not be at the same time; and more specific applications of this, such as that no thing can be both spherical and cubic at the same time, are not known by small babies, who do not yet have the ideas of sphere and cube (my example, Locke's point). Similarly with moral principles and theological doctrines.

This assumes that we could not have a proposition innately built into our fabric without being conscious of it. Locke held to this, being sure that the mind is wide open to itself (§113). Just once he seems to qualify it:

> If there be any innate ideas, any ideas, in the mind which the mind does not actually think on, they must be lodged in the memory, and from thence must be brought into view by remembrance . . . Whatever idea is in the mind is either an actual perception or else, having been an actual perception, is so in the mind that by the memory it can be made an actual perception again. (I.iv.20)

This, he argues, provides no comfort to the innatist, who postulates beliefs that people have before they ever 'actually think on' them. Leibniz, taking this at face value, turns it back against Locke:

> Since an item of acquired knowledge can be hidden [in the soul] by the memory, as you admit that it can, why could not nature also hide there an item of unacquired knowledge? Must a self-knowing substance have, straight away, actual knowledge of everything which belongs to its nature? (NE 78)

This is fair enough, given most of that section of Locke's, which seems to allow that an idea can be actually and episodically 'in the mind' by being lodged in the memory. At one point, however, he says that ideas in the memory are 'said to be' in the mind (97:21, 98:1), and returning to the topic in IV.i.8 he twice writes of what someone is or may be 'said to know'. His considered opinion seems to be that if someone is disposed to be aware of some fact about his past, it is all right to *say* that he remembers it (as it is all right to say 'The sun has set' or 'The shoreline is receding'). This does not admit unconscious mental contents as literal doctrine. In one place Locke is explicit about it: 'Our ideas are said to be in our memories when indeed they are actually nowhere' (II.x.2).

Leibniz thought that point worth arguing because he had rejected the Cartesian view that the contents of any mind are wholly open to it (§113). Universal self-awareness, he argued, far from being necessary to mentality, is not even possible for it: it would prevent one from ever getting from one thought to the next, because first one must have the thought of x, then the thought of the thought of x, and so on *ad infinitum* (NE 118). A Cartesian could respond that self-awareness does not take time: your awareness of your thought x comes with that thought, not after it. Leibniz might still object that this implies that every mental event is synchronous with an infinity of others in the same mind. Spinoza tried to save the Cartesian position by saying that although there is an 'idea of' each idea, there is no infinite pile-up, because the idea of idea x is x itself; hints to that effect had also been offered by Descartes. No one has succeeded in making this plausible. At *NE* 238 Leibniz briefly sketches his own view of self-consciousness, apparently identifying it with short-term memory. On this account, self-consciousness does take time; but in Leibniz's hands it does not generate an infinity of thoughts or tie the thinker down to a single thought. Rocco Gennaro sees this as one part of a larger view which he attributes to Leibniz: namely, that for a monad to be consciously aware of a given perception is for it to have a higher-order thought about it. (See Gennaro 1999 for an interesting discussion in which the matter is linked with contemporary issues in the philosophy of mind.)

171. Dispositional innate knowledge

Leibniz does not defend innate knowledge by appealing to unconscious mental possessions. He does not say that children, idiots, etc. know all those weighty things and are merely unaware of doing so. Rather, he maintains, as most innatists did, that we innately possess some knowledge in a dispositional form. Others did not believe that one could have actual mental contents of which one was not aware; but neither did they contend that we have innate knowledge of which babies, idiots, etc. are aware. 'The supposition that innate knowledge is explicitly possessed from the earliest dawn of consciousness was expressly repudiated by all writers of repute,' writes Gibson (1917: 30). This is certainly true of Descartes, the most famous innatist of the period: 'All those things whose knowledge is said to be naturally implanted in us are not for that reason expressly known by us; they are merely such that we come to know them by the power of our own native intelligence, without any sensory experience' (CSMK 222). On this account, having innate knowledge is being innately subject to certain conditionals to the effect that, if C occurs, you will come to know (in a fully aware manner) that P.

To attack dispositional innatism, Locke must stop harping on the incompetence of babies, disagreements in theology and ethics, and so on, all of which are now irrelevant. Here is what he offers instead:

If any one [proposition] can be said to be in the mind which it never yet knew, it must be only because it is capable of knowing it; and so the mind is of all truths it ever shall know. Nay, thus truths may be imprinted on the mind which it never did nor ever shall know: For a man may live long and die at last in ignorance of many truths which his mind was capable of knowing, and that with certainty. (I.ii.5)

Locke is here attacking the thesis:

For some values of P, we are born with the dispositional knowledge that P, meaning that we can some day come actually to know that P.

This is open to Locke's charge of triviality, because I constructed it to be so. But I doubt whether anyone has offered innatism in this form, and it is certainly not true that a dispositional knowledge kind of innatism 'must' be this trivial doctrine.[1]

It could, instead, be any one of several more robust theses, each replacing the bland 'We can come to know that P', or

> There is some condition c such that, if c comes to obtain, then we shall then actually know that P,

by a thesis about some one specific condition C. Such a more robust thesis will equate a person's dispositionally knowing that P with

> If C comes to obtain, the person will consciously know that P.

For example, she will consciously know that P if she reaches mature years, or if she ever wonders whether P, or if she ever becomes generally reflective. This will not be equally true of everything the person ever comes consciously to have in her mind.

A specific form of innatism will select a particular antecedent for the crucial conditional, or perhaps different ones for different kinds of knowable: if she reaches maturity, she will consciously know that $2 + 2 = 4$; if she raises certain sorts of questions, she will consciously know that it is wrong to lie; and so on.

Despite saying that dispositional innatism 'must be only' the trivial version, Locke does confront and attack two of these non-trivial versions. He starts with this, which he takes to straddle the two: 'All men know and assent to [certain principles] when they come to the use of reason, and this is enough to prove them innate' (I.ii.6). After commenting sarcastically on the sloppy ambiguities in the speech of zealots, he continues:

To apply this . . . with any tolerable sense to our present purpose, it must signify one of these two things; either [1] that as soon as men come to the use of reason, these supposed native inscriptions come to be known and observed by them: Or else [2] that the use and exercise of men's reason assists them in the discovery of these principles and certainly makes them known to them. (7)

So we have two theses about a person's coming to know that P: 1 concerns when, 2 concerns how. Unlike Locke, I shall discuss them in that order.

(1) In section 12 Locke sharply rejoins that this is plainly false, and that many people have the use of reason for many years without giving any thought to the general maxims that are declared to be innate. In section 13 he allows his opponents to retreat out of range of this objection, by weakening their view to this: 'These maxims . . . are never known nor taken notice of before the use of reason, but may possibly be assented to some time after during a man's life; but when is uncertain.' Locke adds dismissively, 'And so may all other knowable truths',

---

[1] Leibniz does not comment on Locke's trivializing move, and seems not to have understood it. Compare Philalethes' speech at NE 77 with what Locke wrote at *Essay* 50:14–20.

rightly implying that this kind of 'use of reason' innatism slumps back into triviality.

In section 14 he adds a further thrust. Even if it were true that everyone comes to know that P precisely when that person acquires the use of reason, why would that show P to be innate? In his flurry of jibes about this, he strikes me as insensitive to what motivates innatism. The innatist can say:

We do take ourselves to know that P (for certain values of P) while having a problem about how we could acquire this knowledge. I propose the following solution. We do not learn that P through any method of discovery; we are given the knowledge that P; it is handed to us on a plate, so to speak, at a certain stage in our lives (namely, when we come to the use of reason). Its coming to us at that time, with no need for inquiry or discovery on our part, is a part of our human birthright.

I do not say that Locke is powerless against this; but it does indicate that some of his moves of the form 'How would *that* show the knowledge that P to be innate?' are a little shallow and quick.

(2) Locke's dense, intricate, difficult treatment of 2 is shaped by his distinction between 'the maxims of the mathematicians, and the theorems they deduce from them' (I.ii.8). He argues energetically that if the maxims were discovered by reason, and that if this showed the knowledge of them to be innate, then the whole of mathematics would be innate, since the deduced theorems are certainly discovered through reason. I do not understand his confidence that no one would claim an innate status for the whole of mathematics. That is false about Descartes, and also about Leibniz, who at *NE* 85 calmly accepts the innateness of everything that can be proved by demonstrative reasoning.

That argument of Locke's was based on allowing that the maxims are discovered by reason; but, he says, they are not: nobody would say that 'It is impossible for the same thing to be and not to be' is 'a deduction of our reason'. Our serious epistemological question concerns the maxims, and he undertakes to explain later how we come to know them. That he does not put this explanation at the front and centre of his attack on innatism is an aspect of the slight lack of focus in this whole discussion. This faint blur prevents him from saying clearly, explicitly, and outright the thing that should be his main objection to version 2 of innatism, namely: 'Innatism was supposed to explain how we come to have certain items of our knowledge. You now offer a different account of how, and simply call it "innatism". It is as though you had said that a person counts as having a dispositional innate knowledge that ripe bananas are sometimes yellow just because she will come consciously to know this if she looks at ripe bananas in a good light.' Locke does at one point remark that the use of reason is *unlike* what innate knowledge is supposed to be: 'All reasoning is search, and casting about, and requires pains and application. And how can it with any tolerable sense be supposed that what was imprinted by nature as the foundation and guide of our reason should need the use of reason to discover it?' (I.ii.10). But he does not properly make what ought to be his central point.

172. Leibniz on dispositional innatism

I have said that Leibniz defends innatism without invoking his idiosyncratic view that there are unconscious mental contents, taking instead the dispositional route, like all other innatists. That report was a stop gap—superficially plausible but in fact not quite right.

Here is Leibniz conceding that we possess our innate knowledge only dispositionally: 'The actual knowledge of them is not innate. What is innate is what might be called potential knowledge of them . . . Items of knowledge (or truths), in so far as they are within us even when we do not think of them, are tendencies or dispositions' (NE 86; see also 106). This is no great concession, he thinks, once we have properly grasped that a disposition is never a 'bare faculty' (110).

Part of what he means by this is safe, true, and irrelevant to our present topic. It is that dispositions supervene on non-dispositional states: sugar is soluble because of its molecular structure, and so on (§103). We all accept this, including Locke, who takes it for granted that a body has its dispositions 'by reason of the particular constitution of its primary qualities' (II.viii.23).

Leibniz's rejection of bare faculties, however, also means something stronger, which Locke would not accept and which bears on the innatism debate. It is hinted at here: 'What makes us call them innate . . . is not a bare faculty, consisting in a mere possibility of understanding those truths: it is rather a disposition, an aptitude, a preformation, which determines our soul and brings it about that they are derivable from it' (NE 80). The word 'preformation' suggests that the basis for a disposition must mirror or prefigure or resemble the disposition itself. That is suggested even more strongly here: 'Ideas and truths are innate in us as inclinations, dispositions, tendencies, or natural potentialities, and not as actions; although these potentialities are always accompanied by certain actions, often insensible ones, which correspond to them' (NE 52). It seems now that a disposition to act in manner M must arise from actual doings which 'correspond to' M. It is hard to see how this can be a doctrine about dispositions generally. How can solubility arise from something in the sugar which corresponds to dissolving? As applied to dispositionally possessed knowledge, however, the doctrine is intelligible: a disposition to be consciously aware that P must arise from a non-dispositional state of the mind which somehow involves the proposition P. Leibniz expounds this through a favourite comparison:

If the soul were like such a blank tablet then truths would be in us as the shape of Hercules is in a piece of marble when the marble is entirely neutral as to whether it assumes this shape or some other. However, if there were veins in the block which marked out the shape of Hercules rather than other shapes, then that block would be more determined to that shape and Hercules would be innate in it, in a way, even though labour would be required to expose the veins and polish them into clarity, removing everything that prevents their being seen. This is how ideas and truths are in us—as inclinations, dispositions, tendencies, or natural potentialities, and not as actions; although . . . etc. (*NE* 52; see also 86)

But the veins in the marble do actually delineate the outline of Hercules; all that is potential here is their reaching the light of day. Leibniz is likening the activities of an arithmetic teacher to those of a sculptor whose statue was already completely marked out by the veins in the marble: each is removing a veil, bringing to light something that was there already. In his version of dispositional innatism, the knowledge is *actually* possessed; the disposition has to do only with the person's becoming aware of it.

That is why I retracted my initial statement that Leibniz defends innatism only in its dispositional form, without invoking unconscious mental contents. It turns out that the 'dispositions' he relies on are, or involve, such contents after all. This brings us to his main point: if P is a necessary truth, then when a person seems to discover that P, she is really just uncovering—bringing to awareness—the knowledge that P which she already possessed.

Leibniz freely allows that our conscious possession of modal knowledge may involve teaching and learning. But when a lesson leads us to conscious knowledge of some arithmetical truth, he writes, 'the teaching from outside merely brings to life what was already in us' (*NE* 76). And a little later:

I cannot accept the proposition that *whatever is learned is not innate*. The truths about numbers are in us; but nevertheless we learn them, whether by drawing them from their source, in which case one learns them through demonstrative reason (which shows that they are innate), or by testing them with examples, as common arithmeticians do. (*NE* 85)

Locke, had he read this, would have thought that Leibniz was leaving himself without a leg to stand on, because he was muddling innate knowledge with what is learned through testing on examples. But Leibniz knows what he is doing, and thinks he is standing squarely on firm ground. His focus is on absolutely necessary truths, such as those of arithmetic and logic; and he contends that appeals to examples, though they may trigger one's awareness of such propositions, cannot prove their necessity. This, he says, is the inner heart of the case for innatism about modal truths: no other account could explain our knowledge of their necessity.

A distraction should be cleared away. We have seen Leibniz writing of truths that are already 'in us', and implying that we cannot learn that a proposition is necessary from teaching which comes from 'outside'. Here he is apparently implying that knowledge of necessity must come from within, not from without:

The mind is capable not merely of knowing them but also of finding them within itself. If all it had was the mere capacity to receive those items of knowledge—a passive power to do so, as indeterminate as the power of . . . a blank page to receive words—it would not be the source of necessary truths . . . For it cannot be denied that the senses are inadequate to show their necessity, and that therefore the mind has a disposition (as much active as passive) to draw them from its own depths. (*NE* 79–80)

This seems to state the issue in terms of looking inward versus looking outward; but that is not the real line of battle, for Locke also holds that modal knowledge comes from looking into ourselves, though not in a way that confirms innatism. In this context, inner/outer throws no light.

Leibniz's better reason why 'the senses are inadequate to show . . . necessity' is not that they look outwards, but that they bring news only about particular events:

Although the senses are necessary for all our actual knowledge, they are not sufficient to provide it all, since they never give us anything but instances, that is particular or singular truths. But however many instances confirm a general truth, they do not suffice to establish its universal necessity; for it does not follow that what has happened will always happen in the same way. (*NE* 49)

This is true whether the 'instances' are inner or outer, so this point does not depend on that difference. It is at least prima facie a good point, for it is problematic to suppose that any particular events, of whatever kind, could enable us to know that some proposition is absolutely necessary, true at all times and places in all possible worlds.

Now let us get into the details of Locke's account of modal knowledge, and of Leibniz's, to see how one does, while the other does not, rely on particular instances.

173. Locke on modal discovery: the relevance problem

Leibniz's main objection to this work of Locke's seems to imply that Locke can show that certain propositions—such as, perhaps,

All triangles have three sides,
All cannibals are carnivores, and
Whenever one thing resembles another, the latter also resembles the former

—are true, but not that they are necessarily true. That may be conceding too much to Locke, however, as I now show.

According to Locke, we learn what is (im)possible by introspectively attending to facts about how our ideas are interrelated. His handling of this confronts him—though he did not see it—with the relevance problem. How can any fact R about relations of ideas be relevant to any proposition that would ordinarily be regarded as necessarily true? Never mind how R can show the proposition to be necessary, or even to be true; before coming to either of those, we need to know how R can point to any one proposition in particular. Which proposition is even a candidate for necessity? And why?

Locke holds that every non-verbal proposition is a pair of ideas: '[In] mental [propositions] the ideas in our understandings are without the use of words put together or separated by the mind, perceiving or judging of their agreement or disagreement' (*Essay* IV.v.5). This opens the door to a relevance problem for any propositional knowledge that Locke might talk about, not only for modal knowledge. Any belief that P—for any kind of P—raises the question of what the constituent ideas in P are, and what relations among them point to P's being true. Locke labels the relations 'agreement or disagreement', but that tells us little.

Now, despite his often asserting it, Locke probably does not really think that *all* our knowledge is based on our awareness of relations amongst our ideas; but this is a controversial matter that I shall not explore. It is at least clear that this is his view about modal knowledge, our present topic.

What facts about ideas count at least prima facie towards the truth of a given modal proposition? Locke has an answer for geometrical propositions. We are pointed towards these, he holds, by seeing them actually instantiated by our ideas, these being images with geometrical properties:

Is it true of the idea of a triangle that its three angles are equal to two right ones? It is true also of a triangle, wherever it really exists. (IV.iv.6)

He that hath got the idea of a triangle, and found the ways to measure its angles, and their magnitudes, is certain that its three angles are equal to two right ones. (IV.xiii.3)

This assumes that mental images have sizes and shapes, which they do not. Also, we now know that the truths of Euclidean geometry are not absolutely necessary, so that this present line of thought does not really belong in our problem area. Locke himself would have agreed that it does not exhaust the area, because he knew that plenty of necessary truths do not belong to geometry.

Furthermore, these geometrical propositions do not involve relations amongst ideas, as can be seen vividly in IV.ii.2. Having undertaken to discuss 'the agreement or disagreement of . . . ideas', Locke there slides into an example concerning 'the agreement or disagreement in bigness between the three angles of a triangle and two right ones'.

For real modal truths, then, he must appeal to other ways in which ideas can represent. He has little theory about this, except to say in connection with secondary qualities that an idea can represent an external quality by having a 'steady correspondence' with it (373:5). His general view, then, is that an idea is a particular mental episode which represents a certain property if its intrinsic nature somehow correlates with or corresponds to that property. If (unlike Locke) we take 'correspondence' weakly enough to cover identity of properties, this also covers his view about ideas of primary qualities—a view implying that an idea can represent a circle by being circular.

Then his view must be this: the fact that my F-representing idea relates in a certain way to my G-representing one points to the proposition that, necessarily, whatever is F is also G. Relates in what way? It should be by *inclusion*, but this is not what Locke says. Rather, he says repeatedly that we are led to modal knowledge through noticing the identity and diversity amongst our ideas:

'The mind perceives that white is not black, a circle is not a triangle, three are
more than two and equal to one and two. Such kind of truths the mind perceives at first sight of the ideas together, by bare intuition' (IV.ii.1).

'Everyone . . . knows . . . when any one [idea] is in his understanding and what
it is; and . . . when more than one are there, he knows distinctly and uncon-
fusedly one from another' (IV.vii.4).

'The idea of white is the idea of white, and not the idea of blue' (ibid.).

'He knows each to be itself and not to be another, and to be in his mind and
not away when it is there' (ibid.; see also IV.i.2,5,7).

These are simple judgements in which one idea is distinguished from another
idea. This seems straightforward enough, as does the assumption that one can
know such things by looking inward at one's ideas.

Locke means to be laying foundations for informal logic, setting out the elements of our knowledge of necessary truth; so he must provide for two relations
amongst concepts—requirement and exclusion. These are a bare minimum. A
logic cannot get by without the notions that nothing can fall under C_1 without
also falling under C_2 (requirement), and that nothing could possibly fall under
both C_1 and C_2 (exclusion).

His only possible candidate for the requirement relation is identity, and that
does not do the whole job, because it is symmetrical, whereas requirement is not.
The identity relation supports *What is square must be square* but not *What is square
must be rectangular*. However, a simple fix enables Locke to take in the asymmet-
rical cases too: where C_1 requires C_2 but not vice versa, he can say that some part
of one idea is identical with the whole of another. His theory of complex ideas
commits him in any case to allowing that ideas have parts, so it would not be a
great stretch to give part/whole some work to do in our present context as well.
Here, as in the account of complexity, the parts must correspond to *conjunctive*
explanations of the meanings of the words, so that *human* will be part of *man* but
not of *inhuman*.

So much for logical requirement. The major problem concerns exclusion.
Locke's only basis for this—namely, diversity or otherness between concepts—is
too weak to carry the load. Square(ness) is not rectangular(ity), and cleverness is
not kindness, but in neither case does one concept exclude the other. Locke
misses this by always illustrating diversity with pairs of ideas that are downright
incompatible—'White is not black', rather than merely 'White is not circular'. In
this way he gets incompatibility into the reader's thoughts without explicitly
mentioning it, and thus without seeing a need to theorize about it.

For example, he contrasts the fact that the ideas of white and black 'do not
agree' with the fact that the idea of equality-to-90-degrees 'does necessarily agree
to and is inseparable from' the idea of angles-of-triangle (IV.i.2; see also I.ii.18,25).
This shows that he is thinking of exclusion and requirement, which are mutually
contrary; but the language of 'agree' and 'do not agree' implies a contrast
between contradictories. Locke has prepared the way for this sleight of hand

with the phrase 'the connection and agreement, or disagreement and repugnancy, of any of our ideas', where connexion is presumably logical requirement, and repugnancy is certainly logical exclusion, that being the word's standard meaning in philosophy at that time.

Using identity and part/whole, we have seen, Locke can ground logical requirement. But from that and negation, can he not get exclusion? Why can he not say that triangularity rules out squareness because the idea of triangular contains as a part the idea of not-square? The answer is that he does not *and cannot* have an acceptable concept of not-square or of any other negative idea.

The problem does not concern negativeness as such. If we could make Lockean sense of each of a pair of ideas which represented logical complements of one another, it would not matter which was positive and which negative. Our problem is to get such a pair of ideas in the first place. Supposing that Locke has safely possessed himself of the idea of *human*, how can he also make room for its logical complement? There are two ways he might go.

He could try to devise an idea that is fit to represent non-humans in the way that the idea of human is fit to represent humans (or that of ball to represent balls, etc.). This requires a natural correlation between the intrinsic features of the idea and the represented property. This is the property of non-humanity—whatever it is that is possessed by all coyotes, balls, lilies, neutron stars, whirlpools, etc., and by no human beings. The only mental property that is suitably correlated with that is the absence of whatever it is that is correlated with humans. That is Locke's opinion, too, it seems; for he would apply to 'non-human' his general statement: 'Negative or privative words . . . relate to positive ideas, and signify their absence' (III.i.4).

(Although a certain mental state represents non-humanity, we can sympathize with Locke's wanting to call it the absence of an idea of humanity rather than an idea of non-humanity. The strain of calling it an idea is part of a more general awkwardness in his theory of ideas—one which he does not adequately recognize. The theory is at its most plausible when treating ideas of easily perceptible properties of things such as shapes and colours. When it comes to ideas associated with terms such as 'human', 'house', and 'dandelion', the account comes under strain, which Locke does not acknowledge. More relevant just now, however, is the strain that comes from moving the other way, towards ever greater generality: human, animal, organism, body . . . ; house, building, artefact, body . . . When he came to the extreme of generality with *thing* or *substance*, Locke finally noticed the trouble, and openly derided the idea which his theory of meaning required him to postulate (§203). Well, an idea of *non-human* would suffer from this problem of extreme generality, as would any other idea that we intuitively counted as negative; so Locke's problem with them is just a special case of the generality problem. The view that negativeness is extreme generality, which I have found in Berkeley, Kant, and Ayer, is developed at length in chapter 6 of my 1995 book *The Act Itself.*)

Now, consider the true proposition that it is absolutely impossible that a cannibal should be a vegetarian. According to our present version of Locke's theory,

I can discover this to be true by inspecting my idea of cannibal, and finding that it includes as a part an idea of non-vegetarian; that is, *includes a part that lacks the features that suffice for representing vegetarian*. But if that established the truth of 'No cannibal can be a vegetarian', it would also establish 'No cannibal can be a human'; because my idea of cannibal contains a part that is not sufficient for representing a human—namely, the part representing eaters. By these standards, no triangle can have three sides, because part of my idea of triangle is not sufficient to represent three-sidedness; and so on through endless other examples. In short, an idea's merely *containing* a part which *lacks* a certain representative feature can never establish a proposition about impossibility. That was Locke's first option.

The second option is to capture non-humanity not through a suitably general representative idea, but rather by operating on the idea of humanity. Locke provides for something like this in his doctrine about the meanings of 'particles':

> The mind in communicating its thoughts to others does not only need signs of the ideas it has then before it, but others also to show or intimate some particular action of its own at that time relating to those ideas. This it does several ways; as *is* and *is not* are the general marks of the mind, affirming or denying. (*Essay* III.vii.1)

He says this only about words that serve to link others to make sentences, or sentences to make arguments and other discourses; but he could agree to extend it to smaller linguistic units that take one from a given classificatory general word to its complement, as from 'human' to 'non-human'.

But that would not combine well with the thesis that we learn modal truths by discovering how our ideas are interrelated. I am to learn that it is absolutely impossible that a cannibal should be a vegetarian by attending to my idea of cannibal and finding that it contains . . . what? The item that you get through a negating operation on the idea of vegetarian? How did it get there? Have I already performed the negation operation and left its upshot sitting there within my idea of cannibal? I can find no way of telling this story without making it unbelievable, even by someone who is not sceptical about Lockean ideas as such, and is comfortable about ideas such as those of humanity and animality.

I should add that the theory of particles looks apt to be useful for the most general modal truths, for which Locke's system of classificatory ideas is quite useless—for example, the proposition that if (if P then not-P) then not-P. But here again the theory that modal truths are learned by introspection seems to be pushed aside. What could we be introspecting?

Locke's troubles with negation and logical exclusion arise from his trying to treat ideas as mental particulars. This aspect of his philosophy is so damaging to it that some students of his work—for example, Ryle (1933)—have held that he is here using 'idea' to refer not to mental particulars at all, but only to qualities or attributes. That would save trouble, but it flies in the face of masses of textual evidence that for Locke intuition is a process of inspecting the particular contents of one's own mind.

174. Other relations

Locke bases many necessary truths on 'relation'; he ought to mean '*other* relations', for identity and diversity are relations too. I have focused on the latter because Locke says most about them; but he seems to hold that the interesting necessities do not arise from those two. Especially in IV.vii and viii, where he proclaims the unimportance of many necessary truths, he cuts some truths down to size by implying that they are verbal or 'trifling' (IV.viii), and this axe falls on precisely the ones whose truth depends on the 'identity and diversity' of ideas when that is enlarged to include part/whole as well as is/isn't. The necessities that Locke counts as instructive all involve some 'consequence' relation other than that of whole to part, and the only place to look for it is among the (other) relations (see especially IV.i.5).

However, when Locke tries to explore this further territory, he loses his compass. Here is the crux:

As to the . . . agreement or disagreement of any of our ideas in any other relation: . . . It is hard to determine how far [this] may extend: Because the advances that are made in this part of knowledge, depending on our sagacity in finding intermediate ideas, that may show the relations and habitudes of ideas . . ., it is a hard matter to tell when we are at an end of such discoveries; and when reason has all the helps it is capable of for the finding of proofs or examining the agreement or disagreement of remote ideas. (IV.iii.18)

The problem, Locke says here, is always to find intermediate ideas that will enable us to construct chains. What are the individual links of such chains? All he says is that they will be such as to show the 'relations of ideas'—presumably the ones at the opposite ends of the chain—and will constitute 'proofs'. Later in that section and after it, he writes of 'necessary consequences', but he does not underpin that with any theory. Throughout these sections, the model he has in mind is demonstration in arithmetic and geometry. He offers to explain why rigorous arguments are easier to find in those areas than elsewhere, while insisting that, in principle, they can be extended much further, and that we could with care 'place Morality among the sciences capable of demonstration' (549:17). In a much misunderstood remark, Locke says that the proposition 'Where there is no property, there is no injustice' is 'as certain as any demonstration in Euclid'; he holds that it can be proved a priori, without help from theology or anthropology. He does not offer it as substantive morality: his point is merely that moral concepts are interlinked conceptually, just as mathematical ones are; this being needed if substantive morality is to be rigorously inferred ('demonstrated') from truths about God and mankind (§170).

From the point of view of our present inquiry, the trouble with all this is that Locke, as we have seen, has no proper account of mathematical demonstration. In trying to give one, he repeatedly slides from the relating of ideas to the relating of numbers, figures, and so on. In short, when discussing the logical powers of the 'other relations', Locke writes as though the problem were to forge demonstrative chains out of links—a consequence relation—for which he has already provided a theoretical grounding; but no such links have been established.

Locke's theorizing about relations is visibly unstable. This is clearly a matter that he could not get to the bottom of. For example, at 322:6 he treats agreement and disagreement as species of relation; but in IV.i.3 'relation' is listed as one species of (dis)agreement.

I should mention a verbal trap that lurks in this material: namely, Locke's repeatedly saying that relations consist in 'referring or comparing two things one to another' (321:3); but he means 'comparing' not in our full sense of the term, but only in the attenuated sense that we still have in the idiom 'to compare notes'. For him, relating involves 'bringing two ideas . . . together, and setting them one by another so as to take a view of them at once' (163:23).

175. Locke on modal discovery: the necessity problem

Pretend now that the relevance problem is solved, perhaps by focusing on geometrical propositions and pretending to read them off from the properties of the ideas. This frees you to focus on the necessity problem. Leibniz brought this to the fore in his complaint that Locke's procedure of attending to particular ideas could establish only contingent truths.

The core of the difficulty has been well stated by Ayers (1991: i. 255): I find in my mind a particular image of a triangle, and perceive that it has (or is an image of something that has) internal angles equal two right angles; but to get a general proposition out of this, I need to know that the image has that property *purely because* it is an image of a triangle. Locke does not try to explain how I could perceive that.

When discussing a different problem, he says something that could be a response to Leibniz's criticism: namely, that the eternity of the truths we learn from inspecting our ideas is ensured by the fact that 'The same idea will eternally have the same habitudes and relations' (IV.i.9). His only grounding for this, however, is a remark about 'the immutability of the same relations between the same immutable things'. But Lockean ideas are not immutable things; they are dated and mentally situated psychological particulars. Locke tells us this openly and often; and, anyway, if ideas were not like that, how could we examine them by looking into ourselves?

Later in book IV, he returns to the problem of eternal truths while holding fast to the status of ideas as psychological particulars:

Such propositions are . . . called *eternal truths* . . . because being once made about abstract ideas, so as to be true, they will, whenever they can be supposed to be made again at any time past or to come, by a mind having those ideas, always actually be true. For names being supposed to stand perpetually for the same ideas, and the same ideas having immutably the same habitudes one to another; propositions concerning any abstract ideas that are once true must needs be eternal verities. (IV.xi.14)

If names really do 'stand perpetually for the same ideas', it follows that a sentence that now expresses a truth will always express that same proposition; but it does not follow that the proposition will always be true. Furthermore, this concerns 'eternity' only in the weak sense of sempiternity at the actual world. The eternity that Locke ought to be treating—the kind associated with necessary truths—is not touched by what he says about what is supposed to obtain 'perpetually'.

Just before this passage, he writes that an event in the mind of one person at one time will be duplicated in the mind of any relevantly similar person at any other time, and we can accept this. But he says it in the language of discovery or even of making-true: if events in my mind teach me that P, or make it the case that P, the mind of any similar person can or will be the scene of similar events—ones in which P's truth will also be revealed or created. If the point concerns discovery, Locke needs, but does not have, an account of what the initial discovery consists in. If it concerns making-true ('being once made about abstract ideas, so as to be true'), he is even further from having explained what he ought to explain. I think this is a mixture of the relevance and necessity problems.

176. Leibniz's first modal epistemology

Throughout book I of the *New Essays* Leibniz seems to propose a modal epistemology in which the relevance problem is solved and the necessity problem does not even arise. It holds that we learn modal truths because they are engraved on our souls. Whereas Locke writes of looking in and finding states of affairs which point to the truth of Q—the relevance problem being the question of what the 'pointing' is—Leibniz's theory of soul-writing says that we look in and find Q itself.

Or so one might think, but let us not go too fast. What is it to find a proposition in my soul? It might be to introspect and discover that I have a certain belief: I find Q in there by finding myself believing that Q. That seems not to be Leibniz's principal view, however. As his metaphor about writing or engraving implies, he apparently holds that in many and perhaps most cases what is written on the soul is something which means a modal proposition—a sentence in soul-script, as it were—and that might seem to raise the relevance problem once more. For Locke it was the question of how a psychological particular can *point to* any one universal proposition; now Leibniz confronts the question of how such a particular can *mean* such a proposition.

Leibniz is silent about this, and seems not to have noticed it. However, this is not really on a par with Locke's relevance problem. It raises a more general question about linguistic meaning, which arises for us all. If it upsets the soul-writing answer to the question of modal epistemology, then it also makes trouble for the question itself; for that is stated in a sentence, which we think we understand. Why does that not also get Locke off the hook? Because he does not simply help himself to fully propositional items in the mind; he tries to say how such items arise and are known about through facts about sub-propositional items; and that is where his relevance problem comes in. Here, as often, Locke has a difficulty because he tackles so much.

As for the necessity problem: surprisingly, Leibniz discusses this only as an objection to Locke, not as a triumph for himself. His best, and perhaps only, way of dealing with it in the present context is to contend that what we find written into our souls are propositions asserting the necessity of various propositions. For example, he should say that what God has inscribed on my soul is not merely Q:

If (if P then not-P) then not-P,

but the stronger modal-Q:

It is absolutely necessary that if (if P then not-P) then not-P.

If Q could be written into me, then so could modal-Q; so there is no need for Leibniz to suffer from the necessity problem.

A question remains. Granted that a given soul-sentence means modal-Q, why should its presence in my soul count as showing me that modal-Q is true? What if I found it inscribed instead on a rock or a redwood? Leibniz might reply by appealing to the supposed phenomenology of the propositions written on the soul—that they 'sparkle in the understanding', and so on. But his main answer would probably be this: the sentence is written on my soul because God wrote it there, and God can be trusted not to write lies in people. This seems reasonable. If I believed in God, I would believe that about him.

Until Leibniz knows some modal truths, he cannot justify his belief in a truthful God. So his procedure is circular if he aims to establish a modal epistemology from a starting-point that assumes nothing about what is possible or necessary. But he may not be attempting that; indeed, it may be that no such attempt could succeed; yet there could still be an epistemology of modality. I have learned this from Alston 1993: ch. 2. Consider the question of how we discover how matter is distributed at the actual world. The right answer has at its core the thesis that material things leave informative traces of their action upon us; but our evidence for this answer relies on things we believe about the material world. Such 'epistemic circularity', as Alston calls it, is not intellectually fatal; and because our epistemic resources are not infinite, we must accept at least one instance of it. So the written-by-God theory may be a coherent epistemology of modal truth.

Still, even someone who accepts this whole story ought to find it disappointing, because it passes on the epistemological problem from humans to another person. 'I got my basic modal beliefs from my brother, whom I trust'—that is not even a down payment on a decent epistemology of modality, because the episte-mological question re-arises regarding my brother. Well, if I substitute God for my brother, shouldn't you react in the same manner? Perhaps not. A believer might think that God knows everything, and that this is a basic fact about him, not the upshot of any epistemic ways or means that might be the topic of an explanatory theory. But if that is your view, and if you also hold that your best explanation of our modal knowledge is that God handed it to us *en bloc*, you ought, as an epistemologist, to be disappointed that this is so.

Return now to the contrast between our two philosophers. Where Leibniz says that I look into myself and find Q inscribed there, Locke says that I look into myself and find states of affairs from which I can work out the truth of Q. Even in the easiest cases, he thinks, there is something we must *do* to arrive at a modal truth; all our knowledge has to be worked for; for him, 'Knowledge is always discovery' (Aaron 1970: 97). The intuitive noticing of identity and diversity in our ideas is easy and elementary, but still it is a method of discovery, not a mere reading of 'natural characters engraven on the mind' (*Essay* I.iii.1). The word 'character' occurs frequently in Locke's polemic against innate principles; characters are letters, and Locke is inveighing against the hypothesis of inner writing, the proposition sitting there waiting to be uncovered. He is eloquent about innatism's work-shy nature:

We may as well think the use of reason necessary to make our eyes discover visible objects, as that there should be need of reason, or the exercise thereof, to make the understanding see what is originally engraven in it. (I.ii.9)

There is a great deal of difference between an innate law and a law of nature; between something imprinted on our minds in their very original, and something that we being ignorant of may attain to the knowledge of by the use . . . of our natural faculties. (I.iii.13)

Gibson warns us against being led by Locke's metaphor of the mind as 'white paper'[2] to think that he sees the mind as generally passive:

The upholders of the theory [Locke] opposes commonly employed the metaphor of the stamp and its impression in describing the source of innate principles. . . . Indeed, so far as the question of mental activity is involved in the controversy at all, one of Locke's objections to the theory he opposes is that it represents certain truths as merely given to the mind, apart from the exercise of that active comparison and examination which he holds to be involved in all human knowledge. (1917: 32–3)

Leibniz also stresses the need for work, and rails against those who plead innateness as a cover for laziness and dogmatism (*NE* 50, 85). But the work he calls for is proving whatever can be proved, using as premises those basic innate truths 'which can be neither doubted nor proved' (108). The latter, according to him, are just given—they are among the 'writings in inner light' which would 'sparkle continuously in the understanding' if we cleared away the sensory clutter.

---

[2] Not *tabula rasa*—a phrase which does not occur in the *Essay* in Latin or in English translation.

177. Leibniz's second modal epistemology

Later in the *New Essays*, Leibniz deserts the modal epistemology which he has seemed to accept in his opening chapters. He is helped in this by his metaphysic of modality—his account of what the truth-makers are of modal propositions. If Locke had such a metaphysic, it must have been the view that modal truths are made true by facts about our ideas—which invites the charge that he has made them psychological and contingent. Leibniz is warier on this topic:

Eternal truths are fundamentally all conditional. For instance, when I say: *Any figure with three sides will also have three angles*, I am saying only: given that there is a figure with three sides, that same figure will have three angles. . . . How can a proposition about a subject have a real truth if the subject does not exist? The answer is that its truth is a merely conditional one which says that if the subject ever does exist it will be found to be thus and so. What is the ground for this connection? The reply is that it is grounded in the linking together of ideas. Where would these ideas be if there were no mind? and what would then become of the real foundation of this certainty of eternal truths? This question brings us at last to the ultimate foundation of truth, namely to that Supreme and Universal Mind who cannot fail to exist and whose understanding is indeed the domain of eternal truths. (*NE* 446–7, slightly streamlined)[3]

Did you expect him to invoke possible worlds? That Leibniz explained necessity in that way is a contemporary myth; he never did so. The account he does give, the one just quoted, is as psychologistic as Locke's: the ideas in question are in minds—some in God's, others in ours. But for Leibniz this does not revive the necessity problem, because his theology is, he thinks, absolutely necessary. Although the truth-makers for modal propositions are relations amongst mental particulars, the latter must exist and be interrelated as in fact they are; so they are eternal and necessary—as rock-hard and durable, logically speaking, as relations within Frege's third realm.

Although Leibniz thought of God as personal, as caring for us, and as a fit object of reverence and love, he writes of God's intellect as though it were an abstract object. In these contexts, his metaphors are notably Fregean: God's understanding is 'the domain [*région*] of eternal truths', we have just seen him say. He says elsewhere that 'the divine understanding is, so to speak, the land [*pays*] of possible realities' (FW 111), and that 'These essences and the so-called eternal truths about them . . . exist in a certain realm [*regio*, Latin] of ideas, so to speak, namely in God himself' (AG 151). Compare this with Frege's 'third realm' and Wittgenstein's 'logical space'.

Out of this Leibniz develops an epistemology that does not involve soul-writing. 'When God displays a truth to us,' he writes in book IV, 'we come to possess the truth which is in his understanding, for although his ideas are infinitely more perfect and extensive than ours they still have the same relationships that ours do'

---

[3] See also Mon 43–4, FW 273–4; UO, AG 151–2; SD, PM 77.

(*NE* 397). Thus, the relations amongst God's ideas make modal truths true; and an isomorphism between our minds and God's enables us to discover which propositions are necessarily true. There is nothing here about truths inscribed on the soul. Indeed, just after writing that the mind of God 'is where I find the pattern for the ideas and truths which are engraved in our souls', Leibniz goes on to explain: 'They are engraved there not in the form of propositions but rather as sources which, by being employed in particular circumstances, will give rise to actual assertions.' So they are *not* engraved there as propositions! This does not have the disappointing feature of the 'God told me and I believe him' theory which he seemed to advance earlier; but, unlike that theory, it revives the relevance problem.

178. Leibniz's relevance problem

The question is: what do relations amongst ideas in a mind have to do with such propositions as that if (if P then not-P) then not-P? Leibniz cannot brush this off with the remark that the ideas in question are in the mind of God, and that we cannot be expected to grasp what they are or how they do what they do. He has said that the relations amongst our ideas are isomorphic with relations amongst God's ideas; so he ought to have some account of what they are and of how they bear on modal truths.

The problem arose for Locke in an acute form because he seems so often to think of his 'ideas' as images; and the relevance of those to modal truths is especially hard to see. Leibniz is spared that trouble, at least, by his insistence on distinguishing images from what he calls ideas. Notice now the terms in which he does so, commenting on Locke's example of the chiliagon:

That example shows that the idea is being confounded with the image. If I am confronted with a regular polygon, my eyesight and my imagination cannot give me a grasp of the thousand which it involves: I have only a confused idea both of the figure and of its number until I distinguish the number by counting. But once I have found the number, I know the given polygon's nature and properties very well, in so far as they are those of a chiliagon. The upshot is that I have this idea of a chiliagon, even though I cannot have the image of one. (*NE* 261)

This fits with Leibniz's general practice of crediting a person with having a certain 'idea' if he is competent in some intellectual matter. Decades earlier he wrote: 'For the ideas of things to be in us is just for God . . . to have impressed a power of thinking upon the mind so that it can by its own operations derive what corresponds perfectly to the nature of things.'[4] That matches our usual way of talking these days about the 'concepts' that people have (§167).

---

[4] 1678, L 208. For further examples and discussion, see Jolley 1984: 179–86.

But while it explains 'He has an idea of x', it does not help with 'idea' standing on its own. Yet that is what Leibniz needs for his second modal epistemology. For ideas to be relata, they must be distinguishable, countable, identifiable *items* of some kind. What sort of items can Leibnizian 'ideas' be? The best answer is that they are competences; my idea of a chiliagon is my competence in thinking about chiliagons. That, however, will not serve in Leibniz's modal metaphysic and epistemology: it is perfectly unclear what the supposed relations amongst competences could be; and Leibniz would blush to say that I know what is necessarily true because my competences interrelate in the way that God's do.

Sometimes he seems to understand the term 'idea' differently. Responding to Locke's statement (which I do not think accurately expressed Locke's own views) that an idea is an object of an act of thinking, Leibniz comments:

I agree about that, provided that you add that an idea is an immediate inner object, and that this object expresses the nature or qualities of things. If the idea were the *form* of the thought, it would come into and go out of existence with the actual thoughts which correspond to it, but since it is the *object* of thought it can exist before and after the thoughts. (*NE* 109)

Perhaps these 'objects' of thoughts are items that could interrelate suitably. They certainly could if they are what Leibniz was referring to in a dismissive comment on Spinoza's view that your mind is the idea of your body: 'Ideas are purely abstract things, like numbers and shapes, and cannot act. Ideas are abstract and universal: the idea of any animal is a possibility' (AG 277). Relations amongst possibilities are just what we need as a foundation for modal truth; but when the term 'idea' is understood in this manner, Leibniz's account of how we get modal knowledge is destroyed. The account makes sense only if ideas are psychological and personally owned ('his ideas', 'our ideas'), as Leibniz usually held them to be. Here, for instance: '[Ideas] are affections or modifications of our mind . . . For certainly there must be some change in our mind when we have some thoughts and then others' (AG 27).

It looks as though the most Leibniz can salvage from this second theory about modal knowledge is this: The truth-makers for modal propositions are items that exist eternally and necessarily in the third realm, or the mind of God; and we are capable of thoughts which somehow map onto, or at least inform us about, relations amongst them. That is a weak offering indeed. I leave it to you to consider whether we have anything better today. If we do, it is probably along the lines of Descartes's theory of modality, which I shall expound in Chapter 24.

179. Innately possessed ideas

A properly innate item of knowledge, Locke argues, would have to be composed of ideas that are also innate:

It may with as much probability be said that a man hath 100 pounds sterling in his pocket and yet denied that he hath there either penny, shilling, crown, or other coin . . . as to think that certain propositions are innate when the ideas about which they are can by no means be supposed to be so. (I.iv.19)

Locke argues that no ideas are innate. According to him, we acquire ideas in two ways: some are forced upon us, others are 'compounded' from ones that have been forced upon us. (I set aside abstraction, for simplicity's sake.) Because of the role of ideas in determining meanings, Locke takes this to imply that you can attach a meaning to a word only if either you have been confronted experientially by items to which it applies or you can define it verbally, thereby laying out the simpler elements out of which it is 'compounded'. Locke sees the doctrine that there are innate ideas as a rival to his theory about these two ways of acquiring ideas.

Unlike Hume, he seldom uses the theory as a weapon of conceptual criticism, a basis for declaring some terms to be meaningless. Still, he thought it to be true, and its innatist rival false; and, as I have just indicated, he thought that by attacking the rival he could undermine the more importantly false doctrine of innately possessed knowledge. Also, he cared about theoretical economy (I.ii.1); and we can see him as arguing that because all the facts about what ideas we have can be explained in his two ways, it is extravagant to postulate a third origin for any of them. (For a different view of Locke's motivation, see Atherton 1983a.)

We must not take 'innate' in its literal sense of 'existing in a person from birth'. The debate is between a pair of views about how, not when, ideas come to be possessed. Locke freely grants that some ideas of sensation may be acquired pre-natally and thus be possessed at birth. The issue as he sees it is not between (1) 'after birth' and (2) 'before birth', but rather between (1) acquired in particular episodes—ones that are accidental, not inevitable—in the life of the person, and (2) possessed as part of the original fabric of the mind. Such pre-natal mental contents as the foetus's hunger pangs are not innate ideas in the sense that matters, Locke says, because they '[come] into the mind by . . . accidental alterations in or operations on the body', whereas innate ideas 'are supposed to be of quite another nature'—namely, 'original characters impressed upon [the mind] in the very first moment of its being and constitution' (II.ix.6).

As well as denying any need to postulate innate ideas, Locke argues positively that there are none. It is hard to lock horns with this argument because the idea concept on which it is based is so elusive. We may think that the worthwhile question in this area is whether there are any innate concepts; but concepts are skills, capacities, or dispositions, and Locke can allow that many of those are innate. In his copy of a book discussing his views he wrote: 'I think nobody who reads my book can doubt that I spoke only of innate ideas and not of innate powers' (quoted in Gibson 1917: 38). He often alludes to our 'natural faculties' and says that it is because of what they enable us to do that we do not need 'the help of any innate impressions' (I.ii.1). He does not deny that some or all of these 'natural faculties' might be innate in the strong sense of being built into us from the outset; he draws the line only at 'innate impressions'. In likening the inexperi-enced mind to a 'white paper', then, he means to be speaking only of its ideas, not of its powers—its content, not its structure or *modus operandi*.

To engage with this philosophically, we have to distinguish structure from content, 'faculties' from 'impressions'. It is useless to draw that line in Locke's official manner—distinguishing intellectual dispositions from sensory-type images—for that would leave us with nothing worth discussing. To have a real topic to consider, we must abide by the fact that the concepts that Locke calls 'ideas' are in fact powers, and must take him to be denying that *those* powers are innate, while admitting that other powers are. A power of the former kind—one that he will call an 'idea'—is a capacity to have thoughts with a certain specific content; so the idea of snow is the ability to have snow-involving thoughts: to think that snow is white, or to think that the white stuff falling outside is snow, or the like. I am not saying that Locke would consent to his position's being stated thus; presumably he would not, though he seems to be moving in this direction when in the final section of book II he speaks of ideas as 'these (I know not whether I may say) instruments or materials of our knowledge'.

On the basis of this rough account of the line around the items that Locke says are never innate, let us consider his reason—his only real reason—for saying so. There is no need to postulate innate ideas, he says, because all our mental pos-sessions can be explained in his way, according to which each of our concepts is either given through the senses or constructed from concepts thus given. The premiss of this argument is false. Not all of our concepts could be attained through 'composition' out of conceptual raw materials that were sensorily given in the way Locke envisages. The idea of existence, for example, could not be learned through selective attention to the perceived world; nor could the idea of unity. He says that 'Existence and unity are two . . . ideas that are suggested to the understanding by every object without and every idea within' (II.vii.7). But if every example of either idea is equally an example of the other, what makes them two ideas rather than one?

One might expect Leibniz to object, as I just have, to Locke's dependence upon exemplars, but he does not. Indeed, he lays himself open to the same objec-tion:

There is a great deal that is innate in our minds, since we are innate to ourselves, so to speak, and since we include Being, Unity, Substance, Duration, Change, Action, Perception, Pleasure, and hosts of other objects of our intellectual ideas. And since these objects are immediately related to our understanding and always present to it . . . , is it any wonder that we say that these ideas . . . are innate in us? (*NE* 51–2)

Later on he says: 'I would like to know how we could have the idea of being if we did not, as beings ourselves, find being within ourselves' (85–6). This implies that these 'intellectual ideas' could not be acquired in Locke's way, and that the only way we could get them is by instantiating them. Locke is right in looking for exemplars for all our ideas (Leibniz now seems to say) but for some exemplars he looks in the wrong place, looking outward for all of them, when really the basis for his 'intellectual ideas' lies in himself. The trick is worked, he says, through the fact that 'as beings ourselves, [we] find being within ourselves'. I can make nothing of this. Granted that only beings can have concepts, how does my status as a being explain my capacity to have the concept of being? Locke's problem about how existence and unity can be two ideas might seem to threaten Leibniz also, but he could outflank it by saying that they are not really two ideas. That little success, however, should not reconcile us to his use of exemplars in this context.

'Locke rightly looks for exemplars but looks for some of them in the wrong place'—that would abolish the debate. Leibniz starts to realize this: having noticed that Locke too says that some of our ideas are based on what we find when we look inwards, he starts to lose his sense of what the debate is about:

[Locke] admits . . . that ideas which do not originate in sensation come from reflection. But reflection is nothing but attention to what is within us, and the senses do not give us what we carry within us already. In view of this, can it be denied that there is a great deal that is innate in our minds, since we are innate to ourselves, so to speak . . . ? (NE 51)

In this Leibniz comes too close to Locke for the quarrel to be interesting, or, I would add, for his own position to be innatism reasonably so-called.

It would have been better for him to say that we have the concepts of being, unity, substance, etc. as part of our natural intellectual endowment—not that we acquire them because we instantiate them, but rather that we do not *acquire* them at all. A good argument for this view, which I think I learned from Kant, runs as follows. Locke's theory purports to explain the acquisition of 'ideas' through learning: ideas reach us through the senses, are grouped into kinds or types, and are then processed—by abstraction, composition, and perhaps in other ways—so as to be fit for intellectual use. To do all this, one must already have some concepts, and so Locke's account cannot apply across the board. The treatment of temporal concepts in *Essay* II.xiv.3–4, owes its plausibility to Locke's confining it to succession and duration. Had he tried to bring in simultaneity, he would have found himself in trouble. He wants to explain the acquisition of concepts as arising from ostensive definitions; but no ostensive procedure could work unless the pupil was already capable of the thought of 'the item that I am confronted with *now*'. Consider again similarity, as in judgements to the effect that x is more like y than z is. For that concept to be acquired in Locke's way, it would have to be possible to do some Lockean learning before having any competence in similarity judgements. But that is absurd, because the core of that learning is grouping many token ideas together as ideas of a single type, which is precisely to bring them under a similarity judgement. All this applies *mutatis mutandis* to at least some of our logical concepts also.

Did Leibniz see that Kantian objection to Locke's theory? He writes: 'Someone will confront me with this accepted philosophical axiom, that there is nothing in the soul which does not come from the senses. But an exception must be made of the soul itself and its states' (NE 110–11). I used to think that he meant to make exceptions of such concepts as are prerequisite for learning anything, and that his point was that the procedures for concept acquisition which Locke described could succeed only for someone who already had some concepts. That was too generous, I now think. As Savile (1972: 123) points out, there is no evidence that Leibniz ever properly saw that 'the very processing of the data of experience presupposes the use of concepts which thus cannot be extracted from experience'. The most Kant-like thing that Leibniz says in this area refers to the 'general principles' that he thinks are innate: 'General principles enter into our thoughts, serving as their inner core and as their mortar. Even if we give no thought to them, they are necessary for thought, as muscles and tendons are for walking. The mind relies on these principles constantly' (NE 84).[5] Perhaps he pointed towards the Kantian argument, but he seems not to have reached it.

The skirmishing between Locke and Leibniz in the general region of the Kantian argument is complex and interesting. Leibniz holds that the mind is a substance, and that necessarily all substances are active; which may seem to give him grounds for objecting when Locke says such things as: 'The mind, in respect of its simple ideas, is wholly passive' (II.xxii.2). But Locke is there thinking of how ideas come to us through the senses—forced in on us independently of our will— and is not suggesting that the mind is passive in every way—for example, in respect of the building up of its intellectual resources. Quite the contrary, as Price (1953: 199n.) has pointed out:

It is, of course, historically false that the Empiricists thought the human mind passive. It would be more just to criticize them for making it more active than it can possibly be. It is the Rationalist Mind, if either, which is the passive one, or at least the lazy one, born, if one may say so, with a silver spoon in its mouth. The Empiricist Mind has to acquire these basic ideas for itself . . . by its own effort and initiative.

Similar points arise from Leibniz's objection to Locke's describing the mind as white paper. This is offensive to Leibniz because he takes it to imply that two (blank) minds might be perfectly alike, and he holds on metaphysical grounds that every two particulars are unalike (NE 109–10; §142). This does not carry weight against Locke, however, even if we accept the discernibility of the diverse. These 'white paper' remarks of Locke's—including the 'closet' metaphor which Leibniz enlivens and enriches at NE 144–5—give a wrong impression of his real views. He held that each human mind is innately endowed with a stock of capacities and powers, and he could have agreed that these must supervene on the mind's intrinsic structure. He was saying only that a mind is blank with respect to content, to what is written on it, until it receives input from inner and outer sense.

However, these points about content versus structure serve to remind us that we do not really know what the issue over innate ideas is, because the term 'idea' is too protean and slippery to support a clear issue.

---

[5] See also NE 101-2. The phrase 'inner core' (for example, the metal spine or armature that supports the wet clay while the sculptor shapes it) translates âme, which also means 'soul'; the French word for mortar, liaison, also means 'connection'. Three translators have Leibniz proclaiming that general principles are 'the soul and the connection' of our thoughts.

Chapter 24

Descartes's Theory of Modality

180. Descartes's voluntarism about modal truths

Descartes seems to be alone among philosophers in holding that God determines not only what is good, but also what is possible, impossible, and necessary. This doctrine—called 'voluntarism', because it says that God voluntarily creates modal truths—has been described as bizarre, curious, incoherent, notorious, peculiar, and strange, but I shall argue that, on the contrary, it comes from a deep and possibly true philosophical insight, one in which Descartes anticipated Wittgenstein. Since I published a paper arguing for this (Bennett 1994), I have had letters from readers pointing to other texts that support my interpretation, and none offering counter-evidence. Some previous writers have offered something like my interpretation (Wilson 1978: 125; Ishiguro 1986; Alanen 1988), but none has stayed with it, followed through its implications, and used it to explain nearly everything in the voluntarism texts. That is what I offer to do.

Descartes really believed his voluntarism about necessary truths; he did not let it slip out inadvertently, or play with it on idle afternoons, or use it to tease his friends. He first declared it in two letters to Mersenne, urging him to 'assert and proclaim [it] everywhere'. That was in 1630, years before he published anything. Voluntarism does not appear in the *Meditations*, the *Discourse on the Method*, or the *Principles of Philosophy*. But it glows luminously just behind something Descartes wrote in the Second Replies (1641); and he announced it openly, without being prodded, in the Fifth Replies. When the authors of the Sixth Objections (having seen that response) took up the voluntarism doctrine in their turn, Descartes responded forthrightly. He also proclaimed it in letters to Gibieuf in 1642 and to Arnauld in 1648. Nobody knows why he kept voluntarism out of sight in the major published works, but it was evidently not because he was unsure about it.

Furthermore, although Descartes does not put his voluntarism on display in the *Meditations*, that work shows him trying to conform to its constraints. It occurs at a point where one might expect him write:

There is no doubt that God is capable of creating everything that I am capable of perceiving in this manner; and *there is nothing that could not be made by him except for what involves a contradiction.*

But the chief theological thrust behind the voluntarism doctrine is an unwillingness to say of *anything* that God could not do it. We see that at work here, for what Descartes actually writes is this:

> There is no doubt that God is capable of creating everything that I am capable of perceiving in this manner; and *I have never judged that something could not be made by him except on the grounds that there would be a contradiction in my perceiving it distinctly.* (CSM 2:50)

When he wrote the *Meditations*, it seems, Descartes's voluntarism was alive in his mind. What else could explain his immediately following one proposition about what *God can* do by another about what *Descartes has believed that God cannot* do? Similarly in a 1642 letter to Regius: 'The only things that are said to be impossible for God to do are those which involve a conceptual contradiction' (CSMK 214).

The voluntarism doctrine has seemed to involve the following two well-known troubles.

The bootstraps problem   On the strength of his a priori argument, Descartes holds that God's existence is absolutely necessary. This seems to imply that a peculiar bootstrapping procedure has gone on: God selected the principles of necessity, which rewarded him by guaranteeing his existence. This has led Curley (1984: 592–7) and Gueroult (1953: 26–9) to suppose that Descartes's doctrine about necessary truths was not meant to apply to propositions about God's own nature and existence. Aided by textual evidence assembled by Wilson (1978: 123–4), Curley argues that Descartes might have had a philosophical reason for this, so that it is not a purely *ad hoc* gerrymander; still, if that was his view, he was oddly quiet about it. I shall later quote him saying that 'the existence of God is the first and most eternal of all possible truths and the one from which alone all others derive', which seems to express a voluntarism from whose scope the proposition that God exists is excluded. I have no other account of what the sentence might mean, which makes trouble for my interpretation; but I do not back down in face of it. This is the only place where Descartes suggests that one necessary proposition falls outside the scope of his voluntarism; if that really was his doctrine, one would expect it to be proclaimed oftener and more clearly.

The libertinism threat   It is natural and reasonable to think that in his voluntarism about necessary truths Descartes has committed himself to this:

> For any necessary P, God could have made it the case that not-P; so it could have been the case that not-P; so P is not necessary after all. Thus, nothing is absolutely necessary or absolutely impossible.

I shall call this 'the libertine thesis'. Many of Descartes's own arguments and doctrines, when conjoined with it, collapse into rubble; and some of us have tried to help him by preventing such conjunctions from occurring. Curley, for example, discussing the separability argument for the real distinction between body and mind, writes:

> If we were to invoke the doctrine of the creation of eternal truths, we might say that a really omnipotent being could cause the mind and body to exist apart even if that were

not logically possible. But in the *Meditations* Descartes is careful not to invoke that extravagant conception of omnipotence, and we would do him no service by bringing it in. (1978: 198)

I too have said that kind of thing in lectures, trying to shield Descartes from his own splatter. But this is intolerable. It implies this: Descartes offered an argument from which he concluded that his mind is one thing, his body another; if voluntarism is true, the argument fails; when he wrote the argument, Descartes believed in voluntarism. I do not believe this. It is one thing to present an argument while suppressing some of its complexities or depths; it is a different and dishonest thing to present an argument while believing it to be no good. More is at stake here than just the separability argument. If Descartes's voluntarism entails that nothing is impossible, it will stampede through the rest of his philosophy like a rogue elephant.

The tandem puzzle   A third question ought to have puzzled writers on this topic. Here is a typical text, written to Arnauld:

[1] I do not think we should ever say of anything that it cannot be brought about by God. For since every basis of truth and goodness depends on his omnipotence, I would not venture to say that God cannot make an uphill without a downhill, or that one and two should not be three. [2] But I merely say that he has given me such a mind that I cannot conceive an uphill without a downhill, or a sum of one and two which is not three, and that such things involve a contradiction in my conception. (CSMK 358-9)

This is one of three or four places where Descartes follows (1) a thesis relating necessary truths to God with (2) a thesis relating them to us: (1) It is not impossible for God to make an uphill without a downhill; (2) we cannot conceive of an uphill without a downhill. These must have struck Descartes as natural companions, because he kept presenting them in tandem—but why? The rationale for pairing them is not obvious.

If voluntarism entails libertinism, the tandem puzzle can be solved: 1 entails that there could be an uphill without a downhill, while 2 explains why we (wrongly) think there could not. There could be, because God could make it so; we think otherwise, because we cannot conceive of this possibility's being actual. One hopes that the tandem puzzle can be explained without rubbing our noses so fiercely in the libertine thesis that everything is possible.

If you think that 1 avoids entailing libertinism, you might relate it to 2 as follows: 1 says that God set up the modal truths, and 2 says that he gave us limits to conception as a guide to what the modal truths are. That is what Wilson proposed (1978: 127). But if the two are related thus, the natural way to say it would be: 'God created the necessary truths, *and* he gave me this way of finding out what they are.' In fact, in each occurrence of the tandem Descartes links the two parts with 'But I merely say . . . (*sed tantum dico . . .*)', a mighty peculiar conjunction if they are a metaphysic of modality followed by an epistemology of modality.

181. The two parts of Descartes's voluntarism: the tandem puzzle

I see Descartes's voluntarism about modal truths as a two-part package. What looks like startling news about God's relation to modality conjoins a fairly routine view about how God relates to mankind with a novel doctrine about how mankind relates to modality. Descartes sincerely means the theological part of this, which also has some interest for us, but the really exciting, surprising, and non-routine part of the voluntarism doctrine is its other half, the conjunct relating modality not to God but to us.

Descartes held, I submit, that our modal concepts should be understood or analysed in terms of what does or does not lie within the compass of our ways of thinking. Roughly speaking: 'It is absolutely impossible that P' means that no human who is thinking efficiently can add P to his system of beliefs without running into outright contradiction. I shall shorten this to 'P is unthinkable by us', but don't understand this in terms of trying and failing to have some thought of P; the crucial idea is that of being drawn by the thought of P into a thought of the form 'Q and not-Q', and thus being brought to a dead halt. Descartes makes much of the notion of self-contradiction. Here, a bit randomly, are some instances of it: 'All self-contradictoriness or impossibility resides solely in our thought, when we make the mistake of joining together mutually inconsistent ideas; it cannot occur in anything which is outside the intellect.' 'Such things involve a contradiction in my conception.' 'We should think that whatever conflicts with our ideas is absolutely impossible and involves a contradiction.' 'I do not boldly deny that he can do what contradicts my conception, but say only that it implies a contradiction' (CSM 2:108, CSM 3:359, 202, 363).

Never mind the fine details. What matters is the thesis that a proposition's modal status is not a monadic property of it, but rather a relation that it has to human intellectual capacities. The only direct evidence that Descartes accepted this subjectivist, conceptualist analysis of modality is a passage in the Second Replies where voluntarism is not in question. That is what one would expect, if I am right: the philosophical core of the doctrine has nothing to do with God. The authors of the Second Objections had questioned whether the concept of God used in Descartes's a priori argument for God's existence is a possible one. Now listen to this small part of his reply:

If by *possible* you mean what everyone commonly means, namely whatever does not conflict with our human concepts, then it is manifest that the nature of God, as I have described it, is possible in this sense because . . . [etc.]. Alternatively, you may well be inventing some other kind of possibility which relates to the object itself; but unless this matches the first sort of possibility it can never be known by the human intellect, and so it . . . will undermine the whole of human knowledge. (Rep 2, CSM 2:107)

Descartes here dismisses the 'possibility which relates to the object itself' as a contrivance, something faked up for argument's sake, and not part of our normal conceptual repertoire. He also denies it a life of its own: if the objective concept does not keep in step with the subjective one, he says, it will be direly subversive. He describes the subjective concept of possibility, which makes it a relation to our concepts, as the common meaning of the term 'possible'. So he is offering an *analysis* of modality; a *conceptualist* analysis—taking concepts as aspects of the human condition.

The analysis provides a solid basis for Descartes's modal epistemology. He frequently moves from something's being distinctly conceivable to its being possible, as here: 'Everything which I clearly and distinctly understand is capable of being created by God so as to correspond exactly with my understanding of it' (Med 6, CSM 2:54). We have already seen one striking instance of this—run contrapositively—in the passage about God's lack of moral limits (§72): 'It is self-contradictory to suppose . . . etc., for it is impossible to envisage . . . etc.' This conforms to the spirit of his writing to Gibieuf that 'We should think that whatever conflicts with our ideas is absolutely impossible and involves a contradiction' (CSMK 202).

Because Descartes chose to keep his voluntarism out of sight in the *Meditations* and *Principles of Philosophy*, the route from conceivability to possibility in those works runs through trust in God, rather than through the conceptualist analysis of modality. This is compatible with his having, ultimately, an analytic basis for the move: theological optimism provides one reason why the move is safe; philosophical analysis another.

The remainder of the voluntarism doctrine practically writes itself: modal truths are facts about our intellectual limits; add the theological commonplace that God made us as we are, willing us to have our limits, and there emerges the conclusion that God voluntarily created all the modal truths.

The tandem puzzle is now easy to solve. The statement (2) about what we can conceive provides all the content we have for our modal statements; and that is why (1) we ought not to think of modal truths as a part of what God has to reckon with. I do not say that logical constraints are independent realities with which God is confronted; but I merely say (*sed tantum dico*) that logical constraints exist as limits on what I can conceive. Not just the framework of the tandem, but the fine details of its wording, fall into place.

Descartes's usual label for necessary propositions is 'eternal truths'. He once refers to 'the mathematical truths that you [Mersenne] call eternal', but I doubt that he is suggesting that perhaps they are not eternally true. A problem arises: how could they be so, if he is right about the source of their truth? For some discussion of the difficulties, see Curley 1984: 576–83.

Descartes solves this by basing the eternity of necessary truths in theology: 'I do not think that . . . mathematical truths . . . are independent of God. Nevertheless I do think that they are unchanging and eternal, since . . . God willed and decreed that they should be so' (Rep 5, CSM 2:261). Given that they are eternally true, Descartes can reasonably speculate that God has decreed that they be so; but what reason can he have for the premiss? On any of the standard

interpretations of his voluntarism, none. On my interpretation, we can do a little better on his behalf.

If the problem is to bite, it must take the form of a threat: If the necessity that
twice two should make four is ultimately a contingent fact about our capacities,
then we might some day find that this arithmetical truth has turned false on us—
waking up one morning to find that we have two noses, rectangular fingers, a
hatred for sugar and . . . minds such that twice two no longer makes four.
Descartes ought to reply that there is no such prospect, and thus no such threat,
because facing it means entertaining the thought of four's not being twice two,
and we cannot do that. Our conceptual limits could have been different, but we
cannot have a specific thought about any such difference: our present use of
modal concepts must reflect our present intellectual limits, even if we are thinking about the past, the future, or other possible worlds.

Still, even if we cannot think of a change in the modal value of any particular
proposition, we can have the general thought that some day the distribution of
modalities across propositions may change. Without that thought, we could not
understand Descartes's analysis of modality. Does that thought not threaten the
eternity of necessary truths? Yes, it does, and Descartes has no reply to this except
his theological one. Something better might be devised through Kantian considerations: personal identity depends on how our thoughts hook into one another
along the time line, so no thinker could survive a conceptual change of the
threatened kind. However, one would not expect that from Descartes, who
helped himself to the notion of continuant thinkers without considering what it
takes for such an entity to last through time.

182. Omnipotence and small achievements

In the passage I have quoted from the Second Replies, Descartes accepts his subjectivist analysis of modal concepts on its philosophical merits: he thinks it is correct, and also sees it as yielding the only metaphysic of modality which explains
how we can have modal knowledge. (He keeps the 'trust God' basis for modal
knowledge out of sight there.) I see no evidence of his being pushed into this
account of modal concepts by his desire to establish voluntarism for theological
reasons; but the philosophical analysis, although it does not dance to a theological tune, does satisfy a demand of piety. Descartes's religious sentiments require
him to maintain the voluntarism doctrine; and he gets an understanding of *how*
it could be true from something that he saw as, on its own merits, sound philosophy. Although the analysis of modality meets a theological need, therefore, it is
also available to an atheist. I once defended a non-theistic version of something
like it (1961), following in Wittgenstein's footsteps and ignorant of Descartes's.

What theological need does it meet? Writers on this topic have usually
assumed that the driving idea is that of God's omnipotence—the doctrine that

God can do *anything*—which Descartes rashly took to mean 'even impossible things!' This is mere folklore. In no voluntarism text does omnipotence carry any load. The only text that mentions God's omnipotence (I have quoted it) does so only in passing, not as a premiss for any argument.

The voluntarism texts are driven by the thought of God not as omnipotent, but as 'great' in such a way that everything else real depends on him. From this Descartes infers that there are no independent principles that constrain God's actions, and no independent standards by which he can be judged. This is akin to the thought of God's omnipotence, but differs from it in not being open to the criticisms of the latter in Geach 1973.

The emphasis on everything's depending on God shines in the first of the three letters proclaiming voluntarism: 'The mathematical truths that you call eternal', he writes to Mersenne, 'have been laid down by God and depend on him entirely, no less than the rest of his creatures. Indeed, to say that these truths are independent of God is to talk of him as if he were Jupiter or Saturn and to subject him to the Styx and the Fates' (CSMK 23). The emphasis remains in the second letter, written three weeks later:

The eternal truths . . . are not known as true by God in any way which would imply that they are true independently of him. If men really understood the sense of their words they could never say without blasphemy that the truth of anything is prior to God's knowledge of it. . . . So we must not say that if God did not exist nonetheless these truths would be true; for the existence of God is the first and most eternal of all possible truths and the one from which alone all others proceed . . . God is . . . the sole author on whom all things depend. (CSMK 24)

This does not say that God can do anything. The same holds for a passage in the response to Gassendi: 'If anyone attends to the immeasurable greatness of God he will find it manifestly clear that there can be nothing whatsoever which does not depend on him. This applies not just to everything that subsists, but to all order, every law, and every reason for anything's being true or good' (Rep 6, CSM 2:293–4).

The 'nothing independent' thought also led Descartes to hold that there are no standards of value independent of God's will. He runs the modal and the moral in a single harness ('truth and goodness') in the passage last quoted, and also here:

God did not will the creation of the world in time because he saw that it would be better this way than if he had created it from eternity; nor did he will that the three angles of a triangle should be equal to two right angles because he recognized that it could not be otherwise, and so on. On the contrary, it is because he willed to create the world in time that it is better this way . . . and it is because he willed that the three angles of a triangle should necessarily equal two right angles that this is true and cannot be otherwise. (Rep 6, CSM 2:291)

The moral half of this has no direct link with 'God can do anything', and Descartes cannot have thought that it does. This further confirms that the same holds for the logical half. What fuels the passage and links its halves is the view that everything true or real depends on God's will. Descartes follows up the quoted passage by saying: 'The supreme indifference to be found in God is the supreme indication of his omnipotence.' Here 'omnipotence' is used in a peculiar manner which I do not properly understand; but Descartes does not argue from it as a premiss.

A substantive issue is at stake in the view that omnipotence was for Descartes the theological driving force behind the voluntarism doctrine. The almost universal belief that this was so has been accompanied by the idea that God's making the eternal truths true is supposed by Descartes to be a stupendously great feat—so great that most believers have thought it to lie beyond even God's reach. On my account, on the other hand, the feat is humdrum by divine standards: it consists only in creating human beings whose thought is constrained in certain ways, and no believer has questioned that God could do that. This can seem to take some wind out of the doctrine's sails when it is understood as saying 'Look at how potent God is!'; but when it is seen as saying 'You see, there is nothing independent of God's will that he has to take into account', it provides exactly what it announces, and is not guilty of false advertising. This adds significance to the fact that Descartes states the theological basis for his voluntarism always in terms of '(in)dependence', never of 'omnipotence'.

183. Subjective and objective: the bootstraps problem

When Descartes's voluntarism is understood as I propose, the bootstraps problem evaporates. Necessarily God exists: that God should not exist is unthinkable by us if we are thinking efficiently; if we accept 'God does not exist', we shall run into contradictions. Because God gave us our limits, it is he who has made it unthinkable to us that he should not exist, but there is no paradox or circle here.

Objection: 'You have extricated Descartes from the tangle of bootstraps by weakening his theology from the momentous and cosmic proposition (1) that it is absolutely necessary that God exists to the modestly local truth (2) that we cannot consistently think that God does not exist.' This implies that 2 is weaker than 1, which amounts to rejecting the conceptualist analysis of modality. Perhaps it should be rejected; but that is not the issue. The accusation which I have answered is that if Descartes accepts it, then he has a problem regarding the thesis that necessarily God exists.

Second objection: 'Inevitably one thinks of God's existing necessarily as explaining *why* God exists. Your Descartes, however, cannot see it in that way. Nobody could think that God's existence is explained by there being certain limits to what we can conceive—let alone by his having set them. So your Descartes has departed radically from some natural ways of thinking, and is therefore probably not the real Descartes.' I respond that the real Descartes was not one of those philosophers who think that 'Why is it the case that P?' might be answered by 'Necessarily P'. At least, not where P = 'God exists'. His a priori argument for God's existence occurs not in the metaphysical context of 'Why does God exist?' but in the epistemological one of 'How can we be absolutely sure that God exists?'

Prodded by critics, he sometimes faces the metaphysical question; and when he does so, it is never in terms of necessity, with one exception that I shall quote near the end of this section. To Caterus he writes that God 'does not need' an efficient cause because he 'possesses such great and inexhaustible power that he never required the assistance of anything else in order to exist' (CSM 2:78). In a 'geometrical' arrangement of his views, one of the axioms says this: 'The immensity of God's nature is the cause or reason why he needs no cause in order to exist' (Rep 2, CSM 2:116). And in reply to Arnauld he wrote that 'the reason why God does not need any efficient cause in order to exist depends on . . . the very immensity of God' (CSM 2:162). In these passages which confront the question 'Why does God exist?', the idea of his existing necessarily is vividly absent.

This is the deepest place in the chasm separating Descartes from explanatory rationalism. According to the latter, when the question arises 'Why is it the case that P?', the answer 'Because it is absolutely necessary that P' could be satisfactory. It is deeply in the spirit of such rationalism to regard necessary truths as self-explanatory, and thus as not needing to be explained through anything external to them. A thorough explanatory rationalist, indeed, is under pressure to conclude that, ultimately, this is the only acceptable answer to a why-question, which means that there are no genuinely contingent truths. There is no such pressure on Descartes, according to his most considered position regarding necessary propositions or 'eternal truths', because he can never explain any proposition's truth by pointing to its necessity, its status as an 'eternal truth'.

(Leibniz's metaphysic of modality cannot similarly be cleared from its own bootstraps problem. As we saw in §177, his position differs from Descartes's. Whereas the latter holds that 'the eternal truths of metaphysics and geometry . . . are only the effects of God's will', Leibniz explains, he takes them to be 'consequences of his understanding' (DM 2, FW 55). He ought to explain how it can be that the necessity by which God is supposed to exist—according to the a priori argument which Leibniz accepts—can be an upshot of relations of ideas in God's understanding. I do not see how he could do so.)

Third objection: 'The position you attribute to Descartes does not let us infer that God exists from its being necessary that he does. More generally, it does not license the inference from *Necessarily P* to P. Descartes must have been aware of that, and would have found it intolerable.' Not so fast! The subjectivist analysis of modality which I have attributed to Descartes does secure the following result: 'If necessarily P, then no human being can believe that not-P. Someone in a muddle might have an affirmative attitude to a sentence which means that not-P, but such a person cannot be thinking clearly, cannot really have his mind around the thought that not-P, be assenting to it, and competently connect it up with his other beliefs; for if he did all that, he would arrived at *P & not-P*, which would stop him in his tracks. While we are thinking clearly, then, the move from *necessarily P* to *P* is settled, an immovably built-in part of our scheme of things.'

Renewed objection: 'Stop pretending not to understand. You point out that on that theory of modality a necessary proposition has to be accepted, in the sense that the acceptance of its contradictory will in competent hands lead to an impasse. But the question we were asking is about how P's necessity relates not to *our acceptance of P* but rather to *P's truth*.' This objector relies on a distinction which Descartes often implicitly snubbed, as we have seen. In his most assiduous epistemological exploration, he frequently replaces the question of what he is entitled to believe by the question of what he is compelled to believe (see Chapter 20). When writing in this vein, you may recall, Descartes

- launched the *Meditations* as a pursuit of beliefs that were 'stable and likely to last';
- highlighted propositions which 'we cannot ever think of without believing them to be true';
- attended to the situation of someone who 'is certain that he is not being deceived, and is compelled to give his assent to' a given proposition;
- accorded a privilege to 'certain common notions' of whose truth our mind, 'for as long as it attends to them, is completely convinced';
- brushed aside a suggestion about falsehood with the words 'What do we care about this [alleged] absolute falsity, since we neither believe in it nor have even the smallest suspicion of it?'
- said of a similar threat that it was 'no objection' because 'the evident clarity of our perceptions does not allow us to listen to anyone who makes up this kind of story'.

In short, Descartes's thought contains a thick, strong vein of subjectivism or pragmatism about truth—a willingness to treat results about the settlement of belief as though they were results about reality, or as though the former mattered and the latter did not. When in that frame of mind, he would equate our finding not-P unthinkable with our discovering that P, and would have the only kind of warrant for 'If necessarily P, then P' that interested him.

I have acknowledged that although the best parts of Descartes's struggle with scepticism in the *Meditations* belong to this subjectivist strand in his thought, there is also a realist strand, which includes his attempt to claw his way across from indubitability to truth (§153). To the elements making up this realist strand we must add Descartes's a priori 'proof' of God's existence, in the course of which he writes: 'From the fact that I cannot think of God except as existing, it follows that existence is inseparable from God, and hence that he really exists. It is not that my thought makes it so, or imposes any necessity on any thing; on the contrary, it is the necessity of the thing itself, namely the existence of God, which determines my thinking in this respect' (Med 4, CSM 2:46). This flatly contradicts my account of Descartes's voluntarism doctrine.

The subjectivist analysis of modality harmonizes *as well as anything can* with the rest of Descartes's work: it fits the subjectivist strand in the *Meditations*; nothing could fit both strands. I have defended here the view that the subjectivist one dominates the *Meditations*. I am also willing to defend the thesis that it is, philosophically speaking, the better of the two—saying not that subjectivism is right, but that Descartes does better with it than with the other. But I cannot go into that here.

184. Theorizing about the basis of modality: the libertinism threat

A voluntarism powered by the idea that God *can do everything* should offer examples of extraordinary *things God can do*, saying for instance that he could make twice two equal five. That implies that twice two *could* equal five, which generalizes to the libertine conclusion that nothing is impossible. But Descartes's actual religious concern—as distinct from the omnipotence idea attributed to him by folklore—does not push him to this disastrous extreme. Whereas the thought that God can do anything leads on to 'for instance he can make twice two equal five', the thought that nothing real is independent of him leads only to 'for instance he does not confront the impossibility that twice two should equal five'.

So the theological impulse behind the voluntarism does not encourage the libertine thesis; and the underlying conceptualist analysis of modality, far from encouraging the thesis, positively condemns it. According to the analysis, the modal status of the proposition that *twice two equals five* is its relation to our conceptual capacities, but the proposition that *twice two could equal five* relates to them in the same way, and therefore has the same modal status.

A problem arises. According to me, the analysis of modality leads to the likes of this ('NI' for 'not impossible'):

(NI) The following is not the case: God absolutely could not have made two plus two equal five,

yet I have congratulated it on not leading to the likes of this ('P' for 'possible'):

(P) God could have made two plus two equal five.

How can this be? From its not being the case that something is impossible, does it not follow trivially that it is possible? How could any coherent theory entail NI without also entailing P? Hostile answer: 'It couldn't. The inference of P from NI is trivially valid, and thus unblockable; a theory that purports to entail NI but not P must be incoherent. Descartes's voluntarism is in as much trouble on your reading as on any other.'

If this objection is sound, it covers every theory of the form:

Because Basis obtains, the modal concepts apply as they do,

where Basis is a contingent proposition. Such a theory should entail that if Basis had not been the case, the modal concepts would not have applied as they do. This entails that (NI) if Basis had not been the case, the following would have been true:

It is not impossible that twice two equals five.

This might seem to entail that (P) if Basis had not been the case, the following would have been true:

It is possible that twice two equals five.

But P entails that at some possible worlds twice two equals five, which means that that is not an impossible proposition. This argument, generalized, implies that all seemingly necessary propositions are contingent, thereby demolishing modality rather than analysing it.

If that is sound, we have a fast a priori proof that the nature and applicability of our modal concepts cannot be grounded in contingent facts. Does that not make you suspicious? In philosophy such large results do not often come so easily. It is not likely that an argument as short as this suffices to destroy, for example, Wittgenstein's life's work on modality.

In fact, the argument is defective. The inference which it calls trivially valid is indeed so in any context which assumes the modal concepts as part of the working apparatus. They cannot be thus assumed, and should not be used to support inferences that would ordinarily be valid, in contexts where we are considering what has to be the case for the modal concepts to be usable at all. A statement of the form 'If Basis were not the case, (NI) *it would not be impossible that Q*' understates something whose full strength is 'If Basis were not the case, our modal concepts would be inapplicable'; and this obviously does not entail that if Basis were not the case (P) *it would be possible that Q*. The inference from NI to P fails when, and only when, we are exploring a theory such as Descartes's conceptualist analysis of modality.

185. Descartes's handling of the threat

In the passages I have quoted, Descartes does not put a foot wrong. Applying his conceptualist analysis of modality to his theological problem, he says only that God does not confront any absolute impossibilities. The passage that I quoted when introducing the tandem problem is strikingly accurate. Here is a shortened version of it:

I do not think we should ever say of anything that it cannot be brought about by God. I would not venture to say that God cannot make it be the case that one and two are not three. But I merely say that he has given me such a mind that I cannot conceive an aggregate of one and two which is not three, and that this involves a contradiction in my conception.

This does not say that one plus two could fail to equal three; Descartes merely *refuses to assert* that God could *not* make this be the case. He does assert that he cannot conceive of one plus two not making three, and that by his standards it is contradictory. This is exactly right when a religious concern with God's greatness is being helped by a conceptualist analysis of modality. The threatened modal limit on God is removed; but it continues to limit our powers of conception. Descartes calls it contradictory, but reminds us that this relates it to us only, and not to God.

Equally flawless is this, written to Mersenne: 'In general we can assert that God can do everything that is within our grasp, but not that he cannot do what is beyond our grasp. It would be rash to think that our imagination reaches as far as his power' (CSMK 23). This makes the general claim that God can do things that are unintelligible to us; but it does not say that God can do everything, nor does it fall into the trap of saying, for a specific Q, that God could make Q obtain although we cannot conceive its doing so.

Passages that create the tandem problem all exhibit Descartes's delicate accuracy in handling this matter. There is another in a letter to More: 'I do not deny that God can do what contradicts my conception, but say only that it implies a contradiction' (CSMK 363). Descartes rightly does not deny that God can do what contradicts his conception; but he does not affirm it either. He only says (*sed dico tantum*) that what contradicts his conception is condemned by *his* modal standards. In all these passages and others like them, Descartes uses the double negative of NI rather than the affirmative of P. 'I do not say that God cannot . . .'; 'We cannot assert that he cannot . . .': 'I do not deny that he can . . .'.[1]

The passage that sits most uncomfortably with my interpretation is in a letter to Mesland: 'The power of God cannot have any limits . . . [This] shows us that God cannot have been determined to make it true that contradictories cannot be true together, and therefore he could have done the opposite' (CSMK 235). If we read 'he could have done the opposite' as meaning only 'he could have brought it about that it was not true that contradictories cannot be true together', this might be only the thought that in that eventuality no modal concepts would apply—all modal bets would be off—rather than that contradictories would be true together. It could, and some friends of my interpretation have suggested that it does; but I am not convinced.

Still, the letter to Mesland does not trouble me greatly, because it also supports a third reading of voluntarism, when Descartes alludes to 'things which God could have made possible, but which he has nevertheless wished to make impossible'. (This has led Curley to suppose that the voluntarism doctrine says not that

---

[1] McFetridge 1990 is a polemic against the view that Descartes had a subjectivist analysis of modality. It is interesting, but does not make me retreat. McFetridge evidently did not notice the tandem problem, or Descartes's careful use of double negatives.

God could have made '2 + 2 = 5' true but only that he could have made it possible. In an earlier treatment of these matters (1994) I have endorsed this as logic but criticized it as theology.) The Mesland letter is a hot potato. There may be an explanation for its failure of fit with the rest of Descartes's work on this topic. In his next letter, to Grandamy, Descartes mentions his recent letters from Mesland, saying: 'I cannot give as much attention to my reply as I would have wished. For I am at present in a place where I have many distractions and little leisure'. Yet the 'reply' in question runs to over five pages in CSM, and must have been written in a terrible hurry. Indeed, Descartes himself writes to Mersenne that 'My letters are normally written with too little care to be fit to be seen by anyone except their addressee', and also that he cannot write at length *and* carefully (CSMK 28, 34).

186. Can Descartes's God deceive?

In presenting to audiences the evidence that Descartes hated and rejected the idea that God confronts any limitations, or comes up against anything independent of his will, I have usually met the challenge: 'What about his insistence that God cannot lie?' I am now placed to answer.

In the majority of the forty-odd passages where God's veracity comes up, Descartes says only that God *does* not deceive, which poses no problem for my account of his thought. He does this even when invited to say something stronger. Mersenne begins an objection with this: 'You say that God cannot lie or deceive', and Descartes in reply removes the modal: 'In saying that God does not lie, and is not a deceiver . . .' (CSM 2:89, 101). Then Hobbes: 'M. Descartes should consider the proposition "God can in no case deceive us" and see whether it is universally true.' Descartes's reply addresses instead the proposition 'We can in no case be deceived' (CSM 2:136). He denies this, and denies that he has committed himself to accepting it; but my interest is in his switch of propositions, removing the modal operator from God's deceiving on to our being deceived. In later Objections, Gassendi and then Bourdin credit Descartes with holding that God 'cannot deceive'; but in neither case does he take the bait.

He sometimes declares it to be impossible that God should be a deceiver. This, however, does not attribute to God any limitation or incapacity; it merely says that a certain proposition is impossible, or unthinkable by us. Objection: 'If it is impossible that God deceives, then God cannot deceive. The impossibility of the proposition implies an inability on God's part to make it true.' I reply that the whole theological point of Descartes's voluntarism is precisely to block that implication. Nearly always Descartes stays with the propositional formulation:

> 'It is a complete contradiction to suppose that he might deceive us or be, in the
> strict and positive sense, the cause of our errors . . . The will to deceive must

always come from malice, or from fear and weakness, and so cannot belong
to God' (PP 1:29).

'It is quite inconsistent with the nature of God that he should be a deceiver'
(PP 2:1).

'It is impossible that God should ever deceive me . . . The will to deceive is
undoubtedly evidence of malice or weakness, and so cannot apply to God'
(Med 4, CSM 2:37).

'It would be a contradiction that anything should be created by God which
positively tends towards falsehood. . . . It is impossible for us to envisage his
being a deceiver' (Rep 2, CSM 2:103).

In two other places CSM wrongly has Descartes asserting that God cannot lie
where the Latin says only that a certain proposition is impossible (2:43*, 105*).
And where CSM 2:289* has Descartes speaking of 'a true God who cannot be a
deceiver', the Latin could as well or better mean 'a God to whom deception is
foreign'.[2]

Just once Descartes openly attributes to God an inability to deceive, writing
that 'It is clear that God cannot be a deceiver' (Med 3, CSM 2:35). This is a clear
exception to his general practice of handling the matter de dicto, in terms of the
impossibility of a proposition rather than de re in terms of an inability in God.
Had he been challenged about this, he might have said that all he meant was that
'God is a deceiver' is an impossible proposition, thus bringing himself into conformity with my account. But I do not know that. Another misfitting turn of
phrase occurs when Descartes writes that even if God made some portion of
matter indivisible by any creature, 'God certainly could not thereby take away his
own power of dividing it' (PP 2:20). This, taken strictly, credits God with an incapacity, though it is a uniquely special one—the inability to give oneself an inability.

In a letter to Mersenne (CSMK 179) Descartes writes that 'God cannot lie' and
'God cannot deceive us'. Little weight should be given to this, I suggest.
Descartes is defending his own thesis that necessarily God never lies against critics who say that sometimes he does; the issue does not involve modality. He says
that Augustine, Aquinas, and others 'over and over again in many places' take his
side on this; and though the letter is written in French, he states the position in
Latin clauses—Deus mentiri non potest, Deus nos fallere non potest—the former of
which comes verbatim from Aquinas.[3] In using the exact wording of his allies,
Descartes need not be endorsing the detail which conflicts with his own view
about God's lack of limitations or inabilities.

---

[2] Incidentally, Descartes's God is veracious because he is powerful, and deceit manifests weakness—
not because he is good, and deceit is bad. For Descartes this topic does not involve 'the traditional problem of evil, as applied to error' (Newman 1999: 561). The problem of evil dissolves in Descartes's views
about how God's will relates to value.

[3] Robert Pasnau tells me that Aquinas wrote Deus mentiri non potest at least three times in his Summa
Theologica (2-2, 2, 4 c; 2-2, 89, 1 c; 89, 3, obj. 2) and at least four times in other works. I suspect that the
other clause, comes from Augustine, but have not yet found it in his writings.

Chapter 25

Secondary Qualities

187. Locke's corpuscularianism

Locke was attracted by the kind of physics he called 'the corpuscularian hypothesis' (*Essay* 547:29)—the hypothesis that the physical world can be comprehensively explained in terms of how corpuscles are assembled into larger structures and how they move. One naturally thinks of the 'corpuscles' as atoms, unsplittable physical minima, but Locke does not confidently do so. Let us consider his troubles with atoms.

Like Descartes, Leibniz, and others at his time, Locke did not believe in attractive forces (§23). This left him, as he knew, unable to explain how bodies hang together so that there are rocks and grains as well as air and water (II.xxiii.23–7). This encouraged the view that there are no atoms because every portion of matter can be divided into still smaller bodies.

Just once Locke openly embraces that conclusion and affirms the infinite divisibility of matter. He is discussing whether God could be a material thing:

> Though our general or specific conception of matter makes us speak of it as one thing, yet really all matter is not one individual thing, neither is there any such thing existing as one material being, or one single body that we know or can conceive. And therefore if matter were the eternal first cogitative being, there would not be one eternal infinite cogitative being, but an infinite number of eternal finite cogitative beings. (*Essay* IV.x.10)

In this astonishing passage Locke implies that every material thing is divisible into an infinite number of basic parts; he calls them 'beings', but drops the adjective 'material', because if they were material, they would be extended, so divisible, so unbasic. He here goes a good distance with Leibniz, but, unlike him, supposes that an extended thing can have unextended things as its ultimate parts (§88). This lets him work his way down to the simple substances, parting company with Leibniz in relating them to bodies as parts to wholes, not as reality to appearance. I do not make much of this passage, however. It was added in the second edition, and Locke seems to have made no other revisions in the light of it. In the *New Essays*, incidentally, Leibniz quotes it without comment.

More often we find Locke writing like a convinced atomist, most notably in II.xxvii.3, where he implies that the material world is composed of 'atoms' that can be neither split nor deformed. This is shown not just by his using the word 'atom', but by the structure of his thought in this chapter. He wants to explain what it is for a single F to last through time, for various values of F, ending famously with F = person (see Chapter 39). He starts with F = atom, and handles it without mentioning parts; then he turns to F = mass-of-matter, saying that mass x is mass y if and only if x has exactly the same atomic parts as y. So he first gets atoms on board in his analytic project, and then starts to use the concept of a part. This would be merely incompetent if he thought of 'atoms' as having separable parts.

These divergent performances of Locke's result from bafflement. On the one hand, matter must be divisible; on the other, we have no notion of infinite division. Take these passages in order:

> 'Since in any bulk of matter, our thoughts can never arrive at the utmost divisibility, therefore there is an apparent infinity to us . . . in that' (*Essay* II.xvii.12).
>
> 'In matter we have no clear ideas of the smallness of parts much beyond the smallest that occur to any of our senses: And therefore when we talk of the divisibility of matter in infinitum, though we have clear ideas of division and divisibility, . . . yet we have but very obscure and confused ideas of [the parts of bodies which are] reduced to a smallness much exceeding the perception of any of our senses' (III.xxix.16).
>
> 'The divisibility in infinitum of any finite extension involv[es] us, whether we grant or deny it, in consequences impossible to be explicated or made in our apprehensions consistent' (III.xxiii.31).
>
> 'We are at a loss about the divisibility of matter' (IV.xvii.10).

The main topic of the present chapter is unaffected by this issue on which Locke wavers so unhappily. All we need is to allow him the notion of micro-structures whose elements are corpuscles of some kind; whether these are thought of as atoms, as splittable but held together by attractive forces, or as held together in some inexplicable manner, will not affect the main lines of the discussion.

188. The corpuscularian thesis about what secondary qualities are

Now, the corpuscularian hypothesis—or Galilean or Cartesian ideal—has to maintain that the qualitative differences amongst material things are really differences in micro-structure. Across some of the territory, this is easily intelligible (§2), but it is not obvious how this could be so for the properties of things that Boyle called 'secondary'. This apple is green, is sweet, is cold; what have such properties as these to do with structures? Let us look at what became the standard answer to this, attending mainly to Locke's version of it.

I shall assume that Locke and his Galilean predecessors each meant to have *one* doctrine about primary and secondary qualities: it may have had several parts or sub-themes, but they were all supposed to be related to a central thesis. I apply that claim to most of the 'twenty odd ways of making a distinction' that are sorted out in MacIntosh 1976. Without claiming to match MacIntosh's knowledge of the history of this matter, I stand by my resolve to find the one distinction that stands at the centre of what is *philosophically interesting* in the primary/secondary distinction. Our first task is to locate this central thesis among all the conflicting statements of Locke and others concerning the topic. Here are the things Locke affirms of secondary qualities and denies of primary ones.

(1) They are dispositions to cause a characteristic kind of sensory state in percipients. 'Secondary qualities . . . are nothing but the powers those substances have to produce several ideas in us by our senses' (*Essay* II.xxiii.9). '[We speak] as if light and heat were really something in the fire more than a power to excite these ideas in us; and therefore are called qualities in or of the fire. But these [are] nothing in truth but powers to excite such ideas in us' (xxxi.2).

(2) They are not in outer objects: 'Yellowness is not actually in gold' (xxiii.10).

(3) They are not intrinsic to the objects that have them, but rather are relations between those objects and something else: The yellowness, solubility, etc. of gold 'are nothing else but so many relations to other substances, and are not really in the gold considered barely in itself' (II.xxiii.37).

(4) They are in minds rather than in outer objects: 'Light, heat, whiteness or coldness are no more really in them than sickness or pain is in manna. Take away the sensation of them; let not the eyes see light, or colours, nor the ears hear sounds; let the palate not taste, nor the nose smell; and all colours, tastes, odours, and sounds, as they are such particular ideas, vanish and cease' (viii.17).

(5) The ideas of them do not resemble anything in the physical world, as do ideas of primary qualities: 'The ideas of primary qualities of bodies are resemblances of them . . . ; but the ideas produced in us by these secondary qualities have no resemblance of them at all. There is nothing like our ideas existing in the bodies themselves' (viii.15).

I contend that the core we are looking for is (1) the thesis that secondary qualities, unlike primary, are dispositions to cause characteristic sensory states in percipients. For Locke and also for Descartes, Boyle, and the others, this was the central, basic, most considered view about how the two sorts of qualities differ.

My first reason for thinking this, so far as Locke is concerned, is textual: there is more of 1 than of any of the others in the *Essay*. I have quoted two instances. Here are five more:

> 'Secondary qualities [are] qualities which in truth are nothing in the objects themselves but powers to produce various sensations in us by their primary qualities' (II.viii.10).
> 'Colours and smells [and] tastes and sounds, and other the like sensible qualities . . . are in truth nothing in the objects themselves but powers to produce various sensations in us' (viii.14).
> '[Secondary qualities are] the powers to produce several ideas in us by our senses' (viii.24).
> 'Gold or saffron has a power to produce in us the idea of yellow, and snow or milk the idea of white' (xxi.73).

'We immediately by our senses perceive in fire its heat and colour; which are, if rightly considered, nothing but powers in it to produce those ideas in us' (xxiii.7).

My second reason is philosophical: of the five theses about secondary qualities, 1 comes closest to being true. I shall say more about this later. My final reason is structural: we can understand a philosopher's entertaining any of the other theses by treating it as an outgrowth of or a slight mishandling of (1) the central thesis. None of the others can play this part as a central organizer of all Locke's disparate pronouncements about secondary qualities. I shall now defend this, showing that, in attributing 1 to Locke, we can mop up 2, 3, and 4 also by treating each as a slight mishandling of 1. I shall return to 5 in §193.

To illustrate 2, I quoted a fragment from this: 'Yellowness is not actually in gold, but is a power in gold to produce that idea in us by our eyes, when placed in a due light.' This seems internally inconsistent—yellowness is not actually in gold but is (a power) in gold—but everything comes right if we suppose that by 'is not actually in gold' Locke meant 'is not an actuality in gold'. Then he is merely saying that yellowness is a power or disposition, which brings 2 within the compass of 1.

With regard to 3: according to 1, a secondary quality is not a relation between its bearer and something else; but it involves a relation, because it is a disposition that its bearer has to relate causally to something else. So a mild stretch brings 3 under 1.

There is more difficulty with 4, which identifies secondary qualities with ideas, rather than with dispositions to cause ideas. Here I think Locke has made a mistake: like Galileo and Descartes before him, he has *slipped* from 1 to a different thesis. Consider this passage:

The power that is in any body . . . to operate after a peculiar manner on any of our senses, and thereby produce in us the different ideas of several colours, sounds, smells, tastes, &c. These are usually called sensible qualities. (II.viii.23)

This has 'power' (singular) and 'ideas' (plural). The second sentence ('These . . .') relates to the ideas, where it should have related to the power. That is, Locke should have written: 'The power that is in any body . . . [etc.] This is usually called a sensible quality.' Here is a more complex and subtle example:

Sweetness and whiteness are not really in manna; [for they] are but the effects of the operations of manna, by the motion, size, and figure of its particles on the eyes and palate: as the pain and sickness caused by manna are confessedly nothing but the effects of its operations on the stomach and guts. (18)

What Locke ought to be doing, according to doctrine 1, is comparing the manna's *whiteness* with its *emeticness*—that is, its tendency to make people sick. Each of these is a disposition to have a certain effect on people. Locke has misfocused slightly, however, and has attended not to manna's emetic quality, but to the sickness that it causes; and this has led him on the other side of the analogy to the *idea of white* instead of to the *whiteness*.

There are many 4-like passages. It is uncomfortable to treat them all as result-ing from Locke's misunderstanding his own central thesis, but I see no escape from this. Consider another example. After providing a prime example of 1, quoted above, about light and heat as a power that the fire has to cause certain ideas in us, Locke continues thus:

Were there no fit organs to receive the impressions fire makes on the sight and touch, nor a mind joined to those organs to receive the ideas of light and heat by those impressions from the fire or sun, there would yet be no more light or heat in the world than there would be pain if there were no sensible creature to feel it. (II.xxxi.2)

This is a slide: from treating heat as a power that the fire has, Locke has drifted into regarding it as an effect of that power. And on the other side, he has gone from comparing heat with the fire's property of being 'painful to the touch' to comparing it with the pain that the fire causes. Read that section carefully, and you will see Locke sliding under your very eyes.

He is not alone in this. Galileo (1623: 274) maintained that secondary qualities do not fall within the scope of physics because they are mental, are 'subjective' properties that 'one is under no compulsion' to attribute to bodies, or 'are merely psychic additions of the perceiving mind'. (I am quoting Drake 1963: 265b and Gaukroger 1995: 345.) This insulates them from physics, all right; if it were true, it would solve the problem for Galilean physics; but it is a sadly implausible solution. I do not think that anyone could be attracted to it once he had conceived of the cor-rect solution, which gives to secondary qualities all the subjectivity that is needed, while still attributing them to the objects that we intuitively think possess them.

Anyway, within 1–4 *something* has to give, because those formulations clash. If we are to avoid concluding that on this subject Locke and the others flailed around with no control from any basic considered view, we must somehow bring 1–4 into harmony. My way of doing so is conservative, requiring less rewriting and less attribution of error than any other.

According to Locke's central thesis, then, the following is true of each sec-ondary quality Q and of no primary quality Q:

There is a kind K of idea or sensory state such that for an object to have Q is for it to be disposed to cause K states in normal percipients in standard cir-cumstances.

(Must it be the same kind of idea for each percipient? Perhaps not. In II.xxxii.15 Locke considers whether marigolds might look to you as violets do to me. We could allow for that by revising the formula:

For an object to have Q is for there to be, for each normal percipient, a kind K of idea or sensory state such that: the object is disposed to cause K states in that percipient in standard circumstances.

I shall skip this detail from now on.) Thus, what makes it the case that a given thing is red is the fact that if a normal person confronted it in sunlight with his eyes open, it would cause in him a red-type idea or sensory state. Locke never mentions the condition of the percipient, and says little about the conditions in which the perception takes place; but the qualification 'standard' or 'normal' is needed for the account to be roughly right, and it does not conflict with anything he says.

189. Why the central thesis is true

It is natural to see Locke's central thesis as implying that secondary so-called qualities are not really *qualities*, but *powers* of the things that have them; unlike primary qualities, which really are qualities and not merely powers. Locke would not agree with this. He is willing to count a thing's powers as a subset of its qualities, if only 'to comply with the common way of speaking' (I.viii.10). When he says that a fire's power to melt wax 'is as much a quality in fire' as its redness, he is nudging us into calling both of them 'qualities'.

He sometimes hints that all qualities are powers, but I do not think he consideredly thought so. If he did, the upshot would be this:

> A quality is a thing's power to effect changes in things, i.e. to alter their qualities, i.e. to alter their powers to effect changes in things, i.e. to alter their qualities, i.e. . . .

and so on *ad infinitum*. This is certainly peculiar, but perhaps not absurd. It yields a world where nothing is ultimately and non-dispositionally F; either there is no ground floor, or if there is one, it consists purely of things and their powers. There are properties, according to this view, but a thing's having a property is just its having a power to confer or gain various other powers in interaction with other things. Shoemaker has defended this (1980: 212): 'What makes a property the property it is, what determines its identity, is its potential for contributing to the causal powers of the things that have it.' It is certainly true that our only way of knowing what qualities a thing has is by knowing what its powers are; and although we can insist that the powers are only manifestations of the underlying quality, that smacks of metaphysical excess. So Shoemaker can make a case for his position, and there is in fact an ongoing debate about this. Locke did not mean to go so far; but I have mentioned the matter as a lead in to a crucial point about secondary qualities—the point about them that makes the central thesis true.

What is special about such qualities is not merely that they are powers, but *what* powers they are. Their specialness would not be lost if primary qualities were also powers, because they would be powers of a wholly different sort. A thing's being spherical, for instance, not only disposes it to cause a characteristic kind of visual state in normal percipients; it also gives it countless other well-known powers: it relates in predictable ways to measuring equipment, rolls smoothly on smooth surfaces, has a circular cross-section, leaves hemispherical indents in soft wax, and so on. If sphericalness is a power, it is the sum of all those powers and of many others. This is a richer set of powers than are associated with secondary qualities, especially colours; it differs also in that many of its members are powers to affect (not percipients' sensory states but) other material things.

The underlying fact is that the secondary qualities of things are almost epiphenomenal. I shall explain this in terms of colours, though it applies to the other secondary qualities as well. For most kinds K of thing, most of what we can infer about x's behaviour from the information that *x is K and red* can also be inferred from *x is K*. In contrast with that, information about a thing's shape or size is relevant, in gross, unignorable ways, to its causal relationships with other things, so that if you try to envisage a shape or size analogue of colour-blindness, the story collapses under its own weight: you cannot inhabit the physical world without knowing the sorts of facts that will let you discover—in many ways—whether a given object is cubic or spherical or whether one thing is bigger than another.

It is because colours are so nearly epiphenomenal that colour-blindness can go undetected throughout a lifetime. The earliest record of it dates from 1794, when the chemist John Dalton reported it in himself; but nobody thinks he was the first. Try to imagine someone having an analogous sensory defect, preventing him from grasping properly the difference between larger and smaller things, or straight and crooked edges! The story is almost untellable, and cannot be told in such a way that the afflicted person would not notice that there was something wrong. This is a point about the primary qualities in general; it is not lessened by the fact that 'it doesn't make much difference whether we perceive, say, soap bubbles as spherical or ovoid' (Wilson 1992: 218).

The nearly epiphenomenal character of colours, tastes, and smells is not possessed by extreme differences of temperature: when metals are hot enough, they become flexible; many things when hot enough catch fire; very cold water turns solid; and so on. We have to suppose that when the Galilean philosophers included heat among the secondary qualities, they saw it as problematic only in the range of the temperature scale in which differences in temperature do not make much obvious difference to most things except for how they feel; and their account of secondary qualities holds only for that middle range. Descartes implicitly acknowledges this when he writes of 'heat and other qualities perceived by the senses, in so far as those qualities are in objects' that 'we often see these arising from the local motion of certain bodies and producing in turn other local motions in other bodies' (*PP* 4:198). My account of this whole matter is not refuted by the fact that large-scale differences of temperature are nowhere near to being epiphenomenal.

Colours and other secondary qualities, I have said, are *almost* epiphenomenal. There is just one large, well-known upshot of a thing's being K and red (for almost any K) that is not an upshot of its being K; I refer to how the thing looks— that is, what visual states it is apt to produce in people when they confront it with eyes open in sunlight. A thing's being spherical has hundreds of obvious upshots; a thing's being red has just this one. This makes it reasonable to say that a thing's being red is just its being disposed to (for short) look a certain way, whereas all there is to a thing's being spherical is its being disposed to . . . and we must fill the gap with hundreds or thousands of propositions about how spherical things interact with other things, what results when they are cut in half, and so on. Thus, we can treat sphericalness as a disposition, yet still have a double contrast between it and redness: between a simple power (redness) and a highly complex one (sphericalness), and between a power to affect minds (redness) and a power to affect minds and bodies (sphericalness).

Let me now amend my account. Strictly speaking, nothing can be nearly but not completely epiphenomenal, for any effect can be amplified. If the light had been red, the driver of the car would have had a visual sensation which caused him to stop; but in fact it was green, giving him one which caused him to go on driving; this led to his being hit by a train and killed; which led to war. The crucial point, however, is that all the other effects came *through* the sensory one: the sensory states of perceivers are the bottle-neck through which the secondary qualities affect the world.

190. A difference of kind

Critics such as Mackie (1976: 33–4) have contended that my account, which has to do with the degree to which various qualities are epiphenomenal, cannot have been what moved Locke because he thought that between primary and secondary qualities there is a difference of kind. I might reply that the epiphenomenalness difference is one of kind, rather than degree. Three bases for this have been suggested to me.

(1) Our access to each secondary quality is through only one sense, while our access to each primary quality is through two, sight and touch; and this difference comes into my account of the epiphenomenalness difference between the two. I cannot adopt this defence, though, for my basic case for distinguishing primary from secondary qualities can be made purely in terms of touch-and-movement; a congenitally blind person could agree with it on the strength of what he knew for himself, without borrowing from what he was told by sighted people. There are also other obstacles to the proffered defence, coming from the fact that an apple can look soft, cheese can smell blue, and so on.

(2) My epiphenomenalness contrast brought out the fact that while colourblindness and its secondary-quality cousins are possible and even actual, a thoroughly developed primary-quality analogue of them turns out to be unintelligible; so there is a difference of kind—that between being and not being intelligible. The critic could reply that my difference is still one of degree, because it leaves open the possibility of a kind of quality which fits into the world

in such a way that the relevant kind of 'blindness' to it is *barely* intelligible or *very hard* to make sense of. That would be a fair reply.

(3) The difference that is brought out by my epiphenomenalness contrast is a very large difference in degree, and our name for that is 'difference of kind'. I accept this: I see it as an important truth, and not a mere claptrap, that differences of kind differ from ones of degree only in degree. And this is made easier to maintain if differences of degree are taken to include (in the manner of the last point in 2 above) ones where there is a sheer precipice at the actual world and gentle slopes only at other possible worlds. But I shall not rest my defence purely on this point either. Here is why.

The difference that I have brought to the surface is one of degree, in the sense that it allows for the possibility that a quality might be *fairly secondary* or *pretty thoroughly primary*. We can envisage a physical world in which surfaces varied along the smooth–rough continuum only in ways that made barely perceptible differences to how things interacted, though they were easily detected through touch. At such a world, smooth/rough would be a fairly secondary quality; and it is a simple exercise to slide across the worlds so as to make smooth/rough thoroughly secondary or (in the other direction) thoroughly primary. I contend that this is, when you reflect on it, plainly the case with the distinction that Locke draws. If he did not notice that it was ultimately one of degree, that was his failure; it does not mean that he was thinking accurately about some other distinction.

The point I have been making is echoed in Locke's own treatment of smooth/rough. In II.iii.1 he discusses 'ideas which have admittance only through one sense which is peculiarly adapted to receive them'. He cites light and colours, sounds, tastes, smells, and then turns to qualities 'belonging to the touch', of which he instances heat and cold, solidity, smooth and rough, hard and soft, tough and brittle. There is much to criticize here, but let us focus on 'smooth and rough': in making this qualitative dimension relate to one sense only, Locke implies that the reality of it is given by how it feels. If he let it bear equally strongly on the implications of smooth/rough for the thing's interactions with other things, he would have to admit sight into the picture (and also allow touch a greater role). Yet in other contexts he seems to imply that rough/smooth belongs on the primary-quality side of the line, as when he includes among the primary-quality facts the ones about 'what kind of particles [there are] and how ranged in the superficies' (II.viii.2). Later, discussing the question of 'what primary qualities of any body produce certain sensations or ideas in us', he speaks of 'what sort of figure, bulk and texture of parts in the superficies of any body were fit to give such corpuscles their due motion to produce [a yellow] colour'. The micro-structures of physical surfaces are primary; and they *could* show up in interactions between material things; but evidently Locke thinks of them as showing up only in tactual feelings, which gives them a status like that of the official secondary qualities. This does not acknowledge that the difference is one of degree; but it shows sensitivity to the facts that make it so.

191. How Locke defends the central thesis

What makes Locke's central thesis about secondary qualities true, I submit, is the latter's being so near to epiphenomenal, having few large, immediate, obvious causal implications other than their sensory effects on us. Locke does not explicitly say this; I do not know of anyone who said it before I did in my 1965b; but Locke must have been subliminally cognizant of the facts that I have adduced, and I think he was guided by them. If someone had put to him the possibility of colour-blindness, asking whether it makes sense to suppose that this might occur and remain undetected (though not undetectable), I am sure he would have said Yes, because of his grasp of the facts about colour which I have brought to the defence of the central thesis.

When Locke says, as he frequently does, that if there were no colour vision, there would be no colours, he is not strictly right: the power to have a certain effect on suitably equipped perceivers is not lost merely by there being none; just as sugar can be soluble in tea even if there is no tea. Still, we can see him in these passages as aiming for the point that apart from the effects of colour on vision we have *no use* for the concept of colour, whereas our primary-quality concepts have plenty of uses apart from how those qualities affect our senses. That is how I understand the passage where, having said that if there were no colour vision, 'there would yet be no more light . . . in the world than there would be pain if there were no sensible creature to feel it', Locke continues with this contrast: 'though the sun should continue just as it is now, and Mount Aetna flame higher than ever it did. Solidity and extension and . . . figure, with motion and rest, whereof we have the ideas, would be really in the world as they are, whether there were any sensible being to perceive them or no' (II.xxxi.2). This, I submit, is the writing of a man who has taken in that secondary qualities are nearly epiphenomenal while primary ones are not.

If we look to Locke for outright arguments in support of the thesis, we find few, most of them weak. The three arguments in II.viii.19–21 are the bulk of what he offers to support the central thesis, and all are defective, though in different ways. In II.viii.19 he writes that porphyry loses its colour in the dark, but no one could 'think any real alterations are made in the porphyry, by the presence or absence of light'; so that change of colour is not a real change in the porphyry; so 'whiteness or redness are not in it at any time'. This assumes that colours are ideas, and so go out of existence when the ideas stop. Remove that mistake— allow that porphyry has colour in the dark—and the argument dissolves. In II.viii.20 Locke writes: 'Pound an almond, and the clear white colour will be altered into a dirty one, and the sweet taste into an oily one. What real alteration can the beating of the pestle make in any body, but an alteration of the texture of it?' This argues that an almond's colour and taste are mere upshots or symptoms of its primary-quality 'texture', *since the latter is all that can be altered by pounding.* Suppose we object that, on the contrary, pounding can also cause changes in a thing's secondary qualities, as is shown by Locke's own example. He can have no answer to this other than a general appeal to the corpuscularian ideal for physics; and that is such a giant stride towards the central thesis that this argument should not convert anyone.

In section 21 Locke says that with the central thesis in hand, 'We may be able to give an account, how the same water at the same time may produce the idea of cold by one hand and of heat by the other'. He is right: a corpuscularian version of the central thesis does yield at least a schematic explanation for this fact, making an initially puzzling phenomenon 'easy to be understood'; and this possible explanatory success counts a little in favour of the thesis.

This modest argument seems to be mingled with something bolder and more vulnerable. Locke writes: '. . . and of heat by the other; whereas it is impossible that the same water, if those ideas were really in it, should at the same time be both hot and cold.' A little later he writes: 'Water may at the same time produce the sensation of heat in one hand and cold in the other, which yet figure never does, that never producing the idea of a square by one hand which has produced the idea of a globe by the other.' In these remarks he seems to infer from the premiss that *the two-hands phenomenon obtains with warmth and not with shape* the conclusion that *the central thesis in right in how it draws the line between warmth and shape*. Crediting Locke with arguing in that manner, Berkeley denied the premiss, pointing out that we *do* see and feel shapes, sizes, etc. differently according to where and how we are. He instances the fact that one thing can feel like two, and that something circular may look square. Locke could have defended a version of the argument thus: 'It is true that one's perception of primary qualities can vary according to circumstances, and I was wrong to imply otherwise. Still, I had a point. Even if one coin held in the hand in a certain way feels like two coins, its being just one shows up in a multitude of ways other than how it feels. Again, a tower might look circular from over there and square from over here, but there is ever so much more to its being (in fact) circular than merely how it looks. That is how primary qualities differ from secondary ones.' A rescue of his argument along these lines would be tantamount to relying on the fact that secondary qualities are nearly epiphenomenal.

We are at the end of what Locke has to say in defence of the central thesis. He affirms several times in the *Essay* that primary qualities are essential to matter, while secondary ones are not, as when he writes that the 'original or primary qualities of body' are the properties which 'are utterly inseparable from the body in what estate soever it be; such as in all the alterations and changes it suffers, all the force can be used upon it, it constantly keeps' (II.viii.9). He means that you cannot stop bodies from having some shape, some size, some velocity, some degree of hardness, and so on. This thesis is sometimes taken to have a central role in Locke's main doctrine about the two sorts of qualities; but it does not, and there is no evidence that he thought otherwise.

Given that shape is essential to matter as such, it is to be expected that its determinates—sphericalness and the like—will not be virtually epiphenomenal as the secondary qualities are. But the converse does not hold. A property that only some bodies have might nevertheless be basic in the bodies that do have it, and might contribute in richly complex ways to the bodies' causal interactions with other bodies (§2). Electric charge is perhaps an example. Such a quality would be 'primary' in the sense laid down by the central thesis, without being essential to matter. This is indeed the situation that physics has reached today, in which there are thought to be several *basic* kinds of constituents in matter, so that not all the key terms of basic physics concern properties that are possessed by matter as such.

In short, the mere fact that the secondary qualities are not essential to matter as such does nothing to solve the problem with which they confront corpuscularian physics. And the existence of more than one basic kind of matter, though it implies that the conceptual repertoire of physics is not confined to properties that all matter has, does not doom the corpuscularian programme as such, but only one special form of it.[1] It is true that Locke was drawn to the latter: in several places where he says that bodies can interact only by pushing and bumping, he rejects 'attractive forces' because they could not be explained through the nature of matter as such. But he showed himself willing, under pressure from Newton, to drop this; and he did not think he was dropping the whole corpuscularian project.

I should add that Locke, unlike Descartes, did not see the commitment to primary qualities as coming from a deep requirement of intelligibility. He seems rather to have had a *faute de mieux* attitude to this, viewing primary-quality physics merely as the best game in town. This committed him to conceding that true final physics might be of some other kind, and he saw this. Secondary qualities, he wrote, depend upon the primary qualities of substances' minute and insensible parts, 'or if not upon them upon something yet more remote from our comprehension' (*Essay* IV.iii.11).

192. How the central thesis solves the problem

For the central thesis to solve the secondary-quality problem for corpuscularian physics, something must be added, namely:

> When a thing is disposed to have a certain effect on the sensory states of observers, it has this because of its structure, that is, because of the primary qualities and interrelations of its small parts.

Descartes says this when he identifies secondary qualities with 'certain dispositions depending on size, shape and motion' (*PP* 4:199).

---

[1] McCann (1985: 242–3 n.) defends this against the view of Ayers (1981) that the seventeenth-century mechanistic programme essentially involved deriving the laws of physics from nothing but the attributes that all bodies must have.

(The primary-quality underlay of redness (say) need not be the same for you as it is for me, nor even the same for you at one time as at another. We now know, as Locke could not have, that it is not the case that each colour supervenes on a single primary-quality texture of surface; the structural underlay of colour perception is not as tidy as that. Whether someone experiences red-type sensations depends on the wavelengths of the light that impinges on him, and which wavelengths are reflected from a given surface depend upon its 'texture'; so that if redness is to be strongly associated with surface texture, it must be through those two dependences. It turns out that the former of them is more complicated than used to be thought. Although colour sensations depend upon wavelengths, there is no continuous range of wavelengths correlated with a given colour. A scatter of mixtures of wavelengths will lead a person to say he is seeing something red, another scatter for blue, and so on. This makes it unbelievable that there is a unitary kind of texture possessed by all the surfaces which are apt to cause R states under normal percipients in standard conditions. I here rely on Hardin 1988. In this important book Hardin rejects the central thesis because he sees so much difficulty in the notions of 'normal' percipients and viewing conditions (67–82). His own position is 'eliminativist' (112); he holds that no objects are coloured.)

Why should anyone in the seventeenth century believe that colours supervene on micro-structures? Well, Descartes and his contemporaries could point to experiences with microscopes for evidence that a thing's surface appearance might supervene on micro-structural features of it that do not appear in ordinary perception of the surface. Microscopes were in their infancy: their most important early pioneer, Antoni van Leeuwenhoek, was only 18 when Descartes died. But Descartes knew about them, was influenced by them in his thinking, and indeed thought about them. Hall writes: 'Descartes was virtually the founder of the scientific study of the apparatus of science, in his investigation of the causes of distortions present in the images of crude microscopes' (1954: 236). Descartes certainly knew that small-scale structural differences can generate surface differences which do not appear to the unaided eye to be structural; and by Locke's time, everyone knew.

This, however, is only a tiny step towards the whole thesis that the secondary qualities of things supervene on their micro-structures. Some writers, including Mackie and Peter Alexander, have maintained that Locke at least could have been encouraged to go further by the successes that Galilean physics had been having. Others, including Margaret Wilson and myself, are unpersuaded by this: the relationship between sounds and wavelengths had been established empirically, but that is about all. The guess that things' colours supervene on their primary qualities was accompanied by a total lack of information about *how* this 'by virtue of' might work: there was active debate, for instance, about whether a glass of claret reddens sunlight by altering it all or by absorbing some of it. Locke was candid about this: 'It [is] one thing to perceive and know the idea of white or black, and quite another to examine what kind of particles they must be, and how ranged in the superficies, to make any object appear white or black' (*Essay* II.viii.2).

Locke seems to have been sure that what explains those 'ideas' are *some* facts about micro-structures. Like other thinkers in the seventeenth century, he had grounds for believing that primary qualities afford the only credible prospect of a theoretically unified physics. So these thinkers could reasonably suppose that the causal explanations of our secondary-quality sensations involve primary-quality facts about the perceived object, the intervening medium, and the sense-organs and brain of the percipient. That leaves only the step from the events in the brain to the sensory states of the mind, and for Descartes at least, that step does not belong to physics. The latter is the science of how bodies relate to other bodies, and the last step in the production of secondary-quality experiences involves the effects of bodies on an incorporeal substance. This is one of the places where Descartes's substance-dualism is helpful to him.

Locke was carefully agnostic about substance-dualism. For all he knew to the contrary, he said, our sensory experiences might be states of an animal body rather than of a separate substance. Still, he evinced no doubts about the sound-ness of property-dualism—the thesis that the properties things can have fall into two non-overlapping classes, the members of only one of them pertaining to mentality (§26). So he can envisage the causal chain from brain events to mental ones as staying within the material world, but running from non-mentalistic properties to mentalistic ones, and he can calmly say that this relationship lies outside physics as he understands it. He can and he virtually does: 'Impressions made on the retina by rays of light, I think I understand; and motions from thence continued to the brain may be conceived, and that these produce ideas in our minds I am persuaded, but in a manner to me incomprehensible. This I can resolve only into the good pleasure of God, whose ways are past finding out' (1706: 217 = sect. 10). In acknowledging this mystery about how body acts on mind, Locke does not lose his right to believe in the feasibility of a corpuscular-ian physics that comprehensively deals with (if substance-dualism is right) the world of bodies or (if it is wrong) with the non-mentalistic aspects of bodies. (For further defence of this, see McCann 1985.) So he too can regard the truth of the central thesis about secondary qualities as a solution to the problem that they pose for his kind of physics.

The solution works also for contemporary materialists who identify sensory states with neural states, thus rejecting even property-dualism. For them, as for all of us today who belong in the Galilean camp, the fundamental scientific study of colours is a matter of finding out how bodies cause these states in percipients; their physics (in the broad sense) is obliged to carry the story through the whole way, but the sensory-neural equation on which their materialism is based clears the way for physics to carry out its obligation. The prospect of bringing colours within the purview of an essentially Galilean physics opens up smoothly for a materialist, once it is clear that the project involves tracing causal chains from surfaces to light waves to neurons, and does not involve trying to reduce colours to primary qualities in a manner analogous to the reduction of solubility, frangi-bility, and the like.

193. The 'no resemblance' thesis

In §188 I reported five things that Locke and others said about our distinction, and discussed four. The fifth says that our ideas of primary qualities do, while those of secondary ones do not, resemble the qualities that they represent. I have quoted Locke as saying this, and here is Descartes:

[Beliefs] which I acquired not from nature but from a habit of making ill-considered judgments [include] the belief that . . . the heat in a body is something exactly resembling the idea of heat which is in me; or that when a body is white or green, the selfsame whiteness or greenness which I perceive through my senses is present in the body. (Med 6, CSM 2:56–7)

I agree that a body's secondary qualities do not resemble any of my sensations, but then nor do its primary qualities.

This thesis about secondary qualities, as well as being philosophically incoherent, also fails in the purpose of reconciling secondary qualities with Galilean physics. Someone wanting to advance the latter, and worried about how to bring the secondary qualities within its scope, will not be consoled by the news that his ideas of them do not resemble anything in the outer world. What help is that to him? He was worried not because he thought the secondary qualities resemble his ideas of them, but because he could not see how to handle them in a Galilean physics.

We can explain why Descartes, Locke, and others who accepted the central thesis, and saw that it solves their problem about secondary qualities, also sometimes slid into the 'no resemblance' account of them. As I remarked in §157, we have almost no vocabulary in which to describe our 'sensations' or sensory 'ideas' except through what they represent. So although my 'ideas' do not have colours and shapes, it is true that I cannot say much about them except in terms of colours and shapes, etc., saying things like 'It's the sort of sensory state people typically get into when they see something red' or '. . . when they feel something circular'. Someone who has noticed this, and who accepts the central thesis, can conclude: 'The adjectives that I need to characterize my sensory states fall into two groups: those that I do and those that I do not also need in doing physics. The former are the primary-quality ideas, the latter the secondary-quality ones.' So far, so good. It is an integral part of the correct solution that physics does not need secondary-quality concepts, once they have been explained. There is trouble only if the philosopher infers that his 'ideas' of primary qualities resemble outer things, while his 'ideas' of secondary ones do not. That is an error, based on a misunderstanding of how primary- and secondary-quality words come into the description of 'ideas'. This treatment of the 'no resemblance' thesis is defended in LBH 106. It has been adopted— 'though on rather different grounds'—by Curley (1972: 451–3) and Alexander (1974: 66–70).

In the twentieth century, some philosophers have flirted with the resemblance account of what is special about secondary qualities. Mackie writes:

[Locke] means, surely, that material things literally have shapes as we see shapes, feel shapes, and think of shapes . . . Even under ideal conditions, when we are as right as it is possible to be about colours, colours as we see them are totally different not only from the powers to produce such colours, but also from the ground or basis of these powers in the things that we call coloured. (1976: 13–14)

This passage depends on 'shapes as we see shapes, feel shapes', etc. and 'colours as we see them'. Mackie does not even try to explain these phrases, and his uses of them are not reassuring. He identifies 'colours as we see them' with 'our ideas of secondary qualities', apparently implying that colours as we see them are mental. A page later, he contrasts shapes with colours by writing of something's 'literally being square, its having a shape-quality which we find in the experiential content to which the thing gives rise'. I can make no sense of this echo of the old idea that our sensations of shapes are shaped.

194. Is the central thesis a semantic one?

Here is Descartes stating the core of the central thesis:

The properties in external objects to which we apply the terms 'light', 'colour', 'odour', 'flavour', 'sound', 'heat' and 'cold' are . . . simply various dispositions in these objects which make them able to set up various kinds of motion in our nerves (which are required to produce all the various sensations in our soul). (PP 4:198)

This is the kind of formulation that I have been using all along, but now I issue a warning with regard to it. It is all right to identify a colour (say) with a certain disposition if *all* one means by that is a tying of the truth of 'x is coloured' to 'x is disposed to . . .', with the latter understood as the truth of a counterfactual conditional. The danger is that, having got that far, we may think that there is a further question about the ontological status of the disposition, and thus of the colour. 'Granted: for a thing to have a certain disposition is for a counterfactual to be true. But what, metaphysically speaking, *is* the disposition?'

The most tempting answer is, we now know, wrong. 'The disposition is the primary-quality constellation upon which it supervenes'—wrong, because a single colour does not have a single primary-quality underlay. This is no problem for the central thesis, which is compatible with there being thousands of micro-textures, any one of which would dispose a thing's surface to cause . . . etc.

A question to which there is at least one plainly wrong answer might seem at least to be a good question; but this one is not. Once you know the truth conditions for 'x has a disposition to . . .', you know the whole story; there is no work to be done by the idle, empty, further question 'But what *is* a disposition?' In general, when philosophers italicize the copula, beware!

That question reflects the *noun fallacy*, the assumption that any properly used noun phrase must refer to some thing, some item with an ontological status. We know better. There is plainly a shortage of wheat in North Korea, but we do not inquire into the ontological status of shortages. We all understand that for there to be a shortage of wheat is for there to be less wheat than is needed, and that the latter formulation—in which the noun 'shortage' does not appear—is a better guide to the ontological commitments of this statement.

Yet the noun fallacy occurs quite often in philosophy. People confronted with a functionalist account of the truth conditions of 'In doing A, x intended to bring it about that P' ask whether the intention should be identified with a behavioural disposition, a neural structure, or what. No such question need arise. Again, a good account of the truth conditions of 'In uttering S, x means that P', rather than being obliged to answer the further question 'What kind of item is a meaning?', shows the question to be dispensable. Similarly, I contend, with dispositions. For a sugar cube to have a disposition to dissolve in water is for it to be such that if it were put in water and stirred it would dissolve. There is no place for any thing or item which is the disposition.

So in contexts where ontological questions loom, it may be wise to avoid such nouns as 'disposition', 'colour', 'redness', and the rest. Instead of equating noun phrases, we should equate fully sentential clauses. Here is Descartes doing exactly that:

When we say that we perceive colours in objects, this is really just the same as saying that we perceive something in the objects whose nature we do not know, but which produces in us a certain very clear and vivid sensation which we call the sensation of colour. (*PP* 1:70)

This tells us how to unpack complete sentences about things' colours. It equates *There is colour in the object* with *Something in the object disposes it to affect us thus and so*. Descartes includes 'we perceive', but that occurs on both sides of the equation, so it cancels out.

Descartes here presents the central thesis as a semantic one; it tells us what statements about things' colours mean. If this were meant to generate definitions of 'coloured' or of specific colour-words, it would fail. Suppose we tried to explain the meaning of 'The object is blue' through something of the form 'The object is disposed to cause . . . a visual sensation of kind K', what can 'K' stand for? If we put '. . . of the kind that people typically experience when they see something blue', the definition is circular. If instead we put '. . . of the kind that people typically experience when they see clear skies on a sunny day, an IBM logo, or . . . etc.', the definition is wrong: it is not part of the meaning of 'blue' that any of those kinds of thing is typically blue. We just have to accept that, typically, when you see something blue, you have a visual state with whose intrinsic nature you are perfectly familiar but for which we have no descriptions other than in terms of what people experience when they see blue things. Descartes shows himself as sensitive to this when he explains colour-statements in terms of 'a certain very clear and vivid sensation which we call the sensation of colour'.

How can the central thesis be semantic without falling into the circularity trap? One way is to retreat into a definition that is confessedly only partial:

> To say that a thing is coloured is to say, in part, that it is disposed to cause [etc.] sensations of a certain kind.

But we can do better than that, thus:

> There is a kind K of sensation such that: to say that a thing is coloured is to say that it is disposed to cause [etc.] sensations of kind K.

This definition is also partial, because it contains a free variable which is bound from outside the definition. All that is needed for completion, however, is for the pupil—the person who is to learn from the definition—to know what kind K is; not the meaning of 'K', for it has none, but just the referent of it which makes the entire statement true. And the way to supply this is the one indicated by Locke—namely, ostensive presentation of good examples. The quantified account says everything about the meaning of 'coloured' (or 'red', 'blue', etc.) that can be expressed verbally, and the rest of the semantic story must be supplied ostensively. Locke would agree with this; and I am not being unduly charitable in suggesting that it is what Descartes had in mind in his semantic statement of the central thesis.

Some philosophers have maintained that statements attributing colours, taken in their ordinary meanings, include a metaphysical commitment that conflicts with the central thesis. They seem to be crediting us with giving our colour-words meanings that have the resemblance thesis built into them. I see no evidence for this. Even if it is right, it is not interesting. If indeed we do all make this mistake, it does not connect significantly with anything else in our thought and talk; it squats there in our scheme of things, isolated, impotent, and boring. It would be easy to amend Descartes's semantic version of the central thesis so that it does not conflict with the alleged facts about this semantic error of ours. For example:

> When we apply 'red' to a thing, it would be best for us to mean only that it is disposed to cause . . . etc.

Or, a little more mildly:

> When we apply 'red' to a thing, all that we need to mean is that the thing is disposed to cause . . . etc. Giving secondary-quality words that sort of meaning, we shall be able to cover all the facts that we now cover with their help.

Although these versions concern meanings, they are proposals, or value-judgements, which are supported by contingent facts about the world as we find it. The semantic proposals are good ones because of how secondary qualities are nearly epiphenomenal.

Chapter 26

Locke on Essences

195. Essences of individuals

Much more than any other of our six philosophers, Locke had language as a major theme; *Essay* III, 'Of Words', constitutes nearly a fifth of the work. Its largest topic is a theory about the meanings of general, classificatory words, a theory presented in conscious opposition to a kind of view that Locke thinks one might be tempted into by optimistic corpuscularianism. Locke's own corpuscularianism is, we shall see, highly pessimistic. A key term here is 'essence', to which I now turn.

A thing's essence consists in a certain privileged subset of all its properties or qualities. Usually these days the privilege is that of absolute indispensability: hardness belongs to the essence of *this stone* if it is impossible that this stone should exist and not be hard, and to the essence of *diamonds* if it is impossible for anything to be a diamond without being hard. That notion of essence, however, is not prominent when Locke discusses essences; until III.vi.4 it is not even mentioned. Locke there contends that no property of an individual thing is essential to it *per se*. Essentialness, he maintains, is not a dyad relating a property to a substance, but rather a triad relating a property, a substance, and a kind: my rationality is not essential to me *simpliciter*, though it may be essential to me *qua* human. Locke means this quite generally—'Essence . . . is considered in particular beings no farther than as they are ranked into sorts'—but he tries to persuade us of it only by applying it to examples, including himself:

> There is nothing I have, is essential to me. An accident or disease may very much alter my colour or shape, a fever or fall may take away my reason or memory or both; and an apoplexy leave neither sense nor understanding, no nor life. . . . None of these are essential . . . to any individual whatsoever until the mind refers it to some sort or species of things. (III.vi.4)

Although he expresses this in terms of properties of mine that I could lose, Locke should be willing to say the analogous thing about properties of mine that I could have lacked from the outset. Believers in individual essences sometimes distinguish these, saying that even if a man could become a woman, someone who was male at the outset could not possibly have started out female. Locke has no reason to treat those kinds of essences differently, and would presumably reject both.

He does not consider any of the most abstract or general properties that an individual can have. That heron over there, for instance: could it become a lizard?

Could it have been one from the beginning? Locke should say Yes both times, which means that his position is less plausible than he thinks. Leibniz presents some hard cases for him (*NE* 305), but there are harder ones still. For example, when Locke says that solidity seems to be 'the idea most intimately connected with and essential to body' (II.iv.1; see also III.vi.5), all he is entitled to mean is that an item's being solid is essential not to *it*, but to *its being a body*; and if challenged, perhaps that is what he would say. But then he must allow that a particular body might cease to be a body without ceasing to exist. He would dislike this, I imagine; but he has committed himself to it.

In addition to basic features of things, such as a body's being a body, there are also extremely general (= negative) features, such as a person's not being a grain of sand or a plate of scrambled eggs. If Locke agrees that it is absolutely impossible that I—this very thing—should become a plate of eggs, or should have been one from the outset, then he is allowing a *de re* essence after all. It is negative, boringly trivial, absurd even to mention, but it looks like a breach in the wall: it stops Locke from saying that no properties of a thing are essential to it *de re*, which should then start us discussing which properties are and which are not essential to this or that thing.

Locke's position on this matter has recently fallen into disfavour, under the influence of lines of thought revived by Kripke (1972); but my sympathies are nevertheless with him. Every sane person will answer No to 'Could I become a plate of scrambled eggs?' and Yes to 'Could I become more forgetful than I am now?' But between these there is a continuum, with many intermediate questions which will be answered affirmatively by some and negatively by others— Could a man become a woman?—with no firm concepts or theory controlling the answers. This view of the matter has been embodied in David Lewis's theory about 'counterparts' (1973: 38–43): if x is an actual particular, then it does not exist at any non-actual world, but some such worlds contain things which are like it in ways that lead us—given our interests and the context—to treat them as 'counterparts' of x, and on the strength of them to assent to sentences of the form 'x could have been F' where x is not actually F. At no possible world is a plate of scrambled eggs a decent candidate for the role of counterpart-of-me; but I still contend that there are no hard-edged facts of the matter, and that it is mere superstition to believe that my properties divide into those that objectively and definitively are essential to me and those that objectively and definitively are not. Perhaps Locke's rejection of individual essences reflected some such view as that.

In *Essay* IV.vi.5 he takes the position that 'It is essential to x to be F', rather than always being false, is unintelligible—'very improper and insignificant'; *OED*'s first meaning for 'insignificant' is 'meaningless'. I hope this is not his considered view, for it is plainly false. The form 'x could not possibly exist without being F' is perfectly intelligible.

196. The first opinion about real essences

Let us turn now to the essences of kinds. Most of Locke's discussion of them involves arguing for the primacy of 'nominal' over 'real' essences; the contrast is between *nomen* and *res*, name and thing. The nominal essence of a kind or species is, or corresponds to, the meaning of the word we use to name it (§198). As for the real essence of a species:

> Concerning the real essences of corporeal substances . . . there are . . . two opinions. The one is of those who, using the word *essence* for they know not what, suppose a certain number of those essences, according to which all natural things are made, and wherein they do exactly every one of them partake, and so become of this or that species. . . . [This] supposes these essences as a certain number of forms or molds wherein all natural things that exist are cast and do equally partake. (*Essay* III.iii.17)

Locke disapproves of this first opinion, without making clear what it is or what is wrong with it. The crucial phrase, I think, is 'a certain number of'—by which he means a certain *relatively small* number of essences. He takes the first opinion to imply that particular things fall cleanly into classes, with nothing straddling a borderline or even closely approaching one; they are constrained to do so by there being only a limited stock of essences to which things must conform. Returning to this topic three chapters later, he alludes to 'the usual supposition, that there are certain precise essences or forms of things whereby all individuals existing are, by nature, distinguished into species' (III.vi.14).

Most scholars have thought that Locke has Aristotle and the scholastics in his sights. That is partly right, but it gets the focus wrong, as I have learned from unpublished work by Christopher Conn. We need to distinguish

> (G) the generic thesis that there is a relatively small set of hard-edged and non-overlapping essences, laid down independently of us by nature, to which our classifications should approximate,

from

> (S) the specific thesis that 'forms' in Aristotle's sense are essences of the kind mentioned in G.

There could be a Lockean (corpuscularian) version of G: the essences of things are primary-quality structural features, and they are hard-edged, non-overlapping, and relatively few in number. Unlike Conn, I think that in our present context Locke does have Aristotle in mind; I shall note two bits of evidence for this shortly. But Conn is right in holding that the focus is on G rather than S. When Locke attacks Aristotelian 'forms' head-on, he rails against 'fruitless inquiries after substantial forms, wholly unintelligible, and whereof we have scarce so much as any obscure or confused conception in general' (III.vi.10). He is more temperate concerning the 'first opinion' about real essences. Although he calls it less 'rational' than the second opinion, he does not suggest that it is unintelligible or disgraceful.

Locke makes three main points against the 'first opinion'. (1) He takes it to imply not merely that all things *do* fall cleanly into species but that 'nature . . . designs them to [do so]' (III.vi.15). This is unclear, he alleges, and 'would need some better explication before it can fully be assented to'. (2) Like many of his contemporaries, Locke believed that females of various mammalian species sometimes give birth to creatures that seem to be borderline members of the mother's species, or even to half-qualify as members of two species. These 'irregular and monstrous births', he says, are evidence that either nature has no such design or else its designs are often thwarted: it is a plain empirical fact, he thought, that the members of the animal kingdom do not fall cleanly into a restricted number of species or kinds (III.vi.16). (3) His third and most powerful point is to suggest that 'those we call monsters' are 'really a distinct species, according to the scholastic notion of the word *species*' (III.vi.17). Each of these strange, not obviously classifiable creatures 'has its particular constitution'; it answers to a certain description, has a determinate set of qualities; so why should not those define the species to which it belongs? It is a different species from that to which its parents belong, but is it not still, metaphysically speaking, a legitimate species? What is the evidence that it falls through the cracks of the one objectively right taxonomy and is thus contrary to nature's plan?

Point 1 is evidence that Aristotle is in question. At any rate, Aristotelian scholasticism was an obvious source for the view that first-opinion essences are normative, guiding what does and dictating what should happen. Notice that Locke also tracks Aristotle by discussing the 'first opinion' purely in terms of biological kinds, saying nothing about its implications for fundamental physics. I shall not follow him through the discussion of organisms which he does vouchsafe; evolutionary theory and microbiological genetics have rendered that controversy out of date.

197. The second opinion about real essences

The second opinion is this:

The other and more rational opinion is of those who look on all natural things to have a real but unknown constitution of their insensible parts, from which flow those sensible qualities which serve us to distinguish them one from another, according as we have occasion to rank them into sorts under common denominations. (III.iii.17)

This is not discomfited by borderline cases: it does not say that there is 'a certain [small] number' of essences of the kind now under consideration, or describe them as 'forms or molds' in which things 'exactly partake'. Another difference: it says that essences are 'constitutions of insensible parts', whereas proponents of the first opinion treat essences as 'they know not what'.

When Locke writes, 'That every thing has a real constitution whereby it is what it is, and on which its sensible qualities depend, is past doubt' (x.21), he makes it clear that real constitutions are possessed by things *per se*. He has a passage 'concerning that parcel of matter which makes the ring on my finger', about which he says: 'It is the real constitution of its insensible parts on which depend all those properties of colour, weight, fusibility, fixedness etc. which are found in it' (iii.18). By the curious phrase 'that parcel of matter etc.' Locke wants to point to the thing and say something about it, considered in itself and not brought under any sortal. (See also *Essay* 380:9, 442:5, 449:22.) Leibniz misses this point, replacing Locke's careful '. . . concerning that parcel of matter which makes the ring on my finger' by '. . . concerning gold' (*NE* 294).

Now, Locke sometimes identifies a thing's real constitution with its essence, as in the phrase 'its real essence, or internal constitution, on which . . .' etc. (379:32). And in one place he explicitly points out that this yields a kind of essence that can be attributed to a thing *per se*:

Essence may be taken for the very being of any thing, whereby it is what it is. And thus the real internal, but generally in substances unknown, constitution of things, whereon their discoverable qualities depend, may be called their essence. This is the proper original signification of the word . . . And in this sense it is still used, when we speak of the essence of particular things, without giving them any name. (III.iii.15)

Such essences, then, can be assigned to things 'without giving them any name', that is, without applying any sortal terms to them; so they are essences that things have *per se*.

This is not Locke's most usual way of using 'essence', however. He nearly always says that real essences, even of the rational 'second opinion' kind, belong to things only *qua* F for some value of F:

By this real essence I mean the real constitution of any thing, which is the foundation of all those properties that are combined in, and are constantly found to co-exist with, the nominal essence; that particular constitution which every thing has within itself, without any relation to anything without it. But essence, even in this sense, relates to a sort and supposes a species; for being that real constitution on which the properties depend it necessarily supposes a sort of things, properties belonging only to species, and not to individuals. (III.vi.6)

When Locke writes that properties do not belong to individuals, he is using 'property' as a technical term which goes back to Aristotle's logic. Aristotle divided the 'predicables' into three:

definition (of which the parts are the genus and the differentia), expressing the thing's essence

property, a quality which follows necessarily from the essence without being part of it, *accident*, a property or quality which could be lacked by something having that essence.

The 'properties' of a thing, in this Aristotelian sense, make up only a subset of its 'properties' in our sense: namely, the set of qualities which do not fall within the essence but follow necessarily from it. See also 439:28–30 and 449:14–17. The technical sense of 'property' explains the otherwise baffling episode at 486:18–21, where Locke rightly challenges the distinction between essence or definition and Aristotelian 'property'.

So we are back to essences again, and these—Locke holds—must be essences of kinds or sorts. Here is a bit of gold. No matter how you describe it, this nugget has a chemical constitution, a 'texture' of minute parts. Some aspects of that constitution (Locke thinks) suffice causally to make the thing have the features that qualify it to count as *gold*; those aspects of it are part of its primary-quality 'real constitution'; it has them in itself, *per se*, not *qua* gold or *qua* metal or whatever; but they count as the essence of it only *qua* gold. This picture of the situation was first made clear to me, in conversation, by Michael Ayers.

Incidentally, although Locke sometimes calls a thing's inner constitution its 'essence', he does not say that it is 'essential to' the thing. He holds steadily to his view that there are no absolutely unlosable properties. Here, for example: 'There is no individual parcel of matter to which any of these qualities are so annexed as to be essential to it or inseparable from it. That which is essential belongs to it as a condition whereby it is of this or that sort. But take away the consideration of its being ranked under the name of some abstract idea and then there is nothing necessary to it, nothing inseparable from it' (III.vi.6). This passage elegantly relates two topics that Locke rightly regarded as entirely separate: one involving the concept *essential-to*, the other involving the concepts of real and nominal essence.

198. How we classify

Locke says a great deal about the primacy, in our thought and language, of nominal essences over real, whether the latter are understood according to the first or the second opinion. In III.iii.17 he presents the first opinion, then the second, then reverts to the first with this scathing comment:

The supposition of essences that cannot be known, and the making them nevertheless to be that which distinguishes the species of things, is so wholly useless and unserviceable to any part of our knowledge that that alone were sufficient to make us lay it by and content ourselves with such essences of the sorts or species of things as come within reach of our knowledge.

That is, we should content ourselves with nominal essences. The phrase 'cannot be known' points to first-opinion real essences: 'they' absolutely cannot be known, because 'they' are conceptually incoherent or empty, whereas second opinion real essences are only *de facto* out of our reach, because they involve structures that are too small for us to discover. (I cannot find Locke explicitly saying that smallness is the whole difficulty, but that was presumably his opinion; IV.xvi.12 is suggestive.) Still, Locke is here rejecting second-opinion real essences, too, as a basis for classification. From now on I shall use 'real essences', *simpliciter*, to refer to real essences according to the second, 'more rational' opinion.

Because we do not know them in any detail, Locke contends, real essences are not our actual basis for classification. When I pick out bits of the world as gold, I must steer by how they relate to something in my mind, and he holds that the relation is this: a certain abstract idea (type) is for me especially associated with the word 'gold'—it fixes what I mean by that word—and when I decide whether to call an item 'gold' depends on how it relates to that abstract idea. Thus:

When general names have any connexion with particular beings, these abstract ideas are the medium that unites them; so that the essences of species, as distinguished and denominated by us, neither are nor can be anything but those precise abstract ideas we have in our minds. And therefore the supposed real essences of substances, if different from our abstract ideas, cannot be the essences of the species we rank things into. (III.iii.13)

This profound passage confronts the question 'What does my mind contain that enables me to connect one "name" with many particulars?' Every time Locke asks this, he answers that we classify on the basis of a match-up between abstract ideas in our minds and observable ('sensible') qualities of the things being classified. We cannot rank and sort and thus name things on the basis of their real essences, because 'we know them not' (vi.9; see also vi.18 and ix.12).

What we do know, and can steer by in classifying, are nominal essences. Considered as properties of the things being classified, they include 'sensible qualities' and also superficially discoverable dispositions like the fusibility of gold. These qualities lie on the surface, where we have access to them, and their guidance of us is mediated by our ideas of them. Too often, however, Locke writes as though the nominal essence of a kind were itself an abstract idea (type), rather than a property or quality represented by an idea (type). This is one part of his tendency to run ideas and qualities together (§168). In our present area it sometimes embodies a mistake, which can be seen here:

Nature makes many particular things which do agree with one another in many sensible qualities and probably too in their internal frame and constitution. But it is not this real essence that distinguishes them into species; it is men who, taking occasion from the qualities they find united in them . . . , range them into sorts in order to their naming. (III.vi.36)

Here as elsewhere, Locke conflates two questions about classification:

Is it done by nature or by people?
Is it done by internal constitutions or by superficially perceptible qualities?

The mix-up is vividly present at vi.36. Where Locke ought to say that we classify on the basis of sensible qualities, etc., rather than inner constitutions, he tends to say that our basis consists in ideas in our own minds rather than qualities in the objects. The former thesis is defensible, the latter not. Locke's tendency to conflate them is probably both a cause and an effect of his propensity for saying that nominal essences are ideas while giving them roles that are appropriate only to qualities. From now on, I shall take it that nominal essences are qualities of the things being classified: they are not ideas in our minds, but we have ideas of them, which is why we can classify on the basis of them.

What makes an essence 'real' is its ontological place in the whole truth about the thing that has it; what makes an essence 'nominal' is its role in giving meaning to some word. So a real essence could also be nominal. Locke says that this 'rarely if ever' happens (iv.3), but he has no reason to allege any difficulty in principle with it.

199. Guessing at real essences

Of any kind whose members we can pick out through their superficially detectable qualities we can ask whether it has a real essence. To take Locke's favourite example: perhaps the properties on the strength of which we recognize things as gold can flow from many different constitutions, in which case there would be no one real essence of the kind gold, just as there is no one real essence of dirt or of rocks. Locke is sometimes optimistic about this. He says he will call what-we-go-by 'the nominal essence, to distinguish it from that real constitution of substances upon which depends this nominal essence and all the properties of that sort; which therefore, as has been said, may be called the real essence' (vi.2). In this sentence 'properties' has its Aristotelian sense.

But we have seen Locke approach this issue more cautiously, writing of things which agree 'in many sensible qualities and *probably* too in their internal frame and constitution', and sometimes he is sceptical about the chances of a given kind's having a real essence—in vi.8, for example. This difficult section seems to aim partly at first-opinion essences, and to use 'property' partly in the Aristotelian sense; it is hard to sort out. But this bit is clear enough: 'We find many of the individuals that are . . . received as being of one species have yet qualities depending on their real constitutions as far different from one another as from others from which they are accounted to differ specifically.' This implies that some nominal essences do not correspond to any unitary real essences. It is not clear to me that Locke is entitled to this conclusion. Suppose we found that some specimens of gold—taking 'gold' to be defined by the Lockean nominal essence—were soluble in a certain acid while others were not. The inner constitution of the soluble gold must differ from that of the insoluble—that is an article of the corpuscularian faith—but the two constitutions might have much in common, and their shared qualities might explain the fact that all this stuff is yellow, heavy, malleable, fusible, ductile, and soluble in *aqua regia*. In that case, the two sorts of gold would be somewhat different, but they would have a shared partial nature which explained their shared sensible properties and which therefore counted as the real essence of gold—*all* gold, soluble and insoluble. Locke seems not to have thought this the whole way through.

Anyway, he did not rate highly our chances of isolating kinds that have real essences. (In IV.vi.11–12 he takes the pessimism very far, and argues for it at length. This magnificent passage repays careful study.) Locke seems oddly complacent about this. He depicts us as swift and opportunistic in our drawings of lines on the basis of things' sensible qualities:

We, having need of general names for present use, stay not for a perfect discovery of all those qualities which would best show us their most material differences and agreements, but we ourselves divide them by certain obvious appearances into species, that we may the easier, under general names, communicate our thoughts about them. (vi.30)

This could be said ruefully, or with regret, or in a report in which the plain man's conduct is contrasted with the pursuit of scientifically fruitful classifications. Locke, however, does not adopt any of those tones. Throughout the *Essay* he sees so little prospect of our learning about real essences that he is not interested in looking for taxonomies that have a good chance of carving up the universe at its real joints. Yet, if we have evidence that some of our classifications *do not* line up with real essences, as he alleges in vi.8, then we should be able to get evidence that some of our classifications *do*.

Leibniz discusses these matters in the *New Essays* at 292–4, 308–29, 352–4, 400–2; for an illuminating examination of these passages see Goodin 1999. Leibniz has a more cheerful and resolute eye on the possibility of getting scientifically sound taxonomies than Locke does; but he does not, and could not, deny that in classifying things into kinds we must go by qualities of them of which we have ideas. On that point Locke is right.

200. Meanings and essences

What we go by in sorting things, Locke contends, is also what we mean by our names for the sorts: our only way of talking about or referring to gold is through (our idea of) the nominal essence of gold—that is, by a word whose meaning is constituted by (our idea of) that nominal essence. When, in expounding this, he writes of what a word 'signifies' or 'stands for', he means its sense, not its reference: word W 'signifies' the idea whose presence in the mind of the W-user gives W its meaning. Here are some examples:

'The names of natural substances signify rarely if ever anything but barely the nominal essences of those species' (III.iv.3).

'. . . without any consideration of real essences . . . , which come not within reach of our knowledge when we think of those things, nor within the signification of our words when we discourse with others' (vi.33).

'[If we suppose] each of those names to stand for a thing having the real essence on which those properties depend . . . we would make [our words] stand for something which, not being in our complex idea, the name we use can no ways be the sign of' (x.18).

'To make our names stand for ideas we have not, or (which is all one) essences that we know not, [is] in effect to make our words the signs of nothing' (x.21).

Thus, Locke believes that our meanings—like our *de facto* bases for classification—are restricted to qualities of things of which we have ideas. For three centuries most English-language philosophers seem to have believed this, and it is indeed plausible. If, in classifying stuff as gold, I go by whether it is yellow, heavy, etc., does this not show that by 'gold' I mean 'stuff that is yellow, heavy, etc.'?

No. There is an escape from that conclusion. Leibniz points it out, quickly and quietly, in the *New Essays*, and it has been well known since it was rediscovered and proclaimed in our day by Kripke (1972: 315–16 and 319–21) and Putnam (1975: 215–38). As I expound it, pretend that we know nothing about the chemical composition of gold: the point is to explore what such ignorance implies about meanings.

Consider this nugget of gold: without knowing what its chemical composition is, I can reasonably guess that it has one, which makes it yellow, etc. and is possessed by all and only the things that are yellow, etc. In this conjecture I have the thought *There is a real essence that has relation R to certain sensible qualities*. This thought quantifies over chemical compositions without referring to any one of them. If there is indeed a real essence of all and only the stuff that is yellow, etc., I can use the phrase 'the real essence of the stuff that is yellow, etc.' to pick it out, without knowing what it is—just as I can use the phrase 'the perpetrator of the crime' to refer to the criminal, without knowing who he is.

Locke evidently did not see this clearly. He concedes that we can somehow speak about essences which we do not know, but he thinks there is some strain or discomfort or difficulty about doing so:

[To] bid the reader consider *man* as he is in himself and as he is really distinguished from others in his internal constitution or real essence, that is, by something he knows not what, looks like trifling. And yet thus one must do who would speak of the supposed real essences and species of things, as thought to be made by nature . . . It is difficult by known familiar names to do this. (III.vi.43)

In fact, it is easy. Concerning any real essence there is (1) the fact about what it intrinsically is, and (2) the fact about what sensible qualities it causes its possessors to have. Facts of kind 2 suffice to enable us to have thoughts—affirmative or negative, general or particular—about essences that we do not know: that is, regarding which we have no facts of kind 1.

According to Kripke and Putnam, we not only *can* but *do* have such thoughts and build them into meanings. When we say that a certain quantity of matter is gold, these philosophers have argued, we mean that it is of the same natural kind, has the same real essence, as . . . and then there is a choice:

(1) . . . as all and only the stuff that is yellow, heavy, etc.,
(2) . . . as most of the stuff we have so far encountered that is yellow, heavy, etc.,
(3) . . . as *this* (accompanied by a pointing to a particular lump of gold).

Of these, 1 implies that 'gold' is necessarily coextensive with 'stuff that has the same chemical composition as all the stuff that satisfies the Lockean nominal essence of gold', though the two do not mean the same; while 2 allows that some of the gold-seeming stuff we have known may not really have been gold, and even that most of the gold-seeming stuff still to be encountered may not really be gold; and 3 allows that through some freak accident we might be wrong in thinking that *any* gold is yellow, heavy, etc.

Various conceptual thought-experiments, encouraged by Putnam and Kripke, will satisfy you that 3 is better than 2, which is better than 1. But even 1 improves on Locke, and Leibniz did get that far:

Philalethes: [To use the word *gold*] to stand for a thing having the real essence on which that property depends . . . is a plain abuse, since the real essence is not included in the complex idea which the word signifies.
Theophilus: Well, I should have thought it was obviously wrong to criticize this . . . usage, since it is quite true that the complex idea of gold includes its being something which has a real essence whose detailed constitution is unknown to us, except for the fact that such qualities as malleability depend upon it. (NE 345)

As soon as one sees that the meanings of natural-kind names such as 'gold' could be like this, it is easy to find reasons for thinking that they are. One good reason is given by Leibniz (NE 312). Here we are in a world containing a lot of stuff which we classify as 'gold' because it is heavy, yellow, etc. Now suppose that we learn how to fabricate some other stuff which, though indistinguishable from the gold now on earth, has a different chemical composition from the latter. For as long as we cannot distinguish it from the gold we have, we shall call it 'gold', but when we discover the chemical difference, we shall say that it is not gold after all, though it is very like it.

Locke, on the other hand, must say that in this situation we would have discovered how to make a new kind of gold—a new kind of heavy, yellow, etc. stuff—and a further discovery about differences between the new kind and the old. A Lockean might add: 'After the chemical facts were discovered, we might change the meaning of "gold" so as to restrict the word to the old kind', but that is untenable. It implies that, as we learn more about the real essences of various kinds of things, our names for those kinds change their meanings, as though Shakespeare meant one thing by 'water', and we mean another. I find it more plausible to suppose that if 'water' has changed its meaning during the past couple of centuries, the change has not been a replacement, but rather an enrichment: Shakespeare used 'water' to mean 'stuff having the same inner constitution as (most of) the stuff that is colourless, thirst-quenching, etc.', and we mean exactly the same thing with the addition of 'namely, H_2O'. Our meaning of 'water' would differ radically only from that of someone who did not think of water as a natural kind, had no sense of all water's sharing some inner constitution, and thought of water somewhat as we do of dirt.

Here is a different version of the 'discovery of new stuff' story. Suppose we find new stuff which is heavy, yellow, etc., and which chemically differs just a little from the stuff we have been calling 'gold' up to now. We can handle this in either of two ways. We can deny that the new stuff is gold, or we can admit it as gold and say that we have just discovered that 'gold' picks out not an ultimate physical species, but rather a genus with at least two species. We can always be tentative about whether our names of natural kinds pick out species that cannot be further subdivided: a confident judgement that there is such a stuff as gold can go with a tentative judgement that gold does not chemically divide into two species. This paragraph is lifted straight from the beautiful, though difficult, passage at NE 401–2.

Incidentally, if scientific discoveries can enrich meanings, can your or my meaning for a word be altered by a discovery of which we know nothing? Putnam answers Yes, because common meanings partly reflect the esoteric knowledge of the experts. Leibniz beat him to this too: see NE 354. Leibniz's anticipations of Kripke and Putnam are well described in Jolley 1978: 201–2.

I have been taking it for granted that the Leibniz–Kripke semantics applies to all and only the names of *natural kinds*; it obviously does not apply to names of artificial kinds, such as 'pencil-sharpener' and 'parliament'. But what about biological classes? They are natural rather than artificial, but there is a question as to whether the Leibniz–Kripke semantics holds for their names, as I now explain.

Consider camels. Do they admit of a distinction analogous to that between the nominal and real essences of gold? The analogue of the nominal essence would be the easily discoverable features of a thing which lead us zoo-visitors or Bedouin to classify it as a camel; the only analogue of gold's real essence is a certain DNA recipe that is common to all camels. Having no notion of this, Leibniz dodges away from inner natures and real essences of biological kinds, with the sole exception of *Homo sapiens*, which he thinks is marked off by *reason*. Leibniz implies that other biological species also have inner natures, as when he writes: 'One would like to guess whether the inner nature which is common to the individuals of a given species (for example reason, in man) is also present—as suggested by the facts of birth—in individuals lacking some of the outer signs which ordinarily occur in that species' (NE 311). But he has no suggestions about what such inner natures could be, and sometimes implies that there are none:

If we found ourselves back in the age when beasts used to speak, we would lose the privilege of being the sole inheritors of reason; and we would thenceforth pay more attention to birth and to outward features in order to be able to distinguish members of the race of Adam from the descendants of some king or patriarch of a community of African monkeys. (*NE* 320)

Let us now set reason aside. Its role in the human condition is at best very unlike that of chemical composition in the total nature of gold; in calling each of them 'inner', Leibniz produces something close to a pun on that term. Furthermore, when he emphasizes reason's role as a mark of humanity, he is not thinking of humans as a *biological* kind.

This leaves him with two bases for classification: the physical facts that are analogous to gold's colour, weight, solubility in aqua regia, and so on; and descent. This last is special to the biological realm, and for that reason Locke declines to allow it to interfere with his general views on classification as such:

Nor let anyone say that the power of propagation . . . keeps the supposed real species distinct and entire. For granting this to be true, it would help us in the distinction of the species of things no farther than the tribes of animals and vegetables. What must we do for the rest? (III.vi.23)

This almost concedes that we ought to consider biological classification on its own, not aiming to bring it under any unitary theory about the meanings of all general terms. I agree. It seems pretty clear that we need one account for biological species, a second for (other) natural kinds, and a third for artificial kinds.

So we have an organism's intrinsic features and its descent. When these two are linked, all is well: camels are animals that have certain features of size, shape, anatomical structure, and so on, and that are born of animals that also have those features. But what if the two came apart? What if an animal bearing all the obvious intrinsic marks of being a camel gave birth to one with all the obvious intrinsic marks of a tiger? I cannot find in Locke or Leibniz a determinate answer to the question of what we should say in this case, and on that I congratulate them. Our actual meanings and concepts do not, and should not, forearm us against such an eventuality.

Include DNA in the mix, and the situation does not alter. Suppose that an animal with the intrinsic marks of camelhood (including its DNA) gave birth to one with the intrinsic marks of tigerhood (DNA included): if this physically impossible event actually occurred, should we—according to the concepts we now have—declare the offspring to be a camel or a tiger? There is no answer to this.

201. The nature and source of Locke's failure

In *Essay* III.x.17 Locke writes that we sometimes try to use 'gold' to refer to the real essence of gold. This sounds Leibnizian/Kripkean, and Mackie (1976:

93–100) thought that it is. While acknowledging that Locke erred in condemning Kripkean meanings, Mackie credited him with at least seeing that they are possible and even actual. This is not right, though. Locke does not present a definite procedure as clearly possible, though also illicit. Rather, in that passage he writes that 'by a secret supposition' we make the word stand for a real essence; that 'we would'—that is, we try to—make the word stand for a real essence; and that in 'no ways' can the word stand for a real essence. Locke asserts each of these, without reconciling them. Even the first does not adumbrate the clear, controlled position of Leibniz and the others. (See also 378:20 and 380:23.)

Why did Locke not do better in this matter? Suggested answer: 'He didn't see that the meaning of a general term might have (as we would say) an existential quantifier embedded in it.' That is wrong, as can be seen from this:

All words that necessarily lead the mind to any other ideas than are supposed really to exist in that thing to which the words are applied are relative words . . . Father, brother, king, husband, blacker, merrier, etc. are words which, together with the thing they denominate, imply also something else separate and exterior to the existence of that thing. (II.xxv.10)

So Locke grasped perfectly well that 'x is a father' means something of the form 'there is an organism y such that $R(x,y)$'. Why, then, did he not see that 'x is gold' might mean something of the form 'there is a real essence y such that $R(x,y)$'?

The trouble is specific to 'real essence'. Locke holds that for us to give real essences *any* respectable role in our semantics, we would have to know what those real essences are, and we never do. Having implied that it is hard or impossible for someone to 'consider gold as it is in itself', because that would be to consider it 'by something he knows not what', Locke continues:

And yet thus one must do who would speak of the supposed real essences and species of things, as thought to be made by nature, *if it be but only to make it understood that there is no such thing signified by the general names which substances are called by*. (III.vi.43; my emphasis)

This implies that the phrase 'real essence' is problematic in any use of it—not only in existentially quantified meanings, but also in saying that names of kinds of substance do not signify real essences. Locke does not abide by this astonishing statement, for he writes many pages asserting and arguing that our names of kinds of substances do not signify real essences. Yet he does think that his own semantic theory condemns his doing so, and this may have inhibited him from seeing what Leibniz and Kripke saw.

Does Locke's own theory of meaning imply that he could mean nothing by 'real essence'? Here is a reason he may have had for thinking so: the sought-after idea must be an abstract one capturing what is common to many detailed ideas of complete chemical compositions; but we have no such ideas; so we cannot form the abstract idea in question; so, for us, 'real essence' is strictly meaningless. But that is wrong, because abstraction is not the only route which Lockean semantics allows to the formation of a somewhat abstract idea. He cannot think that this is how we get meanings for 'good reason' or 'difficult problem' or countless other phrases. His view ought to be that we have meanings for these because we assemble them out of simpler ingredients, and he has no reason to refuse that approach for 'real essence' as well. I am not endorsing this view. Out of the sense-based raw materials that Locke allows, and the purely conjunctive way of assembling them into complexes, he has no chance of actually explaining the meanings of any of those phrases. But this is a failure in his semantic theory generally; it is not something he could adduce to cast doubt on 'real essence' in particular.

202. Essences and universals

Locke's doctrine that all classification goes by nominal essences, as he understands these, seems to imply that all our classifications are artefacts: the lines fall where we choose to put them, our choices being free and unconstrained. Holders of the 'first opinion' about real essences think that all the significant lines are laid down by nature itself, leaving us no role except to observe and obey them. If the 'second opinion' kind of essences entered the classificatory picture, nature would not do all the work, but it would severely constrain us in our classifications. With both of those set aside, however, we are at liberty to classify in any way we choose; or so Locke's theory seems to imply.

That is vague. In one way of taking it, the thesis is that the likenesses and unlikenesses among particulars offer us endless possible groupings, and we are free to choose from these to suit ourselves. In another, stronger interpretation, it says that we are free to group *any* set of particulars into a 'sort' under a general name—that the world does not even present us with possible sortings from which we may choose. All we have seen in Locke's text so far is the weaker thesis: the observable similarities are there in the world, and we select from them in our classifications. Sometimes, however, he hints at the stronger thesis, apparently denying that there are any shared properties, any universals—'All things that exist are only particulars' (III.iii.6). The appearance of universality comes from facts about how we think and speak:

General and universal belong not to the real existence of things but are the inventions and creatures of the understanding, made by it for its own use, and concern only signs, whether words or ideas. Words are general . . . when used for signs of general ideas . . . , and ideas are general when they are set up as the representatives of many particular things; but universality belongs not to things themselves, which are all of them particular in their existence. (III.iii.11)

This seems to imply that our classificatory work is unconstrained, free, answerable to nothing. That is incredible, but I do not think Locke means to be committed to it. He plainly treats real essences as universals, and they cannot get their universality from us, who know nothing of them; so he cannot consistently dislodge real universals in favour of universalizing mental activities. In at least one place, indeed, he declines to take classification out of nature's hands and put it wholly into ours:

I would not here be thought to forget, much less to deny, that nature in the production of things makes several of them alike . . . But yet I think we may say the sorting of them under names is the workmanship of the understanding, taking occasion from the similitude it observes amongst them to make abstract general ideas and set them up in the mind . . . as patterns. (III.iii.13)

This, as Leibniz implicitly notes at *NE* 292, admits that our classificatory doings are, after all, guided by extra-mental universals—similarities that exist among things independently of us. Leibniz repeatedly challenges Locke's implied thesis that species boundaries are created by us, protesting that the boundaries are laid down by nature, our contribution being merely to select some for our notice.

Locke is probably inconsistent on this matter, but I shall not stay with that question. When he stresses human activities and choices, we do better to see him as engaged in his theory about nominal essences, and not as taking a stand about Platonism, objective universals, and so on.

Chapter 27

Substance in Locke

203. The substratum theory

Before I can move on into Berkeley's metaphysic, I have to deal with a strange theory of Locke's about the idea of substance. (The main texts are I.iv.18, II.xiii.17–20, xxiii.1–6, 15, 37, III.vi.21, and IV.vi.7.) A substance is a thing which has properties; Locke is comfortable about our ideas of the various properties; but he struggles with what he says is the idea of 'thing which . . .'. The raw materials of what we experience are properties or their instances, and from these we infer that there is also something that has them:

The mind being . . . furnished with a great number of simple ideas, conveyed in by the senses as they are found in exterior things or by reflection on its own operations, takes notice also that a certain number of these simple ideas go constantly together; which being presumed to belong to one thing . . . are called so united in one subject by one name; which by inadvertency we are apt afterward to talk of and consider as one simple idea, which indeed is a complication of many ideas together; because, as I have said, not imagining how these simple ideas can subsist by themselves, we accustom ourselves to suppose some *substratum* wherein they do subsist and from which they do result, which therefore we call *substance*. (*Essay* II.xxiii.1)

Here, as often, Locke speaks of how this substratum relates to 'simple *ideas*', but his topic is how it relates to qualities or properties. Although the idea/quality mix-up is not confined to the 'substratum' passages, it does occur richly there. Here is another example, in which both 'qualities' and 'ideas' are involved:

[1] Our complex ideas of substances, besides all these simple ideas they are made up of, have always the confused idea of *something* to which they belong, and in which they subsist: [2] and therefore when we speak of any sort of substance we say it is a *thing* having such or such qualities, as body is a *thing* that is extended, figured, and capable of motion . . . [3] These and the like fashions of speaking intimate that the substance is supposed always *something* besides the extension, figure, solidity, motion, thinking, or other observable ideas, though we know not what it is. (II.xxiii.3; emphasis original)[1]

In this passage 1 really is about ideas and 2 about qualities; while 3 speaks of 'ideas', but is talking about qualities. That is the conflation making itself felt (§168). Here, as everywhere, when Locke writes about 'the idea [or notion] of substance in general' and 'substratum', his topic is the instantiation of qualities; he is theorizing about the notion of a thing which . . .

---

[1] See also II.xxiii.5 and 6. For 'idea [or notion] of substance in general', see 2, 3, and xxxi.13.

He could as well have conducted his discussions of 'the idea of *substance*' in terms of 'the idea of *thing*'. In the passage last quoted, his repeated italics for 'thing' and 'something' emphasize that the 'substance' thought is the 'thing' thought. In other passages too, Locke runs the two terms in a single harness (in the first of the following quotations the italics are his):

When we talk or think of any particular sort of corporeal substances, as horse, stone, &c. though the idea we have of either of them be but the complication or collection of those several simple ideas of sensible qualities which we use to find united in the thing called horse or stone; yet because we cannot conceive how they should subsist alone nor one in another we suppose them existing in and supported by some common subject, which support we denote by the name substance, though it be certain we have no clear or distinct idea of that *thing* we suppose a support. (II.xxiii.4)

Those who have far different ideas of a man may yet agree in the notion of a father: which is a notion superinduced to the substance, or man, and refers only to an act of that *thing* called man, whereby he contributed to the generation of one of his own kind. (xxv.4)

Doubts are raised whether we are the same thinking *thing*, i.e. the same substance or no. (336:8)

At 95:30, 176:8, 296:9, and 297:29 the same work is done not by 'thing', but by 'something', also italicized by Locke in two cases.

I said that Locke's topic is the instantiation of qualities, but that is too sweeping. (1) Like Aristotle in the *Categories*, he is concerned with the instantiation of qualities by items that are not themselves qualities; so instantiation by modes lies outside the scope of this theory. Locke sometimes writes as though qualities, universals, were modes; but mostly he thinks of modes as individual accidents or tropes. Either way, modes lie on the right of the thing/property line. Such facts as that the game was violent and that his prurience is disgusting are irrelevant to our present topic.[2] (2) Nor is Locke's topic involved in instantiations which can be reductively eliminated, as when we equate 'The problem of squaring the circle is difficult' with 'Some people would like to square the circle, and nobody can easily do it', and 'The shortage of food in North Korea is worrying' with 'It is worrying that North Korea is short of food'. (3) What about instantiation by ideas? Locke had no considered ontological views about ideas, and in §159 we saw him coming close to mocking the very question about this. But we can see which way the wind is blowing in the *Essay*. Lockean ideas fare best when understood as tropes; and that puts them on the right of the thing/property line, so that their possession of further properties does not bring 'the idea of substance in general' into play. Locke's own tendency to abolish the distinction between ideas and qualities (which is not fully explained by their being tropes) also has the same effect. (4) Nor is 'substance in general' involved in the instantiation of qualities by items that exist necessarily and lie outside time—ones that we (though

---

[2] Bolton (1976) counts instantiation by modes as decisive against the interpretation I am giving. She is helped to do this by her understanding of the substance/mode line in terms not of thing/quality but of natural/artificial. For good evidence against that reading of Locke, see Atherton 1984: 208.

not Locke) would call 'abstract'—such as the number three's being odd. Thinking of these items as belonging to a timeless 'third realm', we can see them as not involving the idea of substance in general, because Locke intends the latter to provide only for the instantiation of qualities by contingent denizens of the temporal world. He himself, however, would not put it like that, because he has no third-realm ontology; but he would agree that our thoughts about these items do not involve the idea of substance in general. The only propositions he allows for are verbal or mental; he treats numbers as ideas and/or modes; he classifies abstract geometrical figures ('triangle') as modes; and so on. Quite generally, any item that we might think of as a timeless, necessary part of the third realm will be either ignored by Locke or classified as some kind of idea and/or mode. From his standpoint, therefore, my 4 is absorbed by 1 and 3.

These limits on the scope of the 'idea of substance in general' are reflected in something Locke says about our progress towards ever more general ideas: 'By the same way the mind proceeds to body, substance, and at last to being, thing, and such universal terms which stand for any of our ideas whatsoever' (III.iii.9). Thus, 'thing' applies to any item that may be referred to, including my present headache and the number seven; 'substance' is less general than that, Locke says here, and his handling of it throughout the *Essay* shows that he is confining it to durable, contingently existing items that are not themselves properties or qualities. We have seen Locke seeming to equate 'substance' with 'thing', and I shall continue to do so, but only in contexts where it is clear that the 'things' in question are substances—that is, where there is no risk of changing the topic to qualities, modes, ideas, numbers, etc.

Many philosophers have said that the notion of pure substance in general, or 'Lockean substratum' as it is often called, is impossible or intolerable. They are right, but why? We can only smile at the idea that unless something lies under the qualities and props them up they will . . . what? Fall flat? Scatter? Disintegrate? But if that were the whole source of the trouble, we could quietly walk away from it as a mere muddled metaphor in which substratum is like a shelf. Setting aside the metaphor, we are left with the notion of a thing that has various properties—for instance, a thing that is orange and spherical and sweet and middlingly heavy. What could be more innocent than this? Where is the problem?

The answer concerns conceptual emptiness: it is thought that because a substratum has to be the bearer of all the qualities it must therefore be, in itself, bare or unqualified in some problematic way. Elizabeth Anscombe (1981: 38) understands this as follows: 'One of the considerations brought forward in erecting this notion (for it is not a straw man, real humans *have* gone in for it) seems so idiotic as to be almost incredible, namely that the substance is the entity that has the properties, and so it itself has not properties.' Anscombe would rather believe something 'almost incredible' about her contemporaries' idiocy than suspect that she has misunderstood them. Sellars was guilty of the same derisive misunderstanding, and was justly reproached for it by Alston (1954: 257). The fact is that the substratum idea does involve a trouble that could be put in terms of the upholder of properties not itself having properties; yet is not idiotic. I shall explain.

When someone thinks about the thing that is orange and spherical and F and G and H . . . and so on through all the qualities of the orange, and rightly takes that thought to involve the notion of a thing, a concrete particular, a substance, he may wonder: 'What kind of item is that? What does an item have to be like— what monadic features must it have—to be fit for the property-bearing role?' This question cannot be answered, and is improper. Suppose it is legitimate, and that there is such a feature—call it 'substantiality'. Then we are saying that an item gets to be a property-bearer if it has substantiality. But that is one of its properties! We were trying to wrestle with the thought of a *thing* on one side of the divide and *all its properties* on the other, but then in asking what qualifies an item as a thing (asking about thinghood or substantiality), we have slid one property across from the right of the line to the left. That means we are no longer working with the conceptual division we started out with. This whole line of thought says, in a nutshell, that *things are not things of a kind*. This criticism of the 'idea of substance in general' as Locke presents it is of a piece with Leibniz's criticism in *NE* 218.

204. Locke's attitude to it

The criticism would appeal to Locke himself. He was apt to be harsh with any general term that he saw as empty, not cashable in terms of actual or possible experience. It is obvious that 'idea of substance in general', on my understanding of it—which I share with Leibniz, Berkeley, Hume, and most readers of Locke down the centuries—could not possibly satisfy Locke's own theory about how we get our ideas. This naturally prompts the thought that we have all been mis-understanding the 'substratum' texts. That is Ayers's view:

It is improbable to the point of impossibility that Locke, who is an anti-Aristotelian cor-puscularian of the school of Boyle, should himself, using the very term *substratum*, advance a view so analogous to what Berkeley described as 'that antiquated and so much ridiculed notion of *materia prima* to be met with in Aristotle and his followers'. . . . Whatever Locke's *substratum* is, if he wrote *compos mentis*, it cannot be an entity that is undifferentiated, or 'other than' its properties. (1975: 78–9)

Locke's substratum notion, according to the standard or Leibnizian interpreta-tion, is indeed like that of *materia prima*, which he himself treats with scorn at *Essay* 499:4. But he is also critical of the 'substratum' concept that he calls to our attention: as well as saying that we have and need it, he is scathing about its deficiencies, implying that it is confused and perhaps even non-existent.

The unwavering doubleness of Locke's attitude to the 'idea of substance in general' or 'substratum' is remarkable; I know of nothing else like it in any philosopher. On the one hand, with only one exception which I shall report late in this section, the substratum notion is presented as implicit in our ordinary ways of thinking and talking. This happens in the 'thing' and 'something' passages I have quoted or mentioned, and also here:

> 'There is another idea which would be of general use for mankind to have, as it is of general talk as if they had it; and that is the idea of substance' (I.iv.18).
> '[In] ideas of substances [the idea of substratum] is always the first and chief' (II.xii.6).
> 'not imagining how these ideas can subsist by themselves, we accustom ourselves to suppose some substratum' (xxiii.1).
> 'These and the like fashions of speaking intimate that the substance is supposed always *something* besides . . .' (etc.). (xxiii.3).
> 'All our ideas of the several sorts of substances are nothing but collections of simple ideas, with a supposition of something to which they belong and in which they subsist' (xiii.37).
> '. . . collections of such qualities as have been observed to co-exist in an unknown substratum' (IV.vi.7).

On the other hand, the notion of substratum is presented as highly criticizable:

> 'the idea of substance, which we neither have nor can have by sensation or reflection' (I.iv.8).
> 'We . . . signify nothing by the word *substance* but only an uncertain supposition of we know not what . . . which we take to be the substratum' (ibid.).
> 'the supposed or confused idea of substance, such as it is' (II.xii.6).
> 'the promiscuous use of so doubtful a term . . . in ordinary use it has scarce one clear distinct signification' (xiii.18).
> 'Of substance we have no idea of what it is, but only a confused obscure one of what it does' (xiii.19).
> 'the confused [idea] of substance, or of an unknown support' (III.vi.21).

The items in these two lists often inhabit a single clause, as when Locke says that the complex idea of any kind of substance is a 'combination' of simple ideas 'in which the supposed or confused idea of substance, such as it is, is always the first and chief'.

Repeatedly he says of the idea of substance in general that it is central and indispensable, and also intellectually disgraceful. No interpretation of these texts can be right that does not adequately explain Locke's stunningly equivocal attitude towards this 'idea'. In *LBH* I guessed that when Locke seemed to tolerate the idea of substance in general, he had his tongue in his cheek; but in offering that unlikely tale, I overlooked a natural and well-supported alternative account of the matter, which I now present.

Locke's theory of meaning is permeated by his view that each meaningful general word W is linked to an idea-type, which serves as a pattern or criterion to help us sort particulars into those to which W applies and those to which it does not. But, for the reason I have presented, and of which Locke was aware, the word 'substance'—meaning 'pure substance in general'—cannot possibly have a meaning of that kind; and he cannot see what other kind of meaning it could have.

So we have a semantic theorist in an impasse. On the one hand, we talk about things that *have* various qualities; we make sense of such expressions as 'the thing or substance that has all the qualities of the orange', and this seems to be an indispensable part of our conceptual stock-in-trade. On the other hand, Locke cannot see how the supposed idea of 'thing which . . .' or 'substance in general' could be made respectable, and he realizes that he cannot validate it along the lines he offers for most general terms—namely, by associating it with an idea that can be intelligibly derived from sensory ideas.

Locke behaves like someone in a jam. Failing to find any account of how there could be a Lockean idea of substance in general, he had to conclude that we really have no idea corresponding to this way of talking; but then he backed off from that, seeing what an important way of talking it is. His ways of backing off vary. Early in the *Essay* he says that men do not have the idea of substance, but talk 'as if they had it'. Later he straddles the fence, speaking of 'the supposed or confused idea of substance, such as it is'. And there are other formulations: Locke writes that 'of substance we have no idea of what it is but only a confused obscure one of what it does', refers to our 'obscure and relative idea of substance in general' (II.xxiii.3), says that 'we have no positive idea' of substance (xxiii.15), remarks that 'Our idea of substance . . . is but a supposed I know not what, to support those ideas we call accidents' (ibid.), and so on.

It is a strange performance, but an understandable one: Locke was caught between the fact that we do, and perhaps must, have the concept of a 'thing which . . .' and the inhospitable treatment of this concept by his theory of meaning. He would not flout 'the familiar party line', Ayers says, in a phrase that does an injustice to Locke's honesty and independence. He finds the notion of an upholder of qualities *embarrassing*, but he grapples with it, the party line notwithstanding. It is no wonder that the substratum texts are two-faced: in them we see a genius in a bind.

In *Essay* II.xiii.19–20, and there alone, Locke treats substratum not as an embarrassing bit of public property, but rather as a gratuitous, dispensable, and criticizable invention of certain philosophers. According to him, the latter were driven to look for a 'support' because they 'ran into the notion of accidents, as a sort of real beings'. This is right, in that the substratum line of thought flows most smoothly if it starts with individual accidents, or tropes. But how is this to be reconciled with Locke's own tolerance of such items all through the *Essay*? And what were these philosophers doing other than what Locke repeatedly says 'we' do all the time? This passage is out of line with all the rest, and I cannot explain the discrepancy.

205. How to avoid Locke's impasse

Leibniz accurately diagnosed the trouble that Locke was in:

If you distinguish two things in a substance [or: in substance]—the attributes or predicates, and their common subject—it is no wonder that you cannot conceive anything special in this subject. That is inevitable, because you have already set aside all the attributes
through which details could be conceived. Thus, to require of this 'pure subject in general' anything beyond what is needed for the conception of 'the same thing'—e.g. it is the
same thing which understands and wills, which imagines and reasons—is to demand the
impossible; and it also contravenes the assumption that was made in performing the
abstraction and separating the subject from all its qualities or accidents. (*NE* 218)

This is good as far as it goes, but when Leibniz remarks that our thing thought
or concept of substance has only to provide 'what is needed for the conception
of "the same thing"', he is letting himself down too lightly. A conception of 'the
same thing' is useless or worse unless it has some empirical moorings; it must
enable us to have reasons for or against various identity-judgements. Leibniz
rightly says that Locke's supposed idea of substance in general does not do that
job, or any other; but nor does he, in this context, try to do it himself.

In other works of his, far from his Lockean concerns, Leibniz does have things
to say on this topic (§311). In the meantime, let us briefly look into the philosophy of this matter on our own account.

Locke's impasse is created by this trio:

(1) The concept of *thing* is a central and indispensable part of our conceptual
scheme.
(2) The meaning of 'thing' is to be explained in the same way as the meanings
of most general terms.
(3) For most general words, knowing the meaning is knowing what conditions an item must satisfy for the word to be applicable to it.

We should let 1 stand, as it is right. To avoid Locke's trouble, then, we need to
deny 2 or 3 or both. I contend that 3 is false. To explain why, I have to take a couple of steps backwards.

Let us think first about the explanation not of meanings but of *meaning*. What
is involved in explaining what it is for any portion of language to have a meaning?
One might naturally think that one should start by explaining what it is for a
word to have a meaning, and then on that basis explain what it is for a longer
expression such as a sentence to do so. Nobody, however, has succeeded in
explaining what word-meaning is without bringing in sentence-meaning. Most
such attempts have assumed that the basic meaning relation is *naming* or *standing for*, so that to understand what it is for a word to mean something we must
grasp what it is for a word to stand for something. This is doubly defective: plenty
of word-meaning does not involve naming or standing-for; and anyway the

'stands for' relation itself makes sense only in a context in which one can *say things* with words—that is, say something which means *that P* for some propositional P. Try to imagine a community which has a repertoire of meaningful expressions but never uses them to say anything. It cannot be done. For more about this, see my 1976: 17–22.

One promising theory about the nature of meaning was invented by Paul Grice, and developed by Schiffer, myself, and others; another stems from J. L. Austin, and has been furthered by philosophers including Alston and Searle; yet another began with Sellars, and has a progeny including books by Brandom and by Hawthorne and Lance. These vigorous, fruitful, promising accounts of what meaning is, unlike as they are, all start with the meanings of whole utterances (typically sentences), and approach the meanings of words through how they affect the meanings of sentences containing them. This analytic order has come to stay.

Certainly, in understanding what particular bits of language mean, word-meanings come first. We understand sentences through our grasp of word-meanings and of the semantic force of word-order in the sentence. We seldom learn the meaning of sentences as wholes; and if that were our only way to learn what sentences mean, we could not understand ones that we had never heard before—whereas in fact we do this all the time, both as hearers and as speakers. Some philosophers have seen this inescapable fact about *how meanings are grasped* as conflicting with the 'sentence first' view about *how the concept of meaning is to be analysed*; this is a mere mistake, and the ablest maker of it—namely, Dummett (1956: 492)—eventually came to realize this (1973: 192–6).

Now, consider what all this implies about explanations of the meanings of individual words. It may seem natural to think that someone who says '"triangular" means "closed and plane and three-sided"' is explaining one word's meaning without bringing sentences into the story; but really he is not. That definition is a shorthand recipe for correct uses of 'triangular', in sentences such as 'Dealy Plaza is triangular' and 'Wenceslaus Square is not triangular', by someone who is already competent in the use of sentences containing 'plane' and 'closed' and 'three-sided'. It is true that in the case of 'triangular' the definition can *also* be seen as laying down the conditions for something to count as triangular, but there is no good reason to expect this to hold good for the explanation of the meaning of every general term.

It obviously does not hold for adverbs. To explain the meaning of 'gracefully', you have to explain how to use it to modify the verb in 'She skates' and 'He apologizes' and the like. Here there is not even the illusion that the word can be explained in isolation. Similarly with the whole category of relational expressions, including prepositions and transitive verbs. Imagine trying to explain the meaning of 'inside' or 'above', or that of 'pushes' or 'loves', in any context except that of use in sentences!

Some nouns and adjectives also refuse even to seem to be explicable in isolation, and the prime exhibit in this category is the noun 'thing'. To explain its meaning, one must present the rules that govern sentences in which it occurs—rules laying down truth conditions for 'There is an F thing' for various kinds of F, and for 'The thing that is F is also G', and for 'The thing that was F is now not F', and so on. Locke's trouble does not come from the details of what he thinks ideas to be, but simply from his thinking that he should be able to explain 'thing' in isolation. He is wrong about that; and a proper grasp of how word-meaning relates to sentence-meaning shows that this is not because 'thing' is categorially special in some way. It is merely a word that is so abstract and general that an explanation of its meaning must openly have the structure that all explanations of meanings have at least covertly.

So we should analyse 'thing' by elucidating sentences that contain it. The sort of elucidation that I find most promising—it has found favour with many philosophers—is of this form:

> To say that there is an F thing at a given location in space-time is to say that at that location an F-ness trope exists in relation R to a number of other tropes.

I cannot replace the dummy predicate 'R' with anything very specific. The general idea, however, is that we attribute tropes to a thing when a number of them are associated through a period of time, the association being spatio-temporal and also perhaps causal. Locke himself points to a part of this story in a passage already quoted, where he says that our thing thought comes into play when we notice that 'a certain number of these simple ideas [he means tropes] go constantly together'. This was a good start on an account of the thing thought; it needed to be continued with an enrichment of 'go constantly together', to get a full statement of what relations amongst tropes are needed for them to belong to a thing. Locke, however, continues thus: '. . . which being presumed to belong to one thing . . . are called so united in one subject by one name'. The phrase 'presumed to belong to one thing' indicates that Locke regards the thing thought as different from, and additional to, the 'go constantly together' thought; so he looks for it elsewhere, in a supposed idea of substance in general; which brings him to his impasse.

To get this right, Locke needed some tools that he did not have, especially a solid account of sentence-meaning. Still, even with the resources at his disposal, he could have moved in the right direction. His theory of meaning has, as we have seen, two parts: one for general, classificatory terms, the other for words like 'if' and 'but' and 'is', which he called 'particles' (§173). The latter, he says, do not stand for ideas but rather express mental operations on ideas:

Besides words which are names of ideas in the mind, there are a great many others that are made use of to signify the connexion that the mind gives to ideas, or propositions, one with another. The mind, in communicating its thought to others, does not only need signs of the ideas it has then before it, but others also, to show or intimate some particular action of its own, at that time, relating to those ideas. This it does several ways; as Is, and Is not, are the general marks of the mind affirming or denying. . . . [Particles] are all marks of some action or intimation of the mind; and therefore to understand them rightly, the several views, postures, stands, turns, limitations, and exceptions, and several other thoughts of the mind for which we have either none, or very deficient names, are diligently to be studied. (III.vii.1,4)

If Locke had applied this part of his meaning theory to 'thing', saying that, although grammatically it is a general noun, its semantics are like those of a particle, he would have done better. For then he could have said something like this: 'When I say "This is an orange" I mean that there are here instances of certain properties such as orangeness, sphericalness, etc., and I indicate that I am operating on my ideas of those instances in a certain combining manner.' This, though crude and only partial, is better than the obviously doomed attempt to associate 'thing' with a type of idea.

206. Ayers's interpretation of 'substance' in Locke

A few philosophers, most recently Ayers, have rejected the Leibnizian interpretation of Locke's writings about the idea of substance in general, in favour of the view that in those texts Locke is using 'substance' to mean something like 'real essence'. (Others are Mandelbaum (1964), Yolton (1970), and Bolton (1976).) That seemed to be Ayers's view in an early paper (1975) on this topic, and his more recent book (1991) tells a similar story. In the book he quotes Locke: 'Besides, a man has no idea of substance in general nor knows what substance is in itself', and comments that this 'may roughly be paraphrased: "What is more, we do not even know the general or determinable nature or essence which constitutes all physical things—i.e. the fundamental nature of matter as such"' (Ayers 1991: ii.41). This is close enough to an equation of substance with real essence to fall within the scope of my 1987, where I attack that equation in minute detail, adducing textual evidence against it and in favour of the Leibnizian reading of the substratum texts. No one has replied to the attack; and I shall not repeat it here, except to remark that Locke repeatedly says that the idea of substance in general is common property and is conceptually disgraceful, and he does not believe either thing about the idea of real essence.

As well as rejecting the standard Leibnizian understanding of Locke's 'idea of substance in general' texts, Ayers offers his own account of what is going on there. It attributes to Locke a special view about the thing thought—one which Ayers does not endorse, though he treats it with respect. It holds that the thing thought is for us a place-holder for thoughts of the fundamental nature of the thing in question. The only reason why we think of matter as a thing (or stuff) that is extended is that extension is not its basic nature, but only one of the upshots of that nature. What makes us wrinkle our noses at a sentence like 'Yellowness, heaviness, malleability, [etc.] is soluble in aqua regia' is that our list of defining adjectives for 'gold' does not include the fundamental nature of that metal, which ultimately explains its being yellow, etc. If we knew that nature, and expressed *it* in an abstract noun phrase (ANP) that is grammatically like 'heaviness', we would not find it awkward to say '[ANP] is soluble in aqua regia'.

According to this view of substance and property, subject and predicate, Ayers writes (1991: ii.53):

The ground of objection to the sentence, 'Rationality is capable of conversation', [is] not so much syntactic as semantic or, indeed, metaphysical. It is not intelligible that rationality should be the real essence [or absolutely fundamental nature] of man, and that is why the sentence appears to us as nonsense. Rationality itself needs explanation: it is too evidently a mode or attribute dependent on some other attribute or attributes from which it flows.

So we would not need a thing thought if we knew the ultimate explanatory natures of the different kinds of thing, and had abstract nouns to express them; for then we could construct abstract noun phrases that would pick out the things perfectly, uttering sentences of the form '[ANP] is capable of conversation' with no sense of linguistic malpractice.

It follows that if we knew and could say enough, we should dispense with the thing thought entirely. For this thesis to recommend itself philosophically, it would need more explanation than Ayers or I have given it, but I shall not go into this here. My main concern is with his attribution of the thesis to Locke, and with the use he makes of this.

Ayers has not favoured my textual arguments with any reply. He has, however, addressed my 'familiar' and 'notorious' line of thought that Locke was led into his embarrassing 'idea of substance in general' by his theory about how general words have meanings:

However much we knew about a substance (even if we knew its most fundamental properties, its essence), it would still, it seems, be definable as a *thing* which possesses these properties. Something like this line of thought has contributed to the interpretation of substance-in-general as an entity unknowable in principle, a bare and entirely indeterminate subject of attributes. The appeal to language, it is thought, at least committed Locke to such a view. Yet that is to suppose Locke's being forced to an absurd conclusion by a premise which, however natural it may appear to us, was explicitly rejected by him. (Ayers 1991: ii.52)

We are left to gather what the 'premise' is. It seems to be the proposition that, in order to think about things, we need a *thing* thought, or—shifting from thought to speech—in order to talk about things, we need either the word 'thing' or some word whose meaning includes that of 'thing'. If Locke explicitly rejected this, that would destroy my explanation of his substratum texts on the Leibnizian interpretation of them, which in turn would cast doubt on the latter. (It would not dislodge the textual obstacles to Ayers's interpretation.) Well, here is the section in which Locke is supposed to have 'explicitly rejected' that premiss:

But since, as has been remarked, we have need of general words, though we know not the real essences of things; all we can do is to collect such a number of simple ideas, as by examination we find to be united together in things existing, and thereof to make one complex idea. Which though it be not the real essence of any substance that exists, is yet the specific essence to which our name belongs and is convertible with it; by which we may at least try the truth of these nominal essences. For example, there be that say that the essence of body is extension: If it be so, we can never mistake in putting the essence of any thing for the thing itself. Let us then in discourse put extension for body; and when we would say that body moves, let us say that extension moves, and see how it will look. He that should say that one extension by impulse moves another extension, would, by the bare expression, sufficiently show the absurdity of such a notion. The essence of any thing, in respect of us, is the whole complex idea comprehended and marked by that name; and in substances, besides the several distinct simple ideas that make them up, the confused one of substance, or of an unknown support and cause of their union, is always a part: And therefore the essence of body is not bare extension, but an extended solid thing: And so to say an extended solid thing moves, or impels another, is all one, and as intelligible as to say, body moves or impels. Likewise to say that a rational animal is capable of conversation, is all one as to say a man. But no one will say that rationality is capable of conversation, because it makes not the whole essence to which we give the name man. (*Essay* III.vi.21)

Locke is talking about nominal essences and the definitions corresponding to them; he maintains that any sortal word is equivalent to its nominal definition, so that the two are interchangeable in any context. Having reiterated that the meanings of the names of the kinds of substances always include the idea of substance in general, he now supports this through an appeal to the interchangeability test. Consider, for example, the ideas that make up our idea of body: Locke thinks that they include, at least, extension, solidity, and substance in general. He may be aiming at Descartes, who left out solidity; but that is not the focal point of the passage, which is chiefly concerned with the omission of substance in general. When Locke writes: 'He that should say that one extension by impulse moves another extension, would, by the bare expression, sufficiently show the absurdity of such a notion,' his point would still have survived if he had instead poured scorn on anyone who 'should say that one extension and solidity by impulse moves another extension and solidity'. He is concerned with the omission of the idea of a *thing* which has the extension, solidity, or whatever. He says so: 'The essence of any thing, in respect of us, is the whole complex idea comprehended and marked by that name; and in substances, besides the several distinct simple ideas that make them up, the confused one of substance, or of an unknown support and cause of their union, is always a part: And therefore the essence of body is not bare extension, but an extended solid thing.'

Locke does seem to have connected 'solid' with 'thing' in a certain way. In his chapter on the 'simple modes of space' (II.xiii), he attacks Descartes for leaving solidity out of the essence of matter, and thus abolishing the distinction between body and empty space. Here is one episode in the attack:

I would ask whether, if God placed a man at the extremity of corporeal beings, he could not stretch his hand beyond his body? If he could, then he would put his arm where there was before space without body; and if there he spread his fingers, there would still be space between them without body. If he could not stretch out his hand, it must be because of some external hindrance . . . And then I ask, Whether that which hinders his hand from moving outwards be substance or accident, something or nothing? And when they [i.e. the Cartesians] have resolved that, they will be able to resolve themselves what that is which is or may be between two bodies at a distance, that is not body and has no solidity. (II.xiii.21)

The suggestion here that solidity = substance, so that Descartes, in leaving out one, has left out the other, is not in line with Locke's real views. In the immediately preceding four sections he has confronted the question of whether empty space is substantial; he dislikes the question and blusters in the face of it, and, conspicuously, does not give the short sharp answer that emerges from the idea that solidity = substance. Furthermore, he elsewhere makes it clear that he thinks of the idea of substance in general as the idea of that which upholds *solidity* along with the other properties of the thing (see, for instance, II.xxiii.2). If in II.xiii.21 Locke really does make the solidity = substance mistake, I see no reason to extend it to the passage to which Ayers calls our attention. There the focus is not on 'solid', but on 'thing'. Locke writes scornfully: 'Let us then in discourse put extension for body; and when we would say that body moves, let us say that extension moves, and see how it will look.' Are we to suppose that he would regard 'Extension and solidity moves' as more proper? No. His topic is not the clear idea of solidity, but the confused idea of substance. This passage confirms the view that Locke was led by his theory of meaning to the idea of substance in general on the Leibnizian interpretation of the latter.

It troubles me that Ayers should announce that III.vi.21 'explicitly rejects' the very thing that it seems to confirm. I am at a loss to understand how the passage can be made, even with twisting and turning, to do what Ayers wants it to do, let alone to do it 'explicitly'. He writes:

The whole argument implies that the reason why 'extension' can stand neither as subject nor object of 'impels' is not because it is the nominalization of an adjective, but because it is the nominalization of the wrong adjective. If x-ness were what extension is not, the essence of body, then to say that one x-ness impelled another would make sense. (Ayers 1991: ii.52)

How does the whole argument imply this? I can find no hint of such a view in what Locke wrote—here or anywhere else.

207. Two exegetical problems

Two textual details are awkward for the Leibnizian interpretation of the substratum texts and not for Ayers's interpretation.

(1) On the Leibnizian account of what substratum is, Locke should find it obvious that substratum as such cannot have a 'nature'. Yet in two substratum con-

texts he uses the phrase 'nature of substance'—once combatively and once sceptically, but not saying anything like 'Of course this is a nonsense phrase; nothing
could possibly correspond to it'. Even if we cannot reconcile these with the
Leibnizian interpretation, the latter does not thereby collapse. Still, it would be
good to find a reconciliation.

In one of the two 'nature of substance' passages, Locke has been discussing
space, and anticipates being asked a question that he cannot answer: 'If it be
demanded (as it usually is) whether this space void of body be substance or accident, I shall readily answer, I know not; nor shall be ashamed to own my ignorance till they that ask show me a clear distinct idea of substance' (*Essay* II.xiii.17).
In his attack on the question, Locke takes it to be of the form 'What kind of item
is space?— that is, as a request for more information about space. And he proceeds to argue that if you think of 'substance' as picking out a kind of item, you
will land yourself in a dilemma. On the one hand, you can say that 'substance'
always picks out the same kind, so that God, spirits, and bodies are all items of a
single kind: 'agreeing in the same common nature of substance, [they] differ not
any otherwise than in a bare different modification of that substance'. Locke
thinks his opponents will find that unswallowable. (His word is 'harsh'. See the
OED's sense 4 of 'harsh', which includes 'repugnant to the understanding' and
'grating upon the mind'.) If, on the other hand, they say that God is a 'substance'
in one sense of the term, spirits in a second, and bodies in a third, we do not know
what to make of their question whether space is a substance. Perhaps, Locke slyly
suggests, it is a substance in a fourth sense. In this context of argument by *reductio ad absurdum*, Locke's use of the phrase 'nature of substance' is innocent.

I cannot explain the other 'nature of substance' passage, but I point out that its
location may be significant. It is a sentence beginning 'Whatever therefore be the
secret and abstract nature of substance in general' (II.xxiii.6), and it follows one of
the five sections in the *Essay* where Locke speaks of the substance of body and of
spirit, and, more specifically, the substance of one's mind and of one's body. This
peculiar 'substance of' locution, which we saw in Descartes (§19), occurs in II.xxiii
and nowhere else in the *Essay*. In this chapter, Locke opposes the materialist who
complacently accepts the concept of material substance while holding that thinking substance is suspect. He counters this with a *tu quoque* argument, maintaining
that any conceptual problems regarding thinking substance ('spirit') are matched
by equally grave ones about material substance, and in sections 5, 16, 23, 28, and
30 he makes this point in the 'substance of' terminology. Each time, he evidently
uses 'substance of' to mean 'nature of', a usage that Leibniz described:

The word *substance* is taken in two ways—for the subject itself, and for the essence of the
subject. For the subject itself, when it is said that the body or the bread is a substance; for
the essence of the subject when one says 'the substance of the body' or 'the substance of
the bread'. (Quoted in Sleigh 1990: 97)

The latter of these fits Ayers's interpretation, which is apparently right for the
cluster of 'substance of' uses; but that does not make it right for the rest of the

Essay. As for 'idea of substance in general' understood in the Leibnizian way: that is also present in this chapter, where Locke maintains that our idea of a bit of gold is the idea of a yellow, heavy, ductile, fusible, malleable *thing*, a complex idea with five unproblematic ingredients and a sixth which is troublesome for the reason given in the Leibnizian interpretation.

It is also worth noting that the two 'nature of substance' passages belong to the tiny number of texts in which Locke writes as though the issue about substance belonged to metaphysics rather than to semantics. Nearly always he treats it as an issue about our concepts: his point is that our thoughts are shot through with the idea of substratum substance, rather than that we believe that such things or stuff exists. Presumably he would say that if there is no substratum substance, then most of our beliefs about the world are false; but his emphasis is on folk semantics, not folk metaphysics. The latter emphasis, including the 'nature of substance' passages, occurs mainly in his treatments of substance early in the *Essay*, which seem to have been written much earlier and not edited out when his thought on this topic matured.

(2) The substratum texts hardly ever bring in causal relations. All we can say about the supposed substratum is how it relates to ideas or qualities, Locke says, and the relations he usually invokes are not causation—which does relate the real essence to the sensible qualities—but possession, containment, and support:

> 'the substratum or support of those ideas we do know' (95:32)
> 'were forced to find out the word *substance* to support them' (175:2)
> 'the supposed but unknown support of those qualities we find existing' (296:15)
> 'the confused idea of something to which they belong and in which they subsist' (297:5)
> 'we suppose them existing in and supported by some common subject' (297:20)
> 'which he supposes to rest in, and be as it were adherent to, that unknown common subject' (298:23)
> 'a supposed I know not what, to support those ideas we call accidents' (305:33)
> 'a supposition of something to which they belong and in which they subsist' (316:27)
> 'all united together in an unknown substratum' (317:15)
> 'such qualities as have been observed to co-exist in an unknown substratum' (582:14)

There is just one break in this pattern. In a passage already quoted, Locke writes of 'some substratum wherein they do subsist *and from which they do result*' (295:15; my emphasis). The suggestion of substratum as cause does not sit well with the Leibnizian reading, which seems to have nothing causal about it.

But perhaps not, after all. There may be something causal about substratum even on the Leibnizian view of what it is. Because there cannot be a thing with only one property, each instance of substratum must uphold not just one idea/quality but a lot of them:

'are called so united in one subject by one name' (295:10)
'we suppose them existing in . . . some common subject' (297:20)
'all united together in an unknown substratum' (317:15)
'such qualities as . . . coexist in an unknown substratum' (582:14)

From this it is a short step to the idea that substratum does not just hold the qualities up, so to speak, but *holds them together*, this being causal. In one place Locke says as much: 'Besides the several distinct simple ideas that make [up our ideas of substances], the confused one of substance, or of an unknown support and cause of their union, is always a part' (III.vi.21). This is not embarrassing to the Leibnizian interpretation. The latter can hardly avoid saying that substratum is a holder-together, a unifier of ideas or qualities, and that seems to imply that it *causes* their unity. Perhaps when Locke wrote 'and from which they do result', he really meant 'and from which their unity results'. I used to think that unlikely, because in the fifth edition that same phrase (near enough) occurs again (295 n.). Two occurrences of the same careless slip? But Matthew Stuart has shown me strong evidence that the fifth edition passage was not written by Locke.[3]

---

[3] Stuart writes: 'Locke died before he saw the fifth edition (1706) to the press, and his editor, John Churchill, inserted passages from the correspondence with Stillingfleet in footnotes to the *Essay*. In the alleged second slip of the pen, it is in fact John Churchill's pen that slipped. This is evident from the fact that the footnote refers to Locke as "our Author," and also from the fact that when Churchill published the first edition of the Works—which of course included all of the correspondence with Stillingfleet—he did not hesitate to remove the footnote altogether.'

Chapter 28

Berkeley against Materialism

208. Foundationalism

Locke, Berkeley, and Hume all inherited something from Descartes's sceptical exercise in the *Meditations*. Each believed that everyone's system of beliefs has a foundation, consisting in what Locke and Berkeley called *ideas*; Hume also had these in his philosophy in a foundational role, though with different terminology. I shall discuss this in terms of Locke, but the discussion will apply equally to the other two.

The 'ideas' that are supposed to found our beliefs about the material world are what Locke sometimes calls 'ideas of sensation'. When you see a material thing, he thought, you are in immediate epistemic contact not with that thing, but with your sensory 'idea' of it; similarly if you hear or smell or taste or touch something. It is immediate because, as Leibniz said, 'Nothing comes between the mind and its object'. Your epistemic contact with the book you touch or see is not immediate; on the contrary, it is mediated by your sensory idea of the thing—the idea comes between the mind and the book. The information that there is a book in front of you comes to you from your visual idea of it. You could (in a hallucination) have an exactly similar idea although there was no book there; and this shows us that even in the normal case your having the idea is one fact, and your seeing the book is another.

Locke did not have, and did not think he needed, any account of how we know about our ideas. Other epistemic items are admitted to our system of beliefs only if they produce credentials, but the foundational items are admitted before the scrutineers are in place. Locke calls our knowledge of those items 'intuitive', and defends its foundational status in only two ways.

One is to proclaim how 'certain' we are about our ideas:

All our knowledge consist[s] in the view the mind has of its own ideas, which is the utmost light and greatest certainty we, with our faculties and in our way of knowledge, are capable of . . . A man cannot conceive himself capable of a greater certainty than to know that any idea in his mind is such as he perceives it to be. (IV.ii.1)

Later in the work, Locke says that he has an 'infallible' knowledge of his own existence, basing this on Descartes's *Cogito* argument (IV.ix.3); but I cannot find him saying that we are infallible about our ideas. He certainly makes no such claim in the above passage, where he writes not of how assured or guaranteed-to-be-true or certain *it is* that I now have an F idea, but rather of how certain *I am* that I do so. Locke typically ignores the difference between these. At no stage does he seriously enter the Cartesian drama of considering whether even the things he is most certain of might be false. It is in character for him to base his thought on human capacities as he sees them, rather than on a theoretical metaphysical possibility.

He also argues for the foundational status of our ideas on the ground that we have no other possible foundation: 'Intuitive knowledge neither requires nor admits any proof, one part of it more than another. He that will suppose it does takes away the foundation of all knowledge and certainty' (IV.vii.19). He does not defend this important claim, presumably finding it self-evident. Nor does he address the thought that belief systems might not have foundations in the way he has in mind—that the popular metaphor of an edifice of belief which rests on something may be misleading.

To see how this might be so, we must first grasp the case that can be made for a kind of foundationalism. I shall state it in terms of possible worlds, but it could be put otherwise. There are countless possible worlds—that is, ways that things could be—and we think we can rule some out as not the actual world. There are worlds at which no planet has any oceans, and ones where the only physical system is a single planet; and we are pretty sure that the actual world is of neither of those kinds. Given that we know somehow which worlds are possible, how do we narrow down the range of them that have a chance of being the actual one? (I do not ask how we discover which world is the actual one, for that would be to discover the whole contingent truth.) How, that is, do we get contingent information?

The now standard answer to the question is as follows. We learn about the actual world because it acts upon us causally; we learn some details about it through how it affects us. This is, at least, a coherent, intelligible, partial theory of the matter, with no rivals that today's philosophers would take seriously.

It can easily draw one into a kind of foundationalism. 'The world's effects on me inform me about its nature'—this seems to imply that my beliefs about those effects serve as premises from which I draw conclusions about the world; and that is foundationalism. Drawing such conclusions would be making an inference to the best explanation: I am immediately presented with these changes in my own state, I want to explain them, and the best explanation is that they are caused by a world which is thus and so.

It is beyond dispute that I am informed about the actual world through its effects on me. However, the foundationalist line of thought I have sketched goes further, saying that those effects are intellectually available to me as premises for arguments. The thesis that I *infer* a theory of the world from its effects on me requires me to be informed about those effects; I have them as conscious epistemic possessions, from which I draw conclusions.

That is Locke's view, as we see here: 'The foundation of all our knowledge of corporeal things lies in our senses. . . . The whole extent of our knowledge or imagination reaches not beyond our own ideas limited to our ways of perception' (III.xi.23). This implies that the foundation of our (other) beliefs is something that happens in us *and that we are informed about*—recall Locke writing of the 'certainty' with which someone can 'know that any idea in his mind is such as he perceives it to be'.

The caused-by-the-world argument says that our knowledge of the world is founded on states that it causes us to be in, but it does not say that these states—be they physical or mental—are ones that we attend to, have beliefs about, infer things from. They might instead somehow underlie all our knowledge without themselves being objects of knowledge or belief. Many philosophers accept something along these lines. Without denying that we can have beliefs about our sensory states, they deny that these could support the rest of our epistemic edifice. They could find support for this in the plausible view (§157) that we have few concepts that we can apply to our sensory states except ones borrowed from the material world—'I am confronted by a visual datum that is typical of seeing something spherical'. If this view is correct, then Locke's kind of foundationalism probably cannot be.

I do not say that Locke's foundationalism is wrong, merely that it is not secured by the caused-by-the-world account of contingent knowledge. So we should not see it as almost trivially true, as I used to. However, this sort of foundationalism is common to Locke, Berkeley, and Hume, and in exploring them, I shall stay within its confines.

209. Descartes on the existence of matter

In the opening paragraphs of the *Meditations*, Descartes asks what entitles him to believe that there are material things, including his belief that he has a body. He considers the answer that the senses clearly tell him that he has hands and legs—he speaks of having 'accepted' things from the senses, and talks about whether the senses might 'deceive' him. But I doubt if he seriously thinks of this in terms of testimony. His considered view about how the senses 'tell the truth' about bodies is that bodies act upon the sense-organs: 'We cannot perceive any body by our senses unless it is the cause of some change in our sense organs—that is, unless it somehow moves the minute parts of the matter of which these organs are composed' (*W* 4, CSM 1:87–8). When he alludes to what the senses *say* about bodies, I think Descartes is really talking about what hypothesis regarding bodies best explains the facts about his sensory states.

Anyway, he sets aside the appeal to the senses, on the grounds that some of his apparently sensory states—as in dreams—are deceptive, and for all he knows they may be deceiving him right now when he thinks he is awake.

When in the Sixth Meditation Descartes restores this appeal to the senses, he relies on theology. He starts with an argument, which he could have offered back in the First Meditation, for the existence of *something* other than himself. His 'ideas of sensible objects', he writes, could not reach him unless something—either myself or something else—had an active capacity to produce or bring about these ideas. But it cannot be I who has this capacity, since clearly it presupposes no intellectual act on my part, and the ideas in question are produced without my cooperation and often even against my will. So the only alternative is that it is in another substance distinct from me. (CSM 2:55)

Descartes assumes here that if he caused his own sensory states, he would know that he did. This comes from two underlying assumptions: the only way in which someone can cause an event is through the exercise of his will; and there can be no unconscious acts of the will—whatever goes on in a mind is known by it. I shall not discuss these.

Descartes's argument from the involuntariness of his sensory states falls short of concluding that there are material things. Indeed, it ought to apply equally to the states that he involuntarily comes to be in during dreams and hallucinations. To get to a world of material things, therefore, he has to say more, which he does:

Since God is not a deceiver, it is quite clear that he does not transmit the ideas to me either directly from himself, or indirectly via some created thing which [is not corporeal]. For God has not equipped me to recognize any such source for these ideas; on the contrary, he has given me a great propensity to believe that they are produced by corporeal things. So [God would be] a deceiver if the ideas were transmitted from a source other than corporeal things. It follows that corporeal things exist. (Ibid.; see also PP 2:1)

Thus, Descartes infers that there are bodies from his theology, which he thinks he has proved through two arguments which presuppose nothing about what exists outside his mind.

210. Locke on the existence of matter

Without embarking on a Cartesian programme of systematic doubt, Locke saw himself as faced with Descartes's question about the existence of a world of material things. Listen to the tone of his introduction to it:

There can be nothing more certain than that the idea we receive from an external object is in our minds; this is intuitive knowledge. But whether there be any thing more than barely that idea in our minds, whether we can thence certainly infer the existence of any thing without us which corresponds to that idea, is that whereof some men think there may be a question made, because men may have such ideas in their minds when no such thing exists, no such object affects their senses. (Essay IV.ii.14)

One gets the impression that Locke does not regard this question as worth tackling on its own merits, and would have ignored it if others had done so. One may even wonder whether he did tackle Descartes's question. When he revisits this topic, he writes of 'the assurance we have from our senses themselves that they do not err in the information they give us of the existence of things without us', and introduces his arguments for the existence of matter as 'concurrent reasons' by which 'we are farther confirmed in this assurance' (IV.xi.3).

This tells us what Locke's opinions were: he was sure that there is a material world, and thought he had arguments which might screw his level of confidence up a notch—just to satisfy the carping questioners. What matters, however, is not his doxastic state, but his view of his argument. Does he hold that his senses have intelligibly *entitled* him to believe in matter, so that in giving his merely 'concurrent' reasons he is entitled to assume that there is matter? If so, then these arguments of his have nothing to do with the materialism issue as raised by Descartes before him and Berkeley after. Locke has sometimes been understood in this way, but wrongly, I believe. The ensuing arguments are addressed to someone taking the sceptical foundationalist stance, asking for reasons for believing that there are any material things. Telling him 'Your senses give you assurance that there are' will not meet his need; nor will giving him arguments which presuppose the existence of matter. Locke presumably saw this. His discussion of the issue in IV.ii.14 and xi.1–8 belongs to the tradition of foundationalist attempts to show that there is a material world. It offers reasons to justify first taking Frege's 'step with which I secure an environment for myself'.

Where Descartes resolves to accept only what cannot be doubted, Locke declines to set so high a standard:

The notice we have by our senses of the existing of things without us, though it be not altogether so certain as our intuitive knowledge . . . yet it is an assurance that deserves the name of knowledge. If we persuade ourselves that our faculties act and inform us right concerning the existence of those objects that affect them, it cannot pass for an ill-grounded confidence; for I think nobody can in earnest be so sceptical as to be uncertain of the existence of those things which he sees and feels. (xi.3)

The second half of this is odd. The phrase 'it cannot pass for an ill-grounded confidence' sounds normative: one naturally takes it to mean that such confidence is well grounded. However, Locke's reason for this is merely that nobody does in fact lack confidence in the proposition in question—drawing an epistemological conclusion from a sociological premiss.

Locke adduces six main arguments or considerations in support of his materialism.

(1) To the question of 'whether there be any thing more than barely that idea', he gives a firmly argued Yes, on the familiar ground that some of his ideas come unbidden:

Sometimes I find that I cannot avoid the having those ideas produced in my mind. For though when my eyes are shut or windows fast I can at pleasure recall to my mind the ideas of light or the sun which former sensations had lodged in my memory; so I can at pleasure lay by that idea, and take into my view that of the smell of a rose or taste of sugar. But if I turn my eyes at noon towards the sun I cannot avoid the ideas which the light or sun then produces in me. So that there is a manifest difference between the ideas laid up in my memory . . . and those which force themselves upon me and I cannot avoid having. And therefore it must needs be some exterior cause, and the brisk acting of some objects without me whose efficacy I cannot resist, that produces those ideas in my mind, whether I will or no. (xi.5)

Up to here, this echoes Descartes, but it does not take Locke to the existence of material things. He needs reasons for holding that the 'objects' that cause his involuntary ideas are indeed many and not just one, and that they are composed of matter. (Locke is like Descartes also in not discussing what causes the ideas received in dreams, most of which we undergo involuntarily.)

He cannot appeal to theology at this point. Locke has an argument for the eternal existence of an all-powerful thinking thing, which he calls God (IV.x); and that argument does not presuppose that matter exists. But it does not conclude that there is an undeceiving God. For this, Locke turns to natural theology, inferring God's goodness from the excellence of the world he has created; and this assumes the existence of matter. In x.7 he clearly implies that the best way to establish the existence and nature of God is by appeal to 'the sensible parts of the universe', and he scoffs at those whose 'only proof of a deity' is 'an over-fondness of that darling invention'—namely, the idea of God that figures in both of Descartes's arguments for God's existence and veracity. Clearly, then, Locke cannot tread a Cartesian path from his ideas to the material world.

(2) He notes how some ideas differ from others:

I ask anyone whether he be not invincibly conscious to himself of a different perception when he looks on the sun by day and thinks on it by night; when he actually tastes wormwood or smells a rose or only thinks on that savour or odour? We as plainly find the difference there is between any idea revived in our minds by our own memory and actually coming into our minds by our senses as we do between any two distinct ideas. (IV.ii.14)

If this were merely the involuntariness argument for the existence of *something* outside oneself, it might be all right; but Locke evidently means it to go beyond that and to count in favour of matter in particular. Thus considered, the argument fails. A non-circular argument for the existence of a material world cannot have a premiss presupposing that people look at the sun and smell roses. Remove that, and there remains only the modest point that some of our ideas are greatly unlike some others. Realizing this, Locke goes on to confront the objection that such differences might occur in a dream. His response is designed to silence the objector rather than to meet his point.

(3) Locke seems to find it obvious that a belief in an external world is needed if one is to make any disciplined use of 'reasoning and arguments', or to have any use for the concepts of truth and knowledge. Later on he implies that if you question the existence of the material world, you are refusing to trust one of your cognitive faculties, and if you distrust one, you should distrust all:

The confidence that our faculties do not herein deceive us is the greatest assurance we are capable of concerning the existence of material beings. For we cannot act any thing but by our faculties, nor talk of knowledge itself but by the help of those faculties which are fitted to apprehend even what knowledge is. (IV.xi.3)

This implies that we cannot talk sense about 'knowledge' unless we trust our faculties enough to be confident that we inhabit a world of material things. This may be true, but it is far from obvious. Kant devoted much of his first *Critique* to defending it by argument. Locke simply asserts it.

(4) 'Those that want the organs of any sense never can have the ideas belonging to that sense produced in their minds' (xi.4). And the sense-organs themselves do not produce those ideas, 'for then the eyes of a man in the dark would produce colours, and his nose smell roses in the winter'. So the sense-organs must be mediating between the mind and a material world out there. This presupposes that Locke already knows a great deal about the material world—about ears and eyes and sunlight—so that it cannot serve to allay the sceptic's doubts.

(5) In xi.7 Locke writes of how 'our senses in many cases bear witness to the truth of each other's report concerning the existence of sensible things without us'. When I write something on a piece of paper, my tactual sensations correlate reliably with my visual ones; to which Locke adds some other details of how interrelations amongst our sensory states are rendered predictable and intelligible if we take these states as perceptions of parts of a material world. This is promising, and I shall explore it later in connection with Hume (§280). It needs a fuller development than Locke accords it.

(6) Faced with a stubborn enough sceptic, Locke cannot win. He seems to know this. In ii.i4, having countered the 'Perhaps you are dreaming' challenger by virtually threatening to put his foot in the fire, he continues:

But yet if he be resolved to appear so sceptical as to maintain that what I call being actually in the fire is nothing but a dream, and that we cannot thereby certainly know that any such thing as fire actually exists without us: I answer that we certainly finding that pleasure or pain follows upon the application of certain objects to us whose existence we perceive or dream that we perceive by our senses; this certainty is as great as our happiness or misery, beyond which we have no concernment to know or to be.

This seems to imply either that the success of the 'matter' hypothesis is tantamount to its being true (Locke as pragmatist?), or that its truth is not important so long as it is successful. All we need, Locke suggests, is to grasp that our belief in material things helps us to act so as to obtain pleasure and avoid pain.

Why is that all we need? The same question arises when Locke returns to the issue: 'God has given me assurance enough of the existence of things without me; since by their different application I can produce in myself both pleasure and pain, which is one great concernment of my present state' (xi.3; see also 8). It is hard not to read this as implying 'There may be no world of material things, but I do not really care'. I would be surprised if Locke consciously intended to go that far, but if he did not, I am puzzled by these passages. He may have meant to echo what Descartes wrote: 'The proper purpose of the sensory perceptions given me by nature is simply to inform the mind of what is beneficial or harmful for the composite of which the mind is a part' (Med 6, CSM 2:57). But I do not know what he meant to do with the echo.

211. Berkeley's first attack: materialism clashes with common sense

Berkeley is famous for his denial that there is matter. His ontology is best called 'immaterialism'. The more usual 'idealism' is inaccurate: he held that there are not only ideas but also the minds or 'spirits' in which ideas occur. I shall follow him in using 'materialism' to name the thesis that there is matter, not the stronger thesis that there is only matter.

His attack is best seen as having four related prongs, or levels. He charges against materialism that:

It contradicts things that every reasonable person believes.
It is unsupported by evidence, and therefore does not explain anything.
It is demonstrably false.
It is conceptually defective—either self-contradictory or nonsensical.

It might seem that the last of these undercuts the other three, but I agree with Berkeley that it does not. If materialism is nonsensical, as he sometimes alleges, it is not so in the manner of unconstruable gibberish: its lack of meaning comes from troubles with the meanings of the parts that make it up, so that even if it is nonsense, it has structure. Similarly if it is self-contradictory. Either way, Berkeley has something to work with; and there is no objection in principle to his temporarily setting aside the conceptual criticisms in order to present the others. I shall take the attacks in order, starting with the thesis that materialism conflicts with common sense.

Refined, intelligent common sense, Berkeley thinks, holds that *only ideas can be perceived*. This threatens to conflict with the view that we sometimes perceive material things, the only escape being to say that material things are ideas. And that is blocked when we bring in Berkeley's reasonable thesis that an idea can exist only while someone has or perceives it, and the standard view that material things can exist when nobody perceives them.

The view that ideas cannot exist unperceived is supported by two premisses: (1) that ideas can exist only in minds, and (2) that all mental content is known to or perceived by its owner. We shall see that Berkeley bases 1 on the assumption that ideas are states of minds (and the silent rejection of unowned tropes). In accepting 2, he aligns himself with that Cartesian tradition, about which I have no more to say. My present concern is with these two: that ideas are perceived, and nothing other than ideas is perceived.

Take it for granted that our sensory ideas are given to us, epistemically available to us—even perceived by us. Why should we also grant that we perceive nothing else? We talk as though we perceived things other than ideas, but Berkeley tries to persuade us that such talk is condemned by standards that we already, if waveringly, accept. He offers three examples to show them at work in our thought. From this we are to learn to distinguish accurately what is perceived from what is not, and thus to be led to agree with him about what we perceive. This all happens in the First Dialogue. The *Dialogues* are a richer source of persuasive examples and aids to intuition than the *Principles*, because their main purpose was to answer critics of the earlier work.

(1) Berkeley's spokesman Philonous presents the first example thus:

In reading a book, what I immediately perceive are the letters, but mediately or by means of these are suggested to my mind the notions of God, virtue, truth, &c. Now, that the letters are truly sensible things, or perceived by sense, there is no doubt: but I would know whether you take the things suggested by them to be so too. (Dia 1, 174)

His opponent Hylas replies: 'No certainly, it were absurd to think God or virtue sensible things, though they may be signified and suggested to the mind by sensible marks with which they have an arbitrary connection.' Philonous concludes: 'It seems then that by *sensible things* you mean those only which can be perceived immediately by sense.' In the context, he clearly means further that nothing is correctly said to be perceived unless it is perceived immediately, rather than through an inferential link like that connecting a word with its meaning. When we read about virtue, Berkeley holds, we do not *perceive* it, because in such reading our thoughts are carried to virtue only through a kind of inference. If that were the whole story about why 'We perceive virtue in reading about it' is false, it would follow that we ought never to take ourselves to have perceived an F if any inferential element is needed to connect our sensory state with the thought of an F.

In reaching this conclusion through that argument, Berkeley is too optimistic by half. Our refusal to say that we have perceived something—whether virtue or an elephant, truth or a catamaran—by reading about it might come not from the bare fact that some inferential element is involved, but rather from facts about what element it is. A similar remark applies to Berkeley's second example.

(2) On the same page, Berkeley makes Hylas concede that 'by *sensible things* I mean those only which are perceived by sense, and that in truth the senses perceive nothing which they do not perceive immediately; for they make no inferences'. Later on Hylas backslides into using 'perceive' more liberally, which gives Philonous a chance to defend and illustrate his position anew. In quoting the passage, I omit Hylas's routine agreements:

Philonous: Is there anything perceived by sense which is not immediately perceived?

Hylas: Yes, Philonous, in some sort there is. For example, when I look on a picture or statue of Julius Caesar, I may be said after a manner to perceive him (though not immediately) by my senses.

Philonous: It seems then, you will have our ideas, which alone are immediately perceived, to be pictures of external things: and that these also are perceived by sense, inasmuch as they have a conformity or resemblance to our ideas.

Hylas: That is my meaning.

Philonous: And in the same way that Julius Caesar, in himself invisible, is nevertheless perceived by sight, real things, in themselves imperceptible, are perceived by sense. . . . Tell me, Hylas, when you behold the picture of Julius Caesar, do you see with your eyes any more than some colours and figures with a certain symmetry and composition of the whole? . . . And would not a man who had never known anything of Julius Caesar see as much? . . . Consequently he has his sight, and the use of it, in as perfect a degree as you. . . . Whence comes it then that your thoughts are directed to the Roman Emperor and his are not? This cannot proceed from the sensations or ideas of sense by you then perceived, since you acknowledge you have no advantage over him in that respect. It would seem therefore to proceed from reason and memory, should it not? . . . Consequently it will not follow from that instance that anything is perceived by sense which is not immediately perceived. (Dia 1, 203–4)

This subtle passage, with its sarcastic phrase 'see with your eyes', asks us to distinguish what is perceived by sense—*perceived* in the strict, careful use of that word—from what is inferred from that through 'reason and memory'. If I cannot know just by looking that I see an F, knowing this without help from any background interpretative information, then it is not strictly true that I see an F; it is not something I 'see with my eyes'. Thus Berkeley. If we agree, we must also agree that we perceive only our ideas.

Berkeley makes Hylas say, 'I may be said after a manner to perceive' Caesar when I see a picture of him, implying that this is the kind of loose perception-talk that is to be rooted out. Actually, there is nothing to be rooted out here. No real person would say that we see Caesar in viewing a Mantegna fresco—any more than in reading Suetonius. But most people would be willing to say 'I saw an oil-painting', thinking of this as a material thing, something outside the mind, not an idea; yet, to judge that one sees such a thing, one must interpret one's visual data through reason and memory. Even if Berkeley is right that one cannot strictly speaking see a physical painting, he should note that most people talk as though they can do this, while not talking as though in seeing a picture they see its subject. He ought to exhibit and discuss this difference.

In his handling of the picture of Caesar, he assumes that you do not see an F unless you know that what you are seeing is an F. Our ordinary careful thoughts about 'what we perceive' do not conform to this tremendously narrow standard: we do not think we are talking in a sloppy or 'vulgar' way when we allow that one may see an F while not realizing that that is what it is. This is yet another way in which Berkeley fails here to adduce the plain careful person's beliefs as support for immaterialism.

How do we draw the line between what we perceive and what we infer from what we perceive? It is mostly—and perhaps wholly—a question of what kind of causal chain is involved. The chain from Sir Peter Strawson to a painting of him is of the wrong kind for my seeing the painting to count as a seeing of Strawson. If we replace the painting by a photograph, the chain is different, but it still does not lead us to say 'I have seen him' except as an acknowledged shorthand for 'I have seen a photograph of him'. What about seeing Strawson on live television? Would it be an unstrict ellipsis to say 'I saw him on television'? Seeing him in a mirror? Seeing him by watching his silhouette? None of this is clear and sharp-edged (for a good discussion of the difficulties see Lewis 1980); but nothing in it threatens to imply that we have genuine seeing only when no causal or other inferential chain is involved.

(3) Berkeley's best-known attempt to bring us around to his view about what we 'strictly' perceive has to do with the hearing of sounds:

> I grant we may in one acceptation be said to perceive sensible things mediately by sense: that is, when from a frequently perceived connexion, the immediate perception of ideas by one sense suggests to the mind others, perhaps belonging to another sense, which are wont to be connected with them. For instance, when I hear a coach drive along the streets, immediately I perceive only the sound; but from the experience I have had that such a sound is connected with a coach, I am said to hear the coach. It is nevertheless evident that in truth and strictness nothing can be heard but sound: and the coach is not then properly perceived by sense but suggested from experience. (Dia 1, 204)

This aims to convince us that ordinary thoughtful speakers, with no philosophical axe to grind, agree that *strictly* what we perceive is just an idea. We sometimes speak of perceiving (hearing) a material thing, although we would agree that strictly speaking what we hear is not that object, but an item from which we infer it. Thus Berkeley, who wants us to take this as a model for how we ought to think about perception generally.

This argument fails because the second item, the one that we strictly perceive, though it is not a material thing is not an idea either. *A sound is not an idea*; it is public, objective, out there. We can speak of two people hearing the same sound, meaning literally the very same objective sound. Two people can have exactly similar auditory 'ideas' at the same moment without their hearing the same sound; this is as plainly possible as two people's having the same tactual sensations although they are not touching the same coach. Any thoughtful person must know that sounds are objective, interpersonal, physical realities. They are located in space and move through it at a known speed, they have volumes and shapes, and so on; their most basic features are all shared with material things, not with ideas. We know more than Berkeley could about what sounds are; but the reasons for regarding them as objective, and not as auditory ideas, were available to him as well as to us.

This mistake of Berkeley's seems to be widespread. Several expositors of the 'coach' passage have failed to see its crucial defect. Even outside philosophy, some people flutter into and out of this Berkeleian mistake. 'If a tree falls when there is nobody to hear it, does its fall make a sound?' Obviously the fall of the tree makes an unheard sound; just as a twig may fall into a pond and make unseen ripples. If sounds were auditory ideas, it would be obvious that the fall does not make a sound. The popularity of this idiotic conundrum must result from people's wavering between Berkeley's error and the truth.

We do perceive plenty of things other than our ideas, I submit—and I now add that we do not perceive our ideas. This is not to challenge foundationalism: ideas could be what we are immediately given or confronted by, and the foundation of all our beliefs, without it being right to say that we 'perceive' them. Part of what is involved in perceiving something is having certain sensory states; if we perceive the latter too, then it must be through some still more immediately given states or ideas, and so on backward.

Recall Berkeley's derisive remark about what you 'see with your eyes'. Given that things can be seen only with eyes, it follows that our visual ideas are not seen; for our eyes play no part in our mental intake of our visual ideas. Berkeley may protest: 'You are talking as though eyes were material things, but that begs the question against me.' I respond: 'Give an immaterialist account of eyes if you wish. I defy you to do it, so that implies that we see ideas with our eyes.' Berkeley cannot meet this challenge. If he is to avoid concluding that we do not see anything, and that—by parity of argument—we do not feel or smell or taste anything either, he must relinquish 'see with your eyes' and its kin. That will deprive him not of doctrine but of one rhetorical device.

The purely verbal point may not matter greatly. Locke wrote: 'Whatsoever the mind perceives in itself, or is the immediate object of perception, thought, or understanding, that I call idea' (*Essay* II.viii.8). That is a misuse of 'perceive', etc., but perhaps no great harm comes of it in Locke's pages. In Berkeley's, though, it is a premiss in one of his arguments against materialism, as we have just seen.

That argument is a bait-and-switch operation. Berkeley contends that our ordinary beliefs imply that islands and trees etc. are 'sensible things', things we can perceive. We accept that, on a certain understanding of it; but then Berkeley tells us that 'perceive' expresses the relation of a mind to its ideas; from which he infers that sensible things are ideas. But that is not what we meant when we accepted his premiss. In switching its meaning, he misrepresents our ordinary beliefs.

Although Berkeley holds that the plain, careful person's beliefs conflict with materialism, he also thinks they entail it; which means that they conflict with themselves. On the one hand, we assume that shoes and ships and sealing wax are extra-mental, because they can exist out of every mind, or, as Berkeley puts it, they can exist when not perceived. That commits us to their not being ideas, which can exist only when perceived. On the other, he argues, by taking shoes, etc. to be sensible things we imply that they are ideas after all. Something has to give, he maintains, because those two are inconsistent:

It is indeed an opinion strangely [= widely and strongly] prevailing amongst men that houses, mountains, rivers, and in a word sensible objects have an existence natural or real, distinct from their being perceived by the understanding. But with how great an assurance and acquiescence soever this principle may be entertained in the world, yet whoever shall find in his heart to call it in question may, if I mistake not, perceive it to involve a manifest contradiction. For what are the forementioned objects but the things we perceive by sense, and what do we perceive besides our own ideas or sensations; and is it not plainly repugnant [= inconsistent] that any one of these or any combination of them should exist unperceived? (*PHK* 4)

This charge of inconsistency is leveled against the pair: (1) We perceive sensible things. (2) Sensible things can exist while they are not being perceived. Berkeley says that we cannot have both, on the strength of his convictions that all we perceive are ideas, and that ideas exist only when perceived. These two have to be absolutely necessary if they are to make 1 outright inconsistent with 2; Berkeley would probably go that far, saying that it is impossible to perceive anything except ideas, and impossible for an idea to exist while not perceived.

212. Second attack: materialism is not supported by evidence

Berkeley argues briefly that materialists such as Locke and Descartes cannot provide conclusive empirical evidence that matter exists:

> I do not see what reason can induce us to believe the existence of bodies without the mind, from what we perceive, since the very patrons of matter themselves do not pretend there is any necessary connexion betwixt them and our ideas. I say, it is granted on all hands (and what happens in dreams, frenzies, and the like, puts it beyond dispute) that it is possible we might be affected with all the ideas we have now, though no bodies existed without, resembling them. Hence it is evident the supposition of external bodies is not necessary for the producing our ideas: since it is granted they are produced sometimes, and might possibly be produced always, in the same order we see them in at present, without their [= bodies'] concurrence. (PHK 18)

This seems right. But even if Locke's arguments are not perfectly conclusive, might they not have some force? Not if they are thought of as ordinary inductive arguments, like arguing that the smell of smoke is evidence that the trees are burning in the next valley. That requires premisses about known connections between evidence and conclusion, but when we want to reach materialism from a foundation of sensory ideas, no such premisses are available. We saw Locke going wrong about this, talking about the mental situation of someone who lacks eyes, for example.

Locke said that our grasp that there are particular finite things outside ourselves 'go[es] beyond bare probability' (Essay IV.ii.14); but that was a mere expression of confidence. So it is appropriate for Berkeley in PHK 19 to address that fall-back position which Locke declines to adopt: namely, that the shape of our experience makes it probable that our sensory ideas are caused by material things. His reason for rejecting that is that nobody can explain how material things could cause ideas, so the hypothesis that they do should not be regarded as probable. I shall set this aside until §213. What Berkeley could have said instead is that we cannot have reasons for this judgement of probability. For example, the materialist cannot say that he has inspected many worlds and found that in most of them, when people's experience is structured thus and so, that is because of the action on them of material things. This would be in the spirit of PHK 105 about the empirically based concept of probability.

However, a hypothesis can be a good one to accept without being empirically probable. It might be legitimate for us to explain the general course of our experience by supposing that we stand in certain causal-perceptual relations to a material world, even though we have no independent evidence for this theory. We might accept it because it helps us in the intellectual management of our experience. I go to a particular place in Palermo, expecting to see Michael there, and sure enough, there he is. (Think of all this as spelled out into a story about a sequence of sensory states that I undergo.) I formed this expectation because of certain auditory experiences that I had a month earlier. How could those have led me to expect the later auditory and visual experiences? We predict in this way constantly, but how? Looked at in purely sensory-state ('idea') terms, it seems to be a prodigious feat. But the trick of it is relatively simple: I took the earlier auditory experiences to be a hearing of Michael saying he would do something which I understood in terms of real time and a place in the material world; and I interpreted some of my own subsequent 'ideas' as experiences of my own travel through that same world; . . . and so on. If we really do predict our later sensory states on the evidence of our earlier ones, we must nearly always do this with help from a theory about how these states arise from our causal-perceptual contact with an external material world; without such help, we could not make the predictions; and without those, we would die. So what justifies us in accepting the 'theory' that there is a world of matter is our having no alternative to it that we can live with. Except for 'alternatives' that conceptually contain it, such as: 'Our sensory states are caused by a powerful spirit which chooses to make it seem to us that we are in perceptual-causal contact with a world in which [insert here an account of our material world].'

(The Palermo example, incidentally, relies also on my interpreting many of my sensory states as perceptions of Michael's expressions of his plans. If while having a fully fledged theory of physical objects I made no use of the view that some physical objects are human animals which believe, want, and intend things, I still could not predict meeting my friend at that place and time. That is why—as Daniel Dennett has pointed out often—the philosophers who scorn 'folk psychology' cannot dispense with it.)

I offer the foregoing as the right thing to say if we adopt the foundationalist starting-point of our philosophers. Why should you accept materialism? Because if you don't, you will soon be dead. How might Berkeley reply to this?

Well, in *PHK* 50 he makes the point that what we basically get out of physics are predictions of some sensory states on the basis of others. 'To explain the phenomena is all one as to show why upon such and such occasions we are affected with such and such ideas.' But he does not openly discuss the seeming fact that these explanations (and the associated predictions) lie within our intellectual compass only if they are conducted with help from the concept of perceptual contact with extra-mental things. He acknowledges that people do talk in that materialist manner, and says he does not want them to stop. This is about people's talking as though there were material causes, but Berkeley would apply it to materialist talk generally:

In such things we ought to think with the learned, and speak with the vulgar. . . . In the ordinary affairs of life, any phrases may be retained so long as they excite in us the proper sentiments, or dispositions to act in such a manner as is necessary for our well-being, how false soever they may be if taken in a strict and speculative sense. Nay this is unavoidable, since, propriety being regulated by custom, language is suited to the received opinions, which are not always the truest. (*PHK* 51–2)

This misrepresents the situation. Berkeley allows that you are bound to *talk* the language of matter because it does you good, and because everyone else is doing so. He does not acknowledge that you absolutely need to *think* in terms of matter because not doing so would be fatal. He gives a mild reason for a way of talking, not a stern one for a way of thinking.

In *PHK* 60–2 Berkeley attends to one aspect of this issue. 'It will be demanded', he writes in 60, 'to what purpose serves that curious organization of plants, and the admirable mechanism in the parts of animals?' He answers that all this intricacy really consists in a subtle orderedness of the patterns that God puts into our sequences of ideas. This, he says, is for our own benefit, and is not evidence for the existence of material structures outside the mind. He elaborates this in 62 (see also 151–2), starting: 'Though the fabrication of all those parts and organs be not absolutely necessary to the producing any effect, yet it is necessary to the producing of things in a constant, regular way, according to the laws of nature.' The laws of nature (§222) consist in God-ordained regularities in our sequences of ideas. Berkeley develops this line of thought in answering his question about mechanical intricacy, but we can generalize it so that it addresses my broader question: What should we make of the fact that we cannot survive without materialist forms of thought? Thus adapted, the section says something like this:

God in his goodness has established 'laws of nature'—that is, regularities in the course of our trains of ideas. It was for him to choose how to do this—that is, what specific form of order to impose upon experience, and he has for 'wise ends' chosen to do it in such a way that the concepts of 'mechanism' are applicable. It is true, therefore, that our intellectual control of our trains of ideas requires us to conceptualize them in ways that seem to imply that we are perceiving an extra-mental world. But this is merely a fact about the order into which they fall—a fact about how ideas relate to other ideas—and it has no metaphysical significance.

The wording is mine, but I offer this as the gist of *PHK* 62 when broadened to cover the whole extent of the need-for-materialism point. If Berkeley were to say all that, yet still to stick by his immaterialism, he would have to distinguish *thinking of most of one's 'ideas' as though they were perceptions of a material world, and therefore acting as though one believed there to be a material world* from *believing that there is a material world*. We can draw this line across small areas, but not across the whole of someone's life. It makes clear sense to say 'He acts as though he believed economic planning can be useful, but really he doesn't', because the person's non-belief could show up in other parts of his behaviour. But when we say that all his behaviour is as though he believed there to be a material world, there is a question about what his alleged non-belief could consist in.

213. Third attack: materialism is certainly false

In *PHK* 61 Berkeley remarks that even if he has not dealt conclusively with the point about mechanical intricacy, that little trouble for immaterialism is 'of small weight against the truth and certainty of those things which may be proved *a priori*', and that materialism is not 'free from the like difficulties'. This introduces his third line of attack. Setting aside the issues about what can be perceived, and about what evidence there could be for materialism, he argues that materialism could not possibly be true. He says this first about any version of the doctrine which holds that bodies cause us to have ideas of them.

Berkeley rejects this on the basis of two views about causation, of which one implies that material things cannot affect minds, the other that they cannot affect anything. Each was popular at the time, and indeed Locke was intermittently hospitable to each, even though the first conflicts with his reason for the second. In this part of his attack, then, Berkeley has ammunition.

(1) Like many of his contemporaries, he held that causing must be a kind of giving: a projectile gives some of its motion to something that was still; a hot poker gives some of its heat to the cold water in a bucket. So a thing can be caused to move only by something that is itself moving, caused to be hot only by what is already hot. The idea that causes must be donors may have been based, in some philosophers' minds, merely on the plausibility of some examples; but for others it had a metaphysical underlay in the thesis that causation is trope transfer (§35).

On the rare occasions when Locke implies that causation is trope transfer, he is challenging the attitude that physics is bright and clear, whereas psychology languishes in darkness. Our plainest examples of causal action involve one body's making another move, he says, and this is mysterious because we can understand it only in terms of trope transfer:

[The idea of] the power of communication of motion by impulse . . . every day's experience clearly furnishes us with: But if . . . we enquire how this is done, we are . . . in the dark. For in the communication of motion by impulse, wherein as much motion is lost to one body as is got to the other, which is the ordinariest case, we can have no other conception but of the passing of motion out of one body into another: Which, I think, is . . . obscure and unconceivable. (*Essay* II.xxiii.28)

Having proclaimed that he cannot make decent sense of the simplest kind of transaction between material things, Locke continues: 'Which, I think, is as obscure and unconceivable as how our minds move or stop our bodies by thought, which we every moment find they do.' Although he here implies that all trope transfer is incomprehensible, I think he regarded the thesis that mental events can cause bodies to move as especially troubling, given that minds have no motion to give. In the *Essay* he does not express an equal concern about how bodies could act on minds, but he does so elsewhere (§192).

Berkeley, then, has a case for his charge that materialism makes causal claims which even some materialists admit are false or worse. Bodies cannot cause thoughts because they have no thought to give.

(2) He argues from the premiss that only minds ('spirits') can be causes. The general popularity of this view, and Berkeley's especial fondness for it, will be my topic in §221. At present I stay with Locke's admission of it:

Two bodies placed by one another at rest will never afford us the idea of a power in the one to move the other but by a borrowed motion; whereas the mind every day affords us ideas of an active power of moving of bodies; and therefore it is worth our considera-tion whether active power be not the proper attribute of spirits, and passive power of matter. (*Essay* II.xxiii.28)

Locke here suggests, on rather general intuitive grounds, that only spirits can act, and that bodies can merely be acted upon. In xxi.4 he supports this through an argument whose oddity he seems not to have noticed. When the white ball hits the red one and makes it move, he writes, 'it only communicates the motion it had received from [the cue], and loses in itself so much as the [red ball] received'. Thus, 'we observe it only to transfer but not produce any motion', so that it 'gives us but a very obscure idea of an active power of moving in body'. For a good 'idea of the beginning of motion' (and, by clear implication, of causal action generally), we must look to 'what passes in ourselves, where we find by experience that barely by . . . a thought of the mind, we can move the parts of our bodies which were before at rest'.

There is no evident inconsistency between (1) 'All causation must be trope transfer' and (2) 'Only spirits can be causes', but 1 does contradict Locke's reason for 2. Did the white ball genuinely cause the movement of the red? According to 1, the answer is 'Yes, if it passed on some of its own motion to the red'; while Locke's reason for 2 says 'Yes, if it did not merely pass on some of its own motion to the red'. Locke seems not to have noticed this clash.

Berkeley relies more on (1) 'Causes are donors' than on (2) 'Causes must be purely active'; but most of his third attack could be based on either. Here he deploys 2:

As to the opinion that there are no corporeal causes, this has been heretofore maintained by some of the . . . modern philosophers, who though they allow matter to exist, yet will have God alone to be the immediate efficient cause of all things. These men saw that amongst all the objects of sense there was none which had any power or activity included in it, and that by consequence this was likewise true of whatever bodies they supposed to exist without the mind, like unto the immediate objects of sense. (*PHK* 53)

Berkeley thinks that all materialists should concede that matter cannot act upon minds: 'How matter should operate on a spirit, or produce any idea in it, is what no philosopher will pretend to explain' (*PHK* 50). In one memorable passage he recites the obstacles to matter's causing anything, reaching a climax with the cau-sation of states of mind:

Do they not pretend to explain all things by bodies operating on bodies, according to the laws of motion? and yet, are they able to comprehend how any one body should move another? Nay, admitting there was no difficulty in [2] reconciling the notion of an inert being with a cause; or in [1] conceiving how an accident might pass from one body to another; yet by all their strained thoughts and extravagant suppositions, have they been able to reach the mechanical production of any one animal or vegetable body? Can they account by the laws of motion, for sounds, tastes, smells, or colours . . . ? (Dia 3, 257)

214. The occasionalist escape

Suppose you think that there are bodies but that they cannot cause anything, where do you go from there? Well, if you are a Christian philosopher, you may bring God to the rescue. One way of doing so lurks in Descartes's work (§38), and is proclaimed by some of his followers: namely, the doctrine that when anything appears to act, God does the causing. When particles collide and change direction, it is God who redirects them at the instant of the collision. When I am confronted by an orange, God causes me to have the kind of visual idea which I associate with seeing spherical things.

All there is here is a regular, dependable pattern in events—one which facilitates predictions, and also allows explanations of a kind ('It swerved because something collided with it'). But the latter merely fit events into larger patterns without giving the real reasons for them. We can trust God not to make mischievous changes in the patterns; but that is all they are—regularities, with no real connections among events.

No Christian philosopher would ever have said that the white ball's hitting the red *caused* God to start the red ball moving. That would imply in God a passivity which the Christian tradition has unanimously denied to him. What was said was that the collision was the *occasion* for God's causing the red ball to start moving; and so this view was called 'occasionalism'.

It could be resorted to also by a philosopher who held that material things can act on one another but cannot act on minds. Such a philosopher could be an occasionalist not about all seeming interaction between created things, but just about the seeming action of bodies on minds. He would say that although a characteristic sort of visual state is correlated with being confronted, eyes open, by something spherical, spheres do not cause such states; but God has decided that they will typically occur just when the person confronts a sphere with his eyes open.

(Locke argued to a world of matter by postulating bodies as causes for his ideas (§210). As an exercise in occasionalist thinking, let us consider how an occasionalist might try, from that same Cartesian starting-point, to infer the existence of matter. Here is one way:

From the effect (ideas) infer the immediate cause (God's action), and from that infer its cause (states of affairs in matter).

Analogously, from a power outage I infer a fallen tree, from which I infer a storm. As I have already noted, Christian occasionalists reject this on theological grounds. Here is a second pattern of inference:

> From the effect (ideas) infer the cause (God's actions), and from that infer another effect of that same cause (states of affairs in matter).

Analogously, from this wind I predict rain, because I think that the causes of the wind will also cause rain. This inference goes upstream to the best explanation (God) and downstream along a different path to the material world. This pattern of inference is available only to the all-out occasionalist, who holds that all the movements of bodies are directly God's work. For the more limited occasionalist, who thinks that bodies can act on one another but not on minds, there remains only one pattern of inference:

> From the effect (ideas) infer the cause (God's actions), and infer a material state of affairs—not as either causing or being caused by God's action on it, but dependably accompanying it as a non-causal trigger, or 'occasion'.

We shall revisit some of this territory in §224.)

Berkeley denies that materialism can be saved from his third attack by resorting to occasionalism. His grounds are theological:

> I . . . ask whether the order and regularity observable in the series of our ideas, or the course of nature, be not sufficiently accounted for by the wisdom and power of God; and whether it doth not derogate from those attributes to suppose he is influenced, directed or put in mind when and what he is to act, by any unthinking substance. (Dia 2, 220)

In short, God's independence and self-sufficiency would be compromised not only by his actions' having material causes, but even by their having material occasions.

Apart from the theological objection, Berkeley has more to bring against occasionalism; but most of it, in PHK 67–72, relies upon his immaterialism. For example, he takes himself to have shown that all the properties commonly attributed to matter can exist only in the mind, so that the postulated extra-mental 'occasions' are impossible; and argues that since space exists only in the mind, the 'occasions' are not in space—so what can it mean to say that they are 'present' to us?

215. Fourth attack: materialism is conceptually defective

We cannot make sense of materialism, Berkeley charges. Whether or not we strictly perceive matter, the materialist must hold that we do at least mentally represent it in our thoughts, thinking of it as having geometrical properties of size, shape, and so on. Remove this element from the materialist position, he thinks, and no proposition remains to be discussed. But it must be removed, for it is provably false; we could not possibly have any thought of matter, any ideas of matter.

Berkeley here depends on a resemblance theory of representation (§156). Being sure that this is wrong, I see no force in his argument; but I shall stay with it for a while, because Berkeley's deployment of it instructs us about his thought, and helps us to learn some philosophy.

Berkeley did realize that language represents states of affairs in some way other than by resembling them, that a graph can represent an algebraic equation which it does not resemble, and so on. In *PHK* 65 he writes that 'the fire I see' is 'the mark that forewarns me' that I shall suffer pain if I go closer; and that 'the noise that I hear' is 'the sign' of 'this or that motion or collision of the ambient bodies'. He also writes there about 'combining letters into words', saying that these are 'artificial and regular combinations'; and he would say the same about combining words into sentences. Behind all this there seems to lie a general thesis that all representation which is not by resemblance is arbitrary, or conventional; it has to be learned through interpreted experience; so it cannot be what which gives us our initial grasp of the representative content of our ideas. The latter has to precede our learning things from interpreted experience, and so there cannot be anything arbitrary or conventional about it; so it must, Berkeley holds, be based on resemblance.

Here he is putting the point about resemblance:

But say you, . . . there may be things like [our ideas] whereof they are copies or resemblances, which things exist without the mind in an unthinking substance. I answer, an idea can be like nothing but an idea; a colour or figure can be like nothing but another colour or figure. If we look but ever so little into our thoughts, we shall find it impossible for us to conceive a likeness except only between our ideas. (*PHK* 8)

Rubbing it in, he adds that if material things are not ideas, they are not perceivable, which makes them obviously unlike ideas:

I ask whether those supposed originals or external things, of which our ideas are the pictures or representations, be themselves perceivable or no? If they are, then they are ideas, and we have gained our point; but if you say they are not, I appeal to any one whether it be sense to assert a colour is like something which is invisible, hard or soft like something which is intangible, and so of the rest.[1]

I agree that 'An idea can be like nothing but another idea' (*PHK* 9), but Berkeley stands this truth on its head. Something hard cannot resemble something intangible, so an anvil cannot resemble an idea; but that is because the anvil is hard, while the idea is intangible. Berkeley's putting it the other way around reflects his willingness—encouraged by his view that ideas alone are perceived—to apply to ideas many adjectives that we ordinarily think of as applicable to material things.

---

[1] See also *PHK* 90, and Dia 1, 206; note also: 'No idea . . . can be like unto or represent the nature of God' (Dia 3, 231).

That view commits him, one would think, to a fairly strong reifying of ideas (§158). Yet we shall find that when he directly addresses the metaphysical status of ideas, Berkeley classifies them as states of minds. I shall return in §219 to the conflict between this and his willingness to describe ideas as hard and soft, red and green, square and round.

I have introduced the thesis that we cannot have ideas of matter as a Berkeleian reason for rejecting materialism. Strictly, it is a reason for judging materialism to be conceptually defective, something we cannot even make sense of. That is because of the role of ideas as concepts and meanings—mental items that we must employ in thinking about something or making sense of sentences about it. Berkeley often ties ideas to meaning, as here: 'yet if you have any meaning at all, you must at least have a relative idea of matter' (*PHK* 16). The following intentionally comic passage again exhibits Berkeley's tendency to treat matters of psychology as though they generated conceptual truths:

Philonous: Tell me sincerely whether you can frame a distinct idea of entity in general, prescinded from and exclusive of all thinking and corporeal beings, all particular things whatsoever.

Hylas: Hold, let me think a little—I profess, Philonous, I do not find that I can. At first glance methought I had some dilute and airy notion of pure entity in abstract; but upon closer attention it hath quite vanished out of sight. (Dia 2, 222)

Philonous's treatment of this shows that he takes it as conceding that Hylas can attach no sense to his own doctrine. For more on logic and psychology, see *PHK* 45.

What kind of conceptual defect is materialism supposed to have? The answer is a little peculiar, for a reason I shall explain through a contrast with Locke. For Locke, an expression is self-contradictory or 'repugnant' if the ideas it involves relate to one another in certain ways; he tries to say *what happens* in your mind when you discover that something is contradictory (§173). Berkeley follows him in saying that you check on modal status by looking into your ideas; but he goes into no detail about what the latter must be like to justify a judgement of 'repugnancy', saying merely that it involves finding the item in question 'inconceivable'. Thus, we find him writing that talk about sensible things existing outside all minds involves 'a direct repugnancy, and [is] altogether inconceivable' (*PHK* 17). This is one of many places where Berkeley says that materialism involves a 'contradiction', which he sometimes calls 'manifest' or 'direct' or 'plain'. (See *PHK* 4, 7, 9, 22. Other relevant uses of 'contradiction' are in *PHK* 56, 79, 88, 124, 132; *Three Dialogues* 195, 197, 200, 230, 240, 244.)

However, 'P is inconceivable', on its most natural reading, means that we have no conception or idea that relates suitably to the sentence purporting to express P; which, for Berkeley as well as Locke, is to say that the sentence in question is meaningless. Berkeley accepts this, writing that 'to assert that which is inconceivable is to talk nonsense' (Dia 2, 215; see also 216).

So we find him writing as though he could not separate repugnancy from meaninglessness. In *PHK* 24 he writes that the words purporting to express materialism 'mark out either a direct contradiction or else nothing at all', and in 54 he says that it 'involves a contradiction or has no meaning in it'. One might think that Berkeley sees the charges as distinct alternatives between which he is not choosing; but his handling of them shows that he has no clear way of keeping them separate. In only one place does he make anything of their distinctness: late in the Second Dialogue (226) Philonous says that a proposal of Hylas's escapes being contradictory only through being meaningless, as though guilt on one charge brings innocence on the other.

In declaring materialism to be incoherent or meaningless, we have seen, Berkeley does not treat it as mere gabble. He rightly concedes that it has enough structure for us to be able to operate with it in a fashion, and to pretend that it is consistent in order to criticize it in other ways. In *PHK* 72 he keeps both balls in the air at once, charging first that materialism does not explain anything and is not supported by evidence, and then going on to imply that it does not even make sense.

Chapter 29

Berkeley's Uses of Locke's Work

216. Why Berkeley cares about abstract ideas

In §§162–4 we saw Berkeley vigorously attacking Locke's theory about abstract ideas. In the Introduction to the *Principles*, which is dedicated to that attack, the theory is treated primarily as an error in the philosophy of mind and of language. Later on, however, we find Berkeley linking it with the metaphysical issues which occupy the rest of the work; and the materials for that link are now before us. If you cannot see it, that is because it is so tenuous as to be almost invisible.[1]

The abstraction doctrine implies (Berkeley thinks) that something can be triangular without being so in any specific manner. He rightly holds this to be impossible: to say that x is triangular, while denying that it is triangular in some specific manner, is just to *assert something while denying one of its entailments*. He links this with his view that the only perceivable things are ideas, which can exist only when perceived. According to Berkeley, those who are willing to say 'x is a sensible thing which exists while not perceived' are guilty of *asserting something while denying one of its entailments*. In his first reference to abstraction after the Introduction, and in some others, he links it with materialism in this way. Of the belief that 'sensible objects have an existence . . . distinct from their being perceived', he writes:

If we thoroughly examine this tenet, it will perhaps be found at bottom to depend on the doctrine of abstract ideas. For can there be a nicer strain of abstraction than to distinguish the existence of sensible objects from their being perceived, so as to conceive them existing unperceived? . . . The things we see and feel [are] so many . . . impressions on the sense; and is it possible to separate, even in thought, any of these from perception? For my part I might as easily divide a thing from itself. (*PHK* 5)

A 'strain of abstraction' is an episode of abstraction that is carried to the limit, and a 'nice' one is one that is delicately precise. (See *OED*, 'strain', *sb²*, sense 5; 'nice', sense 8.) Berkeley is sarcastically commenting on what an exquisitely sharp knife you need to sever a proposition from another which it entails, or to peel a thing off from itself.

The claim that abstractionism and materialism are both guilty of contradicting themselves, by asserting P and denying Q which P entails, merely brings out

---

[1] In the *Principles* abstraction is mentioned in connection with arithmetic (118–22), geometry (125–6), and time (97–100). Other sections where the concept of abstraction occurs significantly are: 5, 6, 10, 11, 13, 17, 116, 143; and there are minor occurrences also in 68, 74, 81, 111. In the *Three Dialogues* the main treatments are at 192–4 and 222–3.

a resemblance between the two. Even if Berkeley were right about this, it does not show, or even suggest, that materialism 'depends on' the thesis that there are abstract ideas.

That supposed logical likeness between the two doctrines is the only link between them in Berkeley's pages. It is embarrassingly thin, whereas Berkeley implies that the two are integrally connected. I have been told that it is uncharitable to allege that this is Berkeley's only way of linking abstractionism with materialism; but nobody has done better on his behalf. Winkler (1989: 188–91) shows that this performance of Berkeley's had historical antecedents, but in his hands it remains as threadbare as I claim it to be.

In one place, Berkeley declares that materialism is one source of error, and the doctrine of abstract ideas is another: 'Beside the external existence of the objects of perception, another great source of errors and difficulties with regard to ideal knowledge is the doctrine of abstract ideas, such as it hath been set forth in the Introduction' (PHK 97). He continues with a reason for hostility to abstraction that does not bear directly on (im)materialism:

The plainest things in the world, those we are most intimately acquainted with and per-fectly know, when they are considered in an abstract way appear strangely difficult and incomprehensible. Time, place, and motion, taken in particular or concrete, are what everybody knows; but having passed through the hands of a metaphysician they become too abstract and fine to be apprehended by men of ordinary sense. Bid your servant meet you at such a time in such a place and he shall never stay to deliberate on the meaning of those words: in conceiving that particular time and place, or the motion by which he is to get thither, he finds not the least difficulty. But if time be taken, exclusive of all those particular actions and ideas that diversify the day, merely for the continuation of exis-tence, or duration in abstract, then it will perhaps gravel even a philosopher to compre-hend it. (PHK 97)

Berkeley here frowns on the asking of abstract questions like 'What is the nature of time?' Some of his other mentions of abstraction are also like this. A hard ques-tion arises about some highly general concept, and he says in effect that a believer in abstract ideas will think it should be answered, implying that everyone else is free to walk out on it and be satisfied with our everyday competence in particu-lar uses of the concept.

It has long been a familiar point that concepts which we can easily use may be hard to describe. Augustine memorably pointed this out, using the same exam-ple as Berkeley: 'What then is time? If no one asks me, I know; if I want to explain it to a questioner, I do not know' (Confessions, bk. 2, sect. 14). But for him it is not an excuse for ducking the question, as it seems to be for Berkeley. Yet, elsewhere in his work, Berkeley does consider some concepts in the abstract; and he would not be a philosopher if he did not. I now set abstract ideas aside.

217. What Berkeley says about secondary qualities

Berkeley uses Locke's doctrine about secondary qualities as a stick with which to beat materialism; see *PHK* 10–11, 14–15, and Dia 1, 187–94. This tactic depends entirely upon misunderstandings. Berkeley takes as canonical the worst one of Locke's various conflicting statements of the doctrine: namely, that *secondary qualities are in the mind, primary qualities outside it*, using this to fuel a battery of arguments contending that if secondary qualities are mental, then primary ones must be also—which is immaterialism.

The best reading of these texts of Locke's is the 'central thesis' that each secondary quality is a thing's disposition to relate to minds in a certain way (§188). This does not put the secondary quality 'in the mind', and so it does not concede immaterialism for some qualities while denying it for others.[2] Let us look into what Berkeley does with his misunderstanding.

First, taking Locke to have said that material things have primary qualities but lack secondary ones, Berkeley objects that we cannot attach sense to the notion of a thing that has the former but not the latter (*PHK* 10; Dia 1, 194). He is evidently thinking of shape, size, and movement on the one hand, and colour on the other, as detected by eyesight. But we also have the sense of touch, which informs us of primary qualities without giving a hint of secondary ones. Would not touch have to give information about texture? Yes, it would; but Locke regularly includes texture among the primary qualities (*Essay* II.xxiii.8, IV.iii.11,25), and Berkeley follows suit. Well, then, hard and soft? Perhaps—that is a complex business that I cannot go into here. When Hume took over this line of argument from Berkeley, he deepened it and made it more subtle, but could not free it of its commitment to sight at the expense of touch (*Treatise* 228–30).

Second, the case for putting secondary qualities 'in the mind', Berkeley thinks, comes from facts about relativity of perception: what colour a thing looks to have depends on the condition of the percipient and of the surroundings, and so on. He then argues that the same holds for primary qualities: for example, how fast a thing appears to be moving depends on the rate of 'the succession of ideas in the mind' of the percipient (*PHK* 11 and 14–15; Dia 1, 190). In fact, Locke does not appeal to relativity of perception in support of his theory about secondary qualities, to which, indeed, it is irrelevant.

Third, the standard list of primary qualities includes 'number', and Berkeley contends that there is a special reason—not having to do with perception—why this must be 'in the mind'. This argument does not occur in the *Three Dialogues* but only here:

---

[2] For a fuller explanation, see *LBH* 112–17. Berkeley's error about secondary qualities was pointed out by R. Jackson 1929: 71–2. For a kinder view, supported by arguments which I respect but am not convinced by, see Wilson 1992: 226–31.

That number is entirely the creature of the mind, even though the other qualities be allowed to exist without, will be evident to whoever considers that the same thing bears a different denomination of number as the mind views it with different respects. Thus, the same extension is one or three or thirty-six, according as the mind considers it with reference to a yard, a foot or an inch. (*PHK* 12)

Berkeley is working towards a point that Frege clearly articulated a century and a half later (1884). According to Frege, any statement applying a cardinality concept—any statement about *how many*—must involve some other general concept, and what is being said must concern the number of instances of that concept. One book, two hundred pages, thirty billion molecules—different numbers, but all applied to the same chunk of the world in relation to different concepts.

Frege's thesis concerns the logical form of a proper cardinality statement, not the state of mind of someone who utters it. The cardinality facts are perfectly objective and extra-mental (unless nothing is so); the ideas in the mind of the speaker are irrelevant. That destroys this point of Berkeley's, which owes any plausibility it has to being muddled with Frege's view. I should add that Frege's widely admired thesis, though plausible where Berkeley's is not, is also false. 'Cicero and Tully are one' is a good cardinality statement which does not count under a concept; 'Cicero and Caesar are two' is another. For details, see Alston and Bennett 1984.

218. What Berkeley says about substratum substance

When he insists that materialism is conceptually flawed, Berkeley has two things in mind. One is his argument that we cannot conceive of matter because none of our ideas can resemble it. The other, which weighed with him equally, depends on another misunderstanding of Locke, specifically of his remarks about 'the idea of substance in general'. Berkeley's fumble with this deceived all his main commentators for many years, but in recent decades it has been clear to most writers in this area that the substratum doctrine is 'quite obviously' distinct from materialism (Tipton 1974: 357 n. 15).

Berkeley runs together two lines of thought.

In addition to our ideas, there is also, out there beyond the veil of perception, something called *matter* which our ideas are *of*. It is not known directly, or in itself, but we conjecture that it exists on the evidence of our ideas.

In addition to quality-instances, there is also something called *substance*, which the qualities are *in*. It is not known directly, or in itself, but we conclude that it must exist because quality-instances could not exist without it.

These are as different as could be. The former is metaphysics, while the latter—at least in Locke's hands—comes from meaning-theory. The former has to do with subjective/objective, or inner/outer, while the latter concerns thing/quality. These two distinctions are at right angles to one another.

Berkeley, however, ran the two doctrines together, treating the attack on 'the idea of substance in general' as an attack on Lockean materialism:

> The sensible qualities are colour, figure, motion, smell, taste, and such like, that is, the ideas perceived by sense. Now for an idea to exist in an unperceiving thing is a manifest contradiction; for to have an idea is all one as to perceive. That therefore wherein colour, figure, and the like qualities exist must perceive them; hence it is clear there can be no unthinking substance or substratum of those ideas. *(PHK 7)*[3]

Subsequent writers, right through into the twentieth century, followed Berkeley in this muddle. For example, Warnock (1953: 110) reports Berkeley as rejecting Locke's 'second, shadowy world, alleged to lie somehow behind or beneath the things that we touch and see'. The prepositions 'behind' and 'beneath' nicely reflect the conflation that I have been talking about. Another example comes from Ayer, doing philosophy in a non-historical way:

> We cannot, in our language, refer to the sensible properties of a thing without introducing a word or phrase which appears to stand for the thing itself as opposed to anything which may be said about it. [Some people wrongly think] that it is necessary to distinguish logically between the thing itself and any, or all, of its sensible properties. And so they employ the term 'substance' to refer to the thing itself. But from the fact that we happen to employ a single word to refer to a thing, and make that word the grammatical subject of the sentences in which we refer to the sensible appearances of the thing, it does not by any means follow that the thing itself is a 'simple entity', or that it cannot be defined in terms of the totality of its appearances. . . . Logical analysis shows that what makes these 'appearances' the 'appearances of' the same thing is not their relationship to an entity other than themselves, but their relationship to one another. (1946: 42)

Ayer slides from 'the thing itself as opposed to anything which may be said about it' (substratum) to 'the thing itself [as opposed to] its appearances' (Lockean matter). The slide is greased by 'sensible properties', which echoes Berkeley's stock phrase 'sensible qualities'.

Berkeley writes as though Yes to substratum substance stands or falls with Yes to matter. But the answers he envisages—Yes–Yes and No–No—are only half of the possibilities. Here is No–Yes: the concept of substance is that of a suitably related bundle of tropes; and there is mind-independent matter. Here is Yes–No: our substance concept involves a sheer irreducible thing thought of some kind (no bundles); and Berkeleian immaterialism is true—there is no matter. So materialist metaphysics and idea-of-substance-in-general semantics are independent.

Berkeley perpetrated this conflation in a strikingly open way, because he held as a matter of doctrine that *qualities are ideas*. This is indicated at the outset, in *PHK* 1, and it appears more openly in 7 and 91 and elsewhere. Berkeley carries this into his case for idealism; it is not merely something he carries out from it. Bad as this mistake is, we can see how Berkeley might come to make it. It might

---

[3] See also *PHK* 16–17, 73, and 77, and Dia 1, 197–9.

be influenced by the old view that sensory ideas are tropes, instances of the properties they represent. I am sure it is also encouraged by the isomorphisms that I discussed in §169 and, most potently, the one discussed in this section.

For Berkeley, our confinement to our own ideas (we do not get behind the veil to the matter that causes them) is our confinement to the qualities of things (we do not get down to the substratum that has them). His thesis that real things are collections of ideas (we do not need matter) is his thesis that a thing is a collection of properties (we do not need a substratum). Thus, he saw Locke's belief in an extra-mental world as tied to, standing or falling with—perhaps even being identical with—his belief in a substratum that supports a thing's qualities. Berkeley does not comment on the fact that Locke is cheerful in one of these and glumly reluctant in the other.

Locke himself, we have seen, tends to conflate ideas with tropes (§159); and I know of one place where this may have infected his handling of the substance issue in a more than merely verbal manner. This is the passage, discussed at the end of §207 above, where he writes that we 'suppose some substratum wherein [ideas] do subsist, and from which they do result, which therefore we call substance'. That uses 'ideas' to refer to tropes, but the conflation may also have influenced it in another way. The notion of a substratum substance as causing the tropes that it supports does not fit comfortably with most of what Locke writes on this topic; I suggested one explanation for it, and now I suggest another: namely, that Locke has briefly slid into thinking of the 'ideas' partly as ideas properly so-called, sensory states or sense-data, and is thinking of the supposed substratum as the real extra-mental thing that causes them in our minds. Berkeley's mistake.

That is a conjectural explanation for one short atypical passage; it does not make Locke responsible for Berkeley's performance. Whereas Berkeley regularly runs the substratum issue together with the issue over materialism, Locke nearly always keeps them apart, sometimes explicitly showing how the substance concept cuts across the mental/material divide:

Putting together the ideas of thinking and willing . . . , joined to substance of which we have no distinct idea, we have the idea of an immaterial spirit; and by putting together the ideas of coherent solid parts and a power of being moved, joined with substance of which likewise we have no positive idea, we have the idea of matter. . . . Our idea of substance is equally obscure, or none at all, in both: It is but a supposed I know not what, to support those ideas we call accidents. (*Essay* II.xxiii.15. Notice the idea/quality slip-up in the last five words.)

I cannot explain Berkeley's thinking, in the light of this, that substratum and matter are essentially connected. Pitcher 1977: 121, though it is the best defence I know for Berkeley's linking of substratum with matter, seems to me strained.

As for the phrase 'material substance' (in the singular): Berkeley uses it about a dozen times in the *Principles*, suggesting that it captures something important in Locke's thought. But it is absent from Locke's *Essay*. Its plural occurs there once, and 'corporeal substances' oftener; but none of those passages concerns the so-called 'idea of substance in general'. In the only passage that uses 'corporeal substance' in the singular, Locke does use it to stand for the troublesome substratum concept, but his point is that we use the concept when thinking about matter *just as we do when thinking about spirit* (II.xxiii.5,15). Every time he explicitly juxtaposes materiality with substance in general, he does so precisely in order to deny that the two are integrally connected. The more carefully one reads Locke, the less excusable does one find Berkeley's misunderstanding of him.

In a few places Berkeley attacks the substratum notion in itself, not as part of an attack on materialism. These passages point towards the real trouble with substratum, but they are not well focused; see *PHK* 16–17; Dia 1, 197–9. Berkeley mocks the word 'support' in the thesis that substances support their qualities. He does not remark that Locke also derides the suggestion that substances support qualities, likening it to the view that the world is supported by an elephant which is supported by a tortoise. 'Support' cannot be meant in its usual sense, Berkeley remarks, and no unusual one has been explained:

Though you know not what it is, yet you must be supposed to know what relation it bears to accidents, and what is meant by its supporting them. It is evident support cannot here be taken in its usual or literal sense, as when we say that pillars support a building: in what sense therefore must it be taken? (*PHK* 16; see also Dia 1, 199)

This is all right as far as it goes; but for Berkeley to get to the heart of the trouble, he would need to understand that he is here confronted primarily by a thesis about what we mean in saying certain things; and he cannot do that while muddling this topic in semantics with the metaphysics of materialism.

Hume is innocent of Berkeley's conflation of the issue about substance with that about material things. Like many philosophers, he found problematic the thought of a single thing's lasting through a period of time (1) for some of which we do not perceive the thing, and/or (2) during which the thing alters. In *Treatise* I.iv.2 he addresses 1 purely in terms of material bodies and perceptions, and in iv.3 he tackles 2 in terms of substances and qualities. Hume does not allow either pair of concepts to spill over into the territory proper to the other.

Chapter 30

Berkeley on Spirits

219. Berkeley on 'spirit'

I remarked that one might answer Yes to 'Substratum?' and No to 'Matter?' That was in challenge to Berkeley's assumption that the only possible pairs of answers are Yes–Yes and No–No. Now, it turns out that Yes–No is his own pair of answers! This will at last take us away from his attacks on materialism and towards his positive metaphysic.

He adopts Yes–No in his doctrine that there are thinking, immaterial substances. He calls them 'spirits', and accords to them the role in the mental realm that Lockean substances play there and in the material realm as well. But whereas Locke worries about the 'idea of substance in general', Berkeley roundly denies that we have any idea corresponding to the term 'spirit', precisely because it fits his specifications for a substratum substance. Here he says what an idea of spirit would have to be like, by setting a challenge for someone who thinks there is one:

Let him but reflect and try if he can frame the idea of any power or active being; and whether he hath ideas of two principal powers, marked by the names will and understanding, distinct from each other as well as from a third idea of substance or being in general, with a relative notion of its supporting or being the subject of the aforesaid powers, which is signified by the name soul or spirit. (*PHK* 27)

Notice that Berkeley here uses the phrase 'substance or being in general, with a relative notion of its supporting or being the subject of the aforesaid powers' in characterizing the concept of spirit which he accepts. This is the language of the Lockean idea of substance in general, and it becomes clear that Berkeley commits himself to a substance concept that owes nothing to any bundle theory.

This means that he regards ideas as qualities or properties of spirits. Sometimes he seems not to, as when he equates 'what I call mind, spirit, soul, or myself' with 'a thing entirely distinct from [my ideas], wherein they exist' (*PHK* 2; see also 49). That seems to reify ideas, treating them as evanescent mental things that are related somehow to minds. More often, though, Berkeley thinks of ideas as states of minds, especially when he insists that spirits are the only substances, the only *things* (*PHK* 7). He says this strikingly in an early note in his *Philosophical Commentaries*: 'Nothing properly but persons i.e. conscious things do exist, all other things are not so much existences as manners of the existence of persons' (*PC* 24). Berkeley needs to take this position in his published work; for if ideas are not states of minds, why cannot an idea exist outside any mind? In *PHK* 3 he writes that 'everybody will allow' that ideas do not 'exist without the mind', but he does not say why. The only clean explanation I can find comes from combining the thesis that ideas are states with the thesis that states (tropes) cannot exist unowned; from these it follows that ideas do not, because they cannot, exist outside minds.

Anyway, it is clear that Berkeley sees ideas as related to spirits analogously to how properties supposedly relate to the substance that supports them. He emphasizes the similarity when he writes that 'a spirit has been shown to be the only substance or support wherein the unthinking beings or ideas can exist' (*PHK* 135).

Why can there be no idea of spirit? Berkeley's usual reason is that any idea of a thing must resemble it, and that no idea can resemble a spirit:

By the word spirit we mean only that which thinks, wills, and perceives; this and this alone constitutes the signification of that term. If, therefore, it is impossible that any degree of those powers should be represented in an idea, it is evident there can be no idea of a spirit. (*PHK* 138)

This dissimilarity comes mostly from the supposed fact that spirits are causally active and can initiate changes in the world, whereas ideas have no causal powers (§221).

That reason for ruling out ideas of spirits depends on the resemblance theory of representation. Berkeley seems also to have something else to offer, though the matter is not perfectly clear. Late in the *Principles* we find this:

It will perhaps be said that we want a sense (as some have imagined) proper to know substances withal, which if we had, we might know our own soul as we do a triangle. To this I answer that in case we had a new sense bestowed upon us, we could only receive thereby some new sensations or ideas of sense. But I believe nobody will say that what he means by the terms soul and substance is only some particular sort of idea or sensation. (*PHK* 136)

This, I suggest, has the same shape as the case for saying: Lockean substratum substance should not be described as having a nature which is unknown to us; it cannot have a nature, because that would be its having an essential property; but then we should have to mentally peel off the property in order to consider the underlying *thing* that has it. Berkeley is saying, similarly, that any mental representation of a mind would have to be a representation of some of its states or activities; but once we have this, we should peel off the states and activities in order to consider the *mind* that has or does them. Though still tainted with the similarity theory of representation, this is better than a mere list of unlikenesses between minds and ideas.

Berkeley criticizes Locke for using '[material] substance' without backing it by a suitable idea; yet he allows himself 'thinking substance', and treats the lack of a corresponding idea as a mere innocent fact. How can he defend this double standard?

He skirts this issue in the *Principles*, by raising the 'idea of spirit' question in a form which assumes that we can talk and think intelligibly about spirits, and confuting those who think that we have ideas of them, or say that we ought to acquire such ideas, or complain about our lack of any. Berkeley replies that it stands to reason that there are no ideas of spirits. I have quoted passages where he does this; *PHK* 135 is another.

This line of thought does not solve the problem I am raising; it creates it. In the Third Dialogue Berkeley at last faces up to it—with great force, making his interlocutor Hylas say this:

You acknowledge you have, properly speaking, no idea of your own soul. You even affirm that spirits are a sort of beings altogether different from ideas. Consequently that no idea can be like a spirit. We have therefore no idea of any spirit. You admit nevertheless that there is spiritual substance, although you have no idea of it; while you deny there can be such a thing as material substance, because you have no notion or idea of it. Is this fair dealing? To act consistently, you must either admit matter or reject spirit.

Here is Philonous's reply:

I do not deny the existence of material substance merely because I have no notion of it, but because the notion of it is inconsistent, or in other words because it is repugnant that there should be a notion of it. Many things, for ought I know, may exist, whereof neither I nor any other man hath or can have any idea or notion whatsoever. But then those things must be possible . . . I say secondly that although we believe things to exist which we do not perceive; yet we may not believe that any particular thing exists, without some reason for such belief; but I have no reason for believing the existence of matter. I have no immediate intuition thereof: neither can I mediately from my sensations, ideas, notions, actions, or passions, infer an unthinking, unperceiving, inactive substance, either by probable deduction or necessary consequence. Whereas the being of myself, that is, my own soul, mind, or thinking principle, I evidently know by reflection. . . . I have a notion of spirit, though I have not, strictly speaking, an idea of it. I do not perceive it as an idea or by means of an idea, but know it by reflection. (Dia 3, 233)

This busy, complex passage concedes that the complaints against 'material substance' were all aimed at 'material' and not at 'substance'. Berkeley now openly disavows any wish to attack 'substratum' as such; the oddity of the required sense of 'support' is forgotten or forgiven. Or perhaps he is claiming that all he ever meant to attack was 'support' when this is understood extra-mentally. If that was his considered intent in the *Principles* and the earlier parts of the *Three Dialogues*, he signally failed to make that fact clear at the time.

Let us now accept Berkeley's apparent change of tune, and consider his treatment of 'spirit' in itself. Why is his term 'spirit' meaningful? He says two things about this.

One is just that he knows things that he can express using that word or some equivalent of it. Thus, for instance: 'The being of myself, that is, my own soul, mind, or thinking principle, I evidently know by reflection', and somehow the knowledge claim can be secure and can pass its security on to the claim that the words make sense. Adams (1975) argues powerfully that Berkeley is working here with a thesis about two modes of awareness, one through ideas and the other not, and associating 'notions' with the latter. I am sure that this is right.

On what does Berkeley base his knowledge claim? He speaks of 'reflection', but that leaves open a certain question, which he seems to answer in two ways. One is that his own existence is somehow immediately given to him as a datum: 'I know or am conscious of my own being' (Dia 3, 233). But there are also indications that he thinks that his own existence is inferred from ideas which are immediately given, through the principle that there cannot be unowned ideas. This is what he ought to think, I suggest, given his insistence that he has no idea of himself. Either way, his knowledge claim has to include this: 'I know . . . that I myself am not my ideas, but somewhat else, a thinking active principle that perceives' etc. (ibid.). This line of thought may seem to go backwards. While we have a question about whether a certain word is meaningful, how can we be sure that a knowledge claim involving it is sound, or an inference using it valid?

There is another difficulty. Berkeley's claim to make sense of 'spirit' rests on the argument: *I am myself, so I know myself, so I have a notion of myself, so I have a notion of spirit*. Even if this provides a legitimate basis for using 'spirit' in application to oneself, it does not clearly legitimize its use in application to anything else.

The second half of Berkeley's defence of 'spirit' belongs to semantic theory. There are two parts to it. (1) One implies that 'spirit' is all right because we have an acceptable, consistent definition of the word (Dia 3, 233, quoted above). This cannot help Berkeley much. He does not in general hold that a word can get meaning just from being linkable with other words. Ultimately, for him as for us, a verbal definition is no good unless its constituent terms are meaningful, so each must also be verbally definable in terms which are . . . etc.; and for Berkeley, as for Locke, the only way to prevent an infinite regress is eventually to arrive at terms that can be explained ostensively—that is, through their associated ideas. He implies this when he says that a definition confers meaning only if it is 'consistent', having earlier implied that consistency comes purely from relations amongst ideas (Dia 2, 225–6). Well, then, let him produce his definition of 'spirit', and tell us what the ideas are that correspond to the several words in the definiens. As we have seen, he firmly denies that anyone could do that. (2) Berkeley's other apparent semantic defence of 'spirit' says that we can understand a term for which we have no idea, so long as we have a corresponding 'notion': 'It must be owned at the same time that we have some notion of spirit, and the operations of the mind, such as willing, loving, hating, inasmuch as we know or understand the meaning of those words' (PHK 27; see also 89, 142). The term 'notion' appears oftener in later editions of the *Principles* than in the first edition, and oftener still in the *Three Dialogues*.

There is a literature on 'Berkeley's theory of notions', based on the assumption that he has an unexplained premiss about 'notions' from which he infers that he can understand 'myself' or 'my mind' without having corresponding ideas.

But that is not how things stand. Rather, he has the premiss that he does understand 'my mind', yet has no corresponding ideas; and he expresses these facts, or at least the former of them, by saying that he has a 'notion' of his mind. The term 'notion' is used to make the meaning claim, not to explain or justify it:

> 'We have some notion of soul, spirit [etc.]—inasmuch as we know or understand the meaning of those words' (PHK 27).

> 'In a large sense indeed, we may be said to have an idea, or rather a notion of spirit, that is, we understand the meaning of the word, otherwise we could not affirm or deny any thing of it' (PHK 140).

> 'I have some knowledge or notion of my mind, and its acts about ideas, inasmuch as I know or understand what is meant by those words. What I know, that I have some notion of' (PHK 142).

In short, Berkeley uses 'notion' not in explaining, but only in reporting, his having meanings for some words for which he has no ideas.

Is 'having a notion of x' a genus of which 'idea' is one species, or does it rather take up where 'idea' leaves off? The text does not say, and it does not matter. Either way, we have Berkeley making some meaning claims that are not supported by ideas; he ought to have some account of what does support them; and 'notion' is no help with this.

He could try to put flesh on the verbal bones of 'notion' by treating a notion as a disposition towards some sort of intellectual or verbal behaviour. That might lead him to treat 'spirit' somewhat as Locke does linguistic particles. But it goes far beyond anything he says or even suggests. It would involve developing some faint hints that we found in the Introduction to the Principles, but it is hardly credible that Berkeley did develop those in that manner.

Incidentally, Berkeley would not have needed to defend 'spirit' in any of these ways if he had stayed with the bundle view, which he did espouse shortly before the Principles appeared, in a sequence of remarks starting with this: 'The very existence of ideas constitutes the soul' (PC 577), and ending with this: 'Say you the mind is not the perceptions, but that thing which perceives. I answer you are abused by the words "that" and "thing". These are vague empty words without a meaning' (PC 581). In the Principles, published only two years later, there is no trace of this, and Berkeley reverts to the position of PC 24, quoted above. Perhaps he shrank from declaring God to be a bundle of perceptions. He ought to have done so, for a reason we shall hear more about in §221: namely, that if he had no metaphysically independent spirits in his ontology, he would have no causes, and his metaphysic would collapse. Tipton (1974: 263–4) holds that in the Principles Berkeley still envisaged spirits as something like collections of ideas, and did not think of them in substratum terms; but his long chapter on spirits in Berkeley has not convinced me.

220. Berkeley against solipsism

In the background of Berkeley's immaterialism, we always have his view that this metaphysic rescues us from the scepticism to which materialism condemns us. He puts it with sharp elegance in *PHK* 18–20, and again here:

[Materialism] is the very root of scepticism; for so long as men thought that real things subsisted without the mind, and that their knowledge was only so far forth real as it was conformable to real things, it follows they could not be certain that they had any real knowledge at all. For how can it be known that the things which are perceived are conformable to those which are not perceived or exist without the mind? (*PHK* 86; see also 87)

Someone who believes in nothing but himself and his own ideas need have no doubts about any of his existential beliefs. But that is the non-scepticism of the solipsist, which is not interesting. Berkeley accepted an ontology in which more things than himself existed, and he thought he could secure it, too, against sceptical doubts.

To get to it, the first step is to refute solipsism. Berkeley starts on this where Descartes and Locke did, with the fact that some ideas come into one's mind without one's willing them to do so:

When in broad daylight I open my eyes, it is not in my power to choose whether I shall see or no, or to determine what particular objects shall present themselves to my view; and so likewise as to the hearing and other senses, the ideas imprinted on them are not creatures of my will. There is therefore some other will or spirit that produces them. (*PHK* 29)

This gives a reason for concluding that Berkeley's ideas of sense are caused by something other than himself. The reason is essentially the one that Descartes gave (§209). His confidence that the causation of his ideas of sense 'presupposes no intellectual act on my part', and Berkeley's that such ideas 'have not a like dependence on my will', probably arise from the shared assumption that nothing can happen in someone's mind without the person's being conscious of it; see Dia 3, 238. A weaker premiss would suffice: if I were causing all my ideas of sense, I would be conscious of causing at least some of them.

Descartes gets from mere non-solipsism to a world of matter with help from two further premisses: (1) He has been made by a perfect God, who would never be a deceiver. (2) He has a great propensity to believe in matter; if that belief is false, though he has not been warned or armed against it, his maker would be a deceiver. Berkeley could not employ 1 at this stage in the argument, because his case for his theology depends on his already accepting the existence of things other than himself. He would probably reject 2 also, claiming that Descartes has misdiagnosed his own condition. Berkeley thinks that the belief in matter is widespread (*PHK* 4); but he would never concede that it is inevitable for anyone.

So far, then, he has only this: there is something other than me. He advances beyond that with help from something, mentioned briefly in §213 above, which now forces itself to centre stage—the thesis that only spirits can be causes.

221. Only spirits can be causes

We are working within the framework of Berkeley's belief that there is no matter, so we need not linger on his denial that matter can act. More to our point is his denial of causal powers to the 'sensible things' which he does believe in. These are—or are composed of—ideas, which Berkeley insists are passive, inactive, unable to make anything happen. He will say: 'Of course there are shoes and ships, properly understood. Can they cause anything to happen? Certainly not!' In his own words: 'All our ideas, sensations, or the things which we perceive . . . are visibly inactive; there is nothing of power or agency included in them.' See for yourself by looking in at your own ideas: 'There is nothing in them but what is perceived. But whoever shall attend to his ideas, whether of sense or reflection, will not perceive in them any power or activity; there is therefore no such thing contained in them' (PHK 25). When we look at our ideas, Berkeley says, we do not find them to be active, and we cannot have overlooked any of their features— we are omniscient about our own present mental states. I cannot evaluate this, because I do not know what thought-experiment I am being invited to perform. How do I go about looking for activity in my ideas? Anyway, even granted that none of *my* ideas is *now* active, why should I infer that this holds for all ideas always?

However, this introspective experiment is not the real basis for Berkeley's position. He continues: 'A little attention will discover to us that the very being of an idea implies passiveness and inertness in it, insomuch that it is impossible for an idea to do any thing, or, strictly speaking, to be the cause of any thing.' I take this to mean that ideas are essentially, necessarily inactive, this being something we can know a priori if we reflect 'a little'.

I cannot find that Berkeley ever states a reason for this, but here is a guess. Perhaps he is moved by the thought that (1) ideas are *states* of minds, whereas (2) active power can be exercised only by *things*, *substances*. Or, more cautiously: (1*) ideas are like states in being metaphysically dependent, unable to exist unsupported; whereas (2*) only independent items can be causally active. Berkeley seems to have believed at least the weaker (1*& 2*). He emphasizes the dependence of ideas here:

That an idea, which is inactive, and the existence whereof consists in being perceived, should be the image or likeness of an agent subsisting by itself, seems to need no other refutation than barely attending to what is meant by those words. But perhaps you will say that though an idea cannot resemble a spirit in its thinking, acting, or subsisting by itself, yet . . . (PHK 137; see also 26)

. . . and so on. Note the repetition of 'subsisting by itself'. When Berkeley says that 'it has been made evident' in *PHK* 25 that ideas are inactive, I hope he was referring to this dependent/independent line of thought, rather than the intro-spective experiment (see *PHK* 61 and 102). The former may not be right, but it is solider than the latter.

So much for the inactivity of ideas. The view that spirits are active at first seems also to be based on introspection:

I find I can excite ideas in my mind at pleasure, and vary and shift the scene as oft as I think fit. It is no more than willing, and straightway this or that idea arises in my fancy: and by the same power it is obliterated, and makes way for another. This making and unmaking of ideas doth very properly denominate the mind active. Thus much is certain, and grounded on experience. (*PHK* 28)

This is Berkeley at his most confident, but he goes too fast. Let us grant that I know for sure that I sometimes voluntarily do things. Berkeley says that this 'doth very properly denominate [my] mind active', meaning that my doings are genuine instances of causation. Now, causation is a heavily laden theoretical notion; and Berkeley takes that load seriously, denying a causal status to many episodes that most of us think have it. Suppose I put this to him:

I find I can excite auditory ideas in my mind at pleasure, and vary and shift the tune as often as I think fit. It is no more than moving my fingers on the piano keys, and straight away this or that auditory idea arises in my mind; and by pressing one of the pedals it is obliterated, and makes way for another. This making and unmaking of auditory ideas makes it proper to say that my hands and feet are active.

Berkeley does not believe a word of this. He agrees that the sequence of ideas that I call pressing piano keys with my fingers is followed by auditory ideas, but he denies that the former cause the latter. What is the difference between this and the voluntary 'making and unmaking' of ideas in my imagination?

Pitcher (1977: 133) answers that for Berkeley 'there is something altogether special about the causality of our own actions; we can just feel ourselves making them happen'. That is wrong; Berkeley never contends that I directly experience the causal efficacy of my will. Hume says that 'Some have asserted that we feel an energy or power in our own mind' (*Treatise* I.iii.14), but Berkeley is not one of them. His description of his own mind's activity fits rather with Hume's own debunking account: all we experience that would relate our volitions to our movements is what also relates the movements to one another—constant con-junction, empirically discovered regularity. I have quoted him as saying 'It is no more than willing, and straightway this or that idea arises in my fancy'. Berkeley does not deny that in willing I experience causal power at work, but he stops short—deliberately, I think—of asserting it. His unpublished work confirms this: see *PC* 107, 461, 499, 699.

Why—I ask again—is Berkeley so sure that volition is causal *making*, and that nothing else plays that role? He seems to think that he has general reasons for hold-ing that 'when we talk of unthinking agents, or of exciting ideas exclusive of volition, we only amuse ourselves with words' (*PHK* 28). I once suggested that he thought of the volition–upshot relation as the only way for anyone to know something about the future non-inductively—that is, other than through knowing about past patterns and trusting them to recur. That cannot be right, though, for we have just seen how inductively Berkeley treats the relation of volition to upshot.

Here is a less vulnerable suggestion. Although there can only be inductively based confidence that a volition will have a certain upshot, *what* upshot it will have is, so to speak, non-inductively written into it. A volition is a willing *that P occur*, which means that a representation of P is built into it. This provides a non-inductive link between volition and upshot, though not a strong enough one to permit non-inductive predictions. Winkler (1989: 130) has offered essentially the same suggestion, saying that Berkeley regards volition as causal because he 'links causation with intelligibility'. The point is that if something is voluntarily brought about by some spirit, the fact that the spirit wanted it and aimed at it helps to makes its occurrence intelligible. We have here an answer to 'Why?' which goes further than merely subsuming the event under some past pattern. There is probably something in this, but it can hardly carry the whole weight of Berkeley's confidence that the spirits alone can act.

This is a puzzling affair. Thomas Reid, who was in a position to write against Hume on this matter, argued at length that the only real causation is agent-causation, so that the only genuine causes are acts of will. I do not fully understand why this able, insightful philosopher took this position, given that he flatly denied that we *find* activity in the will. On the latter topic he is as firm as Hume. Here is one straw in the wind:

Every operation of the mind is the exertion of some power of the mind; but we are conscious of the operation only, the power lies behind the scene; and though we may justly infer the power from the operation, it must be remembered that inferring is not the province of consciousness, but of reason. (Reid 1788: 6)

Later on, we learn that Reid does not think we are entitled to be quite sure—even through reasoning—that volition is an exercise of power:

It is possible . . . for anything we know, that what we call the immediate effects of our power may not be so in the strictest sense. Between the will to produce the effect and the production of it there may be agents or instruments of which we are ignorant. This may leave some doubt whether we be in the strictest sense the efficient cause of the voluntary motions of our own body. (Ibid. 50–1)

Why, then, was Reid as sure as he was that human volition involves real causation? His work, like that of most Christian philosophers, tends towards the unwanted conclusion that really only God does or causes anything.

Anyway, Berkeley, for whatever reason, does confidently hold that only the will is active, and this drives his argument from the involuntariness of his ideas of sense to their being caused by one or more other spirits. That still leaves him well short of Christian monotheism.

222. Berkeley's natural theology

Berkeley argues his way to the Christian God with help from standard natural theology—empirical evidence that there is just one God, who is wise, benevolent, etc. (PHK 146–56). There is little philosophical profit in this, but Berkeley's metaphysical setting for it is rewarding. It concerns his account of what we might (though wrongly) call the 'causal order' that we find in the world. He expounds this mainly in PHK 30–2, 58–9, 62–6, 102–10. It is not a substantial topic anywhere in the *Three Dialogues*, perhaps because the *Principles* did not meet with criticism on this score. It is one of the best things in Berkeley's philosophy.

Start from his basic ontology: there are only spirits and the ideas which they have or support or 'perceive'. There are, Berkeley allows, 'sensible things' like peacocks, islands, and ivory; but these are not listed in the inventory of the ground floor, only because they are not sheerly additional to spirits and their ideas. Rather, all the facts about how sensible things behave in relation to one another are complex facts about the sequences of our sensory ideas.

Many of our ideas, Berkeley writes in PHK 30, occur 'in a regular train or series, the admirable connection whereof sufficiently testifies the wisdom and benevolence of its Author'. This regularity is what we call 'the laws of nature: and these we learn by experience, which teaches us that such and such ideas are attended with such and such other ideas in the ordinary course of things'. He continues:

This gives us a sort of foresight, which enables us to regulate our actions for the benefit of life.... That food nourishes, sleep refreshes, and fire warms us; ... and, in general, that to obtain such or such ends, such or such means are conducive, all this we know, not by discovering any necessary connexion between our ideas, but only by the observation of the settled laws of nature, without which we should be all in uncertainty and confusion. (PHK 31)

There is more, all of it excellent. In these passages Berkeley shows that he sees clearly something which many earlier philosophers noticed, and which later impressed Hume: namely, that in observing the world around us, we perceive only successions. If one person reports 'He made the wall collapse by leaning on it' while another says merely 'The wall collapsed just after he began leaning on it', the former has not noticed something which the latter overlooked. All there is to *notice* are facts about temporal succession and spatial relations. There are patterns or regularities in these facts, and Berkeley writes elegantly about what is involved in discovering nature's regularities, harmonies, analogies, without perceiving any causal connections. Hume holds that these patterns have no ultimate explanation, or none that we could understand (§270); whereas for Berkeley they are intelligibly explained by the will of God. Despite this massive difference, however, they relate causation to perception in exactly the same way.

When Berkeley says that the empirically discovered patterns do not involve any necessary connection, he had better not be implying that without absolute necessity we do not have causation; because his own theory of causation does not meet that standard. The point he wants to make, I think, is just that all we find in our observations of the world is *de facto* regularity, from which he infers that we should beware of undue confidence about the rightness of our science, and should avoid any kind of a priori thinking in science. For example he scolds those who think that gravity is a force that holds between any two bodies, when there is empirical evidence that 'the fixed stars have no such tendency towards each other', and says severely: 'There is nothing necessary or essential in the case, but it depends entirely on the will of the governing spirit, who causes certain bodies to . . . tend towards each other according to various laws, whilst he keeps others at a fixed distance; and to some he gives a quite contrary tendency to fly asunder, just as he sees convenient' (*PHK* 106). There is some tension, but no real contradiction, between this and *PHK* 62.

What the laws of nature reveal—Berkeley sometimes says—are not 'causes' but 'signs'. He means this literally. It is not merely that when we encounter an A, we can take this as evidence that a B is impending, and can profit accordingly; but, further, in the typical case God presents the A to us as evidence (a warning, perhaps) of an impending B. These 'signs', Berkeley holds, are parts of a language: learning the laws of nature is learning to understand how God speaks to us, in a language of warnings and promises about possible or likely future mental states. (See, for example, *PHK* 109.) There is more to this effect in the *New Theory of Vision*, a work which studies how sight relates to touch. It relates, Berkeley concludes, essentially as a word does to the thing it refers to:

The proper objects of vision constitute an universal language of the Author of nature, whereby we are instructed how to regulate our actions in order to attain those things that are necessary to the preservation and well-being of our bodies, as also to avoid whatever may be hurtful and destructive of them. It is by their information that we are principally guided in all the transactions and concerns of life. And the manner wherein they signify and mark unto us the objects which are at a distance is the same with that of languages and signs of human appointment, which do not suggest the things signified by any likeness or identity of nature but only by an habitual connexion that experience has made us to observe between them. (*NT* 147)

I am pretty sure that in the context of the *Principles* and *Three Dialogues* Berkeley would have been willing to extend most of this to all dependable regularities among ideas. Rightly regarding the tactual-kinaesthetic data as the most basic and important to us, he says in *NT* 59 and 140 that visual data are important mainly as warnings about impending tactual data. He cannot consistently treat the latter so dismissively, but he can still say that they are, among other things, statements by God about what other ideas will be had if . . . For example, he can say that the feel of an apple is, among other things, God's way of telling us how it will taste.

We have seen Berkeley supporting his view that spirits can act by noting that he can change some of his own ideas at will. He says nothing about what is involved in the divine spirit's changing ideas in *other* minds at will. Perhaps he lets it pass because this remarkable power is being assigned only to God. Wittgenstein pilloried the tendency in philosophy to assign things to 'hocus pocus in the soul'; there has sometimes been a parallel tendency in philosophical theology.

Berkeley's God is intimately involved in our lives. A natural theologian who believes in matter and in its causal powers cannot do much better than: 'This splendid machine must have been constructed and set going by a divine being.' Berkeley, on the other hand, has reason to say that God acts upon us directly at our every waking moment. He objects to materialism, indeed, partly because it weakens natural theology and thereby encourages atheism. Some passages in the *Principles* and *Three Dialogues* show him rejoicing in his supposed success in weaving God into the fabric of our lives; and he does so even more strongly in *Alciphron*, an immaterialist work of Christian apologetics written two decades later. One spokesman for Berkeley says to Alciphron, his free-thinking opponent: 'You, it seems, stare to find that God is not far from every one of us, and that in him we live and move and have our being. You, who [at first] thought it strange that God should leave himself without a witness, do now think it strange the witness should be so full and clear' (1732, LJ 3:159). Alciphron concedes: 'I must own I do. . . . I never imagined it could be pretended [= maintained] that we saw God with our fleshly eyes as plain as we see any human person whatsoever, and that he daily speaks to our senses in a manifest and clear dialect.' The other Berkeleian in the dialogue weighs in thus:

This optic language hath a necessary connexion with knowledge, wisdom, and goodness. It is equivalent to a constant creation, betokening an immediate act of power and providence. It cannot be accounted for by mechanical principles, by atoms, attractions or effluvia. The instantaneous production and reproduction of so many signs combined, dissolved, transposed, diversified, and adapted to such an endless variety of purposes, ever shifting with the occasions and suited to them, being utterly inexplicable and unaccountable by the laws of motion, by chance, by fate, or the like blind principles, doth set forth and testify the immediate operation of . . . one wise, good, and provident Spirit who directs and rules and governs the world. Some philosophers, being convinced of the wisdom and power of the Creator from the make and contrivance of organized bodies and orderly system of the world, did nevertheless imagine that he left this system, with all its parts and contents well adjusted and put in motion, as an artist leaves a clock, to go thenceforward of itself for a certain period. But this visual language proves not a Creator merely but a provident governor, actually and intimately present and attentive to all our interests and motions. (Ibid. 159–60)

This brings in all four themes: our continuously intimate relation with God, his addressing us through our senses, the denial of power to sensible things, and the thinness of any natural theology that credits them with powers.

223. Human agency

Berkeley has reached, by an intelligible route, a belief in a stupendously powerful and wholly benevolent spirit, God. He now needs evidence that there are other finite spirits like himself, and he finds it in another inference to the best explanation. Before coming to that, let us see what he does say, and consider what he should say, about the agency of finite spirits. Start with this as a first-person question—'What do *I* actually cause?'

This is Berkeley's paradigm: 'I find I can excite ideas in my mind at pleasure, and vary and shift the scene as oft as I think fit.' If varying and shifting the scene is merely seeing things with one's mind's eye, hearing them with the mind's ear, and so on, it is a minor aspect of the human condition. Indeed, some people apparently cannot do this kind of imaging, as we might call it. But Berkeley means to be covering not only that, but also the whole range of thinking, his only account of which is in terms of the mental manipulation of ideas. So this is his version of a time-hallowed dichotomy between thought as active and sense perception as passive: 'Whatever power I may have over my own thoughts, I find the ideas actually perceived by sense have not a like dependence on my will.' Elsewhere he writes that 'thoughts' and 'sensations' are two labels for items of one kind, differing only in that the former come into one's mind voluntarily while the latter do not (*PC* 286).

What of the converse thesis? Although Berkeley does not say outright that thinking is our only true activity, he frequently suggests this. He always illustrates active/passive through thinking/sensing, never through swimming/sensing or the like. Bodily activity, indeed, is never prominent in his picture of the human condition, and is almost invisible when the active/passive distinction is at work.

What can Berkeley say happens when I voluntarily clench my fist? Well, my fist's moving is for him ultimately a fact about the occurrence of various ideas, and if I feel or see my fist clench, some of the relevant ideas are my own. Now, he must say that those visual ideas come to me involuntarily; it is obvious that they do, and he is also pushed that way by theoretical considerations. The ideas are perceptions of a real fist (as we say): they are ideas of sense, not of imagination; and Berkeley distinguishes sense from imagination largely through our being passive with respect to the former (§220). So when I clench my fist and watch myself doing it, I am somehow active, yet I passively undergo a change of visual state. How can Berkeley fit these two facts together? Where can he draw the active/passive line in this case? Not only immaterialists, but all of us who think we have a good active/passive distinction, confront the question of how to apply it in physical activity; and the right answer is not obvious. However, I shall focus on the problem as it arises for Berkeley.

Objection: 'What problem? The movement of your fist is one event, and the change in your visual ideas is another; you are active in one and passive in the other.' That sounds all right if we think only of my change of visual state as I clench my fist, but there can be other changes as well: I have tactual and kinaesthetic feelings in the clenched fist, I clench it so violently that I hear the fingers smack against the palm, and so on. I undergo all these changes passively, because they all belong on the 'sense' side of the sense/imagination divide. Now, if Berkeley agrees that I am passive with respect to all those changes of state, yet active with respect to *the movement of my fist*, he is distinguishing that movement from *all* my sensory evidence for its occurrence. That is an impossible position for him: it amounts to a capitulation to materialism.

If we glance ahead, acknowledging that Berkeley will say that my fist's clenching is a fact about a collection of ideas most of which are in minds other than my own (§225), it becomes clearer than ever that the clenching is not something I do. The passivity with which I take in the sensory evidence of the clenching must be matched in the mind of anyone else who sees, feels, or hears it happen.

Berkeley, it seems, must conclude that when I voluntarily clench my fist, I actively perform a mental act—a *volition*—and that the rest of what happens falls outside the scope of my activity. That would imply that the modest claim that 'We move our legs our selves' (PC 548) is wrong: we do not move our legs; rather, we will that our legs should move, and then, usually, our legs move. Although I have not found Berkeley saying outright that in so-called bodily activity we are really active only in our volitions, he was deeply committed to this view, and probably knew it when he wrote the *Principles*.

We have seen signs of his thinking that volitions are our only acts, even in our imaginative and intellectual lives. When he writes 'It is no more than willing, and straightway this or that idea arises in my fancy', he suggests that if, after the volition, the willed change in mental content occurs, that is because we are lucky or blessed—not because it falls within the scope of our activity. On this view, acts of the will exhaust the range of human activity; this means not that each action of ours starts with a volition, but that each action—mental or 'physical'—is a volition. We say that we swim and think and clench our fists, but, strictly speaking, all we do is to will that these things shall happen; that they do usually happen when we will them to is a gift from God. This view is adumbrated in a haunting early note of Berkeley's: 'Strange impotence of men. Man without God wretcheder than a stone or tree, he having only the power to be miserable by his unperformed wills, these having no power at all' (PC 107). When he wrote that, Berkeley must have thought that volitions are our only activity. If he had thought that we can actively think, he would have said that man without God has a power to think, as well as to be miserable.

In the Third Dialogue, when Philonous is clearing God of guilt for human sins, he offers a defence which confirms the position that I have tentatively attributed to Berkeley:

Sin or moral turpitude doth not consist in the outward physical action or motion, but in the internal deviation of the will from the laws of reason and religion. . . . Since therefore sin doth not consist in the physical action, the making God an immediate cause of all such actions is not making him the author of sin. (Dia 3, 236–7)

Unfortunately, he goes straight on to this second defence:

I have nowhere said that God is the only agent who produces all the motions in bodies. It is true, I have denied there are any other agents beside spirits: but this is very consistent with allowing to thinking, rational beings, in the production of motions, the use of limited powers, ultimately indeed derived from God, but immediately under the direction of their own wills. (Ibid.)

This seems not to fit with my proposed interpretation of Berkeley's thought about human agency, but I do not retract. If Berkeley means to assert the premisses of both defences, then he is saying that 'God [is] the immediate cause of all [physical] actions' and, inconsistently, that 'the production of [some] motions [is] immediately under the direction of [finite spirits]'. The second of those, however, is not asserted; Berkeley merely says that it is consistent with God's not being the author of sin. It is a safety move, I suppose, a fall-back position to be occupied only if he has to give up his view that volitions are our only actions.

224. Other people

Here is how Berkeley relates my changes of sensory state to the activities of other created spirits:

We cannot know the existence of other spirits otherwise than by their operations or the ideas by them excited in us. I perceive several motions, changes, and combinations of ideas that inform me there are certain particular agents like my self, which accompany them and concur in their production. Hence the knowledge I have of other spirits is not immediate, as is the knowledge of my ideas; but depending on the intervention of ideas, by me referred to agents or spirits distinct from myself as effects or concomitant signs. (PHK 145)

Similarly in the *Three Dialogues*, he writes that 'we have neither an immediate evidence nor a demonstrative knowledge of the existence of other finite spirits', but he claims that 'there is a probability' that such spirits exist because 'we see signs and effects indicating distinct finite agents like our selves' (Dia 3, 233). So I am to believe in the existence of finite spirits other than myself because this explains my data better than any other hypothesis.

How does it do that? The simplest answer is that some facts about my ideas are best explained by supposing them to be caused by the activities of other finite spirits. We have seen Berkeley saying that some of my ideas are 'excited by', and are 'effects' of, other spirits. That sounds causal, but it had better not be, for reasons I have given in part. Even if he did allow that spirits can do something other than *will*, Berkeley would have to explain how one finite spirit can act upon another. God's ability to act on others can be swept under the theological rug;

but interaction of finite spirits is something else again, and Berkeley should hesitate to postulate it unless he has a theory about how it is possible.

When you and I both watch you clenching your fist (as we informally say), our visual states alter. Berkeley, we have seen, needs God to mediate between your volition and your visual idea, and equally to connect the volition to my idea. He cannot say that your unaided activity makes a difference to me; your 'effect' on me must be mediated by God.

Berkeley says so in a passage where he approaches the other minds problem by contraposition: from the indirectness of your experience of other human spirits, he concludes that you perceive God at least as directly as you do other humans. Then he pushes on to the stronger conclusion that we are *more* directly in touch with God than with one another, partly because it is God who 'maintains that intercourse between [human] spirits, whereby they are able to perceive the existence of each other' (*PHK* 147; see also 1732, LJ 3:145–8).

So Berkeley is not entitled to argue for the existence of other people before establishing the existence of God. Without his theology he has no account—not even a feeble one—of how your volitions relate to my ideas. He is not properly aware of this; in his argument, other finite spirits precede God. In *PHK* 145 he writes: 'I perceive several motions, changes, and combinations of ideas that inform me there are certain particular agents like myself, which accompany them and concur in their production.' In the *next* section he writes: 'But though there be some things which convince us human agents are concerned in producing them, yet it is evident to everyone that those things which are called the works of nature . . . are not produced by or dependent on the wills of men. There is therefore some other spirit that causes them.' Humans first, God next.

Reverse the order, and things go better: I invoke God to explain the general course of my experience; consulting the latter, I reach the further conclusion that God is motivated by his benevolence towards me; but I notice that some of my experience does not fit that conjecture; so I am led to the supplementary hypothesis that there are other finite spirits whose desires God sometimes acts to satisfy. This possibly Berkeleian line of argument was first presented, I think, by Lorne Falkenstein:

> Among our ideas of reality there are some, those of the motions of animate bodies, which exhibit a degree of irregularity, inconstancy of purpose, greed, stupidity, and sheer perversity which is simply inconsistent with the notion that these ideas are produced by a wise and benevolent being. One plausible way to deal with these phenomena is to postulate that there exist certain other spirits whose wills the divine spirit is disposed to indulge when moving animate bodies. (Falkenstein 1990: 438–9)[1]

One gets the general idea; but Falkenstein's phrase 'simply inconsistent with the notion that these ideas are produced by a wise and benevolent being' is wrong, for the next sentence postulates that the ideas in question *are* caused by such a being.

---

[1] Winkler 1989: 285–6 is also relevant.

Where many people argue from evil to the non-existence of God, Falkenstein's Berkeley argues from evil to the existence of people. This is not surprising. The existence of people is a useful resource for those who defend Christianity against the fact of evil.

Falkenstein relies on 'a degree of irregularity, inconstancy of purpose, greed, stupidity and sheer perversity'. That is broader than 'evil', but it is still too narrow. Some innocent human behaviour still seems pointless for a being like Berkeley's God. I see people walking along a trail beside a river, for several miles upstream and then down again. I ask why God in his goodness should organize that series of ideas for me, and I answer with this complex hypothesis: each of those animal bodies is related to a spirit in the same way as in my own case; those spirits want the experience of (as we informally say) open air, mountain streams, and so on; God in his goodness wants them to have their way, as I find he wants me to have mine; so he 'performs their wills' as he does mine. In performing their wills, he affects my ideas also, because of his overriding desire that the ideas of all finite spirits should be correlated so that they can (as we informally say) inhabit a single physical world.

This fits with Berkeley's evident commitment to saying that the only thing that people actively do is to alter their own ideas of thought and imagination; they do not move their legs themselves, and have no causal effect on anyone else's mind. In light of this, look at Berkeley writing that certain changes in my ideas lead me to believe that 'there are certain particular agents like myself which *accompany* [the changes] and *concur in* their production'. The terms which I have emphasized look like careful attempts to avoid crediting those 'agents' with any causal role in the affair.

Chapter 31

Berkeleian Sensible Things

225. Each sensible thing is a collection of ideas

How does Berkeley propose to establish the existence of books and fingers and boulders in an ontology in which basically there are only spirits and ideas? He sometimes claims to do this in a manner that does full justice to the beliefs of plain people about what there is in the world. 'I am not for depriving you of any one thing you perceive', Philonous tells Hylas (Dia 3, 235); and Berkeley jotted into his notebook that 'I side in all things with the Mob' (PC 405). Sometimes, especially in the *Three Dialogues*, he writes as though he were merely rescuing common sense from the clutches of materialist metaphysics. He describes his philosophy as 'this revolt from metaphysical notions to the plain dictates of nature and common sense' (Dia 1, 172). Then again later: 'I assure you, Hylas, I do not pretend to frame any hypothesis at all. I am of a vulgar cast, simple enough to believe my senses, and leave things as I find them' (Dia 3, 229). Berkeley here misrepresents his own work so blatantly that there is nothing for us to discuss.

Return now to the more moderate claim that Berkeley's philosophy is consistent with common sense. His offer to rescue us from scepticism is a poor affair if it takes the form: 'You can stop being doubtful about the existence of sticks and stones; the appropriate attitude is not sceptical doubt and worry but confident denial.' That is not what Berkeley means to say. He wants to assure plain folk of the existence of the things that they believe in—things like shoes and ships, with these understood in an immaterialist way. This rescue can succeed only if there is an immaterialist account of ordinary physical things such as houses and rocks, frogs and canoes. He does disagree with 'the Mob' in its 'opinion strangely prevailing' that sensible things can exist when nobody perceives them: he is forthright about that. Aside from this, however, he presents himself as aiming to side with the mob and as optimistic about his chances. Let us see.

If each sensible thing were an individual idea, plain people would be wrong in believing that a lake or a cockroach can be perceived by you and by me, yesterday and tomorrow, by sight and by touch. Berkeley often writes as though for him at least two of this trio of beliefs were secure in his philosophy:

The real things are those very things I see and feel, and perceive by my senses. These I know, and finding they answer all the necessities and purposes of life, have no reason to be solicitous about any other unknown beings. A piece of sensible bread, for instance, would stay my stomach better than ten thousand times as much of that insensible, unintelligible, real bread you speak of. . . . I, who understand by those words ['snow' and 'fire'] the things I see and feel, am obliged to think like other folks. . . . Wood, stones, fire, water, flesh, iron . . . are things that I know. And I should not have known them but that I perceived them by my senses. . . . I might as well doubt of my own being as of the being of those things I actually see and feel. (Dia 3, 229–30)

That explicitly allows perception to be inter-modal ('see and feel'), and implicitly allows it to be diachronic ('sensible bread' may 'stay my stomach'). There is plenty of this in Berkeley's texts. Interpersonal perception is harder to find there; I shall come to that later.

Berkeley tries to secure the trio of properties for sensible things by equating each thing with a 'collection' or 'combination' of ideas. This 'collection' concept has to work as follows. Any sensible thing is a collection of ideas whose membership can be represented like this:

$$\{I(t_m, p_m, s_m), I(t_n, p_n, s_n), \ldots, I(t_k, p_k, s_k)\}.$$

Each I-item refers to an idea that occurs at one time (t) to one person (p) in one sense modality (s). The t's need not all be different, nor need the p's or the s's; indeed, there cannot be many different s's. But nearly always there will be some differences, because most sensible things are perceived at different times, by different people, and through different senses; and the 'collection' theory is supposed to provide for this.

Berkeley does not often use the word 'collection(s)' in this way. The only occurrences are in *PHK* 1, 57, and 148, and one I shall quote later from the *New Theory of Vision*. But he expresses the same line of thought with 'combinations' of ideas; and he seems to rely on it when he insists, frequently, that his metaphysic squares with the plain man's careful beliefs except for his belief that sensible things can exist unperceived. For other examples of such plain-person down-to-earthery, see *PHK* 3, 5, and 40, and *Three Dialogues* 224, 228, and 249.

Now, what does it take for a given idea to belong to a thing-constituting collection? In answering this, Berkeley uses the phrase 'real things'. He also calls these 'sensible things', bringing 'real' into play when contrasting illusions and hallucinations with veridical sense perception. Here is the answer:

The ideas imprinted on the senses by the author of nature are called real things . . . [They] are nevertheless ideas, that is, they exist in the mind, or are perceived by it, as truly as the ideas of its own framing. The ideas of sense are allowed to have more reality in them, that is, to be more strong, orderly, and coherent than the creatures of the mind: but this is no argument that they exist without the mind. They are also less dependent on the spirit or thinking substance which perceives them, in that they are excited by the will of another and more powerful spirit: yet still they are ideas, and certainly no idea, whether faint or strong, can exist otherwise than in a mind perceiving it. (*PHK* 33)

These descriptions of ideas fall into two classes. One contains 'vivid', distinct', 'strong', and '[not] dependent', etc., each of which could be true of a single idea considered on its own. The other class contains 'regular', 'constant', 'orderly', and 'coherent', none of which can apply to a single idea but only to a number of ideas occurring at different times. Similarly at Dia 3, 235 we are given a first group containing 'faint', 'indistinct', 'dependent on the will', 'vivid', 'clear', 'dim', 'confused', 'lively', and 'natural'; and a second pair comprising 'irregular' and 'not connected and of a piece with the [rest] of our lives'. For Berkeley, we see, whether my present ideas are a perception of a real thing logically depends on what did or will happen at past and future times, as well as on what is happening now. This commits him to saying that real things are not single ideas, but collections of them.

The term 'regular' and its near-cognates tell us little about what it takes for several ideas to be members of (a collection which constitutes) one sensible thing; but Berkeley gives us nothing more. This might not matter if he could satisfy us as to how in principle the story could be told, showing that mere length and complexity—not any difficulties of principle—barred him from actually telling it. But he does not do that either. This is a serious lack in his 'collections' theory; but too much has been made of it in the secondary literature (including *LBH*). It is minor compared with two deeper problems confronting the theory that sensible things are collections of ideas.

226. Problems with collections

Let us pretend that we have a good account of what makes two ideas belong to a single thing-collection—an account implying that almost every such collection contains ideas had at different times, by different people, belonging to different sense modalities. Now for the problems.

(1) What can it be to perceive a sensible thing, if it is a collection of ideas? If no special provision is made for answering this, we must steer by the ordinary meanings of 'perceive', 'collection', and so on; and that will lead us to the answer that you perceive a collection only if you perceive every member of it. That would undercut the purpose of the theory, which was to achieve a maximal salvage of the plain person's beliefs. So Berkeley must stipulate an answer, saying what he will *count as* perceiving a sensible thing; and if he is to placate 'the Mob', he must stipulate that perceiving any one member of a sensible-thing collection counts as perceiving the thing.

There need be nothing wrong with stipulating a meaning for a theoretical purpose, but this stipulation of Berkeley's is semantically drastic. We have seen him deploring the practice of saying that one sees an item with which one's visual idea is connected through 'reason and memory'. His treatment of the 'picture of Caesar' example culminates in this: 'Those things alone are actually and strictly perceived by any sense, which would have been perceived in case that same sense had then been first conferred on us' (Dia 1, 204). This, it turned out, had to mean: *Strictly speaking, one is not perceiving an F unless one knows, without recourse to reason and memory, that what one is perceiving is an F* (§211). Berkeley insists on this line of thought more than once, offering it as something that we will accept as soon as we clear our minds. Yet now we find that it does not hold for the stipulated sense of 'perceive' which is at work in talk about perceiving houses and cherries.

If a house is a collection of ideas, I can at any one time perceive only a few its members, and I may not know whether the idea I perceive belongs to a real house or rather to a hallucination. I usually have strong grounds for the former, but they involve reason and memory. So if I ever perceive a house by perceiving a member of a real-house collection of ideas, I need reason and memory to tell me that what I am perceiving is a house. So it is not a case of perceiving a house by Berkeley's 'strict' standards, which he insists upon quite often, as here: 'Strictly speaking, Hylas, we do not see the same object that we feel' (Dia 3, 245).

So Berkeley is committed to holding that the sensible things that plain folk believe in—the ones he identifies with collections of ideas—are not things that anyone perceives, carefully and properly speaking. In his works, two senses of 'perceive' are at work, one for

x perceives [idea],

and one for

x perceives [sensible thing].

Only the latter has a chance of accommodating what plain folk believe about peninsulas and pineapples; but the former is what Berkeley insists on nearly everywhere, including the places (such as the 'Caesar' example) where he purports to be, and needs to be, using 'perceive' in a sense which ordinary people would accept. This should make us suspect that he is not serious about the stipulated sense of 'perceive' or, therefore, about the theory that sensible things are collections of ideas. This suspicion will take root and flower in my next section.

(2) What does it take for a sensible thing to exist at time T? Steering purely by the ordinary notion of what a collection is, Berkeley would have to answer that a sensible thing exists at T only if every member of it exists then. That would imply that no sensible thing lasts through time, thus subverting again the collection theory's purpose of rescuing the plain person's beliefs. So Berkeley has to stipulate once more, saying that 'A sensible thing exists now' is to *count as* true if . . . , with the blank filled by something weaker than 'every member of it exists now'.

How should he fill in the blank? The range of options is defeatingly large and complex, and I need to simplify. For my purposes, what matters is just this. Berkeley could stipulate for 'A shoe exists now' a meaning such that:

(a) A shoe can exist now only if at least one member of it exists now;

or he could give it a meaning such that:

(b) A shoe can exist now even though no member of it exists now, perhaps by stipulating that it suffices for the shoe's existing now that some of its members existed recently and others will exist soon. Option *a* requires that in the members of a complete thing-collection

$$\{I(t_m,p_m,s_m),\ I(t_n,p_n,s_n),\ \ldots,\ I(t_k,p_k,s_k)\}$$

the t-components shall form an unbroken sequence of short intervals—a sequence with no gaps in it. Option *b* would allow at least some gaps.

Berkeley chose *a*, writing off *b* as an indefensible 'opinion strangely prevailing'. But why? Either way, it is a stipulation—not something we reach by consulting the normal meanings of the various terms that are in play here. Why should he take the option which he knows puts him in conflict with a central feature of folk ontology: namely, the belief that sensible things can exist while not perceived? A stipulation of type *b* would require hard, inventive work to round out the story; but one might expect Berkeley to regard that as a small price to pay for rescuing so much of what ordinary people believe. Anyway, we have already seen that he is unaware of, or not interested in—and certainly not deterred by—such matters of detail.

It might be thought that he is absolutely barred from accepting option *b* by an argument of his. In this he purports to *prove* that sensible things cannot exist while not perceived, the proof being one that does not rely on anything like the choice of *a* over *b*. This is it:

There is nothing easier than to imagine . . . books existing in a closet and nobody by to perceive them. [But this is no] more than framing in your mind certain ideas which you call books . . . and at the same time omitting to frame the idea of any one that may perceive them. But do not you yourself perceive or think of them all the while? . . . [To] show that you can conceive it possible the objects of your thought may exist without the mind . . . it is necessary that you conceive them existing unconceived or unthought-of, which is a manifest repugnancy. (*PHK* 23)

This purports to prove, by one short snappy argument, that the existence of an unperceived book is inconceivable. The argument rests on a plain error. If it were valid, we could, by parity of argument, prove that it is impossible to tell the story of someone concerning whom no stories are told. Of course one can do that. Hardy wrote a story about Jude, and it was *part of that story* that no stories were told about Jude ('the Obscure'). Berkeley has similarly inferred that because you are conceiving something, the content of your conception must include the thing's being conceived. This argument also involves the running together of perception with conception, but I need not press the point because the rest is so bad. I am reluctant to think that it carried weight with Berkeley. Had he ever taken option *b* seriously, he would have seen what is wrong with the 'conceive them existing unconceived' argument.

The two difficulties discussed in this section are evidence that Berkeley did not mean his treatment of 'sensible things' to be a central and significant part of his philosophy. No doubt he valued the entitlement that he intermittently thought he had to reassure plain folk that he believed in everything they believe in; but it is beginning to appear that he did not even try to earn that entitlement by thinking hard about what an immaterialist account of foxes and hillocks and snow banks must look like.

227. Berkeley's disrespect towards 'sensible thing'

In his *New Theory of Vision* Berkeley asserts the 'picture of Caesar' principle, as we might call it:

A man born blind, and afterwards when grown up made to see, would not in the first act of vision parcel out the ideas of sight into the same distinct collections that others do, who have experienced which do regularly coexist and are proper to be bundled up together under one name. He would not, for example, . . . [unite] all those particular ideas which constitute the visible head or foot. For there can be no reason assigned why he should do so, barely upon his seeing a man stand upright before him: there crowd into his mind the ideas which compose the visible man, in company with all the other ideas of sight perceived at the same time: but all these ideas offered at once to his view, he would not distribute into sundry distinct combinations, till such time as, by observing the motion of the parts of the man and other experiences, he comes to know which are to be separated and which to be collected together. (*NT* 110)

This says that we come to 'parcel out' or 'distribute' ideas into 'collections' or 'combinations', but it does not say that we perceive the latter; and indeed, it offers to explain why we could not do so. In the same work Berkeley says that 'we never see and feel one and the same object' (49), and that 'The things I see are . . . very different and heterogeneous from the things I feel' (108).

This stands in striking contrast to the 'collection' element in the *Principles* and *Three Dialogues*. If that element belongs to Berkeley's seriously considered and valued philosophical position, then the latter must have shifted a lot between the first work and the next two. I contend that there was no shift, and that in the later works the 'collections' account of sensible things is marginal rhetoric, rather than central philosophy. Look again at some of the texts. Here is the first:

As several of these [ideas] are observed to accompany each other, they come to be marked by one name, and so to be reputed as one thing. Thus, for example, a certain colour, taste, smell, figure, and consistence having been observed to go together, are accounted one distinct thing, signified by the name apple. Other collections of ideas constitute a stone, a tree, a book, and the like sensible things. (*PHK* 1)

The members of a collection of ideas, Berkeley says here, 'come to be . . . reputed as one thing' or are 'accounted one distinct thing'. This is the idiom of an anthropologist's report—a mere description of a tribe's verbal and intellectual practice. So when he goes on to say that such collections 'constitute' stones and trees, etc., we can reasonably read that as short for 'are deemed to constitute'.

Philonous says that 'Strictly speaking, we do not see the same object that we feel', and goes on to explain how demotic metaphysics came to part company with this truth (Dia 1, 245). To avoid certain 'inconveniencies', he says, 'men combine together several ideas, apprehended by divers senses, or by the same sense at different times, or in different circumstances, . . . all which they refer to one name, and consider as one thing'. He suggests that Hylas and other materialists do not 'rightly understand the common language of men speaking of several distinct ideas as united into one thing by the mind', and of building a metaphysic 'not so much on notions as words, which were framed by the vulgar merely for conveniency and despatch in the common actions of life, without any regard to speculation'.

Berkeley does not here endorse plain people's belief in sensible things—he condescends to it. His casually dismissive attitude towards folk metaphysics rests on two views of his: that what you and I believe about wheels and smoke and mountains results from how we talk, and that the point of talking as we do is merely to achieve 'conveniency and despatch in the common actions of life'. These are both false. Our folk ontology would serve us well even if we had no language; and what it gives us is not mere ease and speed, but some chance of survival.

At the end of the excerpt Berkeley declares that ordinary ways of speech, though pragmatically justified, do not aim at truth. They are not devised with 'any regard for speculation', which is why philosophical beliefs based on them are apt to be 'erroneous conceits'. Nobody would write like this who thought that accurate truth conditions for plain talk could be constructed, in terms of 'collections of ideas', within the true philosophy. In these passages, therefore, the 'collections' account of sensible things belongs to sociology, not philosophy; to linguistic convenience, not truth.

Several times in the two main works the double theme appears: demotic metaphysics is a product of talk, and the advantage of the talk is just that it makes life easier. That attitude could sap Berkeley's will to try to explain in immaterialist terms the truth conditions for plain talk about daffodils and elbows and oceans. I believe it did: at no time did he seriously consider providing in immaterialist terms for what you and I say about sensible things. I shall try to clarify this.

Here is a possible position for Berkeley to adopt:

On the metaphysical ground floor there are no shoes or ships, and using only ground-floor concepts it must be admitted that ideas can be perceived and shoes cannot. Using 'strict' to mean something like 'basic', I say that strictly we do not perceive shoes. Still, the ground floor provides the means for stating, in terms of the basic set of concepts, truth conditions for plain talk about shoes and the rest. That is, I can construct a sensible-thing concept out of the materials provided at the immaterialist ground floor.

That would be like the situation of Spinoza, who held that 'There are bodies that move through space' is not basically true, because basically there is only one extended thing, namely Space; and the superficial fact that bodies move through space is, at the ground-floor level, the fact that there are alterations in which regions of space are 'thick' and which 'thin' (§54). According to this metaphysic, statements about moving bodies have precise truth conditions—they are not vague or shabby, but merely non-basic, like statements about rumours, epidemics, and freezes.

This position is consistent with immaterialism. But I have offered evidence that Berkeley did not adopt it. He gestures towards the project of constructing sensible things out of his basic ontology—so far as concerns their having histories and their being interpersonally and inter-modally observable—but he does no work on it, and does not trouble to keep it clear of what he mainly says about what can be perceived. And when it comes to the common view that sensible things can exist when not perceived, Berkeley turns his back on the plainly open avenues towards a solution. In particular, he does not reach for the glittering prize of an account of thing-collections which allows for one to exist when not perceived by anyone. If the 'collections' account can be made to work at all, it can be made to yield this result. Yet Berkeley, rather than trying for it, dismisses this part of the world scheme of the vulgar as something they should give up.

In his published works, I contend, Berkeley had little interest in rescuing the plain person's beliefs about sensible things. He did not want to connect them rigorously with his ontology, or even to show that this could in principle be done. Rather than thinking of them as Spinoza thought of 'bodies moving through space', or as we all think of 'epidemics', his attitude was more like that of intelligent people to the question 'When does human life begin?' The mob ask that question, treat it as important, and presumably mean something by it; but whatever they mean is so sloppy and various and undisciplined that it would be a waste of our time to try to express it rigorously in clear language. Although we acknowledge that this way of speaking exists, and admit that it has some structure, our attitude to it is dismissive.

Berkeley's fundamental attitude to the plain person's trees and stones, in the deployment of his philosophy, was this disrespectful one. Once outside his study and walking along the street, he was no doubt wedded to the scheme of continuant and interpersonally perceivable things; he could not have survived otherwise. My conjecture does not concern that, but only the intellectual attitudes at work in Berkeley's philosophy.

228. The vulgar sense of 'same'

A good Berkeleian account of sensible things in terms of 'collections of ideas' would have to provide for a single sensible thing to be perceived by two people, or at two times, or in different sense modalities. In one place Berkeley directly confronts the interpersonal part of this, and his treatment implies something for the other two as well.

Hylas has issued this challenge: 'Does it not . . . follow from your principles that no two can see the same thing? And is not this highly absurd?' (Dia 3, 247). The best and most Berkeleian reply would be this:

I have shown it to be true that no two can see the same thing, and what is true is not absurd. If it sounds absurd to you for a moment, that is because you have drifted from true metaphysics to plain folks' ways of thinking. We can allow for those within the true metaphysic by introducing the concept of a kind of *thing* that is not found on the imma-terialist ground floor, a concept that includes that of a kind of *perceiving* that is also not found there. In terms of those things, and that kind of perceiving, two can indeed see the same thing.

Philonous's actual reply starts in that manner:

If the term *same* be taken in the vulgar acceptation, it is certain (and not at all repugnant to the principles I maintain) that different persons may perceive the same thing; or the same thing or idea exist in different minds. Words are of arbitrary imposition; and since men are used to apply the word *same* where no distinction or variety is perceived, and I do not pretend to alter their perceptions, it follows that as men have said before, *several saw the same thing*, so they may upon like occasions still continue to use the same phrase, without any deviation either from propriety of language or the truth of things.

This implies that when ordinary people say things like 'You and I can both see it', they mainly mean that their sensory states are indistinguishably alike. This is off the mark—yet another example of Berkeley's underrating the complexity and subtlety of our common world-view. Still, the general drift seems appropriate for him, whether he is taking the respectful or the disrespectful attitude to the 'vulgar' ways of speaking.

Here is what Philonous should go on to say:

But if we confine ourselves to the kinds of things and the kinds of perceiving that are sanctioned by *basic* immaterialist metaphysics, then—you are right about this—no two can perceive the same thing.

What he actually says next is strikingly different:

But if the term *same* be used in the acceptation of philosophers, who pretend to an abstracted notion of identity, then, according to their sundry definitions of this notion (for it is not yet agreed wherein that philosophic identity consists), it may or may not be possible for divers persons to perceive the same thing. But whether philosophers shall think fit to call a thing the same or no, is, I conceive, of small importance. (Dia 3, 247)

Any competent reader must have a sense that this performance is twisty, not quite honest. Still, let us learn from it what we can.

The first trouble is that Berkeley thinks the issue concerns different senses of 'same'. In fact, all parties are employing the ordinary, central, familiar, uncontroversial concept of identity—the one we use in saying that the square of 2 is 4, that the kelp now lying in the sun is the stuff we were diving for six hours ago, and that it was you who advised me to invest in asbestos. Debates about personal identity do not concern a kind of identity, or a sense of 'identity'; they are about what a person is. Frege, inquiring after identity-conditions for numbers, said he wanted to clarify the concept of number by linking it with our all-purpose concept of identity, which is clear already (1884: 74). A dispute about 'perceiving the same thing', therefore, is a dispute about 'thing' and perhaps 'perceive', not about 'same'.

(Berkeley makes a similar mistake about the meaning of 'exist': 'The various sensations or ideas imprinted on the sense . . . cannot exist otherwise than in a mind perceiving them. I think an intuitive knowledge may be obtained of this by any one that shall attend to what is meant by the term *exist*, when applied to sensible things' (*PHK* 3). This implies that 'exist' is ambiguous: we are to attend to what it means in one of its senses. The view that 'exist' is ambiguous is a grave error, though it used to be common. Morton White devoted much of a book (1956) to combating the view—prevalent in mid-twentieth-century Oxford—that 'Minds exists' and 'Bodies exist' use 'exist' in different senses; and many philosophers have thought that universals, numbers, and possibilities 'exist' in a sense so special that we should use a different word, 'subsist', for it. There is no ground for any of this. Existence conditions for minds differ from those for bodies, but that is because minds are radically unlike bodies; similarly for numbers and bottles, gods and creatures.)

Secondly, Philonous makes room only for (1) vulgar identity statements and (2) statements using a vicious abstracted notion invented by philosophers; he answers comfortably in terms of 1, and gives the back of his hand to 2. Now, 'abstracted' means almost nothing; here, as in most places, the word is just a label that Berkeley slaps on to a concept before pushing it off a cliff. The more general thesis is that when the 'vulgar acceptation' is set aside, there remain only questions involving a (supposed) concept of identity that is artificial, unexplained, and controversial. This is nasty, because Berkeley does not believe it. He frequently employs the identity-concept at his own basic metaphysical level. 'Strictly speaking, . . . we do not see the same object that we feel.'

Having implied that philosophers should shut up once the plain person has spoken, Philonous switches (after the quoted passage) to a more even-handed treatment. It does not matter which side one takes, he implies, for they are equally respectable. He invites us to consider a number of people 'all endued with the same faculties' who therefore have similar sensory histories. At first they have no language, but they 'agree in their perceptions'. Then they acquire language, and a split occurs: in a particular situation some will say 'We perceive *the same* thing' because of the similarity of our ideas; whereas others will say 'We perceive *different* things' because of our distinctness from one another. Put like this, Philonous says, the issue is patently verbal and thus trivial: 'Who sees not that all the dispute is about a word; to wit, whether what is perceived by different persons may yet have the term *same* applied to it?' He likens this to a second example, where a 'same or different?' issue is more plainly trivial:

Suppose a house, whose walls or outward shell remaining unaltered, the chambers are all pulled down and new ones built in their place; and that you should call this the *same* and

I should say it was not the *same* house: would we not for all this perfectly agree in our thoughts of the house, considered in itself? And would not all the difference consist in a sound? (Dia 3, 248)

The same / different dispute over the house does strike us as verbal and trivial; but the reason for this does not carry over to the dispute about whether two people can perceive the same thing.

For one thing, the issue about 'same house' seldom arises: we are usually unanimous about whether the house that was F at T_1 is the one that was G at T_2. Also, we could legislate in advance for every dispute about this that did arise. Using our concepts of sameness of planks, beams, shingles, and so on, we could set out precise conditions for sameness of house, yielding a definitive answer to every actual question of the form 'Is it the same house?' (Not every possible question about sameness of house—no finite set of rules could do that.) This would be pointless, but we could do it.

By contrast with this, the serious issue about 'perceiving the same thing' divides those who think that countless things are, from those who think that nothing is, perceived by more than one person. There is no way of legislating something that would make the issue go away. If there were a 'same house' dispute, it would arise from different placings of a borderline; but the 'perceived by the same person' dispute is nothing like that.

Secondly, Berkeleian same-house disputes would make no difference to our lives. The Hall of Languages had its floors and inner walls replaced. Probably the inhabitants all think of it as still the same building, but perhaps some think that the old Hall of Languages has been replaced by a new one with the old name and outer shell. Who cares? The issue about interpersonal perception of a single thing is not like this. We cannot simply walk away from it and get on with our lives. The concept of 'same object' is woven into our talk and thought and feeling and conduct so intimately that we cannot live without it.

229. The continuity of sensible things

Berkeley's 'collections' account of sensible things, such as it is, implies that a thing-collection can be perceived (and thus can exist) at a time when most of its members do not exist. Having stipulated this, I have pointed out, he could have gone a step further, stipulating senses of 'perceive' and 'exist' that would allow for a collection to exist at a time when none of its members do. Yet his writings contain no hint of this way of dealing with the continuity question—that is, the question of whether sensible things can exist continuously through gaps in our perceptions of them. This would be a remarkable omission if he were seriously concerned to reconcile his serious metaphysic with plain people's beliefs.

In fact, he is not. He mentions the continuity question only at the shallow end of his philosophy, where he is casually gesturing towards what ordinary people think and say. I shall discuss these passages, partly because it is philosophically instructive to do so, and partly because I want to show that this is indeed the shallow end, and that Berkeley saw it as such. Objection: 'If Berkeley was not dead serious about what ordinary folk believe, why did he put care and energy into considering how sensible things can exist when none of us perceive them?' The answer is that he did no such thing; this supposed care and energy is mythical. Writers who have disagreed with me about this (e.g., McCracken 1979: 291) have mistaken Berkeley's rhetoric for working philosophy.

He simply did not much care about this issue, and did not allow the continuity of sensible things as a legitimate premiss for himself or for plain folk. In *PHK* 6 he fleetingly mentions the possibility that God's ideas enable sensible things to be continuous; the sections that follow include some strenuous ones about scepticism and about the reality of sensible things; but none of this concerns continuity. The latter comes to the fore only in *PHK* 45, where Berkeley introduces it as a new issue: 'Fourthly, it will be objected that from the foregoing principles it follows, things are every moment annihilated and created anew.' Summing up later his treatment of this, he refers back to 'the objection proposed in Sect. 45', not to 'the objection discussed throughout the past fifteen or more sections'. Now let us see what happens in the sections on continuity.

Berkeley is accused of implying that 'things are every moment annihilated and created anew. . . . Upon shutting my eyes all the furniture in the room is reduced to nothing, and barely upon opening them it is again created.' Rather than replying, 'Of course that would be absurd, but I am not committed to it', Berkeley counter-attacks:

If [my accuser] can conceive it possible either for his ideas or their archetypes to exist without being perceived, then I give up the cause: but if he cannot, he will acknowledge it is unreasonable for him to stand up in defence of he knows not what, and pretend to charge on me as an absurdity the not assenting to those propositions which at bottom have no meaning in them. (*PHK* 45)

Only after arguing through two over-ingenious sections that 'the materialists themselves' are committed to denying that sensible things can be continuous, does Berkeley remark that he is not thus committed:

Though we hold indeed the objects of sense to be nothing else but ideas which cannot exist unperceived; yet we may not hence conclude they have no existence except only while they are perceived by us, since there may be some other spirit that perceives them, though we do not. Wherever bodies are said to have no existence without the mind, I would not be understood to mean this or that particular mind, but all minds whatsoever. It does not therefore follow from the foregoing principles that bodies are annihilated and created every moment, or exist not at all during the intervals between our perception of them. (*PHK* 48)

The crucial expressions are 'we may not hence *conclude*', 'there *may* be some other spirit', 'it does not therefore *follow*'. Berkeley does not allow that his accusers are making a just demand or, therefore, that it is important for him to meet it.

He does not even say something like this: 'My accusers have no grounds for their correct belief that objects are continuous. My principles show that the belief can be justified only on theological grounds; in a way, it is itself a covertly theological belief. I wonder how my materialistic opponents like that!' That cries out to be said by an immaterialist who respects the common belief that objects are continuous; and this is the place for it. But Berkeley nowhere argues like that—with one tiny exception to which I now turn.

230. The continuity argument

It used to be widely accepted that Berkeley not only cared about the continuity of sensible things, but argued from it to the existence of God. Things exist when we do not perceive them; so at that time some other being perceives them; so . . . somehow we get through, with help from natural theology, to the conclusion that one other spirit does all this perceiving, and that it is divine. Although this 'continuity argument', as I call it, used to appear conspicuously in commentaries and textbooks, it is almost invisible in Berkeley's texts.

Let us think first about its premiss, that sensible things *do* exist continuously through gaps in human perception of them. We have seen Berkeley giving short shrift not only to this proposition, but also to the question to which it is an answer. When writing the *Philosophical Commentaries* he did care about continuity, and alluded to the problem often. (The evidence is assembled in *LBH* 188–98, a treatment which is somewhat expanded in Tipton 1974: 321–49.) But he later dropped this interest.

He was bound to do so, given his view that sensible things are either single ideas or shakily constructed collections of them, and given that it did not occur to him to reconcile 'collections' idealism with continuity in the manner proposed in §226. We have seen that Berkeley sometimes writes that his immaterialism secures the sensible things that we all believe in; and no doubt he would like his philosophy to leave the thoughtful plain man's scheme of things undisturbed. But he intermittently realized that he could not achieve this. Listen to him:

[Sceptical worries] vanish if we do not maintain the being of absolute external originals, but place the reality of things in ideas, fleeting indeed, and changeable; however not changed at random, but according to the fixed order of nature. For herein consists that constancy and truth of things, which secures all the concerns of life, and distinguishes that which is real from the irregular visions of the fancy. (Dia 3, 258)

This highlights Berkeley's strong tendency to equate sensible things with single ideas. In calling them 'fleeting', he turns his back on collections, and shows himself to be thinking of each sensible thing as a single idea; and this is the version of immaterialism that he needs for the arguments he emphasizes most. I mean his *philosophical* arguments, not the rhetorical assurances that he is preserving our ordinary beliefs. In the above passage he drops that rhetoric, and talks not about what we believe, but rather about what we want—'the concerns of life'—namely, that 'fleeting' things will not subject us to horrid surprises.

In so far as he consents to ask the continuity question—that is, down at the shallow end—Berkeley ought to realize that by his standards there cannot be empirical evidence for continuity, so it poses no problem for him. He ought to think that he could persuade ordinary people that their belief in the continuity of sensible things is wholly unjustified. If he did think this, that would encourage him to downplay this part of his reconciling endeavour. That in turn might explain something else which I have not so far mentioned.

Most of what Berkeley does say about continuity consists in his waving in the plain person's face the thought that God's perceptions *could* secure the existence of sensible things at times when nobody else perceives them. Even this mild position is something to which he is not entitled, and he could hardly have overlooked that if he were taking this reconciliation seriously.

In a treatment of the first five days of creation, Philonous confronts a certain difficulty about what can have been involved in God's creating trees on the third day. He does not suggest that this might have consisted in certain ideas' coming into the mind of God; and he makes clear why. The following sentences, though one appears in the text as a rhetorical question, all express Berkeley's convictions: 'God knew all things from eternity . . . Consequently they always had a being in the Divine Intellect. . . . Therefore, nothing is new, or begins to be, in respect of the mind of God' (Dia 3, 253). Because there are no changes in God's mind, the notion of a datable creation must be construed as something other than 'coming to be perceived or imagined by God'. That is why Berkeley has to tackle the creation differently (§233).

The premiss that 'all things . . . always had a being in the Divine Intellect' destroys Berkeley's reconciling gesture—the one saying that sensible things could exist when we do not perceive them because God could take up the slack. Wanting to be sure that lovely Rock Pond still exists while there are no hikers or boaters to experience it, I am now offered a way of thinking that it may exist right now—along with the oatmeal I ate for breakfast on my fourteenth birthday and the flowers that will some day be laid on my grave. This is no comfort. I want to rescue the pond while not rescuing that oatmeal as late as now, or those flowers so early.

Berkeley does not lump all ideas together: he distinguishes ideas of sense from ideas of imagination and intellectual activity. But he cannot divide God's ideas in that way, because his sense/imagination line divides passive from active, involuntary from voluntary; and Berkeley holds that God is in no way passive. He evidently has no other basis for sorting ideas of God's into two species that would serve the present purpose.

So he is not entitled even to the mild thesis that sensible things *could* exist when creatures do not perceive them; and I think he knew this. The texts purporting to reconcile continuity with immaterialism are throw-away remarks, quick attempts to keep certain opponents at bay without always treating their objection with the contempt that Berkeley thinks it deserves. We get nearer to his considered position in *PHK* 45, where the continuity objection is flung back in the objector's teeth.

In the light of all this, it would be astonishing and disgraceful if Berkeley employed the 'continuity argument', inferring God's existence from the premiss that sensible things exist when no creature perceives them. So it is a relief to find that he does not ever argue like that—well, hardly ever. When I first pointed this out in my 1965a and again in *LBH*, I allowed one exception: a passage where the continuity argument seems to be present, though only for a moment and only as a kind of flickering cloud. The passage in question is puzzling, and perhaps worth study. It starts thus:

Hylas: Supposing you were annihilated, cannot you conceive it possible that things perceivable by sense may still exist?

Philonous: I can; but then it must be in another mind. When I deny sensible things an existence out of the mind, I do not mean my mind in particular, but all minds. (Dia 3, 230)

After I die, sensible things could still exist because perceived by other people; but Berkeley here, through the singular phrase 'another mind', hints at the job's being done by God. And what God could do for Rock Pond after I die, he could do for it when everyone's back is turned. Philonous is not yet trying to prove anything—merely mentioning a basis on which things *could* exist while he does not perceive them. He continues: 'Now it is plain [1] they have an existence exterior to my mind, since [2] I find them by experience to be independent of it.' This is strange. Philonous argues from 2 to 1, but 2 concerns the causation of his ideas, while 1 concerns their existing 'exterior to' his mind. What can he be up to? Nothing will save this inference, but we can understand it. The crucial fact is that when Berkeley uses 'depend on' and its cognates in relating ideas to minds, he sometimes means 'caused by' and sometimes 'exist in'. (This ambiguity was pointed out in Day 1952–3: 448 and Grey 1952: 344. For details, see *LBH* 167–9.) It seems that in this argument he expresses his involuntariness premiss 2 using 'independent of' in the causation sense; he tacitly moves from 'they are independent of my mind' to 'they depend on some other mind', still in the causation sense; and then he thinks of this in its existence sense, in which it is equivalent to 1. Not a creditable performance, but there is no other way to make sense of the passage.

Philonous has now reached the conclusion that his ideas of sense 'have an existence exterior to my mind'. Even if the play with 'independent' were valid, all he would have shown is that every such idea exists in some other mind at the moment when it enters his mind. This is irrelevant to Hylas's question about the existence of sensible things when Philonous (and, by implication, every other human) does *not* perceive them. Philonous continues, however, with something that manifestly is relevant to that:

There is therefore some other mind wherein they exist during the intervals between the times of my perceiving them: as likewise they did before my birth, and would do after my supposed annihilation. And as the same is true with regard to all other finite created spirits, it necessarily follows, there is an omnipresent, eternal Mind, which knows and comprehends all things, and exhibits them to our view.

This, together with the preliminaries, is what I have offered as Berkeley's one use of the continuity argument.

Noel Fleming (1985) has contended that the 'continuity argument' is not present even here. He points out that nothing in the whole passage has any tendency to show that any idea existed in 'some other mind' when not perceived by any human. Its entire force is confined to the time when the idea is forced in upon my mind; and this, Fleming argues, is so obvious that Berkeley cannot have thought otherwise. He concludes that my thesis about the paucity of uses of the 'continuity argument' for God's existence in Berkeley's pages is even truer than I had thought.

I would like to agree, but I do not. Hylas has raised a question about things' existing when Philonous does not perceive them, and Philonous purports to be answering it. The first part of what he says is indeed unresponsive to Hylas's question; but Philonous goes on from there to claims which are saturated with the continuity thought, and his bridges to them are 'therefore' and 'It necessarily follows'. Fleming shows that the argument is even worse than I at first realized—the play on 'independent' is not the whole of its trouble. But I remain convinced that it is meant to be the continuity argument.

231. Idealism and phenomenalism

Now we come to a topic where the difference between single ideas and collections of them can be ignored. I want to contrast what I shall call 'idealism', which is the form of immaterialism which holds that each sensible thing is either an idea or a collection of them, with a different form of immaterialism, commonly known as 'phenomenalism'. Berkeley seems to think that both Singleton and Collection idealism (as I shall call them) imply that no sensible thing can exist while not perceived by anyone, even God; but nobody could think that phenomenalism implies that.

According to phenomenalism, 'ST exists now' is true so long as enough things of the form 'If it were the case that P now, an idea of kind K would be had now' are true; and they could be true at a time when no K ideas were actually being had. Such conditionals let us make sense of the idea of a thing's existing while not perceived (and even existing without ever being perceived). Singleton idealism has no such resources, and Berkeley evidently assumes that Collection idealism lacks them too. Other things that we ordinarily want to say about sensible things can also be coped with better by phenomenalism than by either form of idealism.

For example, the statement that from this position the road looks wet though really it is not: even Collection idealism will make a clumsy job of that, whereas phenomenalism can take it in its stride.

Each of the two forms of immaterialism is committed to this general position:

> GP: Any statement about a sensible thing is equivalent to some statement that can be expressed in the language of 'ideas', without using any physicalistic concepts.

Berkeley would not put it quite like that, and a twentieth-century phenomenalist would not use the term 'idea'—he would be more likely to speak of 'sense data' or 'sensory states'. Still, GP is one way of expressing what the two have in common, bringing out their shared view that what we have to say about shoes and ships and cabbages commits us only to a fundamental reality that is all mental.

Some commentators have thought that while phenomenalism is a thesis about meanings, or about concepts, idealism is offered as a contingent statement of fact, or at least as being substantive in some way that debars it from depending purely upon meanings or upon conceptual analysis. I want no part of that. Berkeley certainly thought of his idealism as an upshot of facts about meanings—he offered it as analytic, as we might say today, just like phenomenalism in that respect. (See *PHK* 24, 45, 54, 88, 89.) Not only Berkeley, but also Leibniz, explicitly makes phenomenalism a doctrine about meanings (see L 605). I offer those facts as an antidote to this: 'Today phenomenalism is pap about the analysis of words. It was once a strong claim about the world. Berkeley thought the world was made only of mental stuff' (Hacking 1976: 141). The supposed 'pap' about the meanings of words connects with a 'claim about the world' as follows. From a phenomenalist or idealist analysis of all our beliefs and statements about the objective realm, it follows that *nothing we say or believe conflicts with the thesis that the world is made only of mental stuff*. That is not the whole of Berkeley's defence of idealism, but he rightly saw it as a large part of it.

Now, phenomenalism involves GP, because the latter follows from this more specific position:

> Phenomenalism: Any statement about a sensible thing is equivalent to a complex of conditional statements about what ideas would be had if such and such other ideas were had.

This freely allows that a sensible thing might exist while nobody has any relevant ideas, that is, while nobody perceives it, and even if nobody ever perceives it. Phenomenalism does imply that sensible things must be perceivable, but that is less drastically implausible than any form of idealism which implies that they must always be perceived.

Berkeley's idealism also includes GP, but derives it from a premiss with which phenomenalism is inconsistent. For Singleton idealism, the source of GP is this:

Singleton idealism: Any statement of the form F(ST), where ST is a sensible thing, is equivalent to one of the form F(I), where I is an idea and F is the same predicate on each side of the equivalence.

Berkeley does not express idealism in terms of equivalence; but this is a fair statement of Singleton idealism, and it helps me to contrast it with phenomenalism. In so far as Berkeley's position is Collection idealism, his source for GP is something along these lines:

Collection idealism: Any statement of the form F(ST), where ST is a sensible thing, is equivalent to one of the form $F^*\{I_1, I_2, \ldots\}$, where each I_n is an idea, and F^* is systematically related to F in some constraining way.

I cannot make this more precise, but it suffices to make the point that even Collection idealism severely constrains what statements about ideas can figure in the analysis of statements about sensible things. Some of the equivalences to which Berkeley plausibly thinks he is committed sound ludicrous, as he realizes:

But, say you, it sounds very harsh to say we eat and drink ideas, and are clothed with ideas. I acknowledge it does so, the word *idea* not being used in common discourse to signify the several combinations of sensible qualities which are called *things*: and it is certain that any expression which varies from the familiar use of language will seem harsh and ridiculous. (*PHK* 38)

Phenomenalism, on the other hand, though it implies that 'I ate an apple' is equivalent to *some* complex statement about ideas, does not imply that we eat ideas, whether nibbling at them singly or wolfing them down in collections. It is patently a better version of immaterialism than either form of idealism. Still, phenomenalism confronts three difficulties which we should look at.

The equivalences which it announces are never fully stated, even for a single sensible-thing statement. One reason is that the conditionals must be expressed purely in terms of ideas or sensory states. One might be tempted to say something like 'If I were to go into my study, I should have an idea of kind K', but that speaks of 'my study', which belongs in the analysandum and thus not in the analysans. That conditional would have to be replaced by something of the form 'If I had such and such visual, tactual and kinaesthetic states, I should then have an idea of kind K', where the antecedent describes the experiential equivalent of my going into my study. The task of writing all this out for just one sensible-thing sentence is worse than daunting. Still, the phenomenalist might say that it is a problem in practice rather than in theory: the equivalences exist, even if we cannot exhibit them; and that is a significant result.

A deeper trouble is this. Phenomenalism aims to rescue sensible-thing statements from having truth conditions that outrun all possible evidence, and thus to spare us from the worst kind of scepticism. So its main thrust is towards getting into the *meaning* of statement S all the sensory *evidence* that one could have for its truth—that is, to equate S with the proposition that most of those evidential statements are true. But we never know for sure what all the sensory statements are that would be evidence for a given sensible-thing statement; what would count as evidence may depend upon technology not yet invented. When such an advance is made, does the meaning of S change? Surely not! Nor is it plausible to say that the actual meaning of S involves only experiential conditionals of a specially basic, elementary, untechnical sort which are all known already. This trouble need not be fatal, however, if the phenomenalist stops offering outright *equivalences* or biconditionals, and settles for many one-way conditionals in each direction. (For some details, see my 1979.)

The third difficulty may be lethal. It is usually thought that a counterfactual conditional can be true only if some non-conditional truth makes it so. If it is true that *If this sugar cube were put into hot water it would dissolve*, that must be because of how the sugar is (actually, categorically, non-hypothetically) structured. Now, in the ordinary affairs of life we believe many conditionals about what our sensory state would be if . . . , and there is no mystery about how these are grounded. Why am I sure that if I had a K-type sequence of ideas, I would next have an idea of kind L? Well, for different values of K and L the grounding will be something like *there is a table in my study* or *the tide is high* or *the car has been repaired*. Phenomenalism, however, cannot ground its conditionals in any such way as this, for an obvious reason. Plenty of phenomenalists, back in the days when there were lots of them, seemed to hold that their counterfactuals about experience are not grounded, and express the most fundamental facts about the material world. This now looks radical and incredible to most of us. Leibniz knew better (see G 1:370), but I was first alerted to the point by MacKenzie (1978).

Even if the need for grounding is fatal to the phenomenalism of Mill and Ayer, however, it would not be so for that of Berkeley if indeed he was a phenomenalist—for he could ground his conditionals in God. According to him, all my ideas of sensible things are caused by God; so he could hold that counterfactuals about ideas are made true by non-conditional facts about God's actual plans. What makes it the case that *If I had a K-type sequence of ideas, I would next have an idea of kind L, rather than one of kind M*, is some fact about how God is now, not a mere fact about how he would behave if . . . Quite generally, God-based forms of phenomenalism can deny that conditionals are ever the fundamental truth about anything, and can give them a firm non-dispositional grounding. When in the *Philosophical Commentaries* Berkeley did consider phenomenalism, it was often in this God-based form (see LBH 188–98).

So phenomenalism has advantages over idealism from Berkeley's immaterialist standpoint; and of the difficulties we have found in the former, two are superable while the third does not exist for Berkeley. A question naturally arises, namely . . .

232. Was Berkeley a phenomenalist?

Mostly he was not, but the story is complex. Vaguely phenomenalistic entries occur at intervals throughout the first half of the *Philosophical Commentaries*. Sometimes he actually uses conditionals of the sort used by phenomenalism, though not always with an 'if'; sometimes he equates the sensible things with 'powers', meaning dispositions, which are reported in conditionals. Here are some examples:

> 'Bodies etc. do exist even when not perceived, they being powers in the active Being' (52).
> 'The trees are in the park, that is, whether I will or no, whether I imagine anything about them or no, let me but go thither and open my eyes by day and I shall not avoid seeing them' (98).
> 'Bodies etc. do exist whether we think of 'em or no, they being taken in a twofold sense. Collections of thoughts and collections of powers to cause those thoughts' (282).
> 'The twofold signification of bodies, viz. combinations of thoughts and combinations of powers to raise thoughts' (293).

These show that at one stage Berkeley seriously, if intermittently, considered the phenomenalist form of immaterialism. But he does not announce it as his considered view in the published works; he evidently changed his mind.

There is a passing turn of phrase that suggests phenomenalism, early in the *Principles*: 'The table I write on, I say, exists, that is, I see and feel it; and if I were out of my study I should say it existed, meaning thereby that if I was in my study I might perceive it, or that some other spirit actually does perceive it' (*PHK* 3). But Berkeley does not cash in on that and develop it into a theoretical option. In the same section he says that it is essential to sensible things that they be perceived. Notice also that the conditional he uses here involves slapdash phenomenalism at best, because it has 'study' in the analysans.

Phenomenalism comes to mind again when Berkeley equates 'the question whether the earth moves' with the question

whether we have reason to conclude from what hath been observed by astronomers that if we were placed in such and such circumstances, and such or such a position and distance both from the earth and sun, we should perceive the former to move among the choir of the planets and appearing in all respects like one of them. (*PHK* 58)

This conditional is even further than the 'study' one from phenomenalistic purity. Also, it does not purport to give a counterfactual version of a statement about the existence of any sensible thing. Rather, the passage goes with Berkeley's treatment of 'the set rules or established methods wherein the mind we depend on excites in us the ideas of sense', rules which he calls 'the laws of nature'. These, Berkeley writes, 'we learn by experience, which teaches us that such and such ideas are attended with such and such other ideas in the ordinary course of things' (*PHK* 30). In this doctrine he aims to explain why there seem to be causal connections among sensible things, why in an immaterialist universe physics is so successful, how God's providence makes itself felt in our lives, and perhaps other things. It is not, ever, made to explain what sensible things are.

In *LBH* I conceded that the *Principles* and *Three Dialogues* contain a phenomenalistic element in Berkeley's treatment of the distinction between appearance and reality. That was clumsy of me. Most of the passages that I had in mind are not even prima-facie phenomenalistic. There is an exception in the Third Dialogue, but even that turns out not to be really phenomenalistic either. It has to do with situations in which, as we would ordinarily say, things are not as they seem. Hylas asks 'How can a man be mistaken in thinking an oar, with one end in the water, crooked?' Philonous replies:

He is not mistaken with regard to the ideas he actually perceives, but in the inferences he makes from his present perceptions. . . . What he immediately perceives by sight is certainly crooked; and so far he is in the right. But if he thence conclude that upon taking the oar out of the water he shall perceive the same crookedness, or that it would affect his touch as crooked things are wont to do, in that he is mistaken. . . . But his mistake lies not in what he perceives immediately and at present . . . , but in the wrong judgment he makes concerning the ideas he apprehends to be connected with those immediately perceived: or concerning the ideas that, from what he perceives at present, he imagines would be perceived in other circumstances. (Dia 3, 238)

This is not an application of phenomenalism, though it reminds one of it. If Berkeley had used conditionals to explain what 'The oar is bent' means, he might have parlayed that into a phenomenalistic account of what 'There is an oar there' means. But the question he is addressing is not 'What does it mean to say "The oar is bent"?', but rather, 'What if anything is the man mistaken about?' Granted, if the man is wrong about 'what he would perceive in other circumstances', he might well express his belief in the words 'That oar is bent'. So Berkeley might be willing to adduce his counterfactual to help explain what the man would mean by the latter sentence. But he is far from offering, as a serious part of his philosophy, a counterfactual analysis of that sentence.

In *LBH* my mishandling of this passage and some others led me to write that Berkeley handles the everyday appearance/reality distinction through an account of 'real things' which is 'a vehicle of a kind of phenomenalism which runs, presumably entirely unrecognized', through the published works. This greatly overstated the amount of phenomenalism those works contain, but Winkler (1989: 201) thinks that I understated this. He writes mockingly: 'I am troubled by an unrecognized phenomenalism that is insistently repeated and developed with considerable care.' Nowhere in the published works does Berkeley either carefully develop or insistently repeat phenomenalism, and Winkler offers no respectable evidence for his assertion that Berkeley does both.

There is some philosophy to be learned from seeing how phenomenalism does figure in Berkeley's work, and why. The topic may be worth the four paragraphs I shall give it, which I offer partly as an exercise in weed control. The phenomenalist reading of Berkeley crops up from time to time; it hinders understanding and learning from his work; so I want to clear it away.

Nowhere in the published works does Berkeley state phenomenalism in its full generality, and he seldom makes even passing remarks that could be seen as phenomenalistic. When his topic really is the meaning of 'existence of a sensible thing', or the ontological status of sensible things, or the like, it is almost always in terms of Singleton or Collection idealism, taken as implying that sensible things cannot exist except when perceived. The only exception to this is in *PHK* 3, an aberration which flits past without Berkeley's trying to cash in on it. On other occasions when he considers whether things can exist when not perceived (by us), he never plays the phenomenalist card. With one exception (see §233), he always says that if sensible things are to exist when we do not perceive them, it must be because some other spirit actually perceives them.

Winkler tries to defuse this last point (1989: 207–16). When we ask Berkeley 'How can the Taj Mahal exist at time T, when no human perceives it?', he answers:

(1) It can exist at T because God has TM-type ideas at T;

but if he is a phenomenalist, we might expect him to answer rather:

(2) It can exist at T because if at T someone were to have such and such ideas, she would also have TM-type ideas.

I have said that Berkeley's always saying 1 and never 2 is some of the evidence that he is not a phenomenalist. Against this, Winkler maintains that for Berkeley 2 implies 1: the counterfactual conditional is true because God intends or resolves that anyone who . . . will have TM-type ideas, and he cannot have that intention unless he actually has TM-type ideas himself. If that is right, then Berkeley's always saying 1 is not so devastating to the reading of him as a phenomenalist, because 1, instead of being a rival to the phenomenalist answer, is a mere consequence of it.

Why would Berkeley hold that 2 implies 1? Winkler answers: because he denied that there can be any 'blind agency'—that is, agency in which a spirit wills or intends that P without having an idea of P's being the case. It is indeed plausible to suppose that genuine willing, resolving, intending, and the like involve some thought about the state of affairs that is willed, etc. And if that state of affairs involves someone's having a K idea, Berkeley would say that the volition must involve having an idea of the very same kind. Thus Winkler. This is a strong form of the denial of blind agency. A weaker form would say that the volition must include some *thought about having* such an idea, but need not involve actually *having* one; but Berkeley's views about what thought is do not permit him this weakening. Now, Winkler shows that many of Berkeley's predecessors and contemporaries explicitly rejected blind agency, and that Berkeley himself was inclined to do so in the *Philosophical Commentaries*. None of the passages asserts the strong form of the denial (which is what Winkler needs), though that could be what was meant, given that the weaker version was probably not accessible to any of these philosophers.

Well, then, why does the 'denial of blind agency' not occur in Berkeley's published works? Winkler: 'Berkeley does not make the denial [of blind agency] explicit in either the *Principles* or the *Dialogues* . . . not because he abandons it, but because he takes it for granted' (1989: 210). That is a guess. Here is a better one: Berkeley abandoned the strong denial of blind agency because he came to realize that it would make a nonsense of his only examples of human activity. Typical of these is the one quoted in §221, which includes: 'It is no more than willing, and straightway this or that idea arises in my fancy . . . This making . . . of ideas doth very properly denominate the mind active' (*PHK* 28). This is Berkeley's standard way of satisfying us that we are agents, and he needs it. But Winkler's Berkeley must say that this activity is impossible, because I cannot will an idea to come into my mind unless it is already there. The strong denial of blind agency had better be irrelevant to Berkeley's published works, and I presume that he saw this and consequently dropped it. So he had no basis for thinking that (2) the phenomenalist option implies (1) the idealist one. For Berkeley the two are genuine rivals, and almost always he opts for 1.

233. Phenomenalism and the creation

A passage which at a quick glance seems to show Berkeley as a phenomenalist concerns the statement, in the first biblical account of the creation, that God created trees on the third day, but did not create sentient beings until the fifth or sixth. Lady Percival had adduced this as a difficulty for him after the *Principles* first appeared, and he replied to it in a letter to her husband, including this:

I do not deny the existence of any of those sensible things which Moses says were created by God. They existed from all eternity in the Divine intellect, and then became perceptible (i.e. were created) in the same manner and order as is described in Genesis. For I take creation to belong to things only as they respect finite spirits, there being nothing new to God. Hence it follows that the act of creation consists in God's willing that those things should be perceptible to other spirits, which before were known only to Himself. (LJ 8:37)

This line of thought is developed a little in the letter, and more still in the Third Dialogue, where Berkeley provides an opening for it by making Philonous remark that sensible things 'always had a being in the divine intellect', so that 'nothing is new, or begins to be, in respect of the mind of God'. Hylas asks 'What shall we make then of the Creation?', to which Philonous replies:

May we not understand it to have been entirely in respect of finite spirits; so that things, with regard to us, may properly be said to begin their existence, or be created, when God decreed they should become perceptible to intelligent creatures, in that order and manner which he then established, and we now call the laws of nature? You may call this a relative, or hypothetical existence if you please. But so long as it supplies us with the most natural, obvious, and literal sense of the Mosaic history of the creation; so long as it answers all the religious ends of that great article; in a word, so long as you can assign no other sense or meaning in its stead; why should we reject this? Is it to comply with a ridiculous sceptical humour of making everything nonsense and unintelligible? I am sure you cannot say it is for the glory of God. (Dia 3, 253)

Then he launches into a diatribe on the disrespect towards God that is inherent in materialism.

In considering how well this reconciles immaterialism with the first biblical account, we must confront an ambiguity in the words 'begin their existence when God decreed they should become perceptible'. This could mean that trees came into existence at T if

God decreed that: at T for the first time if intelligent creatures did such and such, they would have arboreal ideas,

or that trees came into existence at T if

At T God decreed for the first time that: if intelligent creatures did such and such, they would have arboreal ideas.

On the former reading, T is the time *in* the decree; on the latter, the time *of* the decree. Either way, the account is theologically preposterous.

The former reading ('time in the decree') implies that at some earlier time God decreed that something of the following form, having been false throughout the second day of creation, should become true during the third: *If any created spirit were now to do such and such, it would have arboreal ideas.* We have here a God who, knowing there will be no created spirits at T, nevertheless made this conditional about them become true then—not earlier, or later, but just then. Why? You might think that this conduct of God's is no weirder than his decreeing the truth of any other conditional whose antecedent he knows to be false (thus McCracken 1979: 289), but that overlooks a difference. The other conditionals are offshoots of the general laws of nature that God has established for sober reasons, whereas the decree that is now in question is a bizarre singularity.

The latter reading ('time of the decree') is no better. It requires that God did not plan ahead for any stage of the creation: he did his work on the first two days without having decided what to do on the third, *then* he made this decree on the third day; and if it was not absurd for him to do so, that must have been because at that time, for all he had decided to the contrary, he was going to decree the existence of created spirits within the next few seconds. This alternative is as absurd, theologically speaking, as the other.

So phenomenalism does not yield a tolerable immaterialist handling of the first biblical account of the world's creation; and Berkeley could hardly have overlooked this if phenomenalism were something he had developed with care. It is not surprising, then, that this passage has 'ad hoc', 'tentative', and 'marginal' written all over it. To take it as evidence of Berkeley's being a phenomenalist, one must overlook six features of its tactics and tone.

Though late in the Third Dialogue, the passage does not begin with Philonous saying—as he so often does—that his treatment of this matter was implied in things he has explained earlier. He treats the question as a new one, requiring an answer that has not yet been prepared for.

Philonous answers with a question of his own: 'May we not . . .?' This is not one of Berkeley's scornful rhetorical questions; rather, it shows him as atypically tentative.

He says he has provided 'the most natural, obvious, and literal sense of the Mosaic history of the creation'. This continues the idea that this is a new issue, to be considered in its own right. Conspicuously absent is any hint that the preceding materials in the *Dialogues* have shown this to be the *right* sense to give to the creation story.

Philonous recommends his interpretation of the creation story on the grounds that 'it answers all the religious ends of that great article'. To my ear, this sounds like a kind of religious pragmatism, rather than a concern with literal truth. In *Alciphron*, which is openly a work of Christian apologetics, Berkeley argues for the truth of various things in the Bible; but rather than espousing a literalist fundamentalism, he allows for static in the line through which revelation comes. So Genesis 1 did not take him by the throat and demand to be interpreted in accordance with the rest of his philosophy; and he writes as though he were not even trying to meet such a demand. It is true that a little later Philonous speaks up for something like a literal interpretation of 'the historical part of scripture'. Ought this, he asks Hylas, 'to be understood in a plain, obvious sense, or in a sense which is metaphysical and out of the way?', and Hylas expectedly opts for the former. What emerges from this, however, is that a materialist reading of the first creation story would be 'metaphysical and out of the way', because, according to it, what God achieved on those first days was 'the creation of . . . certain unknown natures'. This, he gets Hylas to agree, cannot be what the biblical history asserts. Although this passage at least suggests that plain, literal truth is the standard that has to be met, it does not entirely cancel the evidence that Berkeley thought of his account of the creation as defensible mainly on moral and religious grounds.

Philonous defends this reading of the first creation story on the grounds that Hylas 'can assign no other sense or meaning in its stead'. Whereas on most topics he expresses confidence that he is right, here he adopts the milder tone of 'If you know a better hole, go to it'.

He continues in a manner at once aggressive and plaintive, quite unlike his usual way of handling difficulties. I see it as avowedly *ad hoc*, designed for this special case of a religious text: 'Why should we reject this? Is it to comply with a ridiculous sceptical humour of making every thing nonsense and unintelligible?' Berkeley does not whine like that when straightforwardly arguing for his philosophy.

234. Why was Berkeley not a phenomenalist?

Given the general advantages of phenomenalism over idealism, and given that at one time Berkeley did seriously entertain it, why is it not significantly present in the published works? Winkler (1989: 195) has a conjecture about how this question might be answered by someone who holds, as I do, that Berkeley was an idealist; and he proceeds to show why that answer would be unsatisfactory. The answer he invents for his opponent is indeed absurd, though not for the reason he gives; but the literature contains answers that are not stupid, which he ignores.

In *LBH* I pointed out that idealism yields a completion, in the language of ideas, of the statement 'A sensible thing is . . .', whereas phenomenalism does not. Phenomenalism does not say 'Bring out your sensible things, and I'll tell you in the language of ideas what they are', but rather, 'Bring out your statements about sensible things, and I'll tell you in the language of ideas what they mean'. I conjecture that Berkeley, like any of his contemporaries, would regard that as a serious defect in phenomenalism. (They would be wrong about that, as I have argued in §205.)

In the *Philosophical Commentaries* he does have an essentially phenomenalistic completion for 'A sensible thing is . . .': namely, 'a collection of powers to cause ideas'; but this line of thought did not carry through to the published works, perhaps because Berkeley came to realize that if sensible things were collections of powers, then they could not be perceived, and so would not be sensible after all.

His non-phenomenalism may be partly explained by something else. In one brief, but striking, passage Hylas invites Philonous to play the phenomenalist card, and Philonous declares that it makes no difference.[1] Here is the entire exchange:

Hylas: Yes, Philonous, I grant the existence of a sensible thing consists in being perceivable, but not in being actually perceived.

Philonous: And what is perceivable but an idea? And can an idea exist without being actually perceived?

(Dia 3, 234)

Hylas here enters into the spirit of Philonous's immaterialism while proposing that it be relaxed by shifting from idealism to phenomenalism; and Philonous replies that this supposed relaxation leaves the doctrine unaltered. Philonous is wrong, and it is easy to see what his mistake is. Hylas proposes:

---

[1] I cannot make sense of Winkler's (1989: 227) reason for saying that the passage is 'not inconsistent with the phenomenalist interpretation' of Berkeley. As for his saying that the passage does not concern phenomenalism, because 'it says nothing about statements and nothing about meanings': indeed, it does not contain 'statement' or 'meaning'; but Berkeley regularly bases claims about what it is for sensible things to exist—and what their reality consists in—on semantic considerations. There is no evidence that in this one place he suddenly switches to some other unannounced basis.

(1) ST exists ≡ An idea of kind K is perceivable,

which would be true if this were true:

(2) ST exists ≡ If it were the case that P, then a K idea would be perceived.

Philonous, however, understands it as meaning:

(3) ST exists ≡ There is a K idea such that: if P were the case, it would be perceived.

He rightly says that if there is now such an idea, then it is now perceived; and the apparent weakening from 'perceived' to 'perceivable' is of no avail. But the mistake is his. The natural way to take 1 is as meaning not 3, but 2. On this understanding of it, there is a genuine weakening of the doctrine, the constraints on the existence of a sensible thing are relaxed, and—in particular—a sensible thing can exist when not perceived.

Chapter 32

Hume's 'Ideas'

235. Approaching Hume

Of all Hume's works, I shall attend almost exclusively to book I of his *Treatise of Human Nature*. According to Kemp Smith (1949: p. vi), 'It was through the gateway of morals that Hume first entered into his philosophy. . . . Books II and III of the *Treatise* are . . . prior to the working out of the doctrines dealt with in Book I.' He uses this hypothesis to explain some oddities in Hume's handling in book I of his thesis about the association of ideas. These include one that I shall discuss in §253: namely, Hume's not attending to how a relation's actually holding between two items differs from someone's thinking that it does. The treatment in *Treatise* II.i.4 came first, Kemp Smith says, so the association thesis was originally devised to meet those needs; and in the book II context it was easy to overlook this actual/believed distinction; so Hume did overlook it there, and then carried this through into the book I context where the distinction really matters.

This is neat, but I cannot see that it is true. The distinction between 'R(x,y)' and 'Jones believes that R(x,y)' is needed in book II as much as in book I. Greatly as I respect Kemp Smith, I am not convinced by this hypothesis of his.

As for his general thesis that books II and III were written first and were Hume's chief concern: Kemp Smith adduces, as more direct evidence that moral philosophy was Hume's main focus, his reference in the Introduction to the *Treatise* to some 'late philosophers in England' whom he regards as his predecessors. In a footnote he cites 'Mr Locke, my Lord Shaftesbury, Dr Mandeville, Mr Hutchinson, Dr Butler, &c.'. Four of these were indeed best known as moral philosophers, but that is not decisive. Hume goes on to refer to 'the application of experimental philosophy to moral subjects', and that does not settle the point either. The word 'moral' has often meant something like 'human', and something like 'philosophical'. I was once a Lecturer in the Moral Sciences at Cambridge.

Referring to himself in the third person, Hume repeats his list of favoured philosophers in the Abstract, thus:

He mentions on this occasion Mr. Locke, my Lord Shaftesbury, Dr. Mandeville, Mr. Hutchinson, Dr. Butler, etc., who, though they differ in many points among themselves, seem all to agree in founding their accurate disquisitions of human nature entirely on experience. (Abstract 2)

In short, they are Hume's intellectual forebears not because they are moralists but because they behaved like empiricists. It is worth noting that the Abstract devotes its first twenty-nine paragraphs to Book I, four to Book II, and a final one to the association of ideas. Book III is ignored.

About the order in which the books of the *Treatise* were written, Kemp Smith may be right for all I know. I have no opinion on whether we can often be helped much by seeing book I as secondary to book III; obviously, it is sometimes illuminated by bits of II and III, which is why I sometimes quote from them. But I allow book I to stand on its own feet. The situation here may be analogous to that in Spinoza's *Ethics*—a work which Hume knew well and pondered deeply. Here is how the two works are principally divided:

Hume's *Treatise*	Spinoza's *Ethics*
I: Understanding	I: Nature
	II: Origin of the Mind
II: Passions	III: Affects
III: Morals	IV: Human Bondage
	V: Human Freedom

Greatly as these two philosophies differ in scope and in doctrine, those pairings are fairly accurate. Now, although Spinoza was aiming primarily at IV and V, most philosophically motivated scholars of his work have attended more closely to his I and II than to the rest of the *Ethics*. It has made sense for them to do so, and it is similarly reasonable to attend primarily to book I of the *Treatise*, whatever Hume's ultimate aims were.

236. What kind of philosopher was Hume?

Students of Hume differ widely in how they see his writings: not merely about how to interpret individual arguments and doctrines, but even about what kind of thinker he was. What is at issue is a matter of emphasis: no party to the debate asserts the existence in his work of elements that the other parties deny are there. Opinions differ sharply, however, about which elements are dominant; and this creates disagreements about how to understand particular parts of the text.

Consider, for example, Hume's treatment of our belief that there are 'bodies'—perceptible things which exist independently of our perceiving them, and can therefore exist when we do not perceive them. This is his topic in a section of the *Treatise* which I shall examine in Chapter 37. About the belief in 'the existence of body' we can ask two questions. (1) 'What causes it?' Trying to answer this, we approach the belief in a naturalistic way, as something to be explained as we might try to explain the weather or an epidemic. (2) 'What, if anything, justifies it?' This invites a normative inquiry into the value of arguments or evidence for the belief, which in turn requires us to investigate analytically just what its content is. So there is a naturalistic, causal inquiry, and a normative, analytic one. These exemplify the two sides to Hume's thought about which scholars have disputed. Which should have primacy? Which is uppermost in this or that particular passage? What kind of philosopher was Hume?

The question can be put in various ways. On the naturalistic side, we have the concept of *cause*, and inquiries into the *origins* of various aspects of the human condition; and much of this belongs to *empirical psychology*. The normative side is concerned, rather, with *logical* relations, requiring us to engage in conceptual *analysis*; and there is an emphasis on the *philosophy of mind*. In *LBH* I presented this dichotomy by contrasting 'genetic' questions about where our thoughts and beliefs come from with 'analytic' ones about what they are, the latter being a needed preliminary to discovering what might justify them.

The reasons which lead people to believe P can be causes of their doing so: 'He believes P because he believes R and takes it to be a reason for P' could tell us what causes him to believe P. Some philosophers have thought that if you are caused to believe something, that blocks you from believing it for reasons—as though causes and reasons were rival claimants to a certain role in the life of the mind (§81). Most today would disagree with that, however. A statement about what causes some- one to believe that P, where the causes do not involve anything that he takes to be reasons, has no link with anything normative; and a statement about what reasons there are for P is not in itself a causal one. So the causal inquiry can stand on its own, as can the normative one; but when we ask not just what reasons there are for P, but what reasons move people to believe it, we are in territory that involves both logical and causal relations. None of this is controversial these days.

To get a grip on it, consider a case where someone's beliefs change *because of* some new reasons he acquires. What are we to make of this 'because of'? There are three prima-facie available answers.

(1) Reasons have their own efficacy in making some kinds of thing happen, and it does not coincide with causal efficacy. This answer implies that when rea- sons kick in to alter someone's beliefs, either (a) they thwart the causes that are ready to operate, making something happen that is causally impossible; or (b) they do something which all the available possible causes leave open—something that is causally neither ruled out nor required. I have no arguments against (a) contra-causal reasons, but presumably none of us believes in them. As for *b*: that requires a measure of causal indeterminacy. Well, quantum physics tells us that the world is not strictly deterministic, so there are gaps in which other kinds of agent might operate without offending against the causal order. However, con- sidered as an account of how reasons operate—namely, causing beliefs which would otherwise have been probable but not certain because of quantum inde- terminacy—it is incredible.

(2) Reasons have a kind of efficacy which coincides with, or is helped along by, the efficacy of causes, though the two are distinct. Someone who gives this answer ought to be puzzled about the nature of this collaboration, and his puzzle will not be solved. It has arisen from what Bernard Williams (1972: 143) has called 'the mistake of taking the same facts twice over and then finding the relation between them mysterious':

There are not two facts, first that men are rational creatures who hold beliefs on rational grounds, and second that they have beliefs which quite often cause others in ways which express their rational connexions. . . . The emergence of creatures capable of rational thought just is the emergence of creatures who are capable of having beliefs which are so [causally] related. Some may think it a miracle that any such creatures have emerged, but if it is, it is at least not *another* miracle that the required causal connexions obtain in them: if the causal connexions broke down, they would just cease to be rational creatures.

This fine passage is dead right, and it embodies the third possible answer to our question.

(3) Reasons are causes, or have causal efficacy. A major source of this view is Hume, whose position is neatly compressed into two sentences at the start of *Treatise* (iv.1):

In all demonstrative sciences the rules are certain and infallible; but when we apply them our fallible and uncertain faculties are very apt to depart from them and fall into error. . . . Our reason must be considered as a kind of cause, of which truth is the natural effect; but such a one as, by the irruption of other causes and by the inconstancy of our mental powers, may frequently be prevented.

The mention of certain and infallible rules belongs entirely on the normative side of the line, having to do with what reasons *there are* for this or that belief. On the other hand, the facts about what reasons people *have and apply* when they actually reason are described in terms of causation. Hume does not equate reasons with causes *simpliciter*. Our reason, he says, is *a kind of* cause, allowing that beliefs may have other causes as well; and he suggests that what marks off this cause from others is its having truth as its 'natural effect'. He may intend this as a general thesis about what qualifies a belief-acquisition mechanism as reasonable or justified, though I have not found him saying so explicitly.

237. A case-study: the belief in body

Hume was a naturalistic philosopher who studied how our minds work, the mechanisms through which we form beliefs, and so on, and also a normative one who was interested in our entitlement to our beliefs, the reasons or justification that we can bring to support them. I find him more interesting in the latter role, and that is what I shall focus on in the ensuing chapters. But that account of the choice over-simplifies the issue, as I now explain through an example.

In his great section on 'Scepticism with Regard to the Senses' (iv.2), Hume's topic is 'the principle concerning the existence of body'. At the outset, he announces what kind of inquiry into this he will conduct (referring to himself in the third person, as 'the sceptic'):

He must assent to the principle concerning the existence of body, though he cannot pretend by any arguments of philosophy to maintain its veracity. Nature has not left this to his choice, and has doubtless esteemed it an affair of too great importance to be trusted to our uncertain reasonings and speculations. . . . It is in vain to ask *Whether there be body or not?* That is a point which we must take for granted in all our reasonings.

Although (as he will later try to prove) the belief in body cannot be supported by philosophically respectable reasons, there is still no question of anyone's being led by that fact to give it up. We 'must' have it; nature has not left this up to us, to accept or not accept, depending on how we weigh the arguments.

Beliefs and intellectual procedures that are forced on us by 'nature' are a large theme with Hume. It is at work when he writes that Berkeley's arguments are 'in reality merely sceptical', because 'they *admit of no answer and produce no conviction*' (*Enquiry* xii.2, 122n.). When an invincible argument does not win the battle, that is because it has collided with 'nature'. I am a little puzzled by his writing, in the above passage and elsewhere, about what nature has done for our own good, on the basis of what it has 'esteemed' to be 'important'. Today we might understand this in evolutionary terms, but Hume lived too early for that. Nor can it have been meant theologically, for Hume was virtually an atheist.

So far, he has said that 'Shall I relinquish my belief in body?' is as idle as 'Shall I hold my breath for half an hour?', and that the answer to 'Am I intellectually justified in believing in body?' is No. In the same passage, he mentions a third question, which he does not brush aside so abruptly: 'What causes induce us to believe in the existence of body?' The word 'cause' can mean 'reason',[1] but here it means what you and I mean by 'cause'. This causal question is, in a way, Hume's topic throughout this long section.

He *also* pursues reasons. His snub to 'arguments of philosophy to maintain [the] veracity' of the belief in body merely anticipates what he will argue for, in elaborate detail, later in the section. The prima-facie possible causes of our belief in body, Hume thinks, are three in number: the senses, reason, and imagination; and which of these is the cause will have implications for whether the belief in body is justified; so in finding a cause we can adjudicate the normative question also. He finally opts for *imagination* as the cause, and infers that the belief cannot be supported by reasons: imagination causes the belief by inventing 'fictions', which it does in response to intellectual, conceptual pressures. The part of the section devoted to imagination is chock-full of analytic philosophy. Hume warns us at 217–18 that even if we fully understand why the imagination does what it does, that is not evidence for the truth of its output. 'I am more inclined to repose no faith at all in my . . . imagination, than to place in it such an implicit confidence. I cannot conceive how such trivial qualities of the fancy, conducted by such false suppositions, can ever lead to any solid and rational system.'[2] He briskly sketches the reasons he has found for this, and then continues: 'What then can we look for from this confusion of groundless and extraordinary

---

[1] See *OED*, 'cause', sense 3a. Examples: 'as I have good cause to think' (Lanham), 'to give just cause of suspicion' (Cudworth), 'A reason is often called a cause' (Reid).

[2] Hume's phrase 'the fancy' is a term from scholastic psychology, meaning 'Mental apprehension of an object of perception; the faculty by which this is performed' (*OED*).

opinions but error and falsehood? And how can we justify to ourselves any belief we repose in them?' This is as normative as it could be. In the next paragraph, ending the section, Hume speaks of the two possible rational bases for the belief in bodies—namely, reason and the senses—and says:

It is impossible, upon any system, to defend either our understanding or senses; and we but expose them further when we endeavour to justify them in that manner. As the sceptical doubt arises naturally from a profound and intense reflection on those subjects, it always increases the further we carry our reflections, whether in opposition or conformity to it.

It is clear from all this that Hume thinks that the normative question about justification has been raised in iv.2, which belongs to normative epistemology as well as to naturalistic psychology.

That is how I see Hume in much of his work. He frequently reminds us and himself that every fact about conceptual structures and movements of the mind is, *ultimately*, a natural fact about the sort of animals we are. But, at least in book I of the *Treatise*, he tries to work down to that naturalistic level through careful attention to what he can find at the analytic/normative level. Never does he turn his back on the latter in order to pursue issues about psychological structure and natural causation independently, as though he were only a psychologist.

238. The idea/impression line: distractions

Hume begins his treatment of the intellectual aspects of the human condition, which are the topic of book I of the *Treatise* ('Of the Understanding'), with an account of the kinds of items there can be *in* the mind—that is, with an account of mental content. He initially sets out to describe the human mind in terms of its *contents*, and is repeatedly forced by the facts to make room not only for content, but also for mental *activity*. Here I follow the lead of Wolff (1960). We shall see that Hume gets activity—or at least *process*—into his story by crediting humans with being subject to certain laws about what mental contents are likely to be followed by what others (§255). Some of this has the concept of habit, or custom, at its centre. The emphasis on the laws to which we are subject, and on the role of habit in these, leads to Hume's treating us as more passive than we really are. I agree with Wolff that Hume overdoes 'habit' and 'custom', and that his philosophy would have gone better if mental processes had been treated in a more active way.

Anyway, we start with mental content, which Hume always takes to be introspectible mental items called 'perceptions'. On the first page of the *Treatise* he divides these into two:

Those perceptions which enter with most force and violence we may name *impressions*; and under this name I comprehend all our sensations, passions, and emotions, as they make their first appearance in the soul. By *ideas* I mean the faint images of these in thinking and reasoning.

Here, as often in the *Treatise*'s early pages, too many things happen at once. The reference to 'thinking and reasoning' is a distraction. For Hume, as for Locke and Berkeley, our ideas are important partly because of their role as elements in thinking and believing, and as mental items which must accompany words if they are to be meaningful. And those intellectual aspects of the human condition are more tightly tied to 'idea' by Hume than by the other two philosophers, because they use 'idea' also for the mental contents that come in sensory experience, while he does not. But the thinking–meaning role of ideas is not of their essence *qua* ideas, according to Hume. Although he holds that all thinking and reasoning involve mentally manipulating ideas, he does not hold, conversely, that ideas can occur only in this way. Rather than being meanings or concepts, ideas may be mere mental presences, data, images that mean nothing beyond themselves. So 'thinking and reasoning' ought not to occur in Hume's explanation of the impression/idea distinction.

The phrases 'first appearance' and 'images of' are gestures towards what I call the 'copy thesis', a doctrine of Hume's which implies—roughly speaking—that impressions enter the mind first and then cause the occurrence of ideas. This, however, is no part of what he means by 'impression' or 'idea': he insists that the copy thesis is contingent, and he supports it through empirical evidence, and presents it as vulnerable to counter-evidence. I shall argue that we do best to take it as a conceptual truth, though not a trivial one (§244); but if Hume stipulated it into truth through the meanings of 'impression' and 'idea', it would do no work. So Hume does not, and should not, mean his definition of 'idea' to imply anything about how ideas are caused.

Nor does his meaning for 'impression' imply anything about how impressions are caused. Hume thinks that we have them in ordinary sensory experience, which is why he alludes later to the 'passive admission of the impressions through the organs of sensation' (*Treatise* 73). But in a footnote on the second page he firmly insists that this is not any part of the impression concept: 'By the term of *impression* I would not be understood to express the manner in which our lively perceptions are produced in the soul, but merely the perceptions themselves.'

Hume holds that impressions of reflection are caused by—'derived from'—the ideas that they are *of* (7), but concerning the causes of impressions of sensation he is resolutely agnostic. When someone has an impression because he sees or feels a physical object, Hume refuses to say that the object causes the impression:

As to those impressions which arise from the senses, their ultimate cause is in my opinion perfectly inexplicable by human reason, and it will always be impossible to decide with certainty whether [1] they arise immediately from the object, or [2] are produced by the creative power of the mind, or [3] are derived from the Author of our being. Nor is such a question any way material to our present purpose. We may draw inferences from the coherence of our perceptions, whether they be true or false; whether they represent nature justly or be mere illusions of the senses. (84)

The final sentence reminds one of Berkeley's account of God's providence, the laws of nature, and so on (§222). Of the three possibilities that I have numbered, 1 echoes Locke, and 3 Berkeley. Item 2 is a puzzling thing for Hume to say, given that he tends to treat the mind as necessarily wholly open to itself, and also tends not to grant minds any independent depth or reality which might house 'creative power'. Anyway, Hume is not committing himself to any view about how impressions are caused.

239. The idea/impression line: what it is

Hume intends the two species of perceptions to be distinguished—initially, definitively and wholly—through impressions' having 'force and violence' and ideas' being 'faint'. In drawing this contrast, he usually uses two-noun phrases—mostly 'force and vivacity' (2, 96, 98, 99, 103, 134), though also 'force and liveliness' (1, 5), 'vigour and vivacity' (99), 'strength and vivacity' (19), and 'force and violence'; and sometimes he uses cognate adjectival phrases, such as 'strong and lively' (134, 359). Each of the above occurs more often than I have noted here.

They are used not only to distinguish ideas from impressions, but also to contrast some ideas with others. For example, Hume regards memory and belief as consisting in the having of ideas, these being marked off from other ideas partly by their greater liveliness, vivacity, etc. Elsewhere he writes of the moral value of keeping certain ideas 'strong and lively' in our minds. Usually, though, he is marking off impressions from ideas, and in a majority of cases he says explicitly that the conjunctive phrase expresses the whole essential difference between the two. Thus, 'less faint' is equivalent to 'more strong and lively' etc., so that impressions differ from ideas in some matter of degree along a single continuum. I shall mostly use the one word 'vivacity' for this purpose.

To think about what vivacity might be, we must understand the work that Hume wants it to do. He holds that an idea of F may be copied from an impression of F, for the very same F. This requires that the idea/impression difference must not intrude on the classificatory system for perceptions (represented here by 'F'); that is, what a perception is *of*—what its content is, what kind it represents—must not be affected by how vivacious it is. Hume realizes that this severely limits what vivacity can be.

Let us see how he might respect those limits for two of our sense modalities. With visual ideas, one naturally equates vivacity with something like brightness of colours (as distinct from hues and shapes); with auditory ones, vivacity might seem to be loudness (as distinct from pitch and timbre). If that were Hume's position, he would have to give up his view that some ideas have no vivacity, and stop speaking of a perception that 'entirely loses that vivacity, and is a perfect idea' (8). Obviously, there cannot be a colour sensation with zero degree of brightness, or an auditory idea representing zero decibels. And the proposed account of vivacity faces another difficulty, which is more centrally fatal. Brightness can indeed vary independently of hue and saturation; but those are only two of the three heads under which colours may be classified, and the third is brightness. In short, brightness enters into content, so it cannot be Hume's 'vivacity', which has to vary independently of content. When I experience or think of a meadow with a specific shade of green, I may experience or think of it as having a more or less bright version of that shade; that affects what kind of experience or thought this is, what its content is, for what value of F it is a perception of F. Similarly with loudness.

Perhaps that is why Hume is not content with any of his terms for marking off impressions from ideas. A certain difficulty, he says, involves 'a little ambiguity in those words *strong* and *lively*'; and he moves over to writing of 'the . . . quality, call it firmness, or solidity, or force, or vivacity' (*Treatise* 106). Clearly, he does not know what to call it.

He is firm, though, in holding that impressions differ from ideas only in degree. This doctrine operates in several ways in his philosophy of mind. For example, he locates memory on that same scale. An idea may copy a previous impression in either of two ways, Hume says: either 'it retains a considerable degree of its first vivacity, and is somewhat intermediate betwixt an impression and an idea', or 'it entirely loses that vivacity, and is a perfect idea'. The former of these is memory, which he describes sometimes in terms of 'ideas' and sometimes of 'impressions', the indecisiveness being explained by its middling position on the vivacity scale. We can easily see what is going on here when we recall that impressions are characteristically sensory states and that ideas are characteristically thoughts, though neither of those is true by definition. Consider these:

(1) experiencing being burned by a fire,
(2) remembering being burned by a fire,
(3) thinking of being burned by a fire.

Hume's point is that 2 is more like 1 than 3 is, and is more like 3 than 1 is. That seems reasonable, though we shall find that the 'single continuum' theory exacts a high price for this modest result.

Hume also puts his 'degree of vivacity' theory to use in some of his views about the dynamics of the mind—that is, about how some mental contents cause others. Such vivacity as memories have, he contends, has been communicated to them by the previous impressions which caused them; and he explains the comparative vivacity of beliefs in a similar way.

Although he finds it plausible to suppose that one perception might draw vivacity from another, Hume does not assume a priori that all causing must be giving (§35). On the contrary, he holds that 'To consider the matter *a priori*, anything may produce anything' (*Treatise* 247). Yet sometimes he writes as though it were certain that any degree of vivacity that an idea has must have come from some earlier vivacious perception.

240. An odd problem

That creates a problem which Hume's ingenuity discovers and his honesty compels him to confront (105–6). It involves the theses (1) that ideas get their vivacity from other perceptions that are already vivacious, (2) that a belief is a strong and lively idea, and that (3) all our ideas are derived from corresponding impressions. The problem comes from the truth of 1 and 2 and someone's *believing* 3. Here I am with an idea of a certain kind of sound. Being convinced of 3, I conclude that I once had an impression of such a sound, though I now have no memory of it. This conclusion is an idea (= belief) of mine, which means that it has more vivacity than the idea (= mere thought) had a moment ago. Where did that vivacity come from? It cannot have come from the thought that caused it, because the vivacity gradient slopes the wrong way for that.

Hume might solve this in either of three ways. He could drop 1; and I see no obstacle to his doing so. Or he might say that my belief gets its vivacity from the forgotten impression; but he might be uncomfortable with this because it would involve mental processes, and perhaps mental content, of which I am not aware. Thirdly, he could conjecture that my belief in the past impression gets its vivacity from my belief in 3.

Hume, however, tries none of these, and goes for something else:

From whence are the qualities of force and vivacity derived which constitute this belief? ... From the present idea. For as [a] this idea is not here considered as the representation of any absent object, but as a real perception in the mind of which we are intimately conscious, [b] it must be able to bestow on whatever is related to it the same quality—call it firmness, or solidity, or force, or vivacity—with which the mind reflects upon it and is assured of its present existence. [c] The idea here supplies the place of an impression, and is entirely the same so far as regards our present purpose.

There are two ways of taking this, neither of which fits the entire passage.

If we think of an idea not as contentful or meaningful but just as a mental presence, that gives it vivacity, which can then vivify the belief.

This fits *a*, and perhaps also *c*; but it makes no use of *b*. It also makes a nonsense of the notion of vivacity. Whatever that is, it had better not be something that springs into existence when representative content is absent or ignored! Alternatively,

The idea exists as a mental presence; one can observe that one has it ('reflect upon it'); and this gives one an introspective impression which, because it is an impression, is vivacious.

This fits *b*. It puts *a* out of work, because it does not use the notion of represent-ative content. Also, it conflicts with *c*, which says that the idea takes the place of an impression, whereas the present interpretation says that the work is done by a real impression accompanying the idea. However, *c* might be misleadingly written; Hume may not have meant 'supplies the place of' quite literally.

So the second interpretation may be better. If that is Hume's solution to the problem, however, it cannot be right. It rests squarely on the claim that in reflect-ing on my own ideas I have impressions, but Hume has no grounds for that. In saying it, he is assuming that any perception I have in which I become aware of something other than the perception must be an impression, and thus have vivac-ity ('the vivacity with which the mind reflects upon it'). This, however, is wishful thinking, or else a switch in the meaning of 'impression'. The problem is not solved.

241. Memory

Hume introduces memory in a passage about how an impression may be echoed in later perceptions of two kinds, one more vivacious than the other. He contin-ues:

The faculty by which we repeat our impressions in the first [more vivacious] manner is called the *memory*, and the other the *imagination*. . . . The ideas of the memory are much more lively and strong than those of the imagination; . . . the former faculty paints its objects in more distinct colours than any which are employed by the latter. When we remember any past event, the idea of it flows in upon the mind in a forcible manner; whereas in the imagination the perception is faint and languid, and cannot without difficulty be preserved by the mind steady and uniform for any considerable time. (*Treatise* 8–9)

There is more of this. When distinguishing them from ideas of imagination, Hume describes ideas of memory as 'strong and lively' (628), and credits them with 'force and vivacity' (85, 86, 106).

In a chapter which is a fine thing to read along with i.3 and iii.5, Pears (1990: 36) remarks that there are two stories here: first a 'pictorial' one—ideas of mem-ory are brightly lit, so to speak; and then what he calls a 'behavioural' one—ideas of memory force their way in, and are hard to budge. Compare a 'forceful' per-ception with two pushy guests at a party: one forces his way in, then sits quietly in a corner but refuses to leave; the other arrives by invitation, and then grabs the limelight.

Pears's observation should not lead us to adopt a purely 'behavioural' under-standing of the 'force and vivacity' of impressions. That would imply that impres-sions are essentially involuntary, and that is not Hume's official position. In one place he alludes to 'other impressions, whether gentle or violent, voluntary or involuntary' (195). He uses terms like 'force' and 'strength' mainly in the manner that Pears calls 'pictorial', as when he writes of 'eloquence, by which objects are represented in their strongest and most lively colours' (426).

Still, Pears is right in thinking that for Hume the difference between memory and imagination is not purely pictorial. (For a brilliant exposé of the trouble that Hume would be in if he did pin everything on pictorial vivacity, see Reid 1764: 99–100.) Hume wants an account of how they differ that will do some justice to the ordinary meanings of 'memory' and 'imagination', so it must relate memory to the past. It will not do merely to say that memory involves some kind of copying of past experience, because, according to the copy thesis, that holds equally for imagination. So Hume says this:

Though neither the ideas of the memory nor imagination, neither the lively nor faint ideas, can make their appearance in the mind unless their correspondent impressions have gone before to prepare the way for them, yet the imagination is not restrained to the same order and form with the original impressions; while the memory is in a manner tied down in that respect, without any power of variation. (9)

This raises two questions which Hume ought to be able to answer and probably cannot; but it is a mark of his quality that he prompts us to ask them.

(1) He seems to offer the 'ordering' property of memory as one that identifies it as such, independently of differences in liveliness. Yet he admits that it does not always work, adding that any departure in memory from the actual order of the remembered events 'proceeds from some defect or imperfection in that faculty' (9). But what is Hume entitled to mean by a 'defect' in a faculty? It sounds as though memory is assigned a role or duty—something normative—and he exhibits no basis for that.

(2) *How* does memory 'preserve the order and position' of items that have been encountered in experience? When I remember that I visited Palermo before going to Siracusa, how do I do that? What actually happens in my mind that constitutes my remembering the order of the visits? My remembering the order cannot consist in my having a memory-perception of Palermo before having one of Siracusa; but what else can Hume say? This is a profound difficulty, which Kant first noticed and then correctly solved in his 'Refutation of Idealism' (see my 1966: 222–9). The core of it is that most recollection of temporal order relies on causal judgements about the order in which various experiences must have occurred. Kant does not remark, but I do, that there is a class of exceptions: namely, cases where one remembers A-then-B in a single stroke of memory, so to speak; and those are what Hume would have to appeal to in his theory according to which all causal judgements arise from memories of the order in which certain events occurred (§§269–70).

In iii.5 Hume returns to memory, asking how I can know that a given mental content of mine is a memory rather than an imagining. Sometimes, he rightly says, we are not sure; but often enough we are, and he wants to know what we go by. He reminds us that it is 'a peculiar property of the memory to preserve the original order and position of its ideas, while the imagination transposes and changes them as it pleases' (85); but this does not enable us to recognize a memory as such, because it is 'impossible to recall the past impressions in order to compare them with our present ideas and see whether their arrangement be exactly similar' (ibid.). He means 'recall' in the sense of 'summon up', 'bring back': he is saying that I cannot check on whether my present fairly vivid idea of certain perceptions is a memory by confronting those very perceptions so as to see how they are (were) ordered. This point helps Hume to clear the way for liveliness as the feature that marks memories as such. He is right in thinking that something is needed, and what he offers might do the job; but he does not remark that it brings us to the brink of a precipice—namely, scepticism about the past. It seems to imply that we have no non-circular way of knowing whether any present mental content truly represents the past, or, therefore, of knowing that there is any such faculty as memory, except in the degenerate sense of a faculty whose output comes between sensing and thinking on the liveliness scale.

242. The line between simple and complex ideas

The terms 'simple' and 'complex', which Hume uses to divide ideas, can mark either of two distinctions. I believe that both of these are involved in his use of this terminology, and I am not convinced that he clearly saw how different they are.

(1) One distinction is best understood by thinking of ideas as meanings, or as concepts. Looked at in this way, the complexity of an idea is revealed by a conjunctive definition of the corresponding word; the definition's role is to expose the complex nature of the meaning of the definiendum by laying its simpler elements side by side. For example:

triangle $=_{df}$ item that is a figure and plane and closed and rectilinear and bounded by three lines.
rectilinear $=_{df}$ having to do with straight lines
straight $=_{df}$ . . .

and so on, until at last we must stop, because each word on the right has a meaning that is constituted by a simple idea. Words of that kind cannot be verbally defined, according to Locke and Hume; so they must be explained in some other way.

The definitions that are in question here are all conjunctive. Our idea of *triangle* has as components our ideas of *figure*, of *plane*, of *three*, and so on. So it is complex, because it has these simpler ideas as *parts*. This conjunctive paradigm is nearly as old as philosophy. It is embodied, for instance, in the view that the right way to explain a meaning is through *genus* and *differentia*, as in 'man $=_{df}$ rational animal', and so on. Definitions need not have this form, Locke says (*Essay* III.iii.10), but he means only that a definiens need not be a strictly two-idea affair rather than something longer; he is not rejecting the conjunctive pattern, which Hume took for granted also. It gives a distortingly limited view about how meanings can be verbally explained.

(2) A simple/complex distinction can be applied to ideas considered just as presences in the mind, without reference to any role they may have as concepts or meanings. This line is drawn purely on the basis of what ideas are like phenomenologically—their pictorial features. The paradigm here is provided by visual ideas, thought of as inner coloured surfaces; such an idea of *triangle* can be seen to be complex just by inspecting it. If you look into your mind and find there a triangular idea, you will see that it has enough complexity—now meaning qualitative variety across the surface—for it to involve an enclosed space, enclosing lines, apexes, and perhaps an enclosing space. One idea can be more complex (in this sense) than another by being more qualitatively various than the other is.

(Hume sometimes denies that a certain idea is 'simple', even though it is not qualitatively variegated, if it is extended or has parts. He thinks of visual ideas as coloured pictures, which can be non-simple, or 'compound', without being variegated. The idea of extension is like that: 'It is impossible to conceive extension but as composed of parts, endowed with colour or solidity. The idea of extension is a compound idea' (228). In this he follows Locke, who held that all (ideas of) modes are complex; a subset of those are 'simple modes', which are complex because they have parts yet simple because their parts are exactly alike. I shall say no more about this strand in Hume's thinking. For proof positive that Hume regards 'compound idea' as interchangeable with 'complex idea', see *Treatise* 38.)

The two simple/complex lines are utterly unalike. Inspecting an image and finding it to be heterogeneous is nothing like reflecting on a concept, or on one's meaning for a word, and finding logical structure in it. Moore (1903: 7–8) shows what can happen if you let the two distinctions masquerade as one:

We can . . . make a man understand what a chimera is, although he has never heard of one or seen one. You can tell him that it is an animal with a lioness's head and body, with a goat's head growing from the middle of its back, and with a snake in place of a tail. But here the object which you are describing is a complex object; it is entirely composed of parts, with which we are all perfectly familiar—a snake, a goat, a lioness . . . So it is with all objects, not previously known, which we are able to define: they are all complex; all composed of parts, which may . . . be capable of similar definition, but which must in the end be reducible to the simplest parts, which can no longer be defined.

Moore slides between defining a word and describing an object; and he muddles the logical parts of the meaning of 'chimera' with the spatial parts of a chimera.

The conflation of these two distinctions is a likely upshot of the more general tendency to run thinking together with imaginative depicting; and of that Hume was certainly guilty, as we can see in his discussion of spatial divisibility. (See *Treatise* 26–7.) He holds that there is a limit to how small a portion of matter or space we can conceive, because there is a limit to how small a portion we can imagine, because there is a limit to how small an image can be in our minds. This fatally relies on conflating thinking with depicting.

There is some excuse for Moore's performance, because the two distinctions are related. Qualitatively, various parts can legitimately be mentioned in a definition: it is *part* of the meaning of 'chimera' that anything to which it applies has a lioness's head as a *part*; so the complexity of the meaning of 'chimera' includes a kind of map of some of the qualitative complexity of a chimera; and, conversely, there may be a difficulty about *conjunctively* defining a general word whose meaning does not insist on any qualitative complexity in its instances (§245). Now, I shall contend that the deepest source of Hume's interest in simple / complex is its role in considerations about what cannot, and what can, be defined. I find it natural to think that he just ran together in his mind the two simple / complex distinctions which I have been discussing; but, faced with a challenge from Don Garrett, I admit to having no clear textual evidence for that; and I have to allow that Hume, when he relates the indefinability of a concept or meaning with the qualitative simplicity of instances of it, may be guided not by a confusion but by the legitimate link that I have just pointed out.

243. The copy thesis: problems

Hume holds that all our simple ideas are caused by previous impressions which they resemble in every respect except the degree of vivacity which defines the difference between them. I call this his 'copy thesis'.

He offers it as his contribution to the debate over innate ideas. Rightly saying that the debate is 'frivolous' if it concerns what a baby has when it is born, Hume writes: 'It is probable that no more was meant by those who denied innate ideas than that all ideas were copies of our impressions' (*Enquiry* ii.2, 17n.). If a child is born with an idea of hunger, this does not now count as innate if it is copied from a previous impression of hunger. This is somewhat in the spirit of Locke's insight that the interesting sense for 'innate' is not 'possessed at birth', but rather 'possessed as an inevitable part of our human nature, whether in the womb or later through normal maturation', the contrast being with what we possess because of (and now I quote Locke) 'accidental alterations in or operations on the body' (§179). Hume, however, while adopting Locke's view about what innateness *is not*, tells a different story about what it *is*. He identifies 'innate' simply with 'not caused by a preceding impression', which leads him to the startling conclusion that 'all our impressions are innate' because they are not caused by preceding impressions. This is a perverse misunderstanding of what 'innate' means in this part of the philosophical arena. Now I come to my main topic in this section.

According to Hume's announced way of distinguishing impressions from ideas, the copy thesis says that our simple mental contents ('perceptions') are of two kinds, vivacious and faint, and that any faint one that occurs in a mind is caused by an earlier vivacious one that is otherwise just like it. He tries to make this the foundation of a large philosophical edifice, but it cannot carry the weight.

Hume wants it as a basis for conceptual criticism, a ground for asserting that certain terms that philosophers use are meaningless or unintelligible. Locke had held that a meaningful term must either be complex and thus verbally definable, or simple and thus traceable to sensation or reflection (§155). Hume follows this lead, but more resolutely and aggressively, as here: 'Neither by considering the first origin of ideas, nor by means of a definition, are we able to arrive at any satisfactory notion of substance . . . What possibility then of answering that question, *Whether perceptions inhere in a material or immaterial substance*, when we do not so much as understand the meaning of the question?' (*Treatise* 234).[3]

Compare this with the view of someone who holds, perhaps on strong evidence, that every good chisel either has a steel handle or was made in Japan. If I claim to have a good wooden-handled Canadian chisel, how can he respond? If he has any sense, he will start by trying out the chisel; if it does not serve him well, my challenge dies. If it proves to be serviceable, and visibly has a wooden handle, he could then challenge my claim about its provenance; *but why should he bother?* If his concern is with this chisel, its origin no longer matters.

He might need his theory for some more general reason. If he is a bulk-buyer who has to evaluate more chisels than he has time to test, or has to evaluate them in advance of testing them, then he has an interest in whether all the good wooden-handled ones come from Japan. But the analogy with the meaningfulness of words collapses right there. We have the word in our hands, so to speak; the question is whether it can serve us well; and it is absurd to look for the answer to that in the past rather than in the present and future.

If the best approach to questions about meaningfulness lay in the past, then they could not matter to us now *qua* philosophers rather than biographers. In fact, meaning does matter to us now and in the future, and it can do so because it shows up in how expressions are used. So the important question about whether someone has a meaning for an expression should be tackled in terms of what uses he can make of it, rather than of where he got the meaning from. Our serious interest in meanings is like a carpenter's interest in chisels.

How did Locke and Hume get side-tracked into the copy theory? The natural answer points to another defect in the theory. According to the copy theory, an idea that confers meaning must either (1) be verbally definable or (2) have been derived from sensory experience; and one naturally sees this as reflecting the fact that what matters about meaning is a person's competence in relating words (1) to other words and (2) to the world. That, however, makes their error explicable only if the term 'impression' as used in the copy thesis is understood in terms not of phenomenological 'vivacity', but rather of involving experience of an objective world. Hume firmly denies that 'impression' is to be understood in this way, presumably because later on he will question the belief in an objective world (Chapter 37). But if he holds to that denial, he deprives the copy thesis of its only chance of relating intelligibly to something interesting that might be true.

---

[3] Hume here says 'notion' rather than 'idea', but he equates these in contexts where meaning is at issue. The point about 'substance' is expressed with 'idea' at 15–16 and 244.

He also divorces it from most of the empirical evidence that he thinks supports it—for example, concerning blind people:

Consider [the fact] that wherever by any accident the faculties which give rise to any impressions are obstructed in their operations, as when one is born blind or deaf, not only the impressions are lost but also their correspondent ideas; so that there never appear in the mind the least traces of either of them. (5)

This assumes that people whose eyes do not inform them about the outer world as ours do have no 'impressions' of the sort we deem to be visual. But there is no basis for that if an 'impression' is just a strong perception, not necessarily involving intake from outside.

The divorce from supporting evidence brings with it a fatal immunity to counter-evidence. Of someone who questions whether 'every simple idea has a simple impression which resembles it', Hume comments: 'I know no way of convincing him but by desiring him to show a . . . simple idea that has not a correspondent impression. If he does not answer this challenge, as it is certain he cannot, we may from his silence and our own observation establish our conclusion' (*Treatise* 4). The phrase 'his silence' shows Hume assuming that for someone to 'show' a certain idea is for him to say that he has it. But how could the person describe his putative idea, and how could we understand his description? Suggested solution to this problem: 'It may be that nobody ever does claim to have *any* Humean "simple idea" that is unlike any previous impression; so we need not worry about the semantic predicament we would be in if such a claim were made' (adapted from Garrett 1997: 46–7). This is not so. Our uncertainty about what would count as refuting the copy thesis is an uncertainty about what the thesis is.

244. The copy thesis: a triple revision

I have taken the copy thesis as Hume offers it, as describing how (1) vivid perceptions relate to (2) faint ones: namely, (3) by causing and being copied by them. With the thesis thus construed, we cannot see how to get evidence for or against it, how it could legitimately be used as a weapon of criticism, or why it matters. Yet Hume means the thesis to do vital work in his philosophy. If these parts of his work are to be considerable and worth discussing, we must rescue the copy thesis from these difficulties. This can be done through a triple revision of it, which I now present. It underlies all the uses of Hume's work by twentieth-century logical positivists and other 'meaning empiricists' who acknowledge Hume as their leader. I am original here only in making explicit the changes that must be made if this work of Hume's is to play the role which the twentieth century has assigned to it.

The three needed changes correspond to the three elements in the copy thesis that I have numbered. They are *all* required for the removal of *each* of the difficulties that I have exposed.

(1) Despite all the evidence that 'impression' is defined in pictorial terms, and not in terms of causation or origin, we must understand the copy thesis as saying something about how ideas relate to *sensory contact with the world of material things*. That is indeed how it was understood by its friends before Hume. There were many of these. Something like it passes unchallenged in Descartes at CSM 2:13–14; Locke held it in a form that may have attracted Hume's attention, describing the human mind as a white paper upon which experience writes (*Essay* II.i.2); Geach calls it 'the commonest scholastic clap-trap' (1957: 20); and Leibniz alludes ironically to the 'accepted philosophical axiom that there is nothing in the soul which does not come from the senses' (*NE* 110–11). Reid contrasts Hume's aggressive use of the copy thesis with the 'greater moderation and mercy' of Locke's use of it, leaving no room for doubt that he takes himself to be contrasting the two philosophers' uses of a single principle (Reid 1788: 27).

Indeed, Hume himself sometimes equates 'impression' with 'perception of the outer world', as though that were its meaning. This is implicit in his treatment of blind people, and explicit here: 'It is confessed that no object can appear to the senses—or in other words, that no impression can become present to the mind—without being determined in its degrees both of quantity and quality' (19). With the phrase 'in other words', Hume implies that 'impression' is to be defined in terms of not of vividness but of sensory intake. This is not his official view about what 'impression' means, and in excluding impressions of reflection, it even clashes with his view about the extension of the word. Yet it seems clear that he is somewhat drawn in the direction in which I now push him.

(2) We must understand 'ideas' as restricted, so far as the copy thesis is concerned, to their roles as tools of thought, concepts, meanings, or the like. I do not mean that while continuing to think of them as images we should bear in mind that Hume also assigned to them a conceptual role as meanings or the like. I mean, rather, that in this context we must drop entirely the view that ideas are images, and regard them only as meanings or concepts. Thus, we must take simple ideas to be the meanings of words that cannot be defined verbally; and simplicity as qualitative uniformity will disappear from the story.

Transform the copy thesis in those two ways and you get something like this:

One way for me to come to have a meaning for a given word W is for it to be defined verbally in terms of words for which I already have meanings. If its meaning is not definable in this way because not complex, then I can come to associate it with W only through an ostensive definition—a procedure in which I am told that W applies to things that look thus or sound so.

Philosophers down the centuries commonly held that meanings must be learned through verbal or ostensive definitions, and I see Hume's copy thesis as belonging to that tradition.

However, it is not true that meanings must be learned in one of those two ways. Attend to how a child learns its first language, and you will find that almost none of it consists in exposure to definitions, verbal or ostensive. A child does learn routines of associating single words with objects, and this evidently helps towards knowing what they mean; but it would be a naïve error to suppose that when the child learns to associate a ball with the sound 'ball', she is acquiring a meaning for that word.

In fact, most acquisition of meaning comes piecemeal through gaining competence in the use of a language—learning to say things that are true, learning what follows from what, and so on. Linguistic competence can be seen as having two crucial elements: the ability to link words with other words in proper ways, and the ability to link words appropriately with the world. One needs both, and that is the grain of truth in the thesis that one needs verbal definitions and ostensive ones. That thesis, taken just as it stands, is mostly wrong, however: one does not need definitions; and when a definition is used, it should be understood as shorthand for some instructions about how to use the word in sentences (§205).

Even if our present version of the copy thesis were true, it would be a peculiar basis for conceptual criticism, just as Hume's is. For our version still answers the question 'Does he have a meaning for word W?' by looking to the past, considering where he could have acquired it. If it is best answered in that way (I repeat), meaning cannot be important. What does not matter for the present or the future does not matter much.

So I want to understand the copy thesis in the less constricted way that I have pointed to, in which it skips definitions and emphasizes instead the two elements that go into linguistic competence: skill with word–word relations, and with word–world ones. That brings with it the third revision.

(3) I choose to (mis)read the copy thesis as being concerned not with the sources of, but rather with the criteria for, meaning and understanding. Rather than a doctrine about how one comes to be linguistically competent, I take it to be about what such competence consists in, what sorts of linguistic behaviour constitute the meaningful use or understanding of language.

This provides the only basis on which the copy thesis could be used in Humean criticism. Consider what happens when Hume challenges us on the so-called 'idea of necessary connection', asking in effect: 'Can you define "necessary connection" verbally? If not, can you tell me what preceding impression your idea of necessary connection is a copy of?' We can understand this more broadly and satisfactorily as a challenge to show how statements about 'necessary connection' fit into the rest of our scheme of things. What inferences can they enter into as premises or conclusions? How, ultimately, do they connect with the world as we experience it—what evidence can there be for causal claims, how can they be falsified, what is their predictive value?

A detailed study of Hume's critical work must sometimes attend to the copy thesis as written. Mostly, though, we can stay with the spirit of his thought, in a way that does him most honour and maximizes our chances of learning from him, by holding him to the triply revised copy thesis which I have presented here. I am sure that it was operative in Hume's mind when he wrote, because his actual thesis, taken literally, is dead in the water. Why would such a great philosopher think otherwise? The only coherent explanation ever proposed is that he aimed to offer meaning-criticisms in the light of word–word and word–world relations, but had not the theoretical and terminological tools to do this properly.

245. The missing shade of blue

At *Treatise* 5–6 Hume describes a phenomenon which he says goes against the copy thesis. Consider a graded series of colour samples running through the whole spectrum, each being barely discernible from its immediate neighbours. Each item in this series has its own shade of whatever colour it is, and the shades are all—in Hume's terms—'distinct' and 'really different from each other'. Now, remove one blue sample—its precise hue being named 'M'—from the series, close the spatial gap that this leaves between the neighbouring samples (named 'L' and 'N'), and show the resulting series to someone who has never seen M. With our help, and perhaps even unprompted, he can notice a quality-gap in the series at that place. So he can say: 'The L and N samples are a little more unalike than any other adjacent pair in the series; an intermediate shade seems to be missing at this point.' Hume continues: 'Now I ask whether it is possible for him, from his own imagination, to supply this deficiency and raise up to himself the idea of that particular shade, though it had never been conveyed to him by his senses? I believe there are few but will be of opinion that he can; and this may serve as a proof that the simple ideas are not always derived from the correspondent impressions.'

To get anywhere with this, we must make two of our revisions to the copy thesis. Unless we take impressions to be sensory inputs from a public world, we cannot be entitled to think that the man has not had an impression—a mere vivacious perception—of M. Nor can we have reason to think that the man does have the idea of M if that consists merely in his having a faint perception of a certain kind. What inclines us to agree with Hume that the man may well have the idea of M is that we think of this as showing in his use of 'M'—his ability to conduct good inferences using it, and accurately to pick out physical samples of M-ness. So, I repeat, we need two revisions before we can start to think about the problem of the missing shade of blue.

Does not the third revision abolish the problem? It turns the copy thesis into something *analytic*—a thesis about what it is to understand or have a meaning for an expression; but Hume's missing-shade problem essentially concerns the *genetic* thesis that understanding must be preceded by sensory inputs or . . . etc. His problem has this form: here is a man with a certain kind of mental present who has not had the required kind of mental past. Can we not just walk out on this?

No. In taking the copy thesis to be analytic rather than genetic, we do not wholly turn our backs on questions about how anyone comes to understand anything. If the man in the example can, unaided and confidently, identify instances of M (the missing shade of blue), we must be interested in how he did it. What did he know? What did he steer by? And how did he acquire it? That is what is left over from Hume's problem after the copy thesis has been triply revised. There is a real question here, which we ought to be able to answer.

The answer is obvious: what the man knows is that M is a shade that falls between L and N and is barely discernible from either. He can find that out for himself, or we can tell him. Hume does not give weight to this, because he confines himself to the conjunctive way of explaining meanings, and thinks that 'M' cannot be explained in that way. We can start: 'for a thing to be M is for it to be blue and . . .', but we cannot go on. However, although 'M' cannot be explained conjunctively, it can be explained; and to the man in the example it has been.[4]

You may say that the explanation 'shade that is half-way between L and N' merely postpones the problem, for 'L' and 'N' have also to be understood. I reply that they too can be defined in terms of their relations to one another and to other shades, *including M*. The meanings of all our colour-words could not be exhausted by their relations to one another; at some stage they must touch the world, being linked to physically given coloured things. But this is consistent with there being plenty of colour-words that one understands without their having been explained ostensively; and any given colour-word could be understood like this if suitable others were understood in another way.

It follows, I believe, that there are no 'simple ideas' in Hume's sense. He thinks there are. At least some colour-words, he believes, must have 'simple' meanings; and then, finding no basis for according that privilege to some over others, he declares them all to be 'simple'. Hence his problem with the *simple* missing shade of blue. He ought to have stopped assuming that explanations of meanings must form a one-way hierarchy with, at the bottom, words whose meanings are absolutely logically simple. The explanations I have been talking about escape such a hierarchy because they are not all conjunctive: the logical form of 'M is what comes between L and N' is unlike that of 'A woman is an adult female human'. Once this is understood, the genetic problem disappears. For a related but slightly different—and extremely good—treatment of this matter, see Pears 1990: 24–5.

Hume twice writes that the missing shade of blue 'may' count against the copy thesis (5–6); but if 'may' expresses a doubt, he does not avail himself of it, and he expects his readers to take this as a counter-example. When he walks out on it, that is not because it may not be a difficulty, but because 'The instance is so particular and singular that it is scarce worth our observing, and does not merit that for it alone we should alter our general maxim'. What is going on here?

---

[4] C. L. Hardin tells me that it can be explained conjunctively, because each shade of blue can be pinned down in the form 'n% blue and 100–n% white'. Well, Hume did not know that; and I shall pretend not to know it either, because the problem could equally well arise for a missing sound timbre, where no such conjunctive rescue is available.

Hume sometimes uses 'singular' in its meaning of 'striking' or 'surprising', but obviously not here. Perhaps, then, by 'particular and singular', he means 'single, isolated, not one of a kind', as when he questions whether any cause could be 'of so singular and particular a nature as to have . . . no similarity with any other cause or object' (*Enquiry*, xi, 115). If the shade-of-blue phenomenon were 'particular and singular' in this sense, Hume would be entitled to disregard it. An image that someone had (say) in a certain room on 17 July 1737, which nobody had since duplicated, would be a 'stray result'; and no theory should back down in face of such an event. A refutation needs a recipe for creating endless counter-examples.

But Hume has provided just such a recipe. His account of the missing shade is offered as a confident prediction that could have millions of instances. Not merely with blue and other hues, but also with sounds, tastes, smells, temperatures, and degrees of hardness as measured by felt resistance. These are Hume's standard examples of 'simple ideas', and perhaps his only ones, so that the 'particular and singular' phenomenon really sprawls across his entire domain.

There is no defence for Hume's complacent dismissal of what he ought to have seen as a serious problem, but we can—at least partly and weakly—explain it. He dismissed the problem, I suggest, because he subliminally realized that it does not seriously impede anything he wants to do with the copy thesis. In the Appendix to the *Treatise* he moves towards saying what rescues him from the problem:

Even different simple ideas may have a similarity or resemblance to each other; nor is it necessary that the point or circumstance of resemblance should be distinct or separable from that in which they differ. Blue and green are different simple ideas, but are more resembling than blue and scarlet; though their perfect simplicity excludes all possibility of separation or distinction. It is the same case with particular sounds, and tastes, and smells. (*Treatise* 637)

Hume may in part be thinking of 'simple ideas' as qualitatively unvarious images; but I am sure that he also means to connect ideas with meanings, and simplicity with indefinability. He comes close here to saying that (for example) the concepts of maroon and of scarlet do have a kind of complexity which shows in their logical relations to one another. He does not call it 'complexity' because he thinks of it as the having not of overlapping 'parts', which could be displayed conjunctively (separated and distinguished), but rather of a shared 'point or circumstance of resemblance'. He is coming closer.

Garrett holds that Hume could, relying on this passage, weaken his theory of idea-origins so as to allow that a single idea might be 'ultimately derived from a set of closely resembling impressions' (1997: 50–5). This, Garrett says, would not open the door to supposed ideas that Hume wants to exclude—vacuum, eventless time, necessary causal connections, and so on. Perhaps some such line of thought was at the back of Hume's mind in this performance of his, but it is far from satisfactory. As soon as he admits that the copy thesis is false, and that ideas can be formed in at least one other way, the game is up. The idea of eventless time (say) cannot be formed in either of the two ways so far described, but what now is the argument for holding that it cannot be formed in some third way? To get a mature and philosophically interesting line of thought out of all this, Hume would have to tackle 'eventless time' in its own right, contending that there can be no such concept because there is no way for it to relate appropriately to the experienced world; and that is just to throw overboard the genetic copy thesis that Garrett is trying to rescue on Hume's behalf, and to resort to the triply modified descendant of it.

246. Passion and reflection

Hume distinguishes impressions of sensation from impressions of reflection. A nodding acquaintance with early modern philosophy will suggest that this is the distinction between 'outer and inner sense'—to borrow terminology that was used by Kant often and by Leibniz once (*NE* 388)—separating what we experience when looking in on ourselves from what we experience when looking outward. The second half of that is wrong for Hume, because he does not tie 'sensation' to what is outer. When he first introduces the term, he says that sensations 'arise in the soul originally, from unknown causes' (*Treatise* 7); and later, again calling them 'original', he says that 'without any antecedent perception [they] arise in the soul, from the constitution of the body, from the animal spirits, or from the application of objects to the external organs' (275). This connects with his refusal to characterize 'impressions' in any way except phenomenologically (§239).

The interpretation's other half is right. Hume follows Locke and Berkeley in using 'reflection' to mean, as Locke explained, 'that notice which the mind takes of its own operations, and the manner of them' (*Essay* II.i.4). Thus he writes of an 'impression which the mind by reflection finds in itself' (*Treatise* 36), of 'some internal impression, or impression of reflection' (165), of 'whatever we discover externally by sensation, whatever we feel internally by reflection' (240).

Sometimes, however, he uses the phrase 'impression of reflection' in a seemingly different manner, equating such impressions with 'passions, desires and emotions' (8, 16). This is odd. Given that the phrase 'impressions of reflection' has to do with self-knowledge or introspection, how can it also carry the load of Hume's account of the affective (passions and emotions) and conative (desires) aspects of the human condition? I shall explain. The terminology is regrettable, but it can be understood. In this use of the phrase 'impression of reflection' Hume is deliberately *stretching* the range of the phrase without dropping his basically Lockean meaning for it. Here is the passage that creates the trouble:

An impression first strikes upon the senses and makes us perceive heat or cold, thirst or hunger, pleasure or pain of some kind or other. Of this impression there is a copy taken by the mind, which remains after the impression ceases; and this we call an idea. This idea of pleasure or pain, when it returns upon the soul, produces the new impressions of desire and aversion, hope and fear, which may properly be called impressions of reflection, because derived from it. (7–8)

Thus, desires and emotions are to be called impressions of reflection because they are 'derived from it'—that is, derived from reflection. On any showing, this is a bad terminological decision. Still, let us try to understand what Hume is getting at here.

The key to it is the first paragraph of book II of the *Treatise*. Hume reasonably thinks of desire and fear, etc. as having cognitive causes: I want something because of what I believe it can do for me, I fear something because of what I believe it can do to me. And at the start of presenting his system, he describes such cognitive causes in terms of causation by ideas. So, when I am in a state of fear, it is because I have an idea—perhaps a memory or a belief. My awareness of that idea involves plain Lockean 'reflection', so in that sense my fear is derived from reflection; similarly in other cases, my disgust, my elation, my desire to go swimming.

Thus, ordinary Lockean reflection is one small part of this whole story, and Hume has chosen to take the word 'reflection' in the phrase 'impression of reflection' and apply that to a different part of the story as well. A bad choice, but an intelligible one.

Incidentally, this account will not do for all 'passions'. Some kinds of depression do not arise from beliefs, but just sit like a heavy formless cloud over the soul. Hume may have that in mind when he writes that 'in a great measure' impressions of reflection are caused by ideas; but if they are not always so, that makes his terminology even worse.

Chapter 33

Hume and Belief

247. Propositional thoughts

What does Hume say about thoughts? So far we have noted only his saying that we have 'ideas', which he sometimes treats as thoughts (at other times as images). The kinds of thought they involve or constitute is sub-propositional: we may have an idea of a certain shade of blue, red, scarlet, or orange, sweet or sour, the taste of a pineapple, pleasure or pain, a past event, an object, a triangle, a man—these are all culled from the opening pages of the *Treatise*. When Hume uses the form 'idea of . . .', the blank is always filled by a noun phrase, never a whole sentence. In this he is a child of his times; it was the standard way of starting on ideas.

Yet some of Hume's 'ideas' must be propositional, because some are beliefs. We have not only the idea of *man* but the idea *some man is wise*. So Hume ought to confront the question of how we go about constructing a single propositional thought out of several sub-propositional ones. What happens in our minds when we do this?

This is hard to answer, as Locke found. 'The joining or separating of signs . . . is what by another name we call proposition,' he writes, adding that 'there are two sorts [of propositions], viz. mental and verbal; as there are two sorts of signs commonly made use of, viz. ideas and words' (*Essay* IV.v.2). Let us look at this on the verbal side. The two-word phrase 'man wise' is not a sentence, and does not express a proposition, and Locke may seem to have trampled on this plain grammatical fact and implied that merely by adjoining the two words one makes a (verbal) proposition. Leibniz thought Locke had committed himself to that absurdity, but he was wrong (*NE* 396). On the basis of his theory about the meanings of 'particles' (§173), Locke can say that to express the propositional thought one needs not only to adjoin 'man' and 'wise' but also to include 'is', whose function is to signal to the hearer that one is *joining* manhood and wisdom—signalling 'a particular action relating to those ideas'.

Still, Locke's account of the forming of propositions, though it escapes Leibniz's trap, is not right. Move from the verbal to the mental side, and ask yourself what is involved in having a man-is-wise thought—is it having a man thought and a wise thought in close mental proximity? No. If there is an 'action of the mind' here, it is not joining. Locke admits this four sections later. The mind does something with its ideas to 'put them into a kind of proposition, affirmative or negative', he writes there, adding defensively that he has tried to say what the

something is by using the expressions *putting together* and *separating*. He continues: 'But this action of the mind, which is so familiar to every thinking and reasoning man, is easier to be conceived by reflecting on what passes in us when we
affirm or deny than to be explained by words' (*Essay* IV.v.6). This is more candid
than helpful. Locke, while admitting that his terminology is wrong, implies that
his theory of propositions is true when its key term is replaced by a variable, to
be cashed in on the basis of one's experience of thinking propositional thoughts.
Even that were right, and the process of making propositions were familiar from
introspection, we would still not have a philosophical grasp of how such
thoughts relate to sub-propositional ones. In my next section I shall explain what,
ultimately, got Locke into this bind.

Hume confronts the thesis that fully propositional thoughts must involve at
least two ideas, declares that it 'is universally received by all logicians', and calls
it 'a very remarkable error':

It is far from being true that in every judgment which we form, we unite two different
ideas; since in that proposition *God is*, or indeed any other which regards existence, the
idea of existence is no distinct idea which we unite with that of the object and which is
capable of forming a compound idea by the union. (*Treatise* 96n.)

Even if this is right, Hume should admit that there are some two-idea propositions and say how they are formed. He does not. The passage from which I have
quoted goes on to say a little about thinking/believing/inferring; but it gets there
by silently vaulting the line between sub-propositional and propositional thinking, and thus jumping across Locke's problem.

Before returning to the latter topic, I shall run with Hume's thesis that some
propositional thoughts involve only one idea. He starts with a correct view about
the concept of existence:

When after the simple conception of any thing we would conceive it as existent, we in
reality make no addition to or alteration on our first idea. Thus, when we affirm that God
is existent, we simply form the idea of such a Being as he is represented to us; nor is the
existence which we attribute to him conceived by a particular idea which we join to the
idea of his other qualities and can again separate and distinguish from them. (94)

This is of a piece with Kant's thesis that 'existent' is not a determining predicate:
the phrase 'existent god' means exactly the same as the word 'god', and similarly
with 'existent hyena' and 'hyena', and so on. This is to deny that 'Existing is
something that things do all the time, like breathing, only quieter—ticking over,
as it were, in a metaphysical sort of way' (Austin 1962: 68n.). The point has been
made by various critics of the notorious a priori argument for God's existence, in
an ascending line in which the criticisms become increasingly incisive and eventually fatal: Gassendi, Hume, Kant, Frege.

In arguing that, as he puts it, there is no separate idea of existence, Hume
employs two suspect premises. If there were such an idea, he says, it must be
copied from a preceding impression; but an impression of existence would have
to be an inseparable companion of every other impression, and Hume says that

'I do not think there are any two distinct impressions which are inseparably conjoined' (66). We should have reservations about both the copy thesis (§243) and the doctrine about the separability of distinct impressions (§261), but the conclusion is still right.

The footnote from which I have quoted ('It is far from being true . . .') is doubly defective. For one thing, even if 'A god exists' contains only one idea, there is *more to it* than that; it does have a propositional structure. With help from quantifiers, you and I can give a good account of its structure—namely, the form: 'For some x, Fx' or 'Something is F'. Hume might comment that the quantifier does not convey any 'idea', but he should admit that it expresses a real structural element in the proposition, and that he needs an account of how such structures are formed in the mind.

248. Beliefs and other propositional thoughts

Having accused Hume of evading a problem which he ought to have thought confronted him, I shall now argue that really there is no such problem. Locke said that we can know from introspection what the processes are that he had misdescribed as 'joining' and 'separating'; but the real reason that he could not describe them is that they do not exist.

In general, when a philosopher writes of a familiar yet indescribable process, *caveat lector*! For example, Descartes and other philosophers talked of an alleged process of 'illation': to perform an illation is to infer a conclusion from a premiss, and it proved hard to say exactly what goes on when someone does this. The difficulty evaporates when one comes to the view—which I learned from unpublished work by Ryle—that there need be no such act or process. Inferring Q from P may comprise two distinct elements: (1) a range of different intellectual activities as one explores what P entails, what entails Q, etc., and (2) being able to see that P entails Q. No wonder 'illation' was elusive! There is no one central act or process; there are (1) thousands of them. The essential singularity (2) is not an act or process but an achievement, not a journey but an arrival.

Locke cannot properly describe what happens when someone forms a propositional thought out of sub-propositional ones because there is no such happening. In fact, propositional thoughts come first, and sub-propositional ones—if there are such—are their offspring.

Or so I believe, without a downright proof but with good reasons. I shall argue that the concept of a sub-propositional thought cannot be properly explained without help from the concept of a propositional one, so that we cannot understand the latter through the former. Objection: 'That is like saying that to understand what bricks are, you must first understand what a house is. That is absurd. Bricks come first in the "order of understanding" because they come first in the "order of being": the way to get a house is to take bricks and mortar and put them together appropriately.' Presumably that is how Locke saw the situation, and prima facie it is reasonable; but I shall argue against it.

First, I need to consider how propositional thoughts in general differ from beliefs in particular. Hume, as we shall see, valued his answer to this; but Locke did not even see the question, which he visibly glides over in his treatment of particles. He writes that '*is* and *is not* are the general marks of the mind' doing . . . well, what? It ought to be: doing whatever it is that leads to having an affirmative or negative proposition in one's mind. But Locke says: '. . . are the general marks of the mind, affirming or denying'. This is a mistake. The doctrine of particles is supposed to contribute to 'grammar', but now Locke has strayed beyond that. When I say 'Some men are wise', thereby affirming that some men are wise, I use exactly the grammar that you do in saying 'Some men are wise', merely meditating on this proposition. Locke has overlooked the difference between having an affirmative thought and mentally affirming its truth, thereby smudging the difference between beliefs and other propositional thoughts.

Note the pattern. (1) How do sub-propositional thoughts relate to propositional ones? (2) How do the latter (when they are merely thoughts) relate to beliefs? We saw Hume gliding over 1 in his treatment of 2; now we find Locke gliding over 2 in his treatment of 1.

Hume did not overlook the difference between mere thoughts and beliefs. He saw that one may take different 'attitudes' (not his word) to a single propositional content, illustrating this with the case of disbelieving something that another person believes. He insists that they disagree about the very same proposition: 'Notwithstanding my incredulity, I clearly understand his meaning and form all the same ideas which he forms' (*Treatise* 95). Although he left it at that, we can extend his point: I believe that Ambrose Bierce died in his bed, my wife tentatively suspects that he did, my brother hopes that he did. Each of us is thereby involved with the single proposition that Bierce died in his bed. How are we to understand this situation?

Some philosophers have thought that all those 'propositional attitudes' include as one ingredient the state, process, or act of simply having in one's mind—or 'entertaining'—the proposition that Bierce died in his bed. Each of the attitudes, they have held, can be understood as *entertainment plus* some further ingredient. Thus:

x believes that P = (x entertains the thought that P) & Fx.
x hopes that P = (x entertains the thought that P) & Gx,

and so on. Few philosophers today would agree that this accurately describes beliefs, let alone that it analytically explains what belief is. Explanations along these lines—including Hume's—have always palpably failed. Here is one:

H. H. Price's mentalistic definition of belief equates it with entertainment of a proposition together with assent. To entertain a proposition is to understand and attend to its meaning; when it occurs by itself, it is neutral and uncommitted as regards the proposition's truth or falsehood. Price breaks assent down into a volitional and an emotional part. He describes the volitional part as a mental act of preferring a proposition to any incompatible alternatives that have occurred to one; the emotional element is a feeling of conviction or assurance and may vary in degree. (Quinton 1963: 351b, based on Price 1935)

Price was a fine philosopher, but this is hopeless. The 'preference' of which he speaks cannot be the preference that I have for P when that is the proposition I *want* to be true. So what is it? Presumably, a preference for P over its rivals as a candidate for the title 'true'. But that preference—cutting the cackle now—is just a belief. As for the supposedly 'emotional' component: I deny that any kind of feeling or emotion is essential to belief; and Price's 'feeling of assurance or conviction' is really, yet again, just a propensity to believe the proposition.

Only quite recently did philosophers start to see how to do justice to the Humean insight that different attitudes can be taken to the same proposition, while not being sucked down into the bog of the entertainment-plus analysis of the attitudes. The alternative they have found starts with two of the propositional attitudes, namely (1) belief and (2) desire—thinking that P and wanting it to be the case that P—and explains them *together* in terms of how they collaborate in the explanation of (3) behaviour and how (4) sensory experience modifies beliefs. How this quartet of concepts is interrelated is told in a long, complex story called 'functionalism'. It looms large in the work of many philosophers, including Van Gulick and on up the alphabet to Dretske, Dennett, Davidson, Bennett.

We have looked at a seemingly natural order of explanation, in which

(a) believing that some man is wise, or wanting it to be the case that some man is wise

is analysed in terms of

(b) having the thought that some man is wise,

which is analysed in terms of

(c) having the thoughts *man* and *wise*.

If functionalism is anywhere near to being correct, this has the truth backwards. In fact, we have to explain the seemingly simpler items in terms of the seemingly more complex ones into which they enter. To explain what it is for an animal (human or otherwise) to hope that P, fear that P, wonder whether P, or the like, we must first get clear about what it is to believe that P or want it to be the case that P; and we do this without help from the concept of merely entertaining a proposition. Nor do we have, here or anywhere else, much use for the concept of a sub-propositional thought. We could, I suppose, force it on to the stage by saying (for example) 'At that moment he was having the thought *horse*', on the grounds that at that moment he was wondering whether there are many horses in Tashkent.

The *a-b-c* pattern displayed above has an analogue in meaning theory, namely:

(a) What it means to assert that some man is wise, or to enjoin that some man
    be wise.
(b) What is meant by the sentence 'Some man is wise'.
(c) What 'man' and 'wise' mean.

Here too it is natural to think that explanation or analysis should start at the bottom and work up; and here again the truth reverses the direction (§205).

249. Looking for an account of belief

Having made the point that one person can believe the very thing that another disbelieves, Hume asks: 'Wherein consists the difference betwixt believing and disbelieving any proposition?' (*Treatise* 95). He proceeds to give an account of belief for the special case where the proposition is a priori knowable. I shall set that aside until §286. Turning then to contingent beliefs, he persists: 'I still ask, *wherein consists the difference betwixt incredulity and belief?*' in cases where neither attitude can be established by a priori reasoning.

His answer is right, and perfectly defended, up to a certain point. You think it will rain this morning, and I think it will not; we differ in our doxastic attitudes to the very same proposition; so we differ not in what content we have in mind, but in how we relate to it—or, in Hume's words, we differ not in our ideas, but only in 'the manner of our conceiving them'.

Elsewhere he reaches this conclusion by a different route:

The mind has a faculty of joining all ideas together which involve not a contradiction, and therefore, if belief consisted in some idea which we add to the simple conception, it would be in a man's power, by adding this idea to it, to believe anything which he can conceive. (Abstract 20)

In short, if belief were an added idea, it would be voluntary, which it plainly is not. If I ask you to think about the possibility that your mother is red-haired, you can do that; and if I say 'and include her being one-armed along with her being red-haired', you can do that too. In large measure, thoughts are voluntary. But you could not, even to save her life, immediately alter what you believe about how many arms your mother has.

Both arguments are good, and the conclusion unassailable: belief does not differ from disbelief in the mental content or 'ideas' that are involved.

(Perhaps encouraged by his view that all real beliefs are affirmations or denials of the existence of something, Hume decorates his point about belief with what he takes to be a similar point about existence. We saw him contending that there is no idea of existence, so that conceiving of a god is the same as conceiving of an existent god. He continues:

But I go further; and, not content with asserting that the conception of the existence of any object is no addition to the simple conception of it, I likewise maintain that the belief of the existence joins no new ideas to those which compose the idea of the object. When I think of God, when I think of him as existent, and when I believe him to be existent, my idea of him neither encreases nor diminishes. (*Treatise* 94)

Hume here treats 'There is no idea of existence' as though it were comparable with, and even linked to, 'Belief does not happen through the addition of an idea'. Some of his readers have observed that the two theses are quite different, and are interrelated only by a thin, formal analogy (Geach 1965: 458–9; see also Passmore 1952: 97–9). That Hume was wrong to bracket them is shown by this: *having the thought that P* is really different from *believing that P*, as Hume knew; whereas *the thought of a hyena* is exactly the same as *the thought of an existent hyena*, as he also knew. Neither pair differs in the mental content ('ideas') that are involved; but the members of the first pair do differ, while the members of the second do not.)

How does believing differ from mere thinking? Before considering Hume's answer to this, I shall offer a better one. I shall not quarrel with him about whether thoughts are image-like; nor shall I press my objections to entertainment-plus analyses of belief. In order to highlight certain other points, I shall keep quiet about those two.

What makes a mental content a belief? According to functionalism—broadly defined—the status of *belief* comes from certain relational properties that a mental content has: its responsiveness to experiential inputs and its proneness to collaborate with desires in giving rise to behavioural outputs. Of these two, I shall concentrate on the relation to behaviour. The belief that P may show in behaviour directly ('It will rain this morning') or indirectly and remotely ('Bierce died in his bed'); but relation-to-action is the essential component in our concept of contingent belief, even for the remote cases. The claim, then, is that for someone to believe (consciously, episodically) that it will rain this morning is for her to have the thought of its raining this morning *in a manner that disposes her to behave thus and so*—where 'thus and so' has to be unpacked in different ways depending upon what her desires are.

Hume often emphasizes the strong link between beliefs and behaviour, as here:

Belief . . . is something felt by the mind, which distinguishes the ideas of the judgment from the fictions of the imagination. It gives them more force and influence; makes them appear of greater importance; infixes them in the mind; and renders them the governing principles of all our actions. (*Treatise* 629)

A little earlier he says that beliefs are marked off from other mental contents by the fact that 'the mind has a firmer hold of them, and is more actuated and moved by them' (624). There is more about beliefs' effects on behaviour in iii.10, 'Of the Influence of Belief'. Their influence on the passions is treated at greater length than their influence on behaviour, but the latter also enters the story, at the top of 119 for example. Here, as in the passage last quoted, Hume seems to regard the influence on actions as an important fact about belief, but not as analytically true of it. Even considered just as a fact about belief, Hume does not bring it clearly into focus, because he does not ever zero in sharply and accurately on how belief teams up with desire to explain behaviour. The only hints of that collaboration are fuzzy (*Treatise* II.iii.3).

Probably the thickest barrier to Hume's having the functionalist insight was his lack of a good enough account of desire and of how desire relates to behaviour. He mainly treats desire (a 'passion') as though it were defined by how it feels. 'Certain calm desires and tendencies', he remarks, are 'more known by their effects than by the immediate feeling or sensation' (417), but he regards those as special cases. Also, he explicitly denies that any 'passion' has anything representative in it:

A passion is an original existence, . . . and contains not any representative quality which renders it a copy of any other existence or modification. When I am angry, I am actually possessed with the passion, and in that emotion have no more a reference to any other object than when I am thirsty or sick or more than five foot high. (415)

Applied to desires, this implies that the form of words *wanting it to be the case that* P does not imply that *what* one wants is an intrinsic feature of the wanting. Rather (the view would be), one has a desire with a certain intrinsic nature, and it is a further fact that it will (or the person thinks it will) go away if P comes to obtain. If that was Hume's position, it would block him from trying to explain behaviour through pairs of the form:

x wants it to be the case that P.
x believes that the way to make P obtain is by doing A.

Just as in relating belief to behaviour he omits desire, so when relating desire to behaviour he omits belief: 'Desire arises from good considered simply; and aversion is derived from evil. The will exerts itself, when either the good or the absence of the evil may be attained by any action of the mind or body' (439). This speaks of what may be obtained, not of what the person thinks may be obtained.

The functionalist analyses of belief and desire are relational, but Hume does not mind relational analyses as such. When offering his two famous accounts of what it means to say that x *causes* y, he notes that each analysans speaks of relations that x and y have to other things that are 'foreign to the cause' (§270). He anticipates that others will find this objectionable, but he does not.

Still, he assumes that each of us knows immediately and securely what he believes (wants), and he might think that a content's status as a belief (desire) must be intrinsic to it, and not a matter of how it relates to something outside the mind. If so, he erred. We do know straight off various relational facts about our behavioural dispositions: you know without submitting to tests that you would not accept a pound of marijuana in payment for publicly humiliating a 6-year-old child for twenty minutes. It might be like that with our knowledge of what our own beliefs are.

250. Hume's account of belief

Anyway, for some reason or none, Hume does assume that whatever makes an idea a belief must be intrinsic to it. This gives him a tremendous problem: believing something must differ in some intrinsic way from merely thinking of it, but not so as to affect what idea it is—that is, not affecting *what* is thought or believed. What intrinsic features of ideas or idea-havings are there that do not affect content? Here is Hume's answer:

When you would any way vary the idea of a particular object, you can only increase or diminish its force and vivacity. If you make any other change on it, it represents a different object or impression. The case is the same as in colours. A particular shade of any colour may acquire a new degree of liveliness or brightness without any other variation. But when you produce any other variation, it is no longer the same shade or colour; so that as belief does nothing but vary the manner in which we conceive any object, it can only bestow on our ideas an additional force and vivacity. An opinion, therefore, or belief, may be most accurately defined, a lively idea related to or associated with a present impression. (*Treatise* 96)

Set aside for now the final eight words, and focus on 'a lively idea'. According to Hume, believing that P is having the thought that P in your mind in a 'lively' manner. He uses some other expressions also to characterize belief; differences amongst these are negligible. Notice that his attempt to separate beliefs from mere thoughts without affecting content resembles his attempt to distinguish impressions from ideas without affecting content. The same language occurs in both.

The terms in which Hume defines 'belief' are most naturally understood to involve phenomenal intensity—something on a scale that has bright/dim for visual ideas, loud/soft for auditory ones, strong/weak for tastes and smells, and I do not know what for tactual ideas. That is suggested by his very words, and also by his application of them to colours. That application is a cheat, however, as I showed in §239 in connection with ideas/impressions. Adapting the point I made there: if the vivacity of visual ideas is their brightness, then my state of mind when I believe that the wall behind us is a dim sky-blue must resemble yours when you merely contemplate the possibility of its being a bright sky-blue. This is incredible, and thwarts Hume's intent to distinguish thoughts from beliefs in a manner that does not affect content.

He was at least partly aware of this. Some of his turns of phrase show that he does not assume that 'lively' and the rest have precise ordinary meanings upon which he can rely. He shows uncertainty about that here: 'It must be able to bestow on whatever is related to it the same quality, call it firmness, or solidity, or force, or vivacity, with which the mind reflects upon it' (106). A few lines later, *en route* to implying that a memory differs from a mere thought in having 'more vigour and firmness', he speaks of the difference as 'that certain *je-ne-sais-quoi* of which it is impossible to give any definition or description, but which everyone sufficiently understands'. In the Appendix he concedes defeat: 'Even when I think I understand the subject perfectly,' he complains, 'I am at a loss for terms to express my meaning,' and so on (628–9). The same passage reappears, slightly reworded, in *Enquiry* v.2, 40. Like Locke's apology for 'joining' and 'separating' (§247), it does not retract the theory in question, but only the words used to express it. Hume has failed, he thinks, properly to state the theory, but he still sees it as helping to clear up 'one of the greatest mysteries of philosophy, though no one has so much as suspected that there was any difficulty in explaining it'.

How can a theory whose central concept is inexpressible help to clear up anything? Well, when he has backed off from 'vivacity', etc., Hume has this left: *What marks beliefs off from mere thoughts is their being had with a greater degree of X, an inexpressible kind of feeling.* In what follows, I shall continue to treat 'X' as an abstract noun, with 'X-ish' as the adjective, and 'the X theory' as naming the thinned-out account of belief that is now before us.

Now, here are three core facts about contingent beliefs: (1) they differ from mere thoughts in a manner that does not affect content; (2) they are responsive to experiential input; and (3) they help to explain behavioural output. Although Hume's theory of belief is false, in his handling of it he shows sensitivity to all three of these.

(1) His account of belief in terms of 'vivacity', etc. was his attempt to deal with 1; we are now taking his word for it that he wants to withdraw from that to the X theory; but that still entails that belief is a kind of feeling, which is an attempt to meet the need posed by 1.

(2) Hume links beliefs with sensory intake by combining the X theory with the thesis that degree-of-X also marks off impressions from ideas. He firmly holds that there is a single continuum, with merely entertained ideas at one end, beliefs near the middle, and impressions out at the other end. Thus we find him saying that a belief 'is only an [X-ish] conception of any idea, and such as approaches in some measure to an immediate impression' (97 n.).

This is supposed to help link beliefs with sensory intake. Despite his official account of what impressions are, Hume often assumes that they are sensory— that is, are experiences of something other than themselves. He also classifies passions as impressions (third sentence of i.1). But most of the time he thinks of impressions as elements of sensory intake; and that is so here, where I think passions must be simply set aside.

Now, he seeks to explain how they can produce beliefs by supposing that impressions upgrade mere thoughts into beliefs by passing on some of their own X. This implies that believing there is a cat in the tree stands mid-way on a degree-of-some-feeling slope from perceiving a cat in the tree down to entertaining the thought of a cat in the tree. It is neat, but it is also incredible.

Even within the purely propositional part of the life of the mind, the X theory—specifically its one-continuum aspect—has enough content to be in trouble. Consider this pair:

thinking about your *past belief* that Bierce died in his bed;
believing that you once *thought* about Bierce's dying in his bed.

How can mere degrees of X distinguish these? Part of what is missing, obviously, is any notion of propositional structure. We saw Hume evading this issue, taking cover under propositions that involve only one idea. I pointed out that even there—even with 'God exists'—there is structure; and the further we push on into Hume's thoughts in this area, the more strongly we feel the need for a structural element.

There is an acute need for it to differentiate a proposition from its contradictory. In his theory of belief, Hume is presumably trying to meet (or avoid) this need, by talking not about believing not-P, but rather about disbelieving P. The work is to be done, it seems, by the single proposition P and the opposing attitudes to it. But where is Hume's account of 'incredulity'? He has only a continuum from robustly believing that P at one end to faintly *entertaining the thought that P* at the other, with no place for firmly disbelieving that P.

Had he attended to some of the other propositional attitudes, Hume would have found even more need for not-P as well as P. Imagine trying to sort out relations amongst fears, hopes, and beliefs without P/not-P pairs!

(3) We have seen Hume wanting to explain why beliefs influence behaviour—why belief gives ideas 'more weight and influence, makes them appear of greater importance, enforces them in the mind, and renders them the governing principle of our actions' (*Enquiry* v.2, 40). The final clause of this trades on the assumption that X is force or vivacity; replace those terms by the abstract 'X', and nothing remains that even seems to explain why beliefs influence behaviour more strongly than mere fiction-making thoughts.

I should add that Hume also holds that beliefs have more influence on our other mental states than fictions do. Belief, he writes, is 'that act of the mind which renders realities more present to us than fictions, causes them to weigh more in the thought, and gives them a superior influence on the passions and imagination' (iii.7). For many of us, this misrepresents the difference between (say) reading Gibbon and reading Tolstoy. Knowing that one book is history and the other a novel does not make the emperor Julian more real, present, interesting, and engaging than is Pierre Bezukhov.

251. Belief: feeling versus Intellect

Hume repeatedly calls belief a 'feeling'. He argues independently for this, in a manner we should try to understand. In doing so, I shall revert to his terminology, using 'vivid', etc.; but my main points will hold also for the more abstract X theory.

Someone might object that Hume has not made contingent beliefs intellectual enough, has not founded belief on the 'reasoning and comparison of ideas' which, the objector says, are its true foundations. Awaiting this charge, Hume sticks to his guns, adducing empirical evidence that belief is indeed not always an intellectual matter:

Here we must not be contented with saying that the vividness of the idea produces the belief: we must maintain that they are individually the same. The frequent repetition of any idea infixes it in the imagination; but could never possibly of itself produce belief if that act of the mind was, by the original constitution of our natures, annexed only to a reasoning and comparison of ideas. (*Treatise* 116)

That is a fragment from a longer discussion which, even taken in full, is a little obscure. Its argument seems to be this:

We can understand how frequent repetition (indoctrination) could produce a vivid idea, and so produce belief if that is a vivid idea. But if you say 'A belief is not to be identified with a vivid idea; rather, it is arrived at *on the basis of* a vivid idea', you will have to allow that the route from the idea to the belief runs through an intellectual procedure of some kind. It is not credible, however, that such a procedure should be caused to occur just by a mindless repetition of some idea, such as occurs in indoctrination and most democratic elections.

Hume is on to something here. Beliefs can be caused by indoctrination; a good cognitive psychology should explain this, and a good philosophy of mind must make room for it; and those are not trivial achievements.

Objection: 'You are conceding too much. Granted that in the pathological back alleys of the human condition beliefs are sometimes acquired in such unreasoning ways, it does not follow that all belief is a matter of feeling rather than intellect.' Hume would respond that the phenomenon in question does not, as my term 'indoctrination' suggests, exist only in the back alleys. He holds that all our inductively based predictions—'Given how the sky looks, there will be rain tomorrow'—are non-rationally based on the sheer repetition of certain sequences of perceptions (§269). That, were it right, would increase the range of his point about feeling versus intellect; but it would still not cover the entire territory. There are plenty of ways in which we arrive at beliefs by means that Hume ought to admit are intellectual, and are not captured even by the abstract X form of his theory.

Sometimes he makes room for these other ways, thereby temporarily deserting his own account of belief: 'When I am convinced of any principle, it is only an idea which strikes more strongly upon me. When I give the precedency to one set of arguments above another, I do nothing but decide from my feeling concerning the superiority of their influence' (*Treatise* 103). He ought to say that when one set of arguments is more vivid in my mind than the rest, that is my believing the former. Instead, he says that when one set is more vivid, I note that fact and 'decide from' that datum to opt for that conclusion.

Early in the Appendix he deserts his theory in another way, while purporting to revisit and re-defend it. He does this with two rhetorical questions: 'Whether there be anything to distinguish belief from the simple conception, beside the

feeling or sentiment? And, Whether this feeling be any thing but a firmer conception, or a faster hold, that we take of the object?' (627). This marks a radical
change of tune, in which 'belief is not a hold that the object takes on us, but that
we take on the object' (Wolff 1960: 114). The believing mind's 'firmer hold' is
significantly unlike anything in the main body of the work; it occurs twice more
in the Appendix (624, 626). Such turns of phrase show Hume tending to move,
under pressure from the plain facts, from his inadequate theory to no theory at
all. The Appendix also has a different kind of 'no theory at all' about belief; it is
shrewdly discussed by Flew (1961: 100–3).

Chapter 34

Some Humean Doctrine about Relations

252. The association of ideas: preliminaries

Hume has a doctrine about the association of ideas. He did not invent it, any more than he did the copy thesis. He declines to explain why it is true. Its causes, he says, 'are mostly unknown, and must be resolved into original qualities of human nature', which I take to mean: it is a *basic* fact about us that we are hooked up like this. At *Treatise* 60–1 he suggests a causal explanation, based on a speculative anatomy and physiology of the brain and probably borrowed from Locke (*Essay* II.xxxiii.6) or Descartes (CSM 1:106–7). We need not linger on this. Our first concern will be with the presentation of the doctrine in *Treatise* i.4.

The principles which it comprises all have this form:

When you have an idea I_1 in your mind, this is likely to cause you to move on to having a second idea I_2 such that R(. . . I_1 . . . I_2 . . .).

This abstract schema must be filled in. (1) The dummy predicate 'R' must be replaced by a genuine relational expression. (2) The remainder of that clause—the R-clause, as I shall call it—must be supplied. As stated, it merely indicates *some* proposition involving R and I_1 and I_2, without saying what it is; and merely supplying a value for R does not tell us. Point 1 is familiar in the literature on Hume; 2 is less so.

Hume announces three values for R—resemblance, contiguity, and causation. I count them as a quartet—resemblance, spatial contiguity, temporal contiguity, and causation—because the two contiguities behave differently in this context. Hume later calls these 'natural relations'; see the paragraph at 13–14, the one labelled 7 at 15, the top of 94, and the paragraph at 169–70. He means by this that they enter into the natural dynamics of the human mind as described in the association thesis. The contrasting phrase is 'philosophical relations': these are just relations *simpliciter*, including unlikeness, irrelevance, being bigger than, etc., as well as natural relations. See the last paragraph of iii.6.

How the R-clause is to be completed depends upon what R is. Rather than saying the same thing about each of four relations, the association thesis says one thing about resemblance and another about spatial contiguity, and so on. It may be worthwhile to get this complex business sorted out.

When we see Hume applying his association thesis, we discover that the R-clause can have any of four forms, which come from there being two parameters, each with two settings.

Subjective or objective   Subjective R-clauses stay within the mind, relating ideas to ideas. Objective ones go beyond the ideas, and involve how objects of ideas relate to objects of other ideas. Hume sometimes thinks of the 'object' of an idea as its content or significance, or the *kind* which it represents. But I am here using 'object of idea x' to refer only to a *particular* external item that x represents. That is also a Humean use of 'object', and it is the one I need.

Particular or general   A particular R-clause relates one individual item to another. A general one relates many items of one kind to many of another.

253. Three of the four natural relations

Resemblance   'In the constant revolution of our ideas', Hume writes, 'our imagination runs easily from one idea to any other that resembles it' (*Treatise* 11). The resemblance is said to hold between I_1 and I_2 themselves—thoughts beget similar thoughts—so the clause is subjective. When Hume writes, 'The idea or impression of any object naturally introduces the idea of any other object that is resembling . . . [to] it' (92), I think he means 'object' in the sense of an internal object, a content. So the subjectivity remains. As well as being **subjective**, the association thesis for resemblance is **particular**: the similarity holds between those two ideas.

For resemblance, then, the R-clause has the simple form $R(I_1,I_2)$—it says that the inducing idea resembles the induced one. Thus understood, the resemblance thesis seems to imply that every thought we have leads on to a different but similar one, which leads to a third, a fourth . . . It is not quite as bad as that, Hume says, because this kind of idea association is not irresistible, but is 'a gentle force, which commonly prevails'. Still, the gently induced movement from thought to merely similar thought looks bad. Hume realizes this, and offers the resemblance thesis as an account, not of a human excellence, but merely of a fact about us. Discussing errors that we commit because of the association of ideas (60–1), he says that 'resemblance is the most fertile source of error' of all the natural relations.

Spatial contiguity   Hume held that visual and tactual ideas can be spatially related to one another (236), and apparently his view was that any two such ideas occurring synchronously in a single mind are contiguous. So the contiguity part of the association thesis must concern relations not between ideas, but between the outer 'object' which one 'conceives' in having the ideas. (If it concerned ideas only, it would say that *when you have an idea in your mind, it is likely to cause you to move on to having a second spatially contiguous idea*, which for Hume is just to say it is likely to cause you to have another idea. That would be an impossibly flat reading of this part of the association thesis.) So the R-clause has the form R(object of I_1, object of I_2)—the first idea induces a second whose object is spatially near to the object of the first. (There may not be an I_2 that answers to this description.

When I think of the Taj Mahal, I have no candidates for the role of 'idea of something else that is close to it'. This could happen also with temporal contiguity, and with causation; but not with similarity.) I have been taking it that the thesis concerns the contiguity of one particular thing to another, thus construing it as **objective** and **particular**.

Sometimes, though, Hume construes it as objective and **general**, especially when he connects spatial contiguity with 'custom' or 'habit':

As the senses, in changing their objects, are necessitated to change them regularly and take them as they lie contiguous to each other, the imagination must by long custom acquire the same method of thinking, and run along the parts of space and time in conceiving its objects. (11)

For example, when I began thinking about arbutus trees, that led me to think also about coastal rocks, because usually when I experience such trees, they are growing near such rocks. The general version of the thesis is at work also in the extensive parts of the *Treatise* in which Hume seeks to explain causation in terms of human mental dynamics. Your causally based expectations, he says there, are upshots of my having found that 'like objects are constantly placed in like relations of succession and contiguity' (170).

The spatial contiguity thesis (particular or general) is 'objective' in the sense I explained: it goes beyond the ideas, and involves how objects of some ideas relate to objects of others. Hume sometimes implies that what matters is whether certain objects are or were near to certain others, but that could not be right. The mere fact of their proximity cannot affect what happens in your mind unless you are informed of it. (I brushed lightly against this point in my Taj Mahal example.) So Hume needs to say that I_1 will tend to induce I_2 in the mind of someone who thinks that their objects are spatially contiguous. (That still *involves* how some objects relate to others, which is why I call it 'objective'.) Hume never expresses the thesis in that form, but it insinuates itself into something he says about a Christian pilgrim whose memories of holy places lead his thoughts 'by an easy transition to the facts which are supposed to have been related to them by contiguity' (110). Notice 'supposed to have been': the pilgrim's ideas are affected by his *believing in* a certain contiguity. Hume puts it like this because he does not believe in the 'facts' or, therefore, in the contiguity.

He seems not to have realized that his thesis about spatial contiguity should be expressed in terms of what items the person thinks are, or were, close to what others. Similar omissions occur elsewhere in his philosophy of mind, as when he maintains that one's idea of any object is apt to be livelier if the object is nearby (not: if it is thought to be nearby). 'Distance diminishes the force of every idea . . . When I am a few miles from home, whatever relates to it touches me more nearly than when I am two hundred leagues distant' (100). It cannot do so if I have no opinion about where I am (§235).

Temporal contiguity   Although Hume yokes this to the other by the phrase 'contiguity in time or place', their roles in the association theory have little overlap.

Temporal contiguity, unlike spatial, can hold between ideas as well as between their objects; so Hume can, and always does, understand this part of the association thesis subjectively. Thus construed, the temporal thesis has to be general, rather than particular. The association doctrine as such concerns a second idea I_2 that you will be apt to have just after having a triggering idea I_1; so those two particular ideas will be temporally contiguous in all cases. Thus, the specific temporal contiguity part of the association thesis must be this: having I_1 in your mind is apt to cause you to move on to having an idea I_2 such that: I_1-like ideas have in the past tended to occur at about the same time as I_2-like ideas. So the temporal contiguity part of the association thesis is **subjective** and **general**. Once again, 'custom' comes to the fore. The temporal contiguity thesis is at work in Hume's analysis of causation (§269). I cannot find that it does much other work for him.

254. The fourth relation: causation

Causation We shall later find Hume putting causation under his microscope, and reaching conclusions that may be seen as sceptical. Still, throughout most of the *Treatise* he wields that concept uninhibitedly, as though he were clear about its nature and sure of its credentials.

The association of ideas quite generally concerns patterns in which having idea I_1 causes one to have idea I_2. The two ideas are not linked by 'an inseparable connection', Hume warns us, but still he thinks of the association in causal terms (see 92 for clear evidence of this). That holds for the entire scope of the thesis— that is, for every natural relation R. So the special case in which R is causation must bring the latter into the story in a second way, other than merely through I_1's causing I_2.

Hume supplies it by making the thesis say that I_1 will tend to cause a second idea I_2 such that the 'object' of the former tends to cause the 'object' of the latter: 'There is no relation which produces a stronger connexion in the fancy, and makes one idea more readily recall another, than the relation of cause and effect betwixt their objects' (11). This uses 'object' to refer to particulars outside the mind. For example, I have an idea I_1 of my son, and this induces in me an idea I_2 of my grandson, because my son is a cause of my grandson. Sometimes Hume invokes a causal relation not between the objects of those two ideas, but rather between objects of classes of ideas to which the two belong: if I have an idea I_1 of thunder and lightning, this may induce me to have an idea I_2 of heavy rain, because electric storms have in my experience tended to cause heavy rain. The causal branch of the association thesis, therefore, is **objective** and either **particular** or **general**.

My thought of Guy induces a thought of Miles, not because Guy caused Miles, but because I think he did. With causation, as with the other objective relation, spatial contiguity, what counts is not the holding of the relation, but the person's thinking that it holds. It is true that Hume's account of the causal concept puts something subjective into the concept itself, but that does not meet the present need.

The place of causation in the association of ideas is peculiar. Hume writes: 'Even the union of cause and effect when strictly examined resolves itself into a customary association of ideas' (260). He bases this on his view of causation—to be examined in Chapter 36—according to which:

> If in our experience each F item has been followed by a nearby G item, we are prone when encountering an F item to form a vivid idea of a G item; this is our expectation that a G item will ensue; and this leads us to say that the one causes or necessitates the other.

This is Hume's root account of causation: our propensity for certain expectations and ways of talking, he maintains, is the fundamental truth about causation; there is nothing deeper we can say about it. So he is offering a kind of analysis of causation in terms of the contiguity parts of the association thesis. That is its peculiarity: as well as being one of the four natural (kinds of) relations, it is also a peculiar kind of product of two of the others.

One reason for not dropping it from the association thesis, and handling the latter purely in terms of resemblance and the contiguities, is that it is too early in the *Treatise* for that. Hume has not yet come to his analysis of causation, so it would be clumsy exposition to rely on it here.

Here is a deeper reason. Hume's account of causation in terms of the contiguities is restricted to *immediate* causation—one item's causing another directly and not through an intermediary.[1] His examples of causation are all like this, and his analysis is plausible only when thus understood. On the other hand, the causal part of the association thesis is meant to involve mediate as well as immediate causation. The associative relation is strongest when R is immediate, Hume writes—that is, 'when the one is immediately resembling, contiguous to, or the cause of the other'—and less strong 'when there is interposed betwixt them a third object, which bears to both of them any of these relations' (11). Not only a third, he goes on to say, for the mediation may go to great lengths: 'Cousins in the fourth degree are connected by causation.' So the causal part of the association thesis has far more scope than would the corresponding contiguities part.

255. The importance of the thesis in Hume's thought

Hume prized the association theory as a powerful, versatile weapon in his armoury. He writes:

---

[1] Hume does have that distinction. 'Reason and judgment may indeed be the mediate cause of an action, by prompting or by directing a passion' (462); 'a Supreme Spirit or Deity, whom they consider as . . . the immediate cause of every alteration in matter' (160); 'to have recourse to some invisible intelligent principle as the immediate cause of that event which surprises them' (*Enquiry* vii.1, 54).

Through this whole book there are great pretensions to new discoveries in philosophy; but if anything can entitle the author to so glorious a name as that of an 'inventor', it is the use he makes of the principle of the association of ideas, which enters into most of his philosophy. (Abstract, final paragraph)

To grasp the place of the association thesis in Hume's account of the human condition, notice that he initially emphasizes mental *content*—impressions and ideas which he credits with intrinsic natures and representative features. That is a sadly inadequate basis for an account of the human mind, which engages in so much activity, so many doings and practices. For example, Hume says that a belief is a mental content with a certain intrinsic feel to it; whereas really it is a mental state with a certain dynamic role in the producing of action. Now, nothing can wholly rescue his account of belief; but his thesis regarding the association of ideas does compensate a little for his emphasis on content at the expense of activity. This is strikingly evident in his account of causal thinking: he looks for the impression that is the basis for one vital ingredient in our concept of cause; and what he finally settles for is a supposed impression of a mental event—a *transition* from one thought to another—which he therefore regards as of the essence of our concept of causation. In fact, the greater part of Hume's natural history of the mind consists in regularities and orderings provided by the association of ideas (see the paragraph at 92–3).

Though he needed to move from content to process, Hume's way of doing so has an unfortunate effect: it makes the goings-on in the mind look passive; we get from one thought to another through the association of ideas, in which we are usually caused to have the second thought by some facts about our past experience. This repeatedly shows up when Hume mentions habit and custom: 'As the habit which produces the association arises from the frequent conjunction of . . .' etc. (130). Again, he traces our causal thinking to an 'association betwixt' two ideas, and spells that out in terms of 'custom, which determines the imagination to make . . .', etc. (170). No doubt 'custom' and 'habit' have their place in the human condition: George Eliot is persuasive when she writes of our need for 'regulated channels for the soul to move in—good and sufficient ducts of habit without which our nature easily turns to mere ooze and mud, and at any pressure yields nothing but a spurt or puddle'. I submit, however, that Hume makes us too passive with regard to these matters, too little in control, too much governed by our pasts.

Still, this is the vice of one of his virtues. Many philosophers, before and since, have comfortably credited 'the mind' with an unexplained capacity for orderly, reasonable thought. Berkeley is one of these. Locke is another; although he dug deeper than Berkeley, he still said many things along the lines of 'The mind proceeds . . .', 'The mind takes a liberty . . .', 'The mind arbitrarily . . .', 'Noticing that P, the mind . . .', and so on. Locke holds that in all these activities the mind is employing its 'natural faculties', but he offers no account of what these are, or how they are grounded. Hume, by contrast, tries to get to the root of the mind's doings, not helping himself to any unexplained 'faculties'.

That is the framework within which we must understand the following:

Were ideas entirely loose and unconnected, chance alone would join them; and it is impossible the same simple ideas should fall regularly into complex ones (as they commonly do), without some bond of union among them, some associating quality, by which one idea naturally introduces another. (10)

By contrast, Locke views the association of ideas as a real disturbance to the more orderly, rational processes of 'the mind'. Having these available (he thinks), he can classify the association of ideas as 'madness', write of its 'opposition to reason', and call it 'a weakness' and 'a taint' (II.xxxiii.4). Where Hume starts on this topic at page 10 of his book, Locke waits until page 394 of his.

I should add that Hume does not include minds in his inventory of the world's basic contents (§306). For him, talk about minds is acceptable only as shorthand for talk about sequences of perceptions that are interrelated in certain ways. He would agree with what Berkeley wrote in his notebook: 'Mind is a congeries of perceptions. Take away perceptions and you take away the mind. Put the perceptions and you put the mind' (*PC* 580; see §219). So for him, more hangs on the association of ideas than I have so far revealed. Absent that association, ideas would be so 'loose and unconnected' that even by our ordinary informal standards there would be no mind at all.

256. Seven kinds of relations

When Hume begins to consider the concept of cause, starting at iii.2, low on 74, he asks what kind of impression the 'idea of causation' is copied from, and remarks that it must be an impression not of a monadic quality, but rather of a relation. Logically, cause/effect is like father/son, not like man/boy: we do not identify x as a cause and y as an effect, but rather x as a *cause of* y. Hume's way of getting the spotlight on to this relation in particular is a little peculiar, fitting awkwardly into his overall theoretical scheme. I shall devote this section to how that happens, and the next one to why.

Causation, we have just seen, is one of those (kinds of) relations that Hume calls 'natural', because they play a role in the dynamics of the mind. A relation R is natural if, but only if, anyone's having a K_1 idea will be apt to cause him or her to have a K_2 idea if some R-involving truth relates those two ideas, or those two kinds of ideas, or the objects of those ideas or kinds of ideas. The other three natural relations are resemblance and the contiguities. At *Treatise* 74 where we now join him, Hume writes that causation is the only relation on the strength of which we get beliefs: we have impressions of the senses and of memory, and from these plus causal assumptions we infer matters of fact which we are not experiencing and do not remember. That is true, and Hume does great things with it.

So much for what he affirms. What he denies, though, is odd. Where we would expect him to say that causation leads to new beliefs while *resemblance and spatio-temporal contiguity* do not, he instead says that causation leads to new beliefs while *identity and spatio-temporal relations* do not. Spatio-temporal relations include the contiguities, but that does not explain Hume's switch from species to genus. And resemblance and identity are entirely different relations. Hume puts the concept of identity out of lawful work, saying that whenever we seem to be using it, we have mistaken resemblance for identity (§282). But he does not deny that resemblance is one relation and identity another; so it does not explain the switch. What is going on?

The answer is that long after expounding the association thesis, Hume digs into relations as such, and identifies just seven kinds of them, which, he says, principally divide into a quartet and a trio. The members of the trio are spatio-temporal relations, identity, and causation; and Hume has that classification in mind in the puzzling remark that I have reported. The line he is drawing here is not between natural and philosophical relations. Of the four natural relations, causation and the contiguities belong to the trio (taking it that the contiguities are included in spatio-temporal relations); but the remaining natural relation, resemblance, belongs squarely in the quartet. This may not be a problem for Hume, though I wish he had at least considered whether it might be.

Enough about the change of classifications; my present concern is with the quartet and the trio considered in themselves. I shall say a little about the 'seven kinds of relations' thesis in this section, and in the next I shall explore the four-and-three division of them.

In an early section entitled 'Relations' (i.5), Hume contends that relating two things involves comparing them, whether or not the relation is 'natural'. He characterizes space and time as 'the sources of an infinite number of comparisons, such as distant, contiguous, above, below, before, after, etc.' This is odd and implausible; in saying that Borrego Springs is north-east of San Diego, I am not comparing them. One might guess that Hume means by 'compare' only its etymological meaning of 'consider together', with nothing implied about similarity (§174). But that is not his meaning, for he writes that 'no objects will admit of comparison but what have some degree of resemblance', inferring that in the absence of resemblance there is no relation at all (14). 'The relation of *contrariety* may at first sight be regarded as an exception to [this],' Hume writes (15), and he proceeds to argue that it is not, because a pair of contrary ideas must relate to one another as F does to not-F, and these *have in common* the idea F. I cannot rescue anything coherent from all this.

The dark doctrine that relations involve resemblance leads Hume to say that difference is not a relation, but rather 'a negation of relation'. That may help to narrow down the range of relations, encouraging him to hold that seven categories contain them all—the trio that I have reported and this quartet: quantitative and numerical relations, differences of degree, contrariety, and cause. It is a variously odd classification, but I shall not linger on it.

257. Two dichotomies

Now we come to the denser and more difficult iii.1, which, despite its title 'Knowledge', mainly concerns relations. Here two themes are interwoven—or rather tangled without Hume's realizing this. One divides relations into two classes which Hume characterizes thus:

(1) relations which 'depend entirely on the ideas, which we compare together';
(2) relations which 'may be changed without any change in the ideas'.

A 1-relation, then, holds between two ideas purely by virtue of what each separately is like, so it can cease to relate them only if at least one changes intrinsically. A 2-relation's holding between two ideas is not an upshot of the nature of each separately: it could hold, then later not hold, between two ideas, without either's altering in itself.

This really classifies relations between items of any kind, not only between ideas, dividing them into (1) those that are supervenient and (2) those that are not (§135). Simplifying a little, I shall say that a relation R is supervenient if and only if:

For all x and y, if R(x,y), then there are non-relational properties F and G such that (Fx & Gy) is true and entails $R(x,y)$.

Thus, 'is warmer than' expresses a supervenient relation, because if *x is warmer than y* is true, it is entailed by a truth of the form *x is at m°C and y is at n°C*. By way of contrast, 'is married to' expresses a non-supervenient relation: no conjunction of non-relational statements about Claudius and about Messalina can entail that Claudius is married to Messalina. Spatial relations are non-supervenient too. It is true that 'Syracuse is about 250 miles from New York City' is entailed by a conjunction of statements saying where each city is; but these locating statements are themselves relational—no theory of place treats them otherwise.

In taking Hume to be distinguishing (1) supervenient relations from (2) non-supervenient ones, we must take lightly his claim to be classifying relations between *ideas*; because supervenient/non-supervenient cuts across all relations, not merely relations between ideas. Hume himself seems to sense this when he writes not of 'ideas', but of 'objects', or of 'objects or ideas'. The supervenient/non-supervenient reading is strongly confirmed by what he says about where his 1/2 line falls. He says that 1 contains just four (species of) relations: namely, **resemblance**, **contrariety**, **degrees in quality**, and **proportions in quantity and number**. Instances of these would be, respectively, 'has the same colour as', 'has a different colour from', 'is warmer than', and 'has more legs than', all of which are supervenient. As for the three (species of) relations which Hume says exhaust 2, two of these are clearly non-supervenient, and we can at least see why Hume would place the third in that category. **Relations of time and place** are obviously non-supervenient: 'The relations of contiguity and distance betwixt two objects may be changed merely by an alteration of their place, without any change on the objects themselves or on their ideas.' He thinks that the same holds for **identity**, but some stretching is needed to make this come out right. Hume is thinking of identity as in statements of the form 'The thing that is F at T_1 is the thing that is G at T_2', and making the point that no piling on of monadic descriptions of how the former is at T_1, and the latter at T_2, will decisively settle whether this is one thing or two. The relation of **cause and effect** is not supervenient. It is not the case that every truth of the form 'x causes y' is an upshot of monadic truths about x and about y.

What Hume actually says about causation's being a 2-relation, however, has nothing to do with its not being supervenient. Yet I stand by my interpretation. The fact is that throughout this section Hume is using his 1/2 language to do two things at once: to divide *relations* into supervenient and not, and to divide *propositions* into a priori knowable or not. I shall now explain the place of the latter dichotomy in the section.

Taking 'ideas' as meanings or concepts, Hume is distinguishing (1) propositions that are knowable a priori, because they owe their truth purely to the natures of the concepts they involve, from (2) ones that are knowable only a posteriori, because they owe their truth partly to how the actual world is arranged. To make this fit the 1/2 terminology, we have to say (1) that *Every brother is male* owes its truth purely to the concepts of *brother* and of *male*, so that no change in the actual world could make it false. By contrast, (2), if *Every brother is intelligent* were true, that would come not only from the natures of the concepts of *brother* and *intelligence*, but also from a fact about how intelligence is actually distributed. So the proposition could change in truth-value without any change in what concepts are involved.

Strictly speaking, *Every brother is male* could not be made false by a change in the constituent concepts, whatever that would be. We might get closer to Hume's wording if we had him speaking not of a priori knowable propositions, but rather of analytic sentences. Then he could say that 'All brothers are male' could not become false except through a change in which ideas are associated with those words. Throughout this whole discussion, incidentally, I am not assuming that all a priori knowable propositions owe their truth purely to their constituent concepts; but I do assume that Hume believed this.

We have just seen that my interpretation does not fit the 1/2 language perfectly; but I still maintain that Hume does, partly or sometimes, mean his 1/2 line to be the line between a priori and a posteriori. Consider his account of why 'cause and effect' belongs in 2: 'As the power by which one object produces another is never discoverable merely from their idea, it is evident cause and effect are relations of which we receive information from experience, and not from any abstract reasoning or reflection.' This is irrelevant to whether 'is a cause of' is supervenient; but it bears strongly on whether truths of the form 'x is a cause of y' are knowable a priori. In explaining why the members of his trio belong in class 2, therefore, Hume deals with two in terms of non-supervenience and the third in terms of aposteriority. This is a long slide; but there is no other way to make sense of this passage.

My charge that Hume conflates these two distinctions may seem unkind; but the evidence mounts. He writes that only the quartet in 1 'can be the objects of knowledge and certainty' (70), and later refers to these four as 'the only infallible relations' (79), arguing from this at 463–4. A distinction purely between super-venient and non-supervenient relations could not even *seem* to yield such a result as that. Yet (non-)supervenience is also involved in Hume's 1/2 line. Here he is jumbling the two dichotomies:

It is from the idea of a triangle, that we discover the relation of equality, which its three angles bear to two right ones; and this relation is invariable, as long as our idea remains the same. On the contrary, the relations of contiguity and distance betwixt two objects may be changed merely by an alteration of their place, without any change on the objects themselves or on their ideas. (69)

'On the contrary' here means 'On the other hand': Hume purports to present an antithesis, contrasting the two sides of a single distinction. What he actually offers is: it is a priori (and thus securely) knowable that the internal angles of a triangle add up to 180°; but, on the other hand, spatial relations are non-supervenient. Looked at coldly, this is a nonsensical farrago, but we can see how Hume fell into it: since he conflates a priori/a posteriori with supervenient/non-supervenient, he naturally thinks that a priori/non-supervenient expresses a proper contrast.

It is important that one of Hume's two 1/2 systems classifies relations, while the other classifies propositions. He certainly does sort relations into (1) supervenient and (2) non-supervenient; but there could be no question of sorting relations by drawing any line involving the concept of a priori knowability. Hume seems to think otherwise when he writes of his quartet of non-supervenient relations that 'only [they] can be the objects of knowledge and certainty'. This would be a tremendously powerful result, if it were right; but it is not. In this remark Hume implies that no propositions involving the causal relation are knowable a priori, but this is not so. The proposition that *any earthquake which causes every house to fall down causes every small house to fall down* is knowable a priori, although its central concept is that of causation. It is not an interesting truth, but its existence shows that if Hume is to prove that causal laws are not a priori knowable, he will need something subtler than the block-busting claim that every statement involving the causal relation is contingent. This point, now so obvious, was denied by many philosophers before being finally put to rights by Donald Davidson (§260). Hume behaves as though he agrees with it, because he devotes many pages of the *Treatise* to arguing for a similar result in ways that owe nothing to the view that the causal relation is, for basic, abstract formal reasons, incapable of figuring in propositions that are knowable a priori. Let us now enter that territory.

Chapter 35

Hume on Causation, Negatively

258. Observing particular cause–effect pairs

Of the three (kinds of) relations which cannot 'be the objects of knowledge and certainty'—namely, identity, spatial and temporal relations, and causation—only one will support 'reasoning'. So says Hume. He standardly uses 'reason' and its cognates to cover not only strictly demonstrative a priori reasoning, but also the likes of judging from the look of the sky that it will probably rain tomorrow. Any such inference, carrying one to a conclusion that goes beyond present perception and memory, must be based on causal beliefs, Hume says. He often makes this sound like a thesis in naturalistic psychology: causal beliefs are the only ones that have the power to cause us to draw conclusions that reach beyond what we have experienced. But sometimes the thesis sounds normative: causal beliefs are the only reasonable bases for such inferences. We shall not be placed to sort this out until we have Hume's whole theory of causation before us (§270).

Having decided that only causal reasoning can (should?) give us conclusions about matters of fact which we do not observe or remember, Hume writes: 'This relation, therefore, we shall endeavour to explain fully', and he embarks on his great exploration of 'the idea of causation'.

Wanting to get clearer about this idea, he asks what impressions it is copied from. He sometimes uses the copy thesis as a basis for attacking a given expression, maintaining that it is not backed by a complex idea (is not verbally definable) or by one copied from an impression (is not ostensively definable), and is therefore meaningless. But this is not his only use for the thesis. In ii.3 he writes that impressions 'are all so clear and evident that they admit of no controversy; though many of our ideas are so obscure that it is almost impossible even for the mind which forms them to tell exactly their nature and composition'. So one may hunt for an antecedent impression, not as a preliminary to an attack on a supposed idea, but merely as an aid to understanding better an idea's nature. Hume repeats this in our present section: properly to understand an idea, look at the impression that caused it, because 'the examination of the impression bestows a clearness on the idea' (74–5).

This is not about an idea's *inheriting vivacity* from its parent impression. Rather, Hume is saying that an already existing idea can *acquire clarity* by being related (compared?) to its parent impression. He has no account of how this happens, beyond saying that it depends on the impression's being 'clear and evident'.

I cannot find an account for him. There seems to be no merit in this view about clarifying ideas by relating them to the impressions that caused them. However, if we apply the threefold revision that I proposed in §244, we can take Hume to be inquiring not into the past forceful perceptions which caused me to have my present idea of causation, but rather into the experiences of the outer world on the basis of which I apply my present idea (= concept) of causation. This yields something we can work with. It is still a pursuit of clarity, for we grasp a concept better when we understand how we apply it to the world; but it is not the spurious clarity that is supposed to come from relating a forceful perception to its copies.

Well, what relations do we find to be present whenever we judge that one thing causes another? One is spatio-temporal contiguity, Hume says: every *imme-diate* cause–effect pair is contiguous in space and time. He has no reason to deny that causal chains may run through large stretches of time and / or space.

Hume thus rejects action at a spatial or a temporal distance. He implies that an event at one place (time) can cause an event somewhere else (at another time) only through a spatially (temporally) continuous intervening causal chain. How could he justify this? Some philosophers have thought that it stands to reason. In the fourth edition of the *Essay*, Locke wrote that it is 'impossible to conceive that body should . . . operate where it is not' (II.viii.11). This is offered a priori, but Hume cannot follow suit, for he holds that nothing about causation stands to reason.

Still, he might say: 'I am describing the idea of causation that we actually have. There could perhaps be a coherent concept which allowed action at a spatial or temporal distance; but our actual concept does rule these out.' That would separate him from Locke's position, according to which there could not be such a concept, but would still imply that it is conceptually required that there is no action at either kind of distance. But although we are for some reason strongly opposed to allowing action at either kind of distance, I do not believe that this opposition is required by our causal concept, whether shallowly (Hume?) or deeply (Locke).

Next, Hume says that causes must be temporally prior to their effects, and he argues for this against the plausible view that some causation is synchronous. Some philosophers held the latter; Descartes was committed to holding that all action of matter on matter is synchronous (§20); so there was work for the argument to do. It proceeds in two steps, starting from a 'maxim' which Hume says is 'established . . . both in natural and in moral philosophy', namely:

[1] An object which exists for any time in its full perfection without producing another is not its sole cause, but is assisted by some other principle which pushes it from its state of inactivity and makes it exert that energy of which it was secretly possessed. [3] Now if any cause may be perfectly contemporary with its effect, it is certain, according to this maxim, that they must all of them be so; since [2] any one of them which retards its operation for a single moment exerts not itself at that very individual time in which it might have operated; and therefore is no proper cause. (76)

The argument runs as follows. (1) The occurrence of E_3 at T cannot be caused purely by the obtaining of some state of affairs for the preceding hour; the passage of time has in itself no causal efficacy. So E_3 must have been triggered just then by an event E_2. (2) The same reasoning applies to the latter, which must have been precipitated by an event E_1 that occurred just then; and so on backwards up the causal chain. (3) If in the foregoing we interpret 'just then' to mean at that very instant, then all the events in the chain occur at the same instant; no time elapses. The only escape is to take the 'just then' to mean 'immediately before', which then yields Hume's conclusion that causes immediately precede their effects, rather than being synchronous with them.

Ingenious as it is, this argument is vulnerable. In the backward-running sequence of precipitating events, it might be that some are synchronous with, while others immediately precede, what they trigger. Then there would be some synchronous causation although causal chains would still take time.

Hume argues on:

The consequence of this would be no less than the destruction of that succession of causes which we observe in the world; and indeed the utter annihilation of time. For if one cause were contemporary with its effect, and this effect with its effect, and so on, it is plain there would be no such thing as succession, and all objects must be coexistent.

If all causation were synchronous, he concludes, the world's history would be contained in an instant. That holds only if different times in the world's history must be causally connected with one another; but one might hold—as Descartes sometimes did for the material world—that history is a chronological, but not a causal, chain of events (§§20, 37). Then one could hold that all causation is synchronous, while still allowing history to stretch through time.

Let us pause to consider how the priority of causes relates to their temporal contiguity. If time is discrete, there is no problem about this: an immediate effect of an event E occurs at the next moment after the one when E occurs. But if time is continuous, there is no 'next moment', and it becomes trickier to make sense of contiguity-and-priority. Hume is unworried about this, however, because he has earlier announced that time is discrete:

It is a property inseparable from time, and which in a manner constitutes its essence, that each of its parts succeeds another and that none of them, however contiguous, can ever be coexistent. . . . It is certain then that time . . . must be composed of indivisible moments. For if in time we could never arrive at an end of division, and if each moment, as it succeeds another, were not perfectly single and indivisible, there would be an infinite number of coexistent moments or parts of time; which I believe will be allowed to be an arrant contradiction. (31)

I tentatively suggest that this obscure passage shows Hume being drawn to discrete time because of the problem I have just pointed out.

In defending the priority of causes to their effects, Hume is not trying to ward off the view that a cause might occur later than its effect. Only in the twentieth century did the possibility of temporally backward causation receive any defenders. (Some had thought that God could cause past events not to have happened, but they had not accompanied this with careful thought about causation as such.) On this question, philosophers have sometimes invoked Hume in a way that is worth looking at.

What reason could he give for saying that causes are never posterior to their effects? It looks as though he must answer: 'Well, priority is part of our idea, part of what we mean by "cause of". Causes have to be prior just as squares have to be four-sided.' If that is all there is to it, then priority enters the concept of cause by brute-force conjunction; so we could lop it off and still have a coherent concept—of cause*, let us say. Then a cause* could follow its effect*, even though a cause could not follow its effect; and we might expect the concept of cause* to work for us in approximately the way that cause does, though with some differences because it lacks the priority constraint. Against this, some have said that if priority goes everything goes, posterior causes* could not be used as levers or means, one could not make anything happen by producing a posterior cause* of it, and so on. If they are right, priority is more than a mere conjunctive add-on to the meaning of 'cause'. This is a hard topic which I cannot go into here. For a good sample of the literature see Dummett 1964.

259. The gateway to the neighbouring fields

So far as experience of individual cause–effect pairs is concerned, Hume says, contiguity and priority are the whole story. He instances a collision—it is between billiard-balls once in the *Treatise*, often in the *Enquiry*. When one body hits another and makes it move, he asks, what relations between events can we discover in this episode by looking at it carefully? He answers: contiguity in space and time, succession in time, and nothing else. But, he continues, these two do not exhaust the meaning of 'x causes y', which also means that because of x, y *had* to happen. This is the element of 'necessary connection' or 'production' (Hume says they are synonymous) in our meaning of 'cause'. The first event made the second happen, necessitated its happening.

The trouble with this 'idea' in our complex idea of causation, Hume says, is that it cannot be verbally defined so as to reveal it as complex, but nor can we find any impression for it to copy: when we see the colliding bodies, nothing happens in us that we could call an impression of production. To conclude that the copy thesis is false, he says, 'would be too strong a proof of levity and inconstancy; since the [thesis] has been already so firmly established as to admit of no further doubt; at least till we have more fully examined the present difficulty' (77). This sounds odd when we remember the missing shade of blue (§245), and it is indeed wide open to Reid's criticism:

[The copy thesis] is a conclusion that admits of no proof but by induction; and it is upon this ground that [Hume] himself founds it. The induction cannot be perfect till every simple idea that can enter into the human mind be examined, and be shown to be copied from a resembling impression. . . . No man can pretend to have made this examination of all our simple ideas without exception; and therefore no man can [justifiably] assure us that this conclusion holds without any exception. . . . 'But,' says our author, 'I will venture to affirm that the rule here holds without any exception.' (1788: 26)

Reid is right: this move of Hume's is highly vulnerable. Fortunately, we need not invoke the copy thesis to learn the main things he has to teach us about causation.

Hume's work on causation has profoundly influenced subsequent philosophers, which it could not have done had it relied on a theory of idea-origins that nobody believes and everyone thinks is irrelevant. In fact, most of those who have been stimulated by Hume's treatment of causation have thought of it in terms of the triply revised form of the copy thesis that I laid out in §244. We think that a concept such as that of cause must be applicable to the world as we experience it; and we can hardly be assured that we understand it until we have an analytic grasp of how we apply it—how, for example, we distinguish chance correlations from causal connections among the events and states of affairs that we observe. This requires an analytic inquiry, not a genetic one; and Hume's search for idea-originating impressions can be seen as that in disguise—an inquiry into what we go by when we declare that one event caused another. Someone may say: 'There is more to our concept of causation than is captured by what we "go by"; the empirical cash value of the concept is not the whole story about it.' Hume's inquiry provides the materials for a response to this, because he does not merely ask for the empirical cash value; he profoundly explores *what we are up to* when we use the concept of causation.

Still, empirical content is the starting-point, and so far all Hume has found are contiguity and priority. These plainly do not exhaust our thoughts about causation; there is more to be found, and it must connect with our experience of the world.

Now a peculiar thing happens. Hume writes:

We must therefore proceed like those who, being in search of any thing that lies concealed from them, and not finding it in the place they expected, beat about all the neighbouring fields, without any certain view or design, in hopes their good fortune will at last guide them to what they search for. (77–8)

The familiarity of this famous passage should not blind us to its oddity. 'We must proceed like those who . . .', Hume writes, as though invoking a well-known procedure. Imagine following it today! Imagine a supervisor's saying to a doctoral student: 'So your dissertation work has reached an impasse? Well, I advise you to start beating about the neighbouring fields without any certain view or design, in the hope that by good luck you will find something useful.' The proposal is absurd.

Hume says that it is his procedure, but it is not. The boundaries of his 'neighbouring fields' are marked by two questions, of which this is one: 'Why [do] we conclude that such particular causes must necessarily have such particular effects, and what is the nature of that inference we draw from the one to the other and of the belief we repose in it?' This is not off to one side. It lies on the shortest route from where Hume is now to his destination, and he could have introduced it without implying that it is a detour: 'I want to grasp what happens in our minds when we draw causally based conclusions, and why we come to think that necessity is involved in them. This will prove to be the key to understanding the causal concept. Trust me.' We shall begin looking into Hume's answer to his question in §269.

Here is the other question: 'For what reason [do] we pronounce it necessary that every thing whose existence has a beginning should also have a cause?' This really is a detour, and Hume ought to explain why he follows it. Let us see, anyway, how he answers it.

260. The status of the principle of universal causation

The principle of universal causation says that whatever happens is caused to do so. This is different from determinism, which says that whatever happens was causally inevitable: it could be that everything is caused, but that some causation is probabilistic. But this did not occur to anyone, so far as I know, until physicists began to adopt it in the twentieth century; and Hume presumably thought of universal causation deterministically. About this deterministic principle of universal causation he asks: why do we 'pronounce it necessary'?

That is the topic of iii.3, the upshot of which is that universal causation cannot be established a priori. Hume looks into three arguments through which, he says, philosophers have tried to do this, and he rightly condemns them all. Each argument, he says, depends for its plausibility on assuming universal causation among the premises; and that is right for two of them. The third is guilty of a different sin: namely, treating the word 'nothing' as though it were the name of something. This shaft is aimed at Locke (*Essay* IV.x.2), but Descartes also lies in its path (§33). A fourth argument which Hume mentions is still worse.

He prefaces his criticisms of those bad arguments with an important general reason for holding that the universal causation thesis could never be established a priori. If it could, he says, its denial would be self-contradictory, but it is not:

As all distinct ideas are separable from each other, and as the ideas of cause and effect are evidently distinct, it will be easy for us to conceive any object to be non-existent this moment and existent the next, without conjoining to it the distinct idea of a cause or productive principle. The separation therefore of the idea of a cause from that of a beginning of existence is plainly possible for the imagination; and consequently the actual separation of these objects is so far possible that it implies no contradiction. (*Treatise* 79–80)

He does not mean quite what he says. The ideas (= concepts) of *cause* and *effect* are not logically separable, for a reason that Hume himself gives: 'Every effect necessarily presupposes a cause; effect being a relative term, of which cause is the correlative' (82). One of the bad attempts to prove universal causation depends on this conceptual point; Hume scorns the argument, but does not dispute its premiss. He must mean to be talking here about the concepts of particular causes and effects, rather than the concepts of cause and of effect.

Well, then, what is he saying about concepts of causes and of effects? Try this first:

(1) If event E_1 causes event E_2, the concept of E_1 is distinct and separable from the concept of E_2.

This is useless, because there is no such item as *the* concept of an object or event. Well, then, a second attempt:

(2) If E_1 and E_2 are a cause–effect pair, every concept of E_1 is distinct and separable from every concept of E_2.

That is plainly false, for we can bring E_1 under the concept 'cause of E_2'. The only other cleanly simple proposal I can offer is this:

(3) If E_1 and E_2 are a cause–effect pair, some concept of E_1 is distinct and separable from some concept of E_2.

Where 1 is inapplicable, and 2 is too strong to be true, 3 is too weak for Hume's purpose. From 3 he cannot infer that E_2 could have occurred without E_1's ever occurring. Consider these two items:

New Zealand; the South Island (of New Zealand).

These are not 'separable' in Hume's sense, because New Zealand could not possibly exist if the South Island did not exist. Yet we can easily find pairs of descriptive concepts C_1 and C_2 such that:

C_1 applies to New Zealand, C_2 applies to the South Island, and there is no logical link between C_1 and C_2.

For example, refer to New Zealand as 'the country which first introduced universal adult suffrage', and to the South Island as 'the island containing the Milford track'.

The point is virtually trivial; but many philosophers have seemed to get it wrong, including Hume when he draws the a priori/a posteriori line through relations rather than through propositions (§257). The point has been incisively made by Davidson (1963: 14):

There is something very odd in the idea that causal relations are empirical rather than logical. What can this mean? Surely not that every true causal statement is empirical. For suppose that 'A caused B' is true. Then the cause of B = A; so substituting, we have 'The cause of B caused B', which is analytic. The truth of a causal statement depends on *what* events are described; its status as analytic or synthetic depends on *how* the events are described.

That is exactly right. So what are we to make of what Hume has written? Is it a pure error? I answer that he is getting at something true and important, but that his way of doing so reflects an error which has had noxious consequences in the twentieth century. I shall deal with the error first.

261. Hume's influential error about distinctness of ideas

The trouble lies in the opening clause of the argument: 'As all distinct ideas are separable from each other'. This uses 'distinct' to mean 'different'. Hume is talking about any *two* ideas—any case of an idea and *another* idea—with the ideas being regarded as concepts. He has a much-prized doctrine about this:

> All ideas which are different are separable. . . . It follows . . . that if the figure be different from the body, their ideas must be separable as well as distinguishable; if they be not different, their ideas can neither be separable nor distinguishable. (24–5; see also 18 and 36)

> Whatever is distinct is distinguishable; and whatever is distinguishable is separable by the thought or imagination. All perceptions are distinct. They are, therefore, distinguishable and separable, and may be conceived as separately existent, and may exist separately, without any contradiction or absurdity. (634)

This has the form: if D(x,y), then S(x,y), and if S(x,y), then P(x,y); therefore, if D(x,y), then P(x,y). Less abstractly: if x is an idea (= concept) which is distinct from idea y, then one can imagine or envisage a state of affairs in which x is applicable and y is not; and if that is so, then it is objectively possible for there to be such a state of affairs.

The move from S(x,y) to P(x,y) is made on the faith of Hume's trust in conceiving or imagining as a proof of possibility. Most of us think that possibility can be shown by thought-experiments, though we would think that it is better not merely to 'imagine or conceive' the supposed state of affairs, but to describe it. Even then we have to be careful, as I pointed out in §29. The description has to be given in enough detail to create a presumption that if it had contained a logical impossibility, that would have come to the surface in a plain contradiction. From now on, when Hume writes about what can be imagined or conceived, I shall take what he says in this more cautious way.

There are problems with the move from the psychological or linguistic S(x,y) to the logical P(x,y), but I shall not go into them. My concern is rather with the other part of the argument, the move from D(x,y) to S(x,y)—from 'x is distinct from y' to 'a state of affairs can be fully conceived or described in which x applies and y does not'. What relation is D? What sort of distinctness does Hume have in mind here? I can find no way of making this part of his work even slightly plausible except by understanding 'distinctness' purely logically: for the idea of squareness to be 'distinct from' that of blackness is for there to be no entailment either way between 'z is square' and 'z is black'. But this makes the inference from D(x,y) through S(x,y) to P(x,y) circular, since the criterion for distinctness is the logical possibility that the inference is supposed to establish.

In several places Hume purports to moves from distinctness through separability to possibility, in contexts where he could explain 'distinct' only in terms of 'possible' (86–7; *Enquiry* iv.1, 27). This patent error is part of his legacy to later generations of philosophy. I have been told that no fact can entail 'another' fact; and I have read that 'nothing that happens in the world can be connected . . . necessarily with anything else that happens in the world'; but our only criteria for 'otherness', or for a happening's being something 'else', are such as to trivialize both these claims. For more examples and a fuller analysis, see my 1960–1.

Wrestling with Hume's attempt to show that the principle of universal causation is not necessarily true, I could find no interpretation that would rescue it, and was left thinking that there is no true, non-trivial principle that would enable us to infer *It is not absolutely impossible that x should have existed without y's existing* from a premiss about concepts of x and of y. We have now seen that Hume thinks he has such a principle, and that he is wrong.

262. Steering around it

However, we need not conclude that he has nothing useful to say about the status of the universal causation principle. If we stand back from the quoted passages and the others I have referred to, and try to say what their central contention is, the following seems right: 'Hume is contending that, given any pair of events which are related as cause and effect, it is logically possible that either should have occurred without the other's occurring.' I submit that the phrase 'distinct ideas' has no place here, and that Hume got into trouble through using that terminology when his real concern was with pairs of *events*.

He does sometimes apply 'distinct' directly to events:

The mind can never possibly find the effect in the supposed cause, by the most accurate scrutiny and examination. For the effect is totally different from the cause, and consequently can never be discovered in it. Motion in the second billiard-ball is a quite distinct event from motion in the first; nor is there anything in the one to suggest the smallest hint of the other. (*Enquiry* iv.1, 25)

In the next passage he writes about 'objects'. They could be events, and are certainly not ideas:

The human mind cannot form such an idea of two objects as to conceive any connexion betwixt them, or comprehend distinctly that power or efficacy by which they are united. Such a connexion would amount to a demonstration, and would imply the absolute impossibility for the one object not to follow, or to be conceived not to follow, upon the other; which kind of connexion has already been rejected in all cases. (*Treatise* 161–2)

Those two passages concern the possibility that the effect should not follow, rather than (our present topic) that the cause should not have preceded. But they show that Hume, making points which he sometimes ties to the non-identity of two ideas, also sometimes handles them in terms of the non-identity of two events.

So perhaps his basic position is that it is not absolutely necessary that every event E should have a cause, because, for any cause C that might be proposed for a given E, just because those would be *two* events, it is conceivable, and therefore possible, that either should occur and not the other.

(1) How do we decide whether E_1 is the same event as E_2 or a different one? (2) Why should we believe that if E_1 is not E_2 then it is not absolutely impossible for either to occur without the other? As regards 1, I think that Hume is working with a certain sufficient condition for event-distinctness: namely, E_1 is not E_2 if E_1 occurs at a different time or in a different place from E_2. Here, for example: 'These impulses have no influence on each other. They are entirely divided by time and place; and the one might have existed and communicated motion though the other had never been in being' (164). All Hume needs for his causal purposes is the temporal half of this sufficient condition. Now let us turn to question 2.

Consider the following thesis, which I call the Time and Possibility Principle:

TAPP   If the whole time throughout which x exists has no overlap with the time through which y exists, then it is not absolutely impossible that x should have existed without y's existing.

I use 'x exists' in its normal meaning where x is an object, to mean 'x occurs' where x is an event, and to mean 'x obtains' where x is a state of affairs. TAPP gets the possibility of x-without-y from a premiss not about the ideas or concepts of x and y, but rather about the times at which x and y exist. That is not what Hume says, but I still offer it as the largest salvage we can make from this area of his thought. I believe that he accepts TAPP, and that it helps to convince him that universal causation is not absolutely necessary.

TAPP does support that denial. If y occurs at T_2, the question of whether it was caused to occur is for Hume a question about the occurrence of some event x at an earlier time T_1. If it is absolutely necessary that there was such an event, then we have a necessity stretching from one time to a distinct time, which TAPP says cannot happen.

Should we accept TAPP? Here is an argument for saying No. Last week I played piquet with my wife; that fact absolutely necessitates that at some *earlier* time she and I had married. Half an hour ago I answered my friend, which entails that he had *earlier* said something. Examples like those—and they are endless—seem to miss the point, but how can we defend TAPP against them?

In the spirit of Hume's thought, we can say that statements such as 'I played piquet with my wife' and 'I answered him' can be split into two conjuncts: one that brings in facts about earlier, and perhaps, later times and one that entails no such facts nevertheless tells the whole truth about what actually happened at T. 'I was playing piquet with my wife', on this line of thought, conjoins a statement about what was happening just then with one about how those events related to certain earlier ones. This presents a picture of the *basic* temporally atomistic facts about how the world is at each moment; and TAPP can be understood as saying that no fact of that sort entails a proposition of the same sort relating to a different time. This, though happily weaker than the false version with which we started, is still strong enough for Hume's purposes.

Is it true? It implies that the history of a world could in principle be given as a series of propositions each saying how that world is at a moment, and entailing nothing about how it is at any other moment. That gives us the Start Anywhere Thesis, which says this: If the ordered sequence of momentary series of world states $\{\ldots S_{T-1}, S_T, S_{T+1}, \ldots\}$ is a possible world history, then so is the fragment of it $\{S_T, S_{T+1}, \ldots\}$. Any history can be broken into at any point, and the part of it subsequent to that point *could* have been a total history. This entails that it is not necessary for any event to have a cause, from which Hume's desired result—that it is not necessary for every event to have a cause—trivially follows.

The Start Anywhere Thesis has been disputed by Kant, however. He had reasons, with which Hume ought to have sympathized, for holding that the only possibilities that we can entertain in thought are of *worlds that we could inhabit and know about as self-conscious beings*; and he argued that any such world must be strictly causally ordered. This amounts to saying that we cannot make the cut I proposed between how the world is at one time and how it was earlier: all our conceptualizations of the world are, Kant thought, shot through with causality; to make any sense of what goes on at one time, we must bring it under a causal scheme relating it to earlier events. If that is right, the Start Anywhere Thesis is wrong, and so TAPP is wrong, for both require the truth about the world to be temporally atomized in a way that is not possible for us.

The Kantian line of thought, with which most philosophers today sympathize, is not the sort of thing that occurred to Hume. In various ways he was an atomizer who reduced things to what he saw as their smallest elements—saying, for example, that a mind is a collection of perceptions—without ever asking whether we could know or think about the elements if they were not built into a larger structure. However, he does not really need anything as strong as this for his attack on the view that the thesis of universal causation is a priori provable. Kantian considerations do perhaps show a priori that any world that we could understand must exhibit a fair degree of causal order, but Kant was simply wrong when he thought they showed that causation is universal and exceptionless. What is best in Kant is consistent with this: 'Consider the fall of this tree, occurring now. You can say things about it which logically reach back to earlier times, but there are facts about it that do not reach back in that way, and the totality of those facts captures the whole intrinsic nature of the tree's fall. There is no reason to believe that this event had to be preceded by an earlier event which related to it thus and so. The distinctness of the times creates a terrific presumption in favour of a logical separation, and there is nothing to overcome it.' That is broadly Humean. It also seems to me to be true, though I cannot prove it.

263. The point of the question about universal causation

Having concluded that the belief in universal causation cannot be based on a priori reasoning, Hume says that it must have a different basis: namely, 'experience'—taking this to assign a cause rather than a justifying reason for the belief. How does experience 'give rise to such a principle'? Hume declines to answer this directly, saying that 'it will be more convenient to sink this question in the following, Why we conclude that such particular causes must necessarily have such particular effects, and why we form an inference from one to another?' He will stay with the latter question, he says, though 'it will perhaps be found in the end that the same answer will serve for both questions'.

It is not true that 'in the end' Hume answers the two questions in the same way; his account of why causes are thought to necessitate their effects does not explain the belief that everything must have a cause, and indeed Hume has no explanation for the latter. Furthermore, even if one answer did suffice for both questions, that would not explain why Hume started 'beating about the neighbouring field' of universal causation in the first place.

There seem to be just two links between the latter and the rest of Hume's account of causation. One concerns explanatory rationalism—the doctrine that there is a true answer to every why-question, so that there are no absolutely brute facts (§68). An explanatory rationalist would insist that universal causation must be true, because without it many events would be inexplicable; and would also reject Hume's analysis of causation, which, as we shall see, ultimately makes causal connections matters of brute fact that cannot be further explained in their turn. It follows that anyone who accepts Hume's analysis will no longer insist that universal causation must be true. Hume points this out himself, at the end of his inquiry into the concept of causation. He sums up his results in a pair of definitions of 'cause', about which he remarks: 'If we define a cause [in the first manner], we may easily conceive that there is no absolute nor metaphysical necessity that every beginning of existence should be attended with [a cause]. If we define a cause [in the second manner], we shall make still less difficulty of assenting to this opinion' (172). This is a genuine link between universal causation and Hume's analysis of the causal concept.

It gives Hume a tactical reason for approaching his analysis through an attack on the view that the principle of universal causation can be proved a priori. His analysis, as we shall see, is prima facie open to the objection: 'That cannot be the whole truth about causation. If it were, it would be incomprehensible that we should know a priori that whatever happens must have been caused.' Reid in his criticisms of Hume gives priority to universal causation: 'That things cannot

begin to exist, nor undergo any change, without a cause that has power to produce that change, is so popular an opinion that I believe this author is the first of
mankind that ever called this in question' (1788: 29). That is accurate, as Reid
usually is. Hume did not deny that whatever happens was caused to do so; but
he did deny that there 'cannot' be an uncaused event; and that is Reid's chosen
point of attack against Hume's account of causation. Since he is prima-facie vulnerable on this flank, it makes sense for Hume to cover the flank before moving
in on the analysis.

The second link is connected with the first. We have seen Hume deploying a
certain general thesis which he thinks implies that, in any case where C causes E,
it is not absolutely impossible that E should have occurred without C's preceding
it. On the surface it is a thesis about the distinctness of ideas; I contend that the
substance of it is TAPP, the Time and Possibility Principle, which concerns the distinctness of events and states of affairs. Either way, it is also at work in the next
part of Hume's treatment of causation, in which he contends that in any case,
where C causes E, it is not absolutely impossible that C should have occurred
without E's following it. Hume may have felt that the reader would be helped to
grasp the power of his principle if he applied it to 'possibly no cause' before moving on to 'possibly no effect'. Let us now leave the neighbouring fields.

264. Causal inferences from memory and sensory experience

In iii.4 Hume sets aside universal causation and starts to examine what happens
when we reach conclusions—that is, acquire beliefs—through causal reasoning.
To do this, he says, we must first have something to work *from*; we might work
from beliefs that were in their turn arrived at through causal inferences, but we
cannot run back thus for ever. Eventually causal reasoning must be rooted in
something else, and all it can be is an impression of the senses or of memory. He
acknowledges that we can conduct 'hypothetical arguments' in which we say
'Suppose it were the case that P; what would that cause?'; but no such argument
can lead to a belief, because it has no impressions as input. At this point in the
Treatise, Hume starts to speak of memories as 'impressions' rather than 'ideas',
pivoting on the statement that 'ideas of the memory . . . are equivalent to impressions'. It is also about now that he begins to allow that not only causal inferences
but also sense impressions and memories generate beliefs. For example, in the
final paragraph of iii.5 he speaks of impressions of the senses and 'repetitions' of
them in the memory as beliefs, and of their acquisition as 'the first act of judgment'—and 'judgment' is the faculty of belief.

Section 5 (84–6) opens with a swift sketch of what is involved in a causal inference:

an initial impression,

a transition from that to a belief,
the belief

—a perception, a process, a second perception. So we have three things to investigate, which Hume addresses in sections 5, 6, and 7 respectively. The treatment
of sensation and memory in section 5 mainly repeats things said earlier.

In section 6 things start moving in a positive way, when Hume introduces the
notion of constant conjunction. This relates pairs of event-kinds, not pairs of
events; it could not be observed in any individual pair, which is why it escaped
Hume's net when he first trawled for relevant impressions. But it is a legitimate
part of the story, he says. When we judge that E_1 caused E_2, it is typically the case
that E_1 is of a kind K_1 and E_2 of a kind K_2 such that: K_1 events have in our experience regularly been followed by K_2 events in their immediate spatio-temporal
vicinity. (I say 'typically' because Hume says at 104–5 that a single experiment
may lead us to believe in a causal connection between a certain pair of event-
kinds, and thus to make causal inferences. He explains at 105 that even this
involves reliance on a higher-level, more abstract kind of constant conjunction,
which leads us to think that 'Like objects, placed in like circumstances, will
always produce like effects'.) Furthermore, that is what leads us to connect these
two kinds of event causally:

We remember to have seen that species of object we call flame, and to have felt that
species of sensation we call heat. We likewise call to mind their constant conjunction in
all past instances. Without any further ceremony, we call the one *cause*, and the other
effect, and infer the existence of the one from that of the other. (87)

But this, says Hume, is a peculiar addition to the account of causation: the added
element seems irrelevant to the question of what happens in any individual case,
because it cannot be detected in—and is not a fact about—any such case. But is
not the individual cause-effect pair our primary topic? If so, then what good can
constant conjunction do us? Hume says that 'it may be thought'—and that 'it
seems evident, at least at first sight'—that we cannot get the idea of necessary
connection out of impressions of constant conjunction, because sheer repetition
cannot add anything to our store of ideas. On the other hand, our experience of
constant conjunction evidently does lead us to impute causality, does take us
from *post hoc* to *propter hoc*. How can it affect so powerfully what we think and
say about particular cases, given that it cannot be found in them? Hume's treatment of this problem is subtle and deep.

It is also lengthy, but at 88 he gives a hint about how it will come out, presenting something which 'perhaps' will 'appear in the end'. It is a tiny bit of
swashbuckling—a mere flourish—which is so elegant that it deserves a paragraph. Previous theorists of causation held that what justifies our causal inferences is the fact that causes are necessarily connected with their effects; so that
for them the pattern is this:

necessary connection → inference to future cases.

The 'arrow' is normative: the necessary connections *entitle* us to make causal inferences. Hume, on the other hand, will explain the so-called idea of necessary connection as an upshot of what happens in our minds when we conduct those inferences. For him, then, the proper explanatory order is this:

inference to future cases → necessary connection.

The arrow, whatever it may be, is certainly not normative. One can sense Hume's pleasure in declaring that previous views about causation put the truth backwards: 'Perhaps it will appear in the end that the necessary connexion depends on the inference, instead of the inference's depending on the necessary connexion.' Now let us track the account in detail.

265. Causation and absolute necessity

I encounter a K_1 event and am led to expect a K_2 event to ensue immediately, because in the past I have found K_1 events to be followed closely by K_2 ones. What, Hume asks, is the basis for this 'because'? What sort of reason does the past constant conjunction give me for expecting that it will continue on the present occasion? It cannot be a matter of demonstrative inference, he predictably says: 'We can at least conceive a change in the course of nature; which sufficiently proves that such a change is not absolutely impossible. To form a clear idea of anything is an undeniable argument for its possibility' (89). Most of us will endorse this, or at least the relative of it which I stated in §29 in terms of full descriptions, rather than clear ideas.

In these claims about what is conceivable and thus possible, Hume is, or ought to be, relying upon TAPP. When dealing with universal causation, he needed the backward half of that: what is the case at one time cannot entail anything about what happened earlier. That yields the Start Anywhere Thesis and its cousin the Come Anywhence Thesis. Now he needs TAPP's forward half, one consequence of which has been almost universally accepted: namely, the Stop Anywhere Thesis:

Let Long be a world at which various things exist before, at, and after time T; let Short be exactly like Long up to T, and unlike it from there on, because at Short everything goes out of existence at T. Then, if Long is possible, so is Short.

This echoes Descartes's view that God must keep re-creating the world, as it were, because a thing's existing at one time cannot necessitate its existing later (§37).

More directly relevant to Hume's present theme is another consequence of TAPP: namely, the Go Anywhither Thesis:

Let Straight be any world at which events occur before, at, and after T; let Bent be a world that is exactly like Straight up to T and then unlike it from there on, because at T the course of events at Bent is different—as different as you like—from the course of post-T events at Straight. Then, if Straight is possible, so is Bent.

This has won less acceptance than the other, I believe; but really the two stand or fall together. The only solid basis for Stop is TAPP, which equally yields Go.

A story about what happens before T may entail propositions about what happens after T: in January he met the woman he would marry in November. Hume's basic point, however, is that there are no across-time forward logical leaps that give us *a better than inductive security about the future.* As Pears points out, any uncertainty about whether he will marry this woman is an uncertainty about whether he is now meeting his future wife; and similarly for any other examples that might be given. So it seems fairly certain that we can make a Humean cut through time to insulate the earlier from the later. There is no Kantian obstacle to this line of thought; my intellectual grasp of my world now cannot depend upon what (I think) the world will be like later.

The thesis that causes do not absolutely necessitate their effects may seem like small beer now: who, today, would doubt it? Well, in §268 I shall show that the thesis has a vital role in closing a door that some philosophers still think is open. I think that Hume was half-aware of this, though he did not openly announce it.

He was very open about another relevance that he saw for his thesis that causes do not absolutely necessitate their effects. After sketching the problem—which haunted Cartesians and others—about how matter could cause thoughts, Hume claims that his 'no absolute necessity' thesis abolishes it:

To consider the matter *a priori*, anything may produce anything . . . This evidently destroys the precedent reasoning concerning the cause of thought or perception. For though there appear no manner of connexion betwixt motion or thought, the case is the same with all other causes and effects (247).

Having for many years inordinately admired the two paragraphs at 246–8 from which that comes, I have lately realized that in them Hume cuts a corner. Someone who questions whether motions could cause thoughts or the converse, on the grounds that there is no 'connexion' between any cause and its effect, may have any of three things in mind. A state of affairs in matter cannot cause a mentalistic one, or vice versa, he may hold, because the conceptual divide between the two prevents it from being the case that

(1) one absolutely necessitates the other, or
(2) a relevant trope transfer occurs between the two, or
(3) the two have features which make them inherently suitable to be causally related to one another.

Hume's no-necessity thesis does indeed abolish 1; it removes Spinoza's kind of reason for denying that there is causal flow between the attributes of thought and extension (§68). But in itself it does not touch 2; it leaves Locke with his perturbation about how matter can act upon mind (§35). Nor does Hume's thesis lay a finger on 3—the objection to mind–matter causality that Leibniz would have had even if he had been a realist about matter and transeunt causation (§117).

Hume had no reason to discuss (2) trope transfer, because it does not offer to solve the problem about causation that preoccupied him. Given two events in a spatio-temporal relation, Hume wants to know how one of them can explain, necessitate, or permit the prediction of the other. Where the first event is the white ball's hitting the red, Hume takes the second event to be the latter's starting to move; but if he had instead supposed the second event to be the transfer of a movement trope from the white to the red, he would still have had his entire problem in front of him. One event (impact), *then* a second event (trope transfer); how do we get from *post hoc* to *propter hoc*?

As for (3) Leibnizian standards of reasonableness or suitability, and the principle of sufficient reason upon which they rely, there is no surprise in Hume's not discussing that topic. Leibniz's explanatory rationalism could be a product of his theology, or a deeper-lying feature of his cast of mind. Hume's atheism closes off the former route to him, while the cast of *his* mind closes off the latter.

266. The Lockean inference to power

Even if we are satisfied that the past existence of a pattern in nature does not absolutely necessitate its future continuance, does it perhaps make it probable? Hume will not discuss probability until iii.11–13, but what he says about it here is safe enough. He makes the point that any conclusion of the form 'Because things are thus and so now, they will probably develop in such and such a manner' must be based upon how we have found things to go in the past; so such inferences rely on some assumption about the continuance into the future of past patterns, so probability cannot underlie and justify any such assumption:

Probability is founded on the presumption of a resemblance betwixt those objects of which we have had experience and those of which we have had none; and therefore it is impossible this presumption can arise from probability. The same principle cannot be both the cause and effect of another. (90; see also 137)

This last sentence embodies a joke, as Hume makes plain when he continues: 'and this is perhaps the only proposition concerning that relation which is either intuitively or demonstratively certain'. His point, however, is serious.

At 90–1 Hume deals superbly with a certain kind of argument which has tempted many philosophers and which he found in Locke. As the latter was also committed to something like Hume's theory regarding the sensory limits on our 'ideas' or concepts, he too faces a problem about the empirical cash value of 'cause' or (his preferred word) 'power'. The topic comes up just twice in the *Essay*, in II.vii.8 and, more satisfactorily, here:

The mind being every day informed by the senses of the alteration of those simple ideas it observes in things without, and taking notice how one comes to an end and ceases to be and another begins to exist which was not before; . . . and concluding from what it has so constantly observed to have been that the like changes will for the future be made in the same things by like agents and by the like ways; considers in one thing the possibility of having any of its simple ideas changed and in another the possibility of making that change; and so comes by that idea which we call power. (II.xxi.1)

Hume understood this obscure passage rightly. Locke speaks of the mind as 'concluding' something from certain data: an inference is asserted to take place. Here is Hume's reconstruction of it:

Such an object is always found to produce another. It is impossible it could have this effect if it was not endowed with a power of production. The power necessarily implies the effect; and therefore there is a just foundation for drawing a conclusion from the existence of one object to that of its usual attendant. The past production implies a power; the power implies a new production; and the new production is what we infer from the power and the past production. (*Treatise* 90)

Hume does not mention Locke by name here, but reverting to the topic at 157 he explicitly cites *Essay* II.xxi and seems to have it in mind in the passage just quoted (see also *Enquiry* vii.1, 52n.). The quoted passage is unhappily worded: the phrase 'an object is . . . *found* to *produce* another' implies that causal transactions are sensorily given. But the trouble is in the wording, not in the thought: Locke means to be talking only about our experience of *regularities*, and that is how Hume understood him.

We now have a line of thought that still attracts some philosophers. It is meant to rescue us from having to accept this:

We experience many regularities in the course of the world. The propositions that report those regularities—ones to the effect that K_1 events have been followed by K_2 events—are fundamental, inexplicable, not true because of some underlying fact that K_1 events *make* K_2 events occur.

Some philosophers find this incredible. No intelligent, unconfused person would swallow such a story, they think. If they are right, and if there are no logical jumps across times, we had better believe in some less strenuous kind of making, producing, necessitating, or the like that does interrelate temporally separated events. This is our only escape from the conclusion that the regularities are the fundamental fact of the matter.

267. Four of Hume's objections to the Lockean inference

After reporting the Lockean inference to power, Hume comments:

It were easy for me to show the weakness of this reasoning, were I willing to make use of those observations I have already made, [1] that the idea of production is the same with that of causation, and [2] that no existence certainly and demonstratively implies a power in any other object; or were it proper to anticipate [3] what I shall have occasion to remark afterwards concerning the idea we form of power and efficacy. (90–1)

He declines to bring in 1 and 2, because that might 'seem . . . to weaken my system by resting one part of it on another', and he postpones 3 at this stage, lest he 'breed a confusion' by getting things out of order. Still, I shall briefly discuss the three now.

(1) Supposing it is true that 'the idea of *production* is the same with that of *causation*', what bearing has this on the Lockean inference? None. Our only problem is to understand why Hume thought otherwise, and here is the best explanation I can find. Forgetting the Lockean inference, and looking only at its ending up with a supposed idea of power, Hume thinks of the Lockean as offering 'power' as an explanation of what 'cause' means. This is no good as an explanation or analysis, he thinks, not because 'cause' and 'power' are synonymous, but because 'power' is only a single word, and therefore gives no help in disentangling or laying bare the inner structure of the idea of cause. That is how we have to understand this: 'The terms of efficacy, agency, power, force, energy, necessity, connexion, and productive quality, are all nearly synonymous; and therefore it is an absurdity to employ any of them in defining the rest' (157). One might say that a definition is wrong unless its two sides *are* synonymous; but Hume's point is that you don't give a helpful analysis by equating one word with another word.

Locke's treatment of power, however, is not a mere proposal that we equate 'cause' with 'power' and regard this equation as explaining the former. It is, as Hume usually sees, an argument, an inference, to the conclusion that something underlies and explains the observed regularities. He has to tackle this independently of what it might imply for the meaning of 'cause'.

(2) When Hume writes that 'no existence certainly and demonstratively implies a power in any other object', he invokes his thesis that it is not absolutely necessary that every event has a cause. When he returns to the Lockean inference at *Treatise* 157, he puts it this way: 'Reason, as distinguished from experience, can never make us conclude that a cause or productive quality is absolutely requisite to every beginning of existence.' We can see this as challenging the Lockean inference to power, making the point that it is not licensed by any absolutely necessary principle. Whether anything weaker than this could support it remains to be seen.

(3) What Hume says 'afterwards' (iii.14) about the idea of power and efficacy relies rather heavily on the copy thesis in questioning the meaningfulness of the Lockean term 'power'. I shall not go into this in detail. Suffice it to say that if Locke's handling of that inference were otherwise successful, it could confer a thin meaning on the term 'power', along these lines: 'To say that one event has the power to bring about another is to say that *something is the case about the first event which explains its being followed by the second.*' This would represent power in

a manner similar to Locke's account of 'substance in general'—namely, as a 'something we know not what'—and we might say of it what Locke said about the other: 'We have no idea of what it is but only a confused obscure one of what it does' (*Essay* 175:13), and might echo his description of the idea of substance in general as not 'positive' (305:28) but 'relative' (296:20). It would not be respectable by the canons of Hume's official theory of meaning, but it might be little the worse for that.

(4) Having declined to press objections 1–3 in section iii.6, Hume launches a fresh attack on the 'power' line of thought. Here it is:

[Let us grant] that the production of one object by another in any one instance implies a power, and that this power is connected with its effect. But it having been already proved that the power lies not in the sensible qualities of the cause, and there being nothing but the sensible qualities present to us, I ask why in other instances you presume that the same power still exists, merely upon the appearance of these qualities? Your appeal to past experience decides nothing in the present case, and at the utmost can only prove that that very object which produced any other was at that very instant endowed with such a power; but [it] can never prove that the same power must continue in the same object or collection of sensible qualities, much less that a like power is always conjoined with like sensible qualities. (91)

This is excellent. As powers are not found, but only inferred, we need a link between them and the sensible qualities of things from which we infer them. Our only link is the inductive thesis that past pairings of sensible qualities with powers will continue into the future. What is our basis for this? Apparently we must accept it as a sheer act of faith; but that leaves us no better off than we were with an act of faith that past pairings of K_1 events with K_2 ones would continue into the future.

Consider an example. This lump of iron, with sensible qualities F, G, and H, has softened each time we have heated it, and we believe that it will soften again next time. The Lockean line of thought offers to rescue us from needing an act of faith to believe that events of the kind heating-of-an-FGH-thing will continue to be closely followed by ones of the kind softening-of-an-FGH-thing. The rescue goes like this:

We are entitled to conjecture that FGH things soften when heated because they have an insensible quality which we shall call a power-to-soften-when-heated; an FGH thing's having this power *explains* why it softens when heated, and also provides a basis for predicting that any FGH thing which has it will soften when heated. So we have grounds for predicting that this piece of iron—which we perceive to be FGH—will soften if we heat it.

This, Hume objects, gratuitously *assumes* that this piece of iron still has a power-to-soften-when-heated, and that other untested FGH things also have it. The Lockean line of thought relies on a mere association between a given constellation of sensible qualities and a certain power; the continuance of such an association—across a species, and through time for an individual—is always up for question; and the answer rests on an inductive act of faith such as we were trying to escape from. This argument of Hume's succeeds brilliantly.

268. A further objection

Just after invoking the copy thesis in attack 3, Hume writes:

If we [have] any idea of power in general, we must also be able to conceive some particular species of it; and . . . we must be able to place this power in some particular being and conceive that being as endowed with a real force and energy by which such a particular effect necessarily results from its operation. We must distinctly and particularly conceive the connexion betwixt the cause and effect, and be able to pronounce, from a simple view of the one, that it must be followed or preceded by the other. This is the true manner of conceiving a particular power in a particular body . . . Such a connexion would amount to a demonstration, and would imply the absolute impossibility for the one object not to follow or to be conceived not to follow upon the other; which kind of connexion has already been rejected in all cases. (161–2)

Hume says here that the 'true manner of conceiving . . . power' is in terms of absolute necessity: the power of E_1 to produce E_2 must be such that a proper knowledge of E_1 would enable one to work out a priori that it would be followed by E_2. This says in effect that there is no middle-strength concept of power, intermediate between absolute necessity and mere regularity.

Here, as elsewhere, Hume apparently assumes that only through absolute necessity can one item be effectively linked with another. Is this mere narrow-mindedness? Edward Craig (1987: 77) has castigated those who think so. In a section entitled 'How not to criticize Hume', he remarks that some commentators accuse Hume of wilfully restricting reasons to the absolutely necessitating ones that Craig calls 'deductive reasons'. According to them, he writes, 'Hume's sceptical arguments are easily overcome: just deny the dogma [that all real reasons are deductive] and sit back'. I wholly agree with Craig's repudiation of this attitude, but not with his reason for it. He sees this move of Hume's as an *ad hominem* one: his opponents are wedded to an absolute-necessity view of reasons, this being part (Craig holds) of their wanting to liken human minds to the mind of God, and when Hume discusses causation in terms of absolute necessity, he is meeting them on their chosen ground. Valuable and original as this work of Craig's is, I do not think it helps us to understand Hume's move into the absolute-necessity mode, which is not *ad hominem* at all. I take Hume's word for it: he invokes absolute necessity because it is the *true* manner—not the *prevailing* manner—of conceiving power; and I now argue that he is right about that.

So as to silence Hume's other objections, 2–4, let us boldly suppose: (3) we have an idea of power, (2) we are entitled to insist that there must be powers underlying the regularities, and (4) we have no problem about associating a specific power with a certain cluster of sensible qualities. Now let us, as temporary Lockeans, suppose this:

> Events of kind K_1 all have a power in virtue of which they necessitate the ensuing of events of kind K_2. When we experience a K_1 event, therefore, knowing that it has a K_2-producing power, we can predict that a K_2 event will ensue because it *must* ensue from something that has that power.

This says that the power 'necessitates' a K_2 event, and says that the latter 'must' ensue from an event having the power; but these modal expressions are to be understood in terms of something less than absolute necessity. If not, then we have stopped pursuing a middle-strength position and remain under the axe of Hume's earlier treatment of absolute-necessity approaches to causal regularity. What we are saying, on this reading of it, implies that it could not possibly happen that an event with a K_2-producing power occurred a microsecond before the world ended; and Hume, Descartes, and others have helped us to see that we should reject that. This rejection follows from the Stop Anywhere Thesis.

To keep the 'power' line of thought in business, therefore, we must mean its modal expressions less strongly: the occurrence of an event with a K_2-producing power necessitates the occurrence of a K_2 event in some manner that falls between absolute necessity and mere *de facto* regularity. That, however, opens up the question of why the K_2-producing power should be operative on this occasion. At some possible worlds an event with a K_2-producing power sometimes occurs although no K_2 event ensues; what is our evidence that ours is not such a world, and that this is not one of those times? The only possible answer is an inductive one. Listen to Peirce:

With overwhelming uniformity, in our past experience, . . . stones left free to fall have fallen. Thereupon two hypotheses only are open to us. Either (1) the uniformity with which those stones have fallen has been due to mere chance and affords no ground whatever . . . for any expectation that the next stone that shall be let go will fall; or (2) the uniformity with which stones have fallen has been due to some active general principle, in which case it would be a strange coincidence that it should cease to act at the moment my prediction was based upon it. (1903: 66)

The 'in which case' clause is devastating. Peirce, in his honesty and intelligence, has virtually admitted that his appeal to 'active general principles'—which I take to be middle-strength powers—achieves nothing.

So even if there were no meaning difficulties, and none about the power's existence or its association with the sensible qualities, still the concept of power would not release us from having to make an inductive act of faith. But that release is just what the idea of power is for; if it fails in that, it does not meet any need—like a lifebelt that has every virtue except buoyancy. Hume is right, then, in saying that power should be thought of in terms of absolute necessity.

Although he does not explicitly present this line of thought, I am sure it was at work in his mind. Anyway, I learned it through thinking about what he does say.

Its being subliminally present in his thinking about causation would explain why his discussions of this keep returning to the idea that a causal connection involves necessity that is absolute and a priori knowable. In this section I have mainly relied on *LBH*. The same points are put more elegantly and powerfully in Blackburn 1990: 241–7.

Chapter 36

Hume on Causation, Positively

269. The causes of causal inferences

Lacking *reasons* or justifications for the belief that past patterns will continue into the future, Hume says, all that remains is to find its *causes*—and thus what causes the particular predictive inferences that we make within the belief's framework. For this he draws on the association thesis, which now returns to the spotlight. He reminds us of his doctrine that associations tend to be set up by resemblance, the contiguities, and causation. In the present context he sometimes uses 'connected' rather than 'caused', but he is not deserting the claim that causation sometimes underlies association, as we shall see.

Hume now introduces what looks like a fourth source for an association between a perception and an idea: namely, their being of kinds that have been repeatedly found together. Really, however, this is not a fourth source of associations, but rather the third source—causation—under a different description:

> We have no other notion of cause and effect, but that of certain objects which have been always conjoined together and which in all past instances have been found inseparable. We cannot penetrate into the reason of the conjunction. We only observe the thing itself, and always find that from the constant conjunction the objects acquire a union in the imagination. (93)

And this 'union' or association engenders not just an idea, but a lively idea, which Hume then explains is a belief—this being the topic of his section 7, which I discussed in §250.

In an aside, he seeks to use this principle of association to explain meaning—which he sees as a linking of words with ideas. He writes: 'Because such a particular idea is commonly annexed to such a particular word, nothing is required but the hearing of that word to produce the correspondent idea; and it will scarce be possible for the mind, by its utmost efforts, to prevent that transition' (93). To adapt a question of Wittgenstein's: Why is it hard to say 'It's warm here' and mean that it's cold here? We have Hume's answer.

Hume elaborates his thoughts about associations, about how vivacity is transmitted from perception to idea, and so on, down to the bottom of 101; none of that needs to be discussed here.

In the paragraph at 103–4 Hume emphasizes that an associative track may persist in the mind of a person who has forgotten the sensory episodes that laid it down in the first place. As a matter of psychological fact, he says, we often go from an experience of a K_1 event *immediately* to an expectation of a K_2 event—not through any 'reasoning' about past experience. But the past experience, even if forgotten, is essential to the story.

In section 9 Hume confronts himself with a difficulty. Here is how he has explained what causes us to have most of our new beliefs:

The past experience of K_1 events constantly 'conjoined' with K_2 ones beats a path through our mind, so that a new K_1 event leads us also to have the idea of a K_2 event, and indeed to have one that possesses the vivacity, etc. that qualifies it as a belief.

So far, so good. But Hume has said that such associative mental tracks can also be induced by (past experiences of) resemblance and of contiguity, yet these in general do not lead us to form new beliefs. New ideas, perhaps, but not beliefs. His statement of this problem contains a hazard. 'We find by experience that belief arises only from causation,' he writes, 'and that we can draw no inference from one object to another, except they be connected by this relation' (107). It is hard to avoid a normative reading of 'we can draw no inference', taking the point to be that we cannot validly or soundly draw such an inference; but Hume is not entitled to mean that, because he has laid no foundation for any normative judgements involving such concepts as those of evidence, support, reasonableness, soundness, etc. When he writes that 'we *can* draw no inference', etc., we had better take him to mean only that we *do* draw no inference, etc. This yields a purely naturalistic, non-normative problem: experience of regularities often leads us to new beliefs; experience of resemblance and contiguity hardly ever does so—why the difference?

One might answer like this:

A past K_1–K_2 regularity is evidence that K_1 events generally do, and will, lead to K_2 ones. But no facts about resemblance or contiguity constitute evidence for what is the case beyond the reach of present impressions and memory. So we are led to new beliefs from causal data, but not from data about resemblance and contiguity, because we are reasonable beings.

This tries to get a causal explanation for our causal beliefs out of (1) a normative judgement about evidence or about what supports what, and (2) the thesis that such norms influence our intellectual behaviour ('we are reasonable beings'). But 1 is not available to Hume, after his fierce criticism of every suggested basis for saying that past regularities are evidence for future ones. And 2 is a kind of statement that he will not make without explaining it. A chief purpose of book I of the *Treatise* is to explore in a naturalistic way what our reasonableness consists in. To accept 2 as an undefended premiss would go against Hume's grain.

Hume's solution to his problem runs from near the end of 107 to the middle of 110, primarily in the last two paragraphs of this passage. It depends on changing the content of the association theory: Hume originally took that to concern 'a gentle force, which commonly prevails'; but now he implies that two forces are involved—a gentle one triggered by resemblance and contiguity, and a more powerful one triggered by causation. The latter's greater power shows up both in the vivacity of the ideas it leads us to form, and also in its bringing these ideas about involuntarily, in defiance of the will. (Beliefs are involuntary, Hume thinks, because the causal force that gives an idea the vivacity that makes it count as a belief also makes it irresistible.)

Now, this change in the association thesis is not purely *ad hoc*; Hume offers to explain why one force is weaker. I shall state the explanation in terms of causation versus resemblance; applying it to causation versus contiguity, though possible, is a clumsy business which is not worth the trouble. When I have found that K_1 events are regularly followed by K_2 ones, and am now confronted with a K_1 event, I am pointed unequivocally in a single direction—towards the thought of a new K_2 event. But K_1 events may *resemble* all sorts of different items, and my thoughts cannot be carried to all of those at once. Where constant conjunction yields a river, resemblance yields a delta; in the former, the torrent is confined between one pair of banks, whereas in the latter the water is spread through many distributaries. Seeing a long slim yacht with a blue hull and white sails might lead me, through resemblance, to form an idea of a snake, or a sapphire, or a snow bank, or . . . , and so on. Thus, the potential influence of resemblance is lessened through scattering; this is sheer psychology, with nothing normative in it.

Hume amplifies this answer to his question in a manner that kicks up dust. When we see that resemblance causes in us only loose, scattered associations, he writes, we 'form a general rule against the reposing any assurance in' ideas that come into our minds through resemblance (110). This seems to report our reasonable response to a noticed fact, with 'our' reasonableness assumed without explanation; which is patently un-Humean. Quite aside from its normative element, it transgresses Hume's theoretical bounds in other ways. 'Reposing assurance in' something is presumably the same as believing it; so Hume is here treating belief as voluntary—we *adopt a policy* of not believing certain things—and, connected with this, he makes it sound altogether different from the kind of 'feeling' that he has taken belief to be. The flaws in Hume's statement of his problem and his solution to it may indicate a wavering of attention, or perhaps an intermittent failure of nerve. They should not change our view about what his fundamental project is.

From the middle of 110 to the end of the section (117), Hume tries to show that resemblance and contiguity do play some role in creating associations of ideas in people's minds, offering caustic remarks about superstition, religious observances, and so on. He also allows that a certain kind of indoctrination, which he calls 'education', sometimes leads its subjects to form beliefs on the basis of resemblance and contiguity, rather than of causation (see 112–13 on credulity). His summing up on this topic is remarkable:

As education is an artificial and not a natural cause, and as its maxims are frequently contrary to reason, and even to themselves in different times and places, it is never upon that account recognized by philosophers; though in reality it be built almost on the same foundation of custom and repetition as our reasonings from causes and effects. (117)

He is saying that beliefs founded on anything but causation are not regarded as respectable, are not 'recognized by philosophers'; he does not make that normative judgement himself, and even suggests that it is not sustainable because 'education' as a cause does not differ greatly from the experience of constant conjunction as a cause. He pushes the comparison too far, I suggest. The process of 'custom and repetition' that might get someone to believe in the Athanasian doctrine of the Trinity (which Hume regarded as absurd) consists in repeatedly exposing the person to the reading or hearing of sentences whose meanings involve the absurdity; the 'custom and repetition' to which non-human nature exposes us is not like that.

270. Hume's best account of causation

Passing silently by the next four sections, we come to iii.14 (155), where Hume returns to his question about the idea of necessary connection. Gathering up the threads of what he has said earlier, he comes to this: on several occasions I observe a K_1 event closely followed by a K_2 event; at first I do not think of events of these two kinds as causally connected, then later I do think of them in that way. I do not observe more on the later occasions than on the earlier ones, yet there is a difference. Why? What has changed my thought?

Hume has been patiently laying the foundations for this answer: The difference that comes about through my growing experience of the K_1–K_2 pattern is an increased proneness on my part to infer from observing a K_1 event that a K_2 event will soon follow. To judge that one causes the other is just to be disposed to make that inference. And the point, purpose and meaning of the word 'cause' is to express that disposition.

On this account, the missing element that Hume has heralded as 'the idea of necessary connection' turns out not to be a conceptual element of the ordinary sort, which is why we do not find an experiential model for it. Rather, it is an aspect of the state of mind of the user of causal terminology. The experience of a regular succession does not give the person a new 'idea', but it imprints on his mind a structure that was not there before. Simon Blackburn lays out the elements of Hume's position up to here, leading to this account of the meaning of 'cause':

Upon acquaintance with a regular succession the mind changes, but *not* by forming an impression or idea of anything not given in one instance alone. It changes *functionally*: it becomes organized so that the impression of the antecedent event gives rise to the idea of the subsequent event. No new aspect of the world is revealed by this change: it is strictly *nonrepresentational*, just like the onset of a passion, with which Hume frequently compares it. But once it takes place we think of the events as thickly connected, we become confident of the association, we talk of causation, and of course we act and plan in the light of that confidence. (1990: 247)

Note 'we talk of causation'. I suggest—following Blackburn's lead—that Hume ought to say that this is the whole story about the meaning of 'cause'. It cannot be expressed in the form '"E$_1$ caused E$_2$" means . . .', but then not all meanings can be displayed in this manner. This is one of those cases where a grasp of an expression's meaning directly requires an understanding of its use—in this case, understanding the frame of mind which the term is used to express.

I agree with Blackburn that this is essentially Humean; it is the core of what we can carry away from Hume's discussion, and make our own if we agree with the main lines of his treatment. Furthermore, it fits well with much of his text. It makes the best possible sense of his two definitions of 'cause' (170). Each says that a cause is 'an object precedent and contiguous to another', but then they continue differently:

P: . . . and where all the objects resembling the former are placed in like relations of precedency and contiguity to those objects that resemble the latter.

N: . . . and so united with it that the idea of the one determines the mind to form the idea of the other, and the impression of the one to form a more lively idea of the other.

These present 'a different view of the same object, and mak[e] us consider it either as a philosophical relation or as a natural one; either as a comparison of two ideas or as an association betwixt them'. I base my 'P' and 'N' labels on that remark, but the remark is not really right. Causation's being a natural relation comes from its role in *producing* associations of ideas; but the second definition of 'cause' is about its role as an *upshot* of the association of ideas.

It is a famous fact that these two are not analytically equivalent, or even coextensive. Furthermore, if each purports to state 'necessary and sufficient conditions' for the truth of 'x is a cause of y', they differ enormously in how plausible they are. When I say 'The iron's becoming hot caused it to soften', each analysis says that I mean, in part, that the iron became hot and then softened, and P says that I also mean that *whenever things like the iron become hot, they soften*, while N says that I mean that *observing the iron becoming hot causes me to expect it to soften*. It is not credible that Hume accepted N on this understanding of it.

A better way of viewing the two definitions is as complementary parts of this single story:

When someone says 'x is a cause of y', he means that x occurred closely followed by y, and that x-like events are always closely followed by y-like ones; and he also manifests his disposition to expect a y-like event whenever he encounters an x-like one.

The second part of this—the part of N that is not included in P—states an important part of the truth about how 'cause', etc. are used, and about what is going on when people think about causes. But it is not part of what someone means by saying 'x is a cause of y'. The mental propensity relates to the causal judgement (on this account) somewhat as a certain conative attitude relates to a moral judgement, according to a certain theory about the nature of moral judgements—a theory which may well have been Hume's. The above 'single story' about causation is, I believe, what he was getting at in his two 'definitions'.

271. The elusiveness of impressions of compulsion

The partly functional account of the meaning of 'cause' that we have found in Hume takes us far beyond his view that the meaning you give to a word is fixed by a faded, sensation-like mental content with which you associate it. But we cannot walk out on the latter. Hume told us in advance that he would use constant conjunction to explain individual inferences of effects from causes, which would in turn throw light on 'the idea of necessary connexion', and now we must see how he tries to make good on that promise.

He does it by pointing to a supposed impression which the supposed idea copies. Your experience of regular succession does give you a new impression, he maintains, namely that of your own compulsion to expect a K_2 event:

Though the several resembling instances which give rise to the idea of power have no influence on each other, and can never produce any new quality in the object which can be the model of that idea, yet the observation of this resemblance produces a new impression in the mind, which is its real model. For after we have observed the resemblance in a sufficient number of instances, we immediately feel a determination of the mind to pass from one object to its usual attendant, and to conceive it in a stronger light upon account of that relation. This determination is the only effect of the resemblance; and, therefore, must be the same with power or efficacy whose idea is derived from the resemblance. (164–5)

When Hume asserts that 'we feel a determination', etc., he does not invite his reader to introspect and agree. The tone of this passage reflects its being offered only because Hume's theory of meaning requires it.

In the same spirit, a little later, he writes: 'Either we have no idea of necessity, or necessity is nothing but that determination of the thought to pass from causes to effects and from effects to causes, according to their experienced union' (165). This does not sound like someone who thinks he can feel 'that determination of the thought', thereby having an impression from which his idea of necessity could be copied. Notice also that although Hume ought to mean that the idea of necessity is copied from the impression of the mental determination, he avoids speaking of the impression as such. Earlier in the same paragraph, he does say that the idea of necessity must be copied from 'some internal impression', but then he continues: 'There is no internal impression which has any relation to the present business but that propensity, which custom produces, to pass from an object to the idea of its usual attendant' (165). The only impression is a propensity! Hume has important things to say about the propensity, that is, the determination of the mind to make a certain transition; his theory of meaning requires him to talk about the *impression of* that propensity or determination; he tries to meet this requirement, but the word 'impression' keeps dropping out. It does so also near the start of the section, where he announces that 'we must find some impression that gives rise to this necessity' (155), and works through to the conclusion that 'it is this impression, then, or *determination*, which affords me the idea of necessity' (156)—again bringing in 'impression', and instantly replacing it by 'determination'.

So Hume several times approaches the supposed impression of determination with a long-handled probe; and he never embraces it, showing a robust conviction that this impression lies at the heart of his account of causation. Even in the second definition of 'cause', which focuses on what happens in the mind of the person who uses the word, nothing is said about the person's impressions of his own thought processes. The definiens could be true, and could satisfactorily complete Hume's good account of how 'cause' is used, even if there were no feeling that accompanies the compulsive expectations that occur in causal inferences.

272. The absurdity of 'impression of compulsion'

Why should Hume handle the impression of determination in such a gingerly fashion? Perhaps he partly sensed that his shining analysis of the concept of causation has no room for that impression, and can only be tarnished by the addition of it. There are other reasons as well.

If the impression of determination is real, Hume must think that it is available to introspection. As Pears points out, however, Hume has no account of what makes any item an impression of compulsion: when I am determined to expect a K_2 event, how do I know that this is so? I *do* expect such an event to occur, but what tells me that this is something I am virtually compelled to do? I can be aware that I am powerless in this matter (see Pears 1990: 110–19); but this awareness is nothing like a Humean impression—least of all one that could be copied by an idea.

In another context, indeed, Hume explicitly denies that there is any such impression. When relating the association of ideas to the passions, he writes:

It is evident that the association of ideas operates in so silent and imperceptible a manner that we are scarce sensible of it, and discover it more by its effects than by any immediate feeling or perception. It produces no emotion, and gives rise to no new impression of any kind, but only modifies those ideas of which the mind was formerly possessed, and which it could recall upon occasion. (305)

This flatly contradicts the thesis that when we inductively expect a certain kind of event to occur, we 'feel a determination of the mind to pass from one object to its usual attendant'.

There is also a deep problem about what would result from a theory which took seriously the view that a crucial element in our idea of causal connection is copied from our impressions of our own intellectual compulsions. Consider this, for example:

Necessity is something that exists in the mind, not in objects; nor is it possible for us ever to form the most distant idea of it considered as a quality in bodies. . . . Necessity is nothing but that determination of the thought to pass from causes to effects, and from effects to causes, according to their experienced union. (165–6)

There are two ways of taking the statement that necessity is a 'determination of the thought'. It could mean that traditional thinkers about power, necessary connection, etc. are right about everything except its location: they thought it was out there in the world, whereas really it exists only in minds. This, however, is an impossible reading of Hume, for the whole of his attack on traditional views— both absolutely necessitating and middle-strength—applies as much to changing thoughts as to colliding bodies. The belief in a K_2 event is distinct from, and therefore separable from, the impression of a K_1 event; we do not observe any *making* between them; we may feel something, but whatever we are doing in calling it 'necessity', we are not conceding anything to traditional ways—for example, the Lockean way—of thinking about causation.

So the compulsion, or 'determination', of which Hume speaks is not an instance of the kind of power or necessary connection that he has been pursuing and attacking throughout *Treatise* I.iii. It is precisely the same kind of determination as is involved when one billiard-ball hits another and determines it to start moving, the only difference being that in one case somebody feels the determination, while in the other nobody does. Then what on earth can be going on here? Our ordinary idea of necessary connection is supposed to be a *copy* of our impression of compulsion when we expect a K_2 event; how can this be so?

Hume could answer this if he held that all causal thought and speech is animistic: when we say that the first ball makes the second start to move, our thought is that the will of the second ball is overpowered, just as ours is when we expect it to move. This would be in the spirit of a *jeu d'esprit* by P. F. Strawson:

In a great boulder rolling down the mountainside and flattening the wooden hut in its path we see an exemplary instance of force; and perhaps, in so seeing it, we are in some barely coherent way identifying with the hut (if we are one kind of person) or with the boulder (if we are another); putting ourselves imaginatively in the place of one or the other. (1985: 123)

This fits Hume's statement that 'the mind has a great propensity to spread itself on external objects, and to conjoin with them any internal impressions which they occasion' (167). However, he has already rejected something like this, back when he reported that 'some have asserted that we feel an energy or power in our own mind; and that, having in this manner acquired the idea of power, we transfer that quality to matter, where we are not able immediately to discover it' (632). He rejected the version of this which he discussed, in which the 'energy or power' that we allegedly 'feel' is the power of our minds over our bodies, exerted when we lift weights or speak or snap our fingers. It remains open to him to say that we do feel power in a different way—namely, the power which overcomes us when our causal expectations are formed—and that 'we transfer that quality to matter'. But he gives no hint that he takes this or any other view of the issue.

I contend that Hume has no role in our causal thought and talk for an idea copied from an impression of mental determination. Strawson (1985: 119) quotes Kant's summary of Hume's position on causation—'Only through the perception and comparison of events repeatedly following in a uniform manner upon preceding appearances . . . are we first led to construct for ourselves the concept of cause'—and remarks that this 'omits the boldest element in Hume's doctrine, namely his diagnosis of the source of the illusory belief in necessary connection in nature'. Taking this to mean the doctrine about the idea copied from an impression of compulsion, I submit that 'bold' is not the right adjective. To the slight extent that he wrote as though he did accept this doctrine, Hume was merely paying dues to his theory of meaning. The meagreness of those payments testifies to how far he has worked through that theory to something richer and truer—something involving not only asserted content but also expressed mind-set, and something involving whole sentences as well as single words.

273. Was Hume a sceptic about causation?

Hume is sometimes described as a sceptic about causation, but that is wrong. His famous essay on miracles rests firmly on the premiss of universal causation, or something like it; his great *Dialogues Concerning Natural Religion* regularly assume that whatever is the case is caused to be so. And he did once explicitly address this question in a letter:

I never asserted so absurd a proposition as *that any thing might arise without a cause*: I only maintained that our certainty of the falsehood of that proposition proceeded neither from intuition nor demonstration, but from another source. *That Caesar existed, That there is such an island as Sicily*; for these propositions, I affirm, we have no demonstrative nor intuitive proof. Would you infer that I deny their truth, or even their certainty? There are many different kinds of certainty, and some of them as satisfactory to the mind, though perhaps not so regular, as the demonstrative kind. (Greig 1932: 187)

When Hume calls the proposition 'absurd', he cannot mean that he has reasons to bring against it—not after all the energy he has expended on arguing that there are none. It would accord better with his philosophy if he meant that for someone to accept the proposition would be unnatural, non-human, weird, like having three eyes or liking the smell of excrement. Even that, however, goes beyond anything he has argued for. His account of the habits of mind that compel us to expect *effects* does not explain or imply our regularly believing in *causes*; while in the 'neighbouring fields' he attacked the view that universal causation is necessary, but said nothing about the view that it is true (§260). Anyway, Hume was evidently convinced that whatever happens is caused. So much for scepticism about causation.

However, he was sceptical (or more) about causation considered as a 'making' or 'producing' relation between events, a relation that cannot be fully explicated in terms of regularities or of anything else that is empirically accessible to us. He said over and over, on the basis of intricate argument, that we can make no sense of that:

If we have really no idea of a power or efficacy in any object, or of any real connexion betwixt causes and effects, it will be to little purpose to prove that an efficacy is necessary in all operations. We do not understand our own meaning in talking so, but ignorantly confound ideas which are entirely distinct from each other. . . . There may be several qualities . . . with which we are utterly unacquainted; and if we please to call these *power* or *efficacy*, it will be of little consequence to the world. But when . . . we make the terms of *power* and *efficacy* signify something of which we have a clear idea and which is incompatible with those objects to which we apply it, . . . we are led astray by a false philosophy. This is the case when we transfer the determination of the thought to external objects, and suppose any real intelligible connexion betwixt them; that being a quality which can only belong to the mind that considers them. (*Treatise* 168)

One might try to reduce the force of this by emphasizing '*intelligible* connexion': 'Hume is merely rejecting the existence of absolutely necessitating connections between events; and that leaves room for him to believe that there are connections which necessitate in some less strong manner.' But it does not. We have seen him saying that the 'true manner of conceiving' power is in terms of absolute necessity, and we have seen why.

If we cannot reduce the scope of the quoted passage, perhaps we can reduce its force. When Hume says 'We have no idea of x', perhaps he means not that we cannot talk sense of any kind about x, but merely that we cannot talk about it in a contentful way. That is what Galen Strawson thinks (1989). According to his Hume, we can think in a non-contentful sort of way by means of 'relative ideas', about which Strawson says: 'A relative idea is not the same as no idea at all.' Let us see, first setting the scene.

Locke uses the phrase 'relative idea' just once, in his discussion of the supposed idea of substance in general (*Essay* II.xxiii.2–3). Having alluded to 'a supposition of he knows not what support of such qualities which . . .' etc., Locke calls this 'an obscure and relative idea of substance in general', and tolerates it only because he thinks we are stuck with it. For him, 'relative idea' is a term of derision.

Berkeley uses 'relative idea' in the same way as Locke, though for him the issue about substance is fused with that about matter (§218). We can pull them apart. Substance: Berkeley is attacking a view that postulates a certain relation ('support') of which it cannot make sense. Matter: the targets are resemblance and causation, which could not relate matter to ideas, and so cannot do what materialism wants from them. Without condemning relative ideas as such, Berkeley demands that they include a clear idea of the relevant relation.

So Locke connects 'relative idea' with substance, while Berkeley connects it both with that and with matter, which he muddles with substance. When Hume is discussing substance, there is no hint of anything like a relative idea (see, for example, 222 and 234). It is when he addresses the issue about matter that he brings 'relative idea' into play:

Since nothing is ever present to the mind but perceptions, and since all ideas are derived from something antecedently present to the mind, it follows that it is impossible for us so much as to conceive or form an idea of anything specifically different from ideas and impressions. . . . The furthest we can go towards a conception of external objects, when supposed specifically different from our perceptions, is to form a relative idea of them, without pretending to comprehend the related objects. (67–8)

The 'relative idea', I take it, would be the idea of 'things which our perceptions are *of*', with 'of' standing for the perception–object relation that makes the idea a 'relative' one.

The above passage is Hume's only use of 'relative idea', though something like it occurs at 241, also in a discussion of matter. In that passage and the one I have quoted, it might seem that he is being a little tolerant of matter, allowing that we can think of it in an indirect 'relative' manner with the help of our grasp of the perception-of relation. What could he think that relation to be? It could not be resemblance, any more than it could be for Berkeley; and the only other candidate is the relation of being-caused-by. Hume could not have been comfortable with this, I think, but he was not in a position, as Berkeley thought *he* was, to dismiss it a priori. So perhaps the having of a relative idea of matter really is being treated as a way of thinking about it, making sense of it, getting some kind of intellectual contact with it.

If that is right, then this tolerance may also be at work when Hume allows that we can 'suppose' a difference between perceptions and matter. Something like that also happens at 218: 'We may well suppose in general, but it is impossible for us distinctly to conceive, objects to be in their nature any thing but exactly the same with perceptions.' Perhaps these turns of phrase show Hume leaving room for the possibility that we should in a thin, formal way think about matter as something *of* which we have perceptions, even though we have no thoughts about what matter is like intrinsically. If so, then he is entertaining—in an oblique and cautious fashion—something like the Kantian notion of things in themselves.

These entertainments are brief and cool. Elsewhere Hume writes: 'As to the notion of external existence, when taken for something specifically different from our perceptions, we have already shown its absurdity' (188), and in a footnote to this he refers to the section containing 'relative idea'.

That completes my survey of the textual basis for attributing to Hume a working concept of 'relative idea'. There isn't much of it; it all concerns matter; it all sounds more dismissive than tolerant; and Hume never builds upon it. Yet Galen Strawson offers this as the device through which Hume thinks we can get some intellectual grip on items of which we do not have contentful ideas. Even if Hume did mean to be tolerant about matter, it is another question whether this tolerance—expressed in the term 'relative idea'—could have been extended to the causation issue. Before coming to that, we should ask what drives Strawson's view about where Hume stood.

274. The great objection to the 'Humean view of causation'

The principal, and almost the only, driver is Strawson's opinion that the view usually attributed to Hume is unbelievable. No competent thinker, he maintains, could believe that the most basic fact about the world's order is that certain regularities obtain, without any underlying reality that produces and explains them. This is a natural thought, but philosophical reflection drains it of most of its plausibility.

In order to assess it, I introduce the concept of a basic regularity in how the world works. That does not mean a regularity for which there is no explanation, but merely one whose obtaining is not explainable in terms of some deeper-lying (more general) *regularity*. Consider the fact (R_{nb}) that gold regularly dissolves in aqua regia. We are sure that there is an underlying explanation for R_{nb}—one that brings in micro-structural facts about gold and about aqua regia, and even more general ones about how various kinds of particles regularly relate to one another. (I keep this vague because I do not know the details, and also to make the example one that Hume might have used.) Our experience of the world makes us sure that some mechanism underlies the events that make up R_{nb}; if someone questioned this, and suggested that this pattern in the world's behaviour might be basic, and not explicable in terms of a finer mechanism, we would be puzzled, wondering why he had such an eccentric picture of how the world is organized. Our reluctance to agree with him would have two notable strengths. (1) We have empirical evidence that ours is not a world at which the likes of R_{nb} are basic. We have found that most such interactions can be explained chemically—that is, in terms of deeper-lying regularities. (2) We have a clear enough idea of what we are asserting that he denies. There is a graspable pattern of explanation that we think applies to R_{nb}: it involves more general regularities plus linking structural facts about the two kinds of stuff.

Now consider some regularity R_b which is basic, not an upshot of any more general regularity that we might discover if we had sensitive enough instruments, or knew how to probe for it. Any example I might offer would differ from any that Hume was in a position to adduce, but that does not matter. It suffices that we and Hume (and Strawson) think there are basic regularities in the world's working, and agree that our present question concerns how *they* are to be explained.

If R_b is such a regularity, what should we say to the suggestion that its obtaining is a brute fact, a mere case of 'That is how things happen at our world' with nothing to explain why? Strawson invites us to reject this as madly implausible. and there is no denying the intuitive pull of this attitude to R_b, like the pull towards the corresponding attitude to R_{nb}. As we move from non-basic down to basic regularities, though, the situation changes in two ways.

(1) Those who insist that something must explain the basic regularities cannot have any empirical evidence that they are right. Strawson concedes that it is possible that the world's basic regularities should have no explanation; yet he is sure that they actually do have an explanation. Why? Evidently there is no answer to this. Perhaps it can be rational to be sure of things for which one does not have evidence; and I feel the tug of the Strawsonian insistence that actual basic regularities must be explained by something that lies deeper. Still, if the only objection to the so-called Humean view of causation is a conviction of that ungrounded kind, we should be aware of that, and correspondingly wary of it. In these remarks, I aim for the centre of Strawson's position, and not for such vulnerable outposts as his suggestion (1989: 26 n. 11) that the 'Humean view' may be more credible for someone who is, in the manner of David Lewis, a realist about possible worlds.

(2) When someone claims that R_b is an upshot of something that explains it, though not of deeper-lying regularities, it is not clear what he is saying. He will, if he is Strawson, use the language of causation, saying something to this effect: 'When I deny that R_b is a brute fact and affirm that there is a reason for it, I am implying that R_b obtains because K_1 events *make* K_2 events occur.' Hume himself, in a passage which Strawson takes to be in agreement with him, uses the phrase 'the cause of these causes'. Now, this use of 'make' or 'cause' cannot have any of the empirical content of our ordinary concepts of making and causing, for those are shot through with empirically discovered and trusted regularities. We are looking here for something that underlies and explains all the regularities. So— this is my present point—the whole content of the claim is just that something is the case that explains the regularities without itself requiring explanation in its turn. We have no thoughts about what sort of explanation it might be, and we have arguments *that we have learned from Hume* for the view that there is no sort of explanation it could be.

I refer to Hume's reasons for holding that the explanation could not be a 'demonstrative' one, conducted in terms of absolute necessity, and that any explanation falling short of that severe standard would fail to do what is wanted. Hume gave one reason for the latter claim, and in §268 I added another, with help from Peirce. The crucial point is that anything less than absolute necessity leaves open the question of whether whatever-it-is will continue to be effective; if there is a guarantee that it will, then the question re-arises concerning the guarantor, and we are off on a regress; if there is no guarantee that it will, then the inductive act of faith in the regularities which is supposed to be so intolerable has been replaced by an inductive act of faith in the guarantor—which is no better.

Strawson's guarantor is something he calls the 'nature' of things. He brings this into play by denying that there is a clean cut between (1) what things are like and (2) how they behave. Much of what we might include in 2, he maintains, belongs integrally to 1. That is right, but useless for his purposes. To the extent that a thing's having nature N entails things about how it will behave if . . . , just so far does the inductive question about its future behaviour become an inductive question about whether it still has its erstwhile nature N. Strawson says at 28 that this response 'wholly mistakes the point at issue'; but he does not patiently and effectively explain why.

Though Strawson's protest against the 'Humean view of causation' is natural, we have learned from Hume that it must be wrong. The protester wants a special, non-inductive, *safe* guarantee about the world's future course; and there is reason to believe that he cannot have what he wants unless he resorts to theology. Hume was not the first to believe this; Descartes beat him to it (§37).

Strawson's heated defence of what he sees as Hume's robust good sense is based, in my view, on a failure to learn from Hume the best things that he has to teach.

275. Did Hume accept the 'Humean view of causation'?

Famously, Hume sometimes writes as though he regards his treatment of causation as limited in the way that Strawson says it is. Some of his turns of phrase suggest that while he denies that we have any experience of, or evidence regarding, or contentful thoughts about, extra-mental causation, he assumes that *there is* such causation. That might be thought to be what is going on here:

My intention never was to penetrate into the nature of bodies, or explain the secret causes of their operations. For, besides that this belongs not to my present purpose, I am afraid that such an enterprise is beyond the reach of human understanding, and that we can never pretend to know body otherwise than by those external properties which discover themselves to the senses. (*Treatise* 64)

What comes just before that, however, shows that it should not be read in Strawson's manner. Hume has been talking about space as separating bodies, and imagines someone objecting that he has given no physics of space—that is, has said nothing 'to explain the cause which separates bodies after this manner, and gives them a capacity of receiving others betwixt them' (63–4). This is a demand for a deeper physics, an account of ordinary discoverable causes (regularities); the topic is not the underlying explanation of basic regularities. Also after the displayed passage, having declared what he does try to do and what he does not, Hume continues: 'As to those who attempt any thing further, I cannot approve of their ambition till I see, in some one instance at least, that they have met with success.' The allusion to visible success shows that he is not talking about unknowable causes lying deeper than any regularities.

That passage is in the spirit of this: 'Experience . . . never gives us any insight into the internal structure or operating principle of objects, but only accustoms the mind to pass from one to another' (*Treatise* 169). This reference to 'the internal structure of bodies', like the earlier one to 'the nature of bodies', shows that Hume is writing in the spirit of Locke's kind of pessimism about our chances of learning enough to explain perceptible events in terms of basic physics. It has nothing to do with the metaphysics of causation as such.

Other passages could go either way, including the one that yields the title of Strawson's book. This is in the *Enquiry*, where Hume, having offered evidence for his claim that in the exercise of the will one is not 'conscious of any power', continues: 'We learn the influence of our will from experience alone. And experience only teaches us how one event constantly follows another; without instructing us in the secret connexion which binds them together and renders them inseparable' (*Enquiry* vii.1, 52). This could be read in Strawson's way, but it need not be. The 'secret connexion' to which Hume refers might be something that could be discovered empirically—the mechanism of the will, so to speak, the more general regularities upon which its working depends—rather than a metaphysical whatnot that underlies all the regularities. That is somewhat confirmed by his saying that we do not, rather than that we cannot, learn about it from experience.

Another passage in the *Enquiry* seems more clearly to go Strawson's way:

No philosopher who is rational and modest has ever pretended to assign the ultimate cause of any natural operation, or to show distinctly the action of that power which produces any single effect in the universe. It is confessed that the utmost effort of human reason is to reduce the principles productive of natural phenomena to a greater simplicity, and to resolve the many particular effects into a few general causes by means of reasonings from analogy, experience and observation. But as to the causes of these general causes, we should in vain attempt their discovery; nor shall we ever be able to satisfy ourselves, by any particular explication of them. These ultimate springs and principles are totally shut up from human curiosity and enquiry. Elasticity, gravity, cohesion of parts, communication of motion by impulse; these are probably the ultimate causes and principles which we shall ever discover in nature; and we may esteem ourselves sufficiently happy, if, by accurate enquiry and reasoning, we can trace up the particular phenomena to, or near to, these general principles. The most perfect philosophy of the natural kind only staves off our ignorance a little longer. (*Enquiry* iv.1, 26)

It is natural to read this as saying that *there is* something that underlies and explains R_b—the pattern of 'general causes'—but that we cannot find out anything about it. But Hume does not quite say that this 'something' cannot be found empirically—merely that it would be 'in vain' to attempt to discover it, and that the general causes are 'totally shut up from' empirical inquiry. Although these are likely phrases for someone who thinks the items are in principle undiscoverable, remember that Hume does not explicitly say so; and consider that the words '*probably* the ultimate causes and principles which we *shall* ever discover' count the other way.

I see Hume as here expressing a scientific pessimism like Locke's, saying something like this:

We know of four kinds of regularity or law that jointly explain what happens in the physical world: elasticity, gravity, cohesion, and impulse. I believe that the real world is causally more unified than this; so I do not accept those four as basic; I'll bet that some deeper and more general regularity underlies and unifies them. However, I do not like our chances of digging down to it.

If we had to read the *Enquiry* passages as Strawson does, I would infer that Hume's thinking in that work had softened and become less deep and thorough. In his 'Conclusion' to book I of the *Treatise* he wrote:

We would [like to be] acquainted with that energy in the cause by which it operates on its effect . . . [But what I have shown] not only cuts off all hope of ever attaining satisfaction, but even prevents our very wishes; since it appears that when we say we desire to know the ultimate and operating principle as something which resides in the external object, we either contradict ourselves or talk without a meaning. (266)

If his views as expressed in the *Enquiry* go against this, that is because he drifted away from his earlier insights. It would be perverse to let drift-caused passages dominate our understanding of Hume's great achievement in the *Treatise*.

His Abstract of the *Treatise* is illuminating. Its sketch of his treatment of causation is clear and helpful. It runs from (8) 'It is evident . . .' to (26) '. . . the difficulty itself '—which is nearly half of the Abstract. A bit that is relevant to our present topic is this crisp declaration: 'Upon the whole, then, either we have no idea at all of force and energy, and these words are altogether insignificant, or they can mean nothing but that determination of the thought, acquired by habit, to pass from the cause to its usual effect' (26). These are not the words of a causal realist.

In the final sentence of the Abstract, Hume writes that the associations amongst our ideas 'are really *to us* the cement of the universe'. He means that any views we have about how the universe hangs together must consist in hangings-together of our thoughts about bits of the universe; so we have a coherent world-view only to the extent that our minds cohere in a certain way, and they can do that only through the association of ideas. Talk if you wish about the 'cement' that there must be 'out there', but you do not mean anything by such talk; Hume's own arguments have shown that nothing could satisfy your yearnings.

Chapter 37

Hume on the Existence of Bodies

276. The project in *Treatise* I.iv.2

In iv.2, entitled 'Of Scepticism with Regard to the Senses', Hume considers the plain person's 'belief in the existence of body'. This long, dense section is orderly and disciplined: it will be worthwhile to work through it page by page.

Hume starts by asking 'What causes induce us to believe in the existence of body?', and then immediately proceeds to discuss both this and what reasons we have to support our belief in the existence of body. Right at the outset, then, causal and normative considerations are interwoven; but Hume has the weaving under control.

He writes that The Belief (as I shall call it) must have its causes in some one of our three mental faculties—the senses, reason, or imagination. Hume discusses the role of the senses in 'To begin with the senses . . .' on 188 through to '. . . manner of their existence' on 193; the role of reason in the remainder of 193; and the role of imagination throughout the final twenty-six pages of the section, though in some of those reason also comes back into play.

These three possible causes for The Belief align with three views about what reasons support it. (1) If any belief is caused by the senses, it may be supported by direct empirical evidence, or the senses may cause it without giving it evidential support—'by a kind of fallacy and illusion', as Hume says at 189. (2) If The Belief is caused by reason, it can be defended either a priori or by some argument whose premises are empirically established. Here, as elsewhere, he equates 'It comes from reason' with 'It is reasonable', meaning this normatively. (3) If The Belief is caused purely by imagination, it is not supported by reasons or evidence, and therefore is not supported at all. Then it is an invention of ours—causally explicable, but not intellectually defensible.

In short, given that a certain belief is caused by this or that faculty, is there legitimate support for it? The senses: perhaps. Reason: yes. Imagination: no.

Hume, we shall see, regards The Belief as indefensible—lacking support from any source—but he thinks we are stuck with it. Kant thought so too, holding that we cannot think about anything unless we take ourselves to be in perceptual contact with an objective realm. There is no hint of this in Hume's writings. That we cannot dispense with The Belief is, for him, a contingent psychological fact. 'Nature is obstinate, and will not quit the field, however strongly attacked by reason' (215).

Our concept of body, Hume says, has three elements which are not equally important. (1) *Continuity*: bodies can exist through gaps in our perceptions of them; for him this is the crucial ingredient in The Belief. (2) *Independence*: it is not the case that bodies exist only because they are perceived. (3) *Externality*: bodies exist somewhere other than where we are. Independence and externality, unlike continuity, are properties that a thing might manifest while being perceived. Hume sometimes lumps the two together under the heading of 'distinctness'. This technical sense of 'distinct' is stronger than the ordinary meaning in which 'x is distinct from y' means merely 'x is not y'.

Hume remarks on 191 that externality matters less than the other two properties of bodies, and even hints that it is dispensable: if we believe that an object is continuous and independent, we do not insist that it also be located at a distance from us. I do not know what he had in mind here. Perhaps it was the possibility of an objective realm—a system of continuous independent items—which was not spatially organized.

For Hume, continuity and independence stand or fall together. Necessarily, if bodies exist when no one perceives them, then their existence does not depend on their being perceived; and conversely, if objects are 'independent of the perception and distinct from it', they 'must' continue to exist when not perceived. That converse thesis is less obviously right, but Hume could make a case for it. Although the two stand or fall together, he says that our belief in independent things is based on our belief in continuous ones (§280). So he has several reasons for holding that continuity is the most basic and important of the three formal properties we attribute to bodies.

Nevertheless, he holds that a thorough treatment of The Belief will attend separately to our belief in continuous objects and our belief in distinct ones. Be warned that Hume uses 'distinct' not only in his technical sense, but also in its ordinary meaning. With the word taken in its technical sense, the phrase 'independent and distinct' is pleonastic; but a paragraph back I quoted 'independent of the perception and distinct from it', which is all right because, in it, 'distinct from' carries its ordinary meaning.

Hume notes a certain ambiguity in 'external', which we can understand either spatially or in such a way that 'There are objects external to us' entails that some objects are fundamentally unlike our perceptions. This need not be discussed, he writes: 'As to the notion of external existence, when taken for something specifically different from our perceptions, we have already shown its absurdity' (188). He showed this, he says, in his section on 'external existence', where he wrote:

Nothing is ever really present with the mind but its perceptions or impressions and ideas, and . . . external objects become known to us only by those perceptions they occasion. . . . Now since . . . all ideas are derived from something antecedently present to the mind, it follows that it is impossible for us so much as to conceive or form an idea of anything specifically different from ideas and impressions. . . . The furthest we can go towards a conception of external objects, when supposed specifically different from our perceptions, is to form a relative idea of them, without pretending to comprehend the related objects. Generally speaking we do not suppose them specifically different, but only attribute to them different relations, connexions, and durations. (ii.6, 67–8)

At this point he refers forward to iv.2. The phrase 'specifically different' occurs only in the above two passages and one other (241). Each time Hume is arguing that we can make no sense of 'object that is different in fundamental kind [= specifically] from perceptions'. We can make no sense of there being anything other than perceptions, he maintains, except perhaps for the thin sense that a 'relative idea' might give, yielding the empty thought of items which perceptions may be *of*.

Now, in iv.2 Hume sets aside as dead the question of bodies which are 'external' in the sense of 'specifically different from perceptions'. So when he discusses the continuity and independence of 'objects', he assumes that the latter are perceptions. When he discusses their 'externality', therefore, he understands this spatially, that being the other half of the ambiguity.

From his standpoint this is not as bizarre as it may seem to us. Hume has not said or implied that perceptions exist only when, or only because, some mind has them; so, even though perceptions are our topic, the questions of their continuity and independence remain open. Furthermore, he sees nothing odd in this stance: we have seen him write that 'generally speaking, we do not suppose' that external objects are specifically different from perceptions; all we do is to 'attribute to them different relations, connexions, and durations'—that is, take them to be independent and continuous. Hume evidently agrees with Berkeley's view that the plain person does believe that bodies exist when she does not perceive them, but has no opinion on whether bodies are items of a categorially different kind from her perceptions—the opinion that they are is a philosophical one, a Lockean intrusion into the plain person's non-committal world-view.

So The Belief involves continuity and independence, which are therefore to be examined. Spatial externality is also still on our plate, Hume holds, because some perceptions may be situated outside us. He broaches this topic later:

An object may exist and yet be nowhere, and . . . the greatest part of beings do and must exist after this manner. An object may be said to be nowhere when [it is] not so situated . . . with respect to other bodies as to answer to our notions of contiguity or distance. Now this is evidently the case with all our perceptions and objects, except those of the sight and feeling. A moral reflection cannot be placed on the right or on the left hand of a passion. (235–6)

The crucial phrase is 'except those of the sight and feeling', meaning sight and touch. Wrongly, but confidently, Hume regards ideas of those two senses as spatially located. So perceptions can be located, he thinks, and therefore we should take seriously the possibility that bodies—even if they are perceptions—are spatially external to us.

277. The role of the senses

Hume denies that the senses alone cause The Belief in us. (1) They could not do it by sensorily showing us—or even by wrongly suggesting to us—that something is continuous, because 'continuous' here means 'existing at times when we do *not* perceive them'. That the senses should present anything as having this property is 'a contradiction in terms'. If they are to have any role, therefore, it must have to do not with continuity but with distinctness, which Hume discusses next, breaking the topic into two.

(2) The senses could not *show* us that anything exists other than them. If from our perceptions we get any glimmer of a thought of 'anything beyond', this must be the work of reason or the imagination; the senses could not do it alone. Here and in what follows, Hume is using 'distinct' to mean 'distinct from—other than—the perception', not emphasizing independence and externality. He is asking whether a sensory perception could show me the existence of something else.

(3) Perhaps the senses could 'suggest an idea of distinct existences ... by a kind of fallacy and illusion', Hume suggests. Granted that they could not honestly point us to something beyond them, might they deceitfully do so? There is something fishy about this question. One would have thought that any sensory 'fallacy and illusion' would also involve reason and imagination. Even familiar illusions concerning which of two equal lines looks shorter, and the like, are not immediate illusions of the senses, owing nothing to any other faculty. In the first half of 190, Hume seems to say this himself, rejecting the whole category of purely sensory illusion. Before that, however, he suspends judgement on that general question in order to make a more specific point about a sensory illusion that there are items distinct from myself. Notice: distinct from *myself*. Hume first introduced his concept of distinctness through the phrase 'an existence distinct from the mind and perception'; his discussion 2 concerns items that are distinct from *my perceptions*; but now in 3 he shifts to 'distinct from the mind'—meaning distinct from oneself. Concerning this, he argues as follows. Any kind of sensory presentation of x as distinct from myself must present both x and myself; so if our senses are to tell us (even falsely) that there are objects distinct from ourselves, we must be 'ourselves the objects of our senses'. Hume infers that we are not, from the premiss—anticipating iv.6—that the concept of personal identity is not given through the senses. He had to shove pretty hard at 189–90 to work this point into iv.2. It would have been better omitted.

He anticipates critics' saying: 'Whatever your arguments purport to show, it is a blunt fact of experience that we see things to be at a distance from our bodies, and thus from ourselves.' This claims that the unaided senses do present objects as external, in the plain sense of being at a distance from us. Hume replies to this with a weak point about secondary qualities, and two better points. One is that our bodies are not just sensorily given: the belief that I have a body situated in public space 'is an act of the mind as difficult to explain as that which we examine at present'. It is indeed a part of the latter; the question 'Is this a hand I see before me?' is, in the context of iv.2, as much of a challenge for me when the supposed hand is mine as when it is yours. Secondly, 'Even our sight informs us not of distance or outness . . . immediately and without a certain reasoning and experience, as is acknowledged by the most rational philosophers' (191). Hume focuses on sight because it is the home ground of the view that material things are sensorily given as being at a distance from us. His point about eyesight is one that Berkeley established in his *New Theory of Vision*: namely, that visual distance is not an immediate sensory datum, but rather is inferred (§222). (For more about this, see my 1966: 29–32.)

Having finished with externality, Hume swiftly dispatches independence. 'This can never be the object of the senses', he says—reasonably, but without argument—so that any belief that objects exist independently of our senses 'must be derived from experience and observation' rather than being immediately sensorily given. The crux is 'derived': Hume's point is that for the belief in independent objects, we have to look beyond the senses.

278. The role of reason

After three more paragraphs Hume turns to arguing that The Belief does not come from reason. The single paragraph that he gives to this is compressed, and its structure does not appear clearly on its surface. The key to it is his distinguishing the 'vulgar' version of The Belief from what he will later call its 'philosophical' version. This distinction dominates the remainder of iv.2.

The Belief of the 'vulgar'—that is, plain folk—requires them to 'attribute a distinct continued existence to the very things they feel or see'. This cannot have been caused in them by reason, Hume says, because it is 'entirely unreasonable'. In defence of this severe judgement he writes: 'Philosophy informs us that everything which appears to the mind is nothing but a perception, and is interrupted and dependent on the mind'; so the vulgar attribute continuity to items which, philosophy informs us, do not have it. Thus, their position is 'unreasonable' and so cannot be a product of reason.

Hume is not saying that the vulgar believe that their perceptions exist continuously, but only that they believe in the continuity of certain items which are in fact their perceptions. This implies that the vulgar version of The Belief is false; so there are no good reasons for it; so it is not caused by reason.

On what basis does philosophy inform us that perceptions are 'interrupted'—that is, never exist outside any mind? Hume does not base this on a Berkeleian confidence that a perception could not possibly exist out of any mind—a view that he later rejects outright (§284). He will argue, however, that there is empirical evidence that perceptions never do exist out of any mind; and that is presumably what he is referring to here.

Perhaps because he is rightly uneasy about the supposed empirical evidence, Hume adds this:

As long as we take our perceptions and objects to be the same, we can never infer the existence of the one from that of the other, nor form any argument from the relation of cause and effect; which is the only one that can assure us of matter of fact. (193)

One might wonder how 'the same' relates to 'the one . . . the other'! The point about causation is straightforward, but it will be more convenient to discuss it later.

So much for the vulgar version of The Belief. The 'philosophical' version, in which 'we distinguish our perceptions from our objects', is a belief in items that are categorially different from perceptions. Arguments for this, Hume says, are not what lead ordinary folk to The Belief:

Whatever convincing arguments philosophers may fancy they can produce to establish the belief of objects independent of the mind, . . . these arguments are known but to very few; and . . . it is not by them that children, peasants, and the greatest part of mankind are induced to attribute objects to some impressions and deny them to others. (193)

This, Hume thinks, disposes of reason's claim to cause The Belief in people in general, but does not show that reason does not support it. Even if sophisticated philosophical arguments in defence of Lockean materialism are not at work in folk metaphysics, they might be sound. This would support only the philosophical version of The Belief; but that has a lot in common with the vulgar version, so the reasonableness of the one might confer some credit on the other. However, Hume tells us, 'it will appear presently' that no such argument is sound.

In neither of its versions, then, is The Belief caused by reason or defensible through it. With the senses and reason thus disqualified, Hume concludes that The Belief 'must be entirely owing to the imagination', to which he now turns. He still has pending his demonstration that the philosophical form of The Belief is unreasonable, that being all he now needs (he thinks) to secure *that* imagination causes The Belief. His larger remaining task is to find out *how* it does so.

279. Imagination: creaking and contradiction

The vulgar believe that only some of their impressions are perceptions of independent continuous objects ('bodies', for short). So what we are looking for, as hooks for the imagination to grab on to, are features that are common to all those impressions and not to any others.

Some that we do not treat as perceptions of bodies are involuntary and/or have great force and violence: one may involuntarily suffer a violent pain without being inclined to treat it as a perception of something independent of oneself. So these popular candidates for the role of experiential basis for the belief in an external world must be disqualified: they are, at any rate, not the whole story. Thus Hume at 194.

In two paragraphs at 194–5 Hume tells us what features of our perceptions *are* imagination's basis for The Belief: namely, 'constancy' and 'coherence'. He is not careful enough to present these as features of our perceptions. Constancy:

Those mountains and houses and trees which lie at present under my eye have always appeared to me in the same order; and when I lose sight of them by shutting my eyes or turning my head, I soon after find them return upon me without the least alteration.

This is about the constancy of mountains, not of perceptions. Coherence:

When I return to my chamber after an hour's absence, I find not my fire in the same situation in which I left it; but then I am accustomed in other instances to see a like alteration produced in a like time, whether I am present or absent, near or remote. This coherence, therefore, in their changes, is one of the characteristics of external objects, as well as their constancy.

Here Hume is explicit about it: his topic is the fact that *objects* often remain unchanged for long periods, and when they change they do so in regular ways.

Yet, immediately after this, he speaks of 'the coherence and constancy of certain impressions'. His strategy requires him to be talking about features of sequences of perceptions, and he is valiantly trying to do so. He wants to highlight the fact that:

Some of our perceptions do, while others do not, fall into patterns that are uniform or orderly along the time line in such a way that they can be interpreted as perceptions of objects that are constant or coherent, respectively.

From now on I shall replace Hume's 'constancy' by 'uniformity': we talk about things that remain constant or unchanged, but his interest is in the subjective counterpart of that: namely, a sequence of perceptions—perhaps an interrupted one—whose members are all alike. I shall also replace Hume's 'coherence' by 'orderliness': we talk about things that alter in coherent ways, the subjective counterpart being a sequence of perceptions which varies in an orderly manner—that is, in conformity to general patterns of variation found elsewhere in our experience.

Hume next asks *how* these features of our perceptions 'give rise to so extraordinary an opinion' as that of 'the continued existence of body'. He says 'continued', not 'continued and distinct'; distinctness drops out of sight for several pages. Here is my understanding of his how-question:

Some of our impressions fall into subsets that are uniform or orderly; our imagination fixes on these features, taking them as its basis for believing that these impressions are perceptions of continuous bodies. How does it do this? What is the imagination up to in this activity? How does it *connect* the uniformity, etc. of impressions with the continuity of bodies?

Hume devotes the long paragraph on 195–7 to an extended example, which is supposed to show what happens when the imagination leads us to believe in bodies that exist while we do not perceive them. I select two episodes from it: (1) I hear a creaking noise and believe that a door is opening behind me, and (2) I read a letter 'from a friend, who says he is two hundred leagues distant', and I 'spread out in my mind the whole sea and continent between us'. For episode 1 to serve Hume's purposes, we have to assume—as he evidently does—that hearing a door creak does not count as perceiving it.

Here is part of what he says about the door:

> I never have observed that this noise could proceed from anything but the motion of a door; and therefore conclude that the present phenomenon is a contradiction to all past experience unless the door, which I remember on t'other side the chamber, be still in being. Again, I have always found that a human body was possessed of a quality which I call gravity, and which hinders it from mounting in the air, as this porter must have done to arrive at my chamber unless the stairs I remember be not annihilated by my absence. (196)

Things have gone wrong here. Hume is supposed to be telling us how we get from facts purely about perceptions that we have to the belief that some items exist when we do not perceive them. His basis—the facts that the imagination steers by—must not themselves involve The Belief. In the quoted passage, however, he includes in this experiential basis the fact that he has found that such a noise always 'proceeds from the motion of a door', that 'a human body possesses gravity', and so on. Where he ought to be explaining how we answer the question 'Are there independent and continued objects—doors, for instance?', he is merely explaining how we answer the question 'Is there a door behind me now?', as asked by someone who knows a lot about doors.

It is also wrong for Hume to say that 'the present phenomenon is a contradiction to all past experience unless . . .'. Experience at one time cannot contradict experience at another: we all agree about that, and many of us learned it from Hume. He has to mean that the present phenomenon threatens to contradict not past experience but some general proposition to which the latter has led him. If it is a proposition expressing his theory of doors, then this trouble of Hume's belongs to the preceding one. But perhaps it is a general proposition which does not involve concepts of independence, continuity, or the like, namely:

GP: Whenever I have a creaky perception, I also have a door-move perception,

where 'creaky' and 'door-move' are short for purely phenomenal descriptions of two kinds of sensory event. Now, I might be led by my experience to accept GP; and then it could be contradicted by an experience in which I have a creaky perception and no door-move perception. This seems to be Hume's position later in the paragraph, where he writes:

> To consider these phenomena . . . in a certain light, they are contradictions to common experience, and may be regarded as objections to those maxims which we form

concerning the connexions of causes and effects. I am accustomed to hear such a sound and see such an object in motion at the same time. I have not received, in this particular instance, both these perceptions. These observations are contrary unless I suppose that the door still remains and that it was opened without my perceiving it.

Though better, this still will not do, as it stands. GP says that creaky perceptions are accompanied by door-move ones, and now we have an episode where the antecedent is true and the consequent false. That refutes GP, which obviously cannot be rescued by supposing that on this occasion there is an unseen door. Look back at GP, and you will see why. If the unseen door is to rescue anything, it must be a proposition which mentions doors. Perhaps this:

GP*: Whenever I have a creaky perception, I am in the presence of a door,

on the understanding that one can be in the presence of a door without perceiving it. That, however, is at least as bad. The 'particular instance' in question—where Hume hears a door, but does not perceive it—is not even prima facie in conflict with GP*. Also, the previous trouble is now back: the present episode is said to threaten a conflict with previously accepted parts of The Belief; but the episode is supposed to show us what goes into accepting any part of it.

I shall return later to some of this trouble. First, though, let us look at a more successful part of Hume's long example.

280. Imagination: oceans and explanation

The door opens and a porter enters with a letter:

I receive a letter which upon opening it I perceive by the handwriting and subscription to have come from a friend who says he is two hundred leagues distant. It is evident I can never account for this phenomenon, conformable to my experience in other instances, without spreading out in my mind the whole sea and continent between us and supposing the effects and continued existence of posts and ferries according to my memory and observation.

This can be read as another instance of the previous trouble: memory and observation have given Hume a theory about posts and ferries, and his present experience is not 'conformable' with this unless he supposes that the posts and ferries still exist, though he does not perceive them. Something better is suggested, however, by the phrase 'account for': the problem is not to *reconcile* the present experience with anything, but rather to *explain* it in some manner that connects it with past experience. Let us see where we can get with this reading, taking 'account for . . . conformable to my [past] experience' to mean 'explain, without contradicting my past experience', rather than 'render consistent with my past experience'.

The emphasis on explanation points towards the best account Hume could give of what we are up to in supposing there to be objects that exist when we do not perceive them. I mean the best he could do once the question had been set up in his way: I have the facts about my own perceptions; now I want to understand how I get from them to my belief in a world outside me. This account says that my belief in a world of independent, continuous physical things—a large, loose, complex theory about how such things relate to one another and to my perceptions—enables me to connect my various sensory episodes to form a coherent whole. This service that my theory of 'bodies' does for me includes helping me to predict some of my future perceptions.

Think about the amount of your experience that does not take you by surprise, because it is approximately what you expected; and ask yourself what enabled you to have that expectation. I have expounded this point in §212, but here is a little more about it, I take water from a stream, taste it, and find it muddy; I am not surprised, because I have seen heavy rain falling in the hills from which this stream flows, and I know the ground in this catchment area to be mostly clay. Now, think of all this in purely subjective terms—the perceptions involved in observing the rain, learning about the clay, knowing the stream's location, and all the rest. How out of all this could I have generated a prediction that if I gave myself these tactual-kinaesthetic perceptions I would then have that gustatory one? Elementary as the example is, by the standards of life as we live it, the feat of computation which it requires is astronomically far out of my reach. What enabled me to get from all those other experiences to my expectation of this latest one is my having interpreted all the former in terms of The Belief— taking them as perceptions of clouds, of physical terrain, of a stream, and so on.

Prediction is not the whole story. Many kinds of intellectual management of our sensory states is made possible by our treating them as perceptions of an objective realm. Not necessarily a realm of material things: Strawson (1959: ch. 2) has described a simple world whose only objects are sounds; and even in this the management of sensory states can be greatly helped by the theory that some auditory perceptions are hearings of independent and continuous sounds (Bennett 1966: 33–41).

Hume first launches this 'utility' account of The Belief in connection with the sea and the continent; but it applies just as well to the creaking door, which he handles, alas, in terms not of utility but of removing contradictions.

If that account of what The Belief does for us justifies it, Hume might say, it does so merely pragmatically, and not by giving evidence of truth. So he could accept the account while still thinking that he is in the province of our imagination, rather than our senses or reason. I shall shortly produce more textual evidence that he was indeed drawn to an account such as I have sketched.

In this section I have lumped continuity and independence together, because I had to. (Spatial externality also, I suppose, but I set that aside so as to keep the discussion within bounds.) According to Hume, independence is the junior partner: we believe in bodies that are independent of our minds because we believe in ones that exist when we do not perceive them: 'The opinion of the continued existence of body . . . is prior to that of its distinct [= independent] existence, and produces that latter principle' (199; see also 210). This implies that we could explain what the imagination is up to in supposing that things exist when we do not perceive them, while not yet supposing that they exist independently of our perceiving them. I doubt it. The utility account that I have given seems to imply that the help The Belief gives us is inextricably bound up with independence as well as with continuity.

Hume seems to anticipate a certain worry about whether continuity should have any place in the account. The Belief helps me to forge links between some of my perceptions and others; how can that help involve postulating things that exist when I do not perceive them? How can a belief in items of which I have no perceptions help me in the intellectual management of perceptions that I do have? Hume faces this question, and gives approximately the right answer if the 'utility' account is what he has in mind:

> On no occasion is it necessary to suppose that [our passions] have existed and operated when they were not perceived in order to preserve the same dependence and connexion of which we have had experience. The case is not the same with relation to external objects. Those require a continued existence, or otherwise lose in a great measure the regularity of their operation. (195–6)

This is exactly right. Suppose I see a door, turn my head away, and then turn back and see it again: the second visual perception does not surprise me; it is just what I expected; and this is because I interpreted the first as a seeing of a door—an independent object which would not suddenly vanish. Now, that concept of *door*—and the physical theory to which it belongs—has as an integral part the thesis that doors often stay in existence when I do not perceive them.

I stress 'an *integral* part'. The benefits of 'perceived independent object' come through a theory which has 'unperceived object' woven densely into it: we cannot lop off statements attributing continuity to objects while retaining the 'useful' statements which interpret some of what happens as perceptions of objects. My belief that the sea and the continent exist now is inextricably bound up, through my theory of the world, and thus through the conceptual framework on which it hangs, with statements about perceptions which I do have at some time or other—what I shall observe if I take a certain journey, what I heard my friend say when asked 'What route will you take?', and so on. The only theory that helps me to manage these perceptions which I do have is one which also implies that the sea exists now when I do not perceive it.

An analogy may help. Think of arithmetic purely in terms of its utility to us in our daily lives. Much of it is obviously useful, helping us to distribute portions, decide elections, estimate journey times, plan food stores, budget for retirement, and so on. But why should our arithmetical theory also imply that there are numbers such as 7,352,866,914,008,253, even adding the extravagant claim that this item is divisible by three? What has that to do with everyday life? Nothing, in that we shall never have a practical use for that number. Everything, in the sense that endlessly many numbers like that one are an inevitable part of the total package.

The proposal to have the useful parts of arithmetic without those unusable numbers is like a proposal to trim the body by amputating the immune system. It cannot be done; there is no plane of cleavage; the two are interwoven.

The coin that I dropped over the ship's railing in 1953 is still down on the ocean bed, I am sure. That belief is not useful to me; but it is implied by a general theory of object stability that *does* help me—to remember perceptions that I have had, to predict ones that I later had, and to avoid ones that would have hurt me if I had not ducked. That theory, together with particular facts which I remember, implies that the coin is on the ocean bed; and I cannot trim it to remove that implication. All this I learned from Hume.

281. The 'what genus?' question

The utility account is in the spirit of Hume's view that The Belief comes from the imagination. To explain The Belief in terms of its utility is not to defend its truth, he would say, and so it does not intellectually *justify* it. The core of the account seems to be given by Hume himself. So the account is complete—iv.2 can end here—right? Indeed not. Two-thirds of it lies ahead: Hume reaches the rest by throwing out what he has done up to here. Let us look into this puzzling turn of events, which occupies two paragraphs at 197–8 and three lines of the paragraph after that.

Hume might have thought that his story is incomplete because the utility account of The Belief explains why it is a good thing to have but does not explain what led us to acquire it in the first place. What he actually says in launching the rest of his account, however, is nothing like that. Having presented his long door/letter example and described what the imagination is doing in such a case, he silently asks a question; that is, he discusses answers to it in a manner implying that one of them had better be right. He wants to know what *kind* of operation this attributes to the imagination. Under what general heading does it fall? What else in our mental lives can we liken it to?

Hume first tries the answer that 'this conclusion from the coherence of appearances [is] of the same nature with our reasonings concerning causes and effects, as being derived from custom and regulated by past experience' (197). He has already endorsed this. When we suppose that a single object is successively 'absent from and present to the senses', he has written, this belief which 'goes beyond the impressions of our senses' must be 'founded on the connexion of cause and effect' (74). Speaking of being in France while believing that Rome still exists, he has said that what distinguishes this belief from 'other ideas which are merely the offspring of the imagination' is that it 'arises from custom and the relation of cause and effect' (108).

Yet now in iv.2 Hume flatly rejects this. I shall report his reason mostly in his own words—all from 197–8—but not in exactly his order. 'We remark a connexion betwixt two kinds of objects in their past appearance to the senses, but are not able to observe this connexion to be perfectly constant, since the turning about of our head or the shutting of our eyes is able to break it.' What we are doing is to 'suppose that these objects still continue their usual connexion, notwithstanding their apparent interruption'. Quite generally, then, 'whenever we infer the continued existence of the objects of sense from their coherence and the frequency of their union, it is in order to bestow on the objects a greater regularity than what is observed in our mere perceptions'. This cannot be the effect of custom and habit. The only possible basis for a habit is 'the regular succession of [one's] perceptions', and it is impossible 'that any habit should ever exceed that degree of regularity'. Hume concludes: 'Any degree . . . of regularity in our perceptions can never be a foundation for us to infer a greater degree of regularity in some objects which are not perceived; since this supposes a contradiction, viz. a habit acquired by what was never present to the mind.'

This seems to imply that a Humean 'habit' can never lead to anything but the experiences that caused it in the first place—which is just to abandon the concept of habit and, with it, the entire theory of the association of ideas. That cannot be what Hume means. He must be aware of how it conflicts with his own theory according to which every causal prediction outruns its experiential basis. I am baffled by the 'degree of regularity' remarks.

Having concluded that the imaginative conduct in question cannot be 'the direct and natural effect' of custom, etc., Hume infers that 'the co-operation of some other' causes must be involved. The 'other principle', he suggests, may come from this imaginative activity's being an instance of a rounding-out, perfecting, carrying-to-the-limit propensity of the mind that he has reported earlier when discussing our thoughts about space. He has offered this as 'the reason why, after considering several loose standards of equality and correcting them by each other, we proceed to imagine so correct and exact a standard of that relation as is not liable to the least error or variation'. He applies this to the imagination's postulating unperceived objects, as follows: 'Objects have a certain coherence even as they appear to our senses; but this coherence is much greater and more uniform if we suppose the objects to have a continued existence; and as the mind is once in the train of observing a uniformity among objects, it naturally continues till it renders the uniformity as complete as possible.' Hume evidently accepts this description of what goes on, but thinks that it does not adequately explain our belief in the continuity of objects. It is, he says abruptly, 'too weak to support alone so vast an edifice as is that of the continued existence of all external bodies' (198–9).

Perhaps that is right. Notice, though, that Hume here describes the postulation of continuous objects as something we do because our minds happen to be built like that. It is as though he has forgotten the view that we do this in order to get certain benefits—the benefit to us of The Belief as a whole, and the *integral* role of continuity within it.

I suspect that he has not forgotten anything. At no time does he renounce any part of his treatment of the long example; he simply walks out on it, and devotes most of iv.2 to a different account of how the imagination produces The Belief. Rather than building on or contradicting the other, this second story is unrelated to it. My guess is that Hume, having discovered this second account and been dazzled by its ingenuity, was resolved to work it in somehow, and was not fussy about how he cleared space for it.

Does this seem uncharitable? Ought we to insist that something more philosophically respectable is afoot on 197–8? If you think so, then consider this. Hume has asked, in effect, 'When the imagination supposes there are continuous objects, in the manner I described in connection with the sea and the continent, what general kind of mental activity is this?'; and he declares two answers to this to be inadequate, assumes that they cannot be improved or supplanted, and starts afresh.

This is extraordinary. The true answer to the 'What genus?' question might be that the imaginative activity described in the utility account is *sui generis*, not like anything else in the life of the mind. Hume does not even mention this possible answer; from which I infer that he is not much engaged with the question, and that when he raises it, he is really bustling towards his second account of how imagination produces The Belief. This presents The Belief as a pure-bred offspring of error, with no sober advantages; from now on we hear nothing about getting serious help in intellectually managing our data. Because I believe the utility account, I do not believe this second one. Still, here as often, Hume wrong is more interesting than most philosophers right.

282. Hume's 'system': the identity move

In the whole paragraph on 199 Hume sketches his new account of what leads us to The Belief. Suppose that I have a pair of experiences which would ordinarily be described as 'seeing a mountain' and then, after an interval, 'seeing the same mountain for the second time'. The two impressions are so alike that I am drawn to think of them as identical; but the gap forces me to notice that they are two, not one; so I try to hide the interruption from myself 'by supposing that these interrupted perceptions are connected by a real existence of which [I am] insensible'. This supposition is my Belief in objects that exist continuously through gaps in my perception of them.

That is a summary. To fill in the details, Hume says, he must break the account into four parts, of which I shall discuss one here and the other three in §283.

The first part of Hume's 'system' concerns the concept of identity: the three paragraphs on 200 imply that there is no satisfactory work for it to do. What he will say later about misuses of the identity concept will make more sense if we first understand why he holds that no uses of it are fully correct.

Though he does not state it so bluntly, Hume knowingly implies that every identity statement is somewhat improper. He puts the difficulty in terms of the ideas of 'unity' and 'number', but its main thrust can be understood without that. I invite you to work through the text and then agree that at best it comes down to the following. Hume is contending that there can be no informative, a posteriori, true identity statements, because 'x is x' is always trivial (unity), and 'x is y' is always false (number). The second half of that claim is wrong: an identity statement can be true and informative if its noun phrases *refer* to the same thing, but refer to it through different *senses*, as in 'That man standing in the corner is the person who has been bidding against you for all the best pieces' and 'This is the river we waded across last summer'. Something like the sense/reference distinction of Frege (1892) was needed for this matter to become clear, or anyway clearer; in Hume's day nobody, I think, was equipped to deal well with identity.

Hume was especially badly placed to do so. In our present context he is assuming that all we ever *refer to* are our perceptions; and his equivalent for Frege's *senses* are ideas, which are also perceptions. For him, then, the sense/reference distinction is especially hard to draw.

From 200, line 4 up, to the foot of 201 Hume explains what he regards as the nearest we can get to a true, informative identity statement. It concerns 'a single object, . . . surveyed for any time without our discovering in it any interruption or variation'. This, he says, yields 'an idea which is a medium betwixt unity and number; or, more properly speaking, is either of them, according to the view in which we take it: and this idea we call that of identity'.

As that wording might suggest, he thinks that this, although it is the best we can do, still involves an element of 'feigning' or 'fiction'. Both words come from the Latin *fingo* = 'I make', and its past participle *fictum* = 'made'. The item that exists at one time is not identical with the item that exists at another time, he holds: the times are different, so the objects must be so as well. We are aware of this when we 'survey [the two points in time] at the very same instant; in which case they give us the idea of number, both by themselves and by the object; which must be multiplied in order to be conceived at once, as existent in these two different points of time'. I sit here at time T_3 and think about the rock at T_1 and the rock at T_2, and my present thought of those *two* items brings in number, and thus excludes identity. But I may instead 'trace the succession of time by a like succession of ideas and, conceiving first one moment along with the object then existent, imagine afterwards a change in the time without any variation or interruption in the object'. If in this manner I let my thought run along the time line with the rock, nothing intrudes into it to create a thought of number, so instead it comes up with 'the idea of unity'. As Hume puts it later: 'The thought slides along the succession with equal facility as if it considered only one object, and therefore confounds the succession with the identity' (204; see also 256).

That choice between number and unity, and our ability to toggle between them, lets us approximate to the unachievable ideal of asserting a true, a posteriori identity statement. Here and elsewhere, Hume holds that diachronic identity beliefs are at their imperfect best when the relevant sequence of perceptions is neither interrupted nor qualitatively various.[1] That is implied when he says that when we believe in the continuous existence of an object, 'notwithstanding the interruption of the perception', this is because we believe 'that if we had kept our eye or hand constantly upon it, it would have conveyed an *invariable and* uninterrupted perception' (74; my emphasis). Just now, though, all the weight falls on interruption.

Hume fails to do justice to identity-statements, I have remarked, because his tool kit lacks the sense/reference distinction. He fails also in another way, which is philosophically more interesting. Let us apply his line of thought to one case. From noon to 3 p.m. I get on with my life while suffering an unvarying headache. Because it does not vary, I am drawn to the fiction that the headache that I endure at 1 p.m. is the headache that afflicts me at 2 p.m. Really they are different, however, and I grasp this in the evening when I think back to both pain episodes at once. Here I am in the evening, recalling both the 1 p.m. pain that spoiled my lunch-time and the 2 p.m. one that stopped me from sleeping; and their distinctness—their being two pains, not one—is obvious to me when I lay them side by side in my mind.

Should we accept this part of Hume's position? Well, it is open to question. There seems to be nothing wrong with saying that I had a three-hour-long pain with many parts that were briefer pains. (The long pain is an event, so its briefer parts are also events.) Now, it need not be a *fiction* to suppose that the headache that I was suffering from at 1 p.m. was the headache that I was suffering from at 2 p.m., because in each case we can understand 'the headache that I was suffering from at T' as referring to the big three-hour headache. Still, Hume could reply that this way of talking is artificial: the fundamental reality consists of many brief pains; they are all I have to report; and while I may quaintly lump them together as parts of a single long one, that is a contrivance which does not capture any real aspect of how the world is.

That reply is plausible enough to make one wonder, at least, whether the concept of identity has any robust a posteriori application to 'perceptions' such as pains. The point concerns *diachronic* statements of identity—that is, ones of the form

The item that is F at T_1 is the item that is G at T_2,

where T_1 differs from T_2, and F may differ from G. We should also consider—though Hume shows no theoretical interest in them—*synchronic* statements, of the form

The item that is F at T_1 is the item that is G at T_1.

[1] Leibniz wrote: 'It is impossible for us to . . . find any way of precisely determining the individuality of any thing *à moins que de la garder elle même*' (NE 289). This has a grammatical defect which, I am told, could be repaired either by making it mean '. . . except by keeping hold of the thing itself' or by making it mean '. . . except by keeping it unchanged'. Leibniz thus, exasperatingly, throws a cover of bad French across the choice between perceptual gaps and qualitative variation.

(These are two sorts of statement, not two sorts of identity. The phrases 'diachronic identity' and 'synchronic identity' are solecisms.) It is hard to find any solid examples of these in which the 'items' are perceptions. What would be needed for such an example is a single brief perception which could be recognized under either of two non-equivalent descriptions; and little of this sort is available to us. It seems hardly possible that I should be in a position to identify a perception of mine as the item that is now F, and to identify it as the item that is now G, and have it come to me as news that the F item is the G item.

When we move from perceptions to objects out there in the world—ones that we relationally perceive—the picture changes. The concept of identity, which has so little a posteriori use with perceptions, is richly usable on outer objects. They provide all the best examples of a single item falling under two non-equivalent descriptions and being identifiable under either. Outer objects have histories, through which they can alter; and even when they do not, the statement that the object which was F at T_1 is the object that was F at T_2 may be substantive and even surprising. Also, an outer object can have many properties at once and be identifiable under different subsets of them, because of differences in person, sense modality, and angle of approach: the thing that I now feel resting on my hand is the thing that you now see from above (§225).

Following Quine's classic 1950, some philosophers think that physical objects have temporal parts, sometimes called 'stages', just as events do. (The most thorough defence is Heller 1990.) Because Picasso's *Guernica* has lasted from about 1940 at least through to 2000, they hold, there is such a thing as the 1950 stage of that painting and a distinct 1990 stage of it. They are right about the identity-conditions of temporal stages, if there are such things. A stage that is confined to one period of time cannot be identical with a stage that is confined to another. Still, these stages can be brought into diachronic identity statements: 'The F painting that was in the Metropolitan Museum of Art at T_1 is the G painting that was in the Prado at T_2' asserts a certain relation between two painting-stages, *but the relation is not identity*. What relates the relevant stages is not '. . . is identical with . . .', but rather '. . . is a stage of a thing of which . . . is also a stage' (§304).

Similarly with my long headache, which certainly has temporal parts. The 1 p.m. episode is distinct from the 2 p.m. one, but they are related by '. . . is part of a continuous headache of which . . . is also a part'; and that makes it true that the headache I was suffering from at 1 p.m. is the one I was still suffering from at 2 p.m.

Here is a contrast between objects and events. Sometimes we treat an aggregate of brief events as parts of one longer one; in other cases we do not. What governs this discrimination? How do we decide whether the battle which raged on Tuesday was the one that had begun on Monday? Or whether the fire that burned down my house on Tuesday was the one that had burned down yours on Monday? We decide by consulting the semantic conventions governing 'same fire' and 'same battle'. It cannot be the same fire, we hold, unless some continuous spatio-temporal zone linking the two incinerations of houses is fiery throughout; but we allow that it can be the same battle even if the two episodes are not linked by a zone that is combative throughout, for the armies can sleep and then resume a battle. This is mere superficial convention, however; we could easily handle 'same battle' differently, as we could 'same fire'. When, on the other hand, we judge whether certain brief object-stages belong to a single enduring object, the principles guiding us are neither superficial nor easily alterable. The constraints governing this are stern and deeply embedded in our scheme of things, and we get at them not through shapeless intuitions of verbal propriety, but through structural facts about what inferences are valid, what statements are self-contradictory, and so on. There are such facts because the physical object concept does hard, central, disciplined work for us.

Perceptions are events. So statements of identity about them are thin in two ways. There is little grip for substantive synchronic identity statements about them, because they do not have a rich array of different features under any one of which they might be recognized. Secondly, diachronic identity statements involving them—like such statements about events generally—reflect only shallow linguistic conventions; they do not hook up with anything weighty in our conceptual scheme. I conclude that a posteriori identity statements come into their own when, and only when, the topic is objective, external objects which have histories and which are, at any given time, richly endowed with properties through subsets of which they may be identified. I came to understand this through wrestling with Hume's work, and realizing how right he was to connect objectivity with identity. His way of connecting them, however, is less good, as we shall see.

283. Hume's 'system': the remainder

The second part of Hume's system starts in the paragraph on 201–2, where he explains that he is here considering the thoughts of the vulgar, who take their objects to be the very things they perceive. Without saying that they believe these to be perceptions, Hume denies that the vulgar distinguish 'betwixt the objects and perceptions of the senses' as a Lockean materialist does—he thinks of that distinction as a technical, philosophical affair. This non-committal aspect of the vulgar scheme of things gives Hume a problem with terminology, which he solves thus:

In order, therefore, to accommodate myself to their notions, I shall at first suppose that there is only a single existence, which I shall call indifferently *object* or *perception*, according as it shall seem best to suit my purpose, understanding by both of them what any common man means by a hat or shoe or stone or any other impression conveyed to him by his senses. (202)

But on his own view about the non-committal element, there is no such thing as 'what any common man means by "a hat"'. In practice, Hume makes his own terminology more stable and determinate by pushing the vulgar in the direction of identifying bodies with perceptions. He probably believes, as Berkeley did, that any intelligent plain person could be induced to accept this if things were properly explained to him.

Now to the substance. When I am in the same perceptual state for some time, this inclines me to judge that the perception I have at T_2 is the one I had at T_1—as with the parts of the long headache. According to Hume, the time difference ensures that it will not really be the same perception, but I am apt to think the two are one if they are alike and linked by a smooth sequence of intervening perceptions which also resemble both. This happens because (Hume says he has shown in ii.5) we tend to mistake resemblance for identity, thinking that x is y because x is like y. In our present case, the act of surveying two of my similar perceptions which are linked by a smooth sequence of similar ones is enormously like the act of the mind that occurs when I survey a single perception. So I tend to think that these are the same (kind of) act, and thus to think that the case of resemblance-and-no-interruption is really a case of identity.

(Hume develops this in detail, from the foot of 201 to the end of 204. There are complexities which I shall ignore; but I note a nice wrinkle to which Hume calls our attention in the footnote at 204–5. First, we have the theory

T: My mind is so constituted that when two items are extremely alike, I shall be apt to think they are one.

There is also the plain fact that

F: The movement of my mind from one thing to a second similar one resembles the mental process of contemplating a single item.

That has the following consequence:

C: When my mind moves from one thing to a second similar one, I am apt to think that I am merely contemplating a single item.

Now, if we ask what makes T true, Hume will reply that it is true because of the truth of F and therefore of C. We mistake similarity for identity because contemplating similarity is so like contemplating identity. But if we ask why F leads to C—why the similarity of those two mental processes leads us to identify them—Hume's answer is that F implies C on the strength of T. That the similarity of the processes leads us to identify them is both *the source* of the phenomenon that T speaks about and *an instance* of that phenomenon. This is not circular or otherwise invalid. It is a wrinkle.)

Even when the sequence linking a pair of resembling perceptions is interrupted, we still tend to think of the two as one: 'An easy transition or passage of the imagination along the ideas of these different and interrupted perceptions is almost the same disposition of mind with that in which we consider one constant and uninterrupted perception' (204). Note the word 'almost'—there is some difference. 'The interruption of the appearance seems contrary to the identity, and naturally leads us to regard these resembling perceptions as different from each other,' Hume writes on 205, and this puts us in a bind: 'The smooth passage of the imagination along the ideas of the resembling perceptions makes us ascribe to them a perfect identity. The interrupted manner of their appearance makes us consider them as so many resembling but still distinct beings, which appear after certain intervals.' In this dilemma, we need to do something to 'reconcile such opposite opinions', or at least to produce the illusion of a reconciliation—something to give us 'relief from the uneasiness' (206) which that opposition creates in us.

Why do interruptions make that difference? We can make good sense of this only against the background of the view, which I attribute to Hume, that no diachronic identity statement is strictly true. I cannot square this with his saying on 209 that 'the interruption of our perceptions . . . is the only circumstance that is contrary to their identity'. He ought to mean that the interruption is the only circumstance that is contrary to their constituting *the best possible approximation to* a genuine identity. He usually seems to accept the view, to which he has committed himself, that even without interruptions there is still no identity along the time line. Similarly, when he implies that in some cases we can 'in propriety of speech' assert an identity statement (201), he may mean that those are the paradigm statements of that kind, while still seeing them as tainted.

The central, predictable element in the third part of Hume's 'system' is given just above the paragraph break on 205: 'The perplexity arising from this contradiction produces a propension to unite these broken appearances by the fiction of a continued existence '; and so we get the belief in things' existing when we do not perceive them. A later restatement of the position is useful: 'This resemblance gives us a propension to consider these interrupted perceptions as the same; and also a propension to connect them by a continued existence, in order to justify this identity and avoid the contradiction in which the interrupted appearance of these perceptions seems necessarily to involve us' (208).

In the next two paragraphs Hume sets up the situation again, emphasizing our need for 'relief', and re-emphasizing that he is concerned with The Belief as it is held by the vulgar, whom he has characterized as 'the unthinking and unphilosophical part of mankind (that is, all of us at one time or other)' (205), and now calls 'all mankind, and even philosophers themselves for the greatest part of their lives' (206). This version of The Belief, Hume thinks, attributes continuity, etc. to our perceptions themselves, these being 'the very things we see and feel'. So two questions arise.

One of them reflects Hume's having cleansed the vulgar version of The Belief of its non-committal element, and begun taking it to be purely about perceptions. He asks 'how we can satisfy ourselves in supposing a perception to be absent from the mind without being annihilated' (207). Anticipating his coming treatment of personal identity, he says that a mind 'is nothing but a heap or collection of different perceptions'; each perception is distinct from each other; and so there is 'no absurdity' in supposing that a perception might exist without belonging to any such collection—that is, without being in any mind. This does not explain the willingness of the vulgar to 'feign' the existence of unowned perceptions; it may clear them of a charge of logical absurdity, but only on the strength of an analysis of mental ownership—that is, of what a mind is—which they would reject if it were put to them. Perhaps here again he is concerned with what the vulgar could be got to see if they were taught properly.

The second question demands that the picture be filled in. When a plain person thinks 'I saw it for a few minutes around noon, and again for a few minutes around 1 p.m., but not in between', what is going on in his mind? How can we re-express his thought in fundamental terms—that is, in terms of perceptions? Hume's answer, in the paragraph on 207–8, is not ideally clear, but I am fairly sure of what it comes down to. The vulgar belief in continuous objects, he holds, amounts to this:

> An uninterrupted all-similar sequence of perceptions occurs, some of its earlier and later members belonging to some person's mind while intermediate ones do not belong to any mind.

Once again the vulgar form of The Belief emerges free of conceptual defect.

In the fourth and final part of his 'system', Hume undertakes to show how the ideas involved in the 'feigning' of un-had perceptions come to qualify as beliefs. This is straightforward: we do this feigning under the influence of 'lively impressions of the memory' of past feignings; the liveliness is passed along to the ideas that constitute the feigning; and so they acquire enough vivacity to qualify as beliefs.

Hume is right in thinking that identity is inextricably linked with objectivity (which includes continuity), but he takes them in the wrong order, depicting us as having an identity-concept and being forced by it to believe in independent continuous objects. It is a curious starting-point. Why do we have this concept, and why are we so determined to employ it, if there are no strictly correct uses for it, and if tolerable 'imperfect' uses involve us in lying to ourselves? What a strange performance Hume sees us as going through! He would be nearer to the truth if he stayed with the first, utility-providing account, and added to it the mirror image of the second account: our views about independent continuous objects are explained by how they help us to cope with our experience; and they also provide solid a posteriori work for our concept of identity to do.

284. What is wrong with The Belief

Although we arrive at The Belief 'by the natural propensity of the imagination', 'a very little reflection and philosophy is sufficient to make us perceive the fallacy of that opinion'. The trouble with it, Hume surprisingly says, is that we have empirical evidence that perceptions do not have 'any independent existence', and therefore do not exist unowned. He gestures towards the evidence in a paragraph (210–11) about how our perceptions depend on our bodily organs. This is distressingly unsatisfactory, given what Hume has riding on it. He points out that what perceptions we have varies with the state and situation of our sense-organs, and takes this to confirm that 'all our perceptions are dependent on our organs and the disposition of our nerves and animal spirits'.

The facts that Hume adduces show at most that our organs affect what perceptions *we have in our minds*, and not what perceptions *there are*. The vulgar form of The Belief, as he understands it, implies that some perceptions exist when nobody has or perceives them. His empirical data have no force against that, precisely because they are confined to perceptions that do occur in our minds. If unowned perceptions are to be ruled out, it must be on other grounds—presumably conceptual ones. Hume, however, has declined to follow that route.

I cannot explain his going as far wrong as he does at 210–11. I understand his wanting to show that the vulgar form of The Belief is false, and he has a strong reason—his account of what an enduring mind is—for not rejecting it as conceptually flawed; so he is under pressure to find empirical fault with it. But that does not explain his being satisfied with the empirical evidence that he actually produces.

Hume has brought us to this point: People's imagination naturally leads them to think that perceptions like theirs exist without being had by anyone, but then philosophy and reflection lead some of them to realize that this is not so. Those thoughtful people are again caught in a bind, from which they try to extricate themselves:

They change their system, and distinguish (as we shall do for the future) betwixt perceptions and objects, of which the former are supposed to be interrupted and perishing, and different at every different return; the latter to be uninterrupted, and to preserve a continued existence and identity. (211)

This is not the point at which we arrive at The Belief; we passed that some distance back. It is the point at which some of us—the philosophers—arrive at the Lockean form of The Belief. Not that Hume puts it like that; he mentions Locke in the *Treatise* only in connection with abstract ideas and causation. But his understanding of the distinction between perceptions and objects must remind us of Berkeley's criticisms of Locke. Above all, Hume firmly assumes that if our objects are the things we perceive, then they are our perceptions; so that the 'philosophical' position which distinguishes objects from perceptions concedes that we do not perceive the objects it speaks of.

Although thoughtful people will be led to it, the philosophical version of The Belief (Hume insists) is worse than the vulgar one, for two reasons. One is that it is not supported by reason, even when 'reason' is understood broadly. Only causal reasoning could lead us 'from the existence of one thing to that of another'; but that must be based on regularities that we have experienced; all we ever experience are perceptions; so we can never have any basis to infer the existence of 'objects' understood as being different from perceptions. Secondly, the philosophical version of The Belief is not directly supported by the imagination either. The latter does have some interest in preserving the illusion of identity by 'feigning' that a gap in a series of perceptions is filled by an unperceived item of the very same sort—that is, an unowned perception. But such an illusion would not be protected or nourished by the pretence that the gap was filled by an item of a different sort from those on each side of it. Or so Hume conjectures, challenging opponents to prove otherwise.

These two criticisms, he concludes, indicate that the philosophical version of The Belief is parasitic on the vulgar one. People are led to the latter by certain intellectual and imaginative needs; then, finding trouble with what they have been led to, they shift across to the philosophical version. But this 'has no original authority of its own'. The energy and elaborateness of Hume's arguments on this point show irritation with Lockean materialists who exclaim at the weirdness of Berkeley's metaphysic.

Chapter 38

Reason

285. Reasoning in man and beast

Of the other five of my six philosophers, Hume is the least like Spinoza personally, and the most like him in some large philosophical respects (§235). They are,
for example, the most openly committed to a naturalistic account of the human
condition—one that postulates no deep difference of kind between man and
beast. 'Man' is one of Spinoza's examples of the kind of general term that is not
fit for serious theoretical use (§84). The term 'human' figures in the titles of parts
4 and 5 of the *Ethics*, but the concept of humanity has no structural role there.
Everything Spinoza says about our bondage and our freedom could equally
apply—for all he says or thinks to the contrary—to other animal species as well,
though in lesser degree as one moves down the scale of complexity. For Hume
the sliding scale from man to beast is something to be militantly proclaimed and
tenaciously defended.

He announces the sloping ramp at the place where many had thought there is
a cliff—namely, the use of reason. Man is a rational animal—and the thought was
that man is *the* rational animal. In iii.16, 'Of the Reason of Animals', Hume combatively treats it as obvious that 'beasts are endowed with thought and reason as
well as men' (176), and boasts that his account of causal reasoning highlights and
partly explains this similarity. He does not notice that this clashes with his treatment of abstract ideas, according to which thought involving general concepts
requires the use of language (§165).

I stress *causal* reasoning. Hume uses 'reason' and its cognates to cover the faculty or capacity for any sort of thinking. His famous thesis that 'Reason is and
ought only to be the slave of the passions' (415) concerns not merely demonstration, but also reasoning about causes and effects, means to ends. He writes:
'The understanding exerts itself after two different ways, as it judges from
demonstration or probability; as it regards the abstract relations of our ideas or
those relations of objects of which experience only gives us information' (413).

The section on the reason of animals ignores demonstrative reasoning, and
confines itself to what Hume calls 'the second operation of the understanding'.
On his way to his topic, he separates (1) 'those actions of animals which are of a
vulgar nature, and seem to be on a level with their common capacities' from (2)
'those more extraordinary instances of sagacity which they sometimes discover
[= turn out to have] for their own preservation and the propagation of their
species' (177). He illustrates 1 with a dog's avoiding fire and precipices, and 2 with

a bird's elaborate nest building. It is behaviour of type 1, Hume says, that 'proceeds from reasoning'; he implies that 2 does not, but without saying why. I suppose he thinks of the 'more extraordinary' behaviour as instinctive: it is too elaborate for the animal to have learned it through trial and experienced error, so it must be wired in somehow—'for their own preservation', etc.—and thus not result from reasoning. (See *OED*, 'sagacity', sense 3 ('of animals').)

The more ordinary kind of animal behaviour, Hume says, manifests thought in exactly the way that human behaviour does: The animal is triggered to behave thus and so by some present impression, and the triggering occurs because of the animal's past experience. This is exactly what happens when humans think causally, he says; and we have seen why he thinks so (§269). Leibniz disagrees:

Here on earth reason is exclusive to man alone and does not appear in any other animals on earth; for . . . the shadow of reason which can be seen in beasts is merely an expectation of a similar issue in a case which appears to resemble the past, with no knowledge of whether the same reason obtains. And that is just how men behave too, in cases where they are merely empirics. But they rise above the beasts in so far as they see the connections between truths—connections which themselves constitute necessary and universal truths. (*NE* 475)[1]

The central point of this is one that Hume could accept (though not the implications of the word 'necessary' in the final clause). Hume does see men as empirics—that is, as steering by the regularities that experience forces on their notice, without trying to deepen and broaden their picture of the world's order. But his philosophy poses no obstacle to adding that we sometimes engage in such broadening.

Hume concludes this section with a lively declaration which is meant to tease or irritate his conservative readers:

Men are not astonished at the operations of their own reason, at the same time that they admire [= wonder at] the instinct of animals . . . To consider the matter aright, reason is nothing but a wonderful and unintelligible instinct in our souls, which carries us along a certain train of ideas. (178)

The faculty for probabilistic and cause–effect thinking, he implies, is unlike nest building, in that it 'arises from past observation and experience'; but it is none the less an instinct. Hume's understanding of 'instinct' seems to fit Leibniz's definition of it as 'an inclination which an animal has—with no conception of the reason for it—towards something which is suitable to it' (*NE* 351). Hume issues this challenge: 'Can anyone give the ultimate reason why past experience and observation produces such an effect, any more than why nature alone should produce it? Nature may certainly produce whatever can arise from habit: nay, habit is nothing but one of the principles of nature, and derives all its force from that origin.' This is beautiful. Hume's point could be put thus:

Nature could have made children so that (1) they instinctively dread fire, but it actually made them so that (2) they learn to dread it. This is a real difference, but do not think of

---

[1] See also PNG 5, FW 261.

it as involving a contrast between (1) the dread's being psychologically caused by the perception of the fire, and (2) its coming about not through causes but through reasoning.
The difference is really just between two causal patterns, two ways for nature to cause
children to fear fire.

Hume's deep, central naturalism is what powers this *jeu d'esprit* about reason as
an instinct.

Most philosophers today would agree with its main thrust; but it goes too fast,
gliding over crevices that ask to be explored. One is the difference between
empirics and broadeners. Here is another. Many philosophers, including Leibniz,
have thought that humans are the only terrestrial animals who reason demonstratively. Hume is silent about that. When he writes about the reasoning of 'animals', he is thinking only of causal reasoning. Why not a priori demonstrative
reasoning as well? Perhaps because he is not sure that other animals do engage
in it. Well, what makes him sure that (other) human beings do so? Language
plays a large part in the most obvious answer to this, but is it required for any possible answer? If beasts do not reason demonstratively, is this because they have no
languages, or none of a certain required sort? This is splendid terrain for Humean
investigations, but Hume did not equip himself to explore it.

286. Demonstrative reasoning

Hume understands demonstration in the same general way as his predecessors
and contemporaries did, and as many philosophers understand 'deduction', 'logical proof', etc. today. Everyone in this tradition accepted this thesis, which I
shall call Necessity:

> If anyone can show by demonstration that P is true, then P is absolutely nec-
> essary.

This concerns showing P through demonstration alone, not rigorously deriving
it from contingent premises. Hume's acceptance of Necessity shows up several
times, as when he writes that a certain line of thought 'must amount to a demonstration, and must imply the absolute impossibility of any contrary supposition'
(111), and when he writes that if a certain proposition were 'demonstratively
false', it would 'imply a contradiction' (*Enquiry* iv.1, 21).

Here is a defence of Necessity:

> In demonstrating that P, one shows its truth without resorting to one's senses
> and thus without inquiring into how things stand at the actual world. If this
> can be done, P's truth does not reflect any difference between the actual world
> and any other possible world; for if it did, one would have to *look* to see which
> of those worlds one lives at. So P's truth at the actual world must be assured
> because P is true at every possible world; which is to say that P is absolutely
> necessary.

That line of thought may well have weighed with Hume and others in the tradition, although none would have expressed it in those terms.

This argument succeeds so well that we should be suspicious of it. In fact, it makes a substantive and disputable assumption, namely: *For some values of P it is possible to show by demonstration alone that P is true.* As traditionally understood, this means that we can engage intellectually with a proposition in such a manner as to get a guarantee of its truth. How can this be? What kind of intellectual process could possibly have that feature? Hume's answer, we shall find, is that none could, and that the traditional view of demonstration—and of the supposed faculty of reason which enables us to demonstrate—is wrong. 'Our reason', we shall find him saying, 'must be considered as a kind of cause, of which truth is the natural effect.' This implies that a demonstration could lead to a false conclusion, but that this would be unnatural or pathological and, for that reason, surprising; so that our trust in demonstration to conform to truth is like our trust in our diaphragms to keep our lungs on the move. That, I am sure, was Hume's considered opinion about reason and demonstration.

What happens when you engage in demonstrative reasoning? Hume answers that you relate your ideas to one another. Sometimes he implies that all this relating is 'comparing' (§256), but I shall not press that here. The ideas in question are the ordinary ones that are involved in all our thinking, believing, imagining, and so on, as Hume insists in a paragraph tacked on to iii.1 in opposition to mathematicians who maintain 'that those ideas which are their objects are of so refined and spiritual a nature that they . . . must be comprehended by a pure and intellectual view, of which the superior faculties of the soul are alone capable'. Hume rejects this on the grounds that 'All our ideas are copied from our impressions', and, since the latter are plain enough, our ideas 'can never, but from our fault, contain anything so dark and intricate [or] imply any very great mystery' (72–3). This may be less than fair, but it serves to declare a position: demonstrative reasoning is a plainly describable mental happening, not hidden in clouds surrounding some 'superior faculty of the soul'.

Demonstration, Hume tells us, involves a compulsion—there is something the thinker is compelled to do, or something he or she cannot do. One might expect it to be a compulsion to *assent to the proposition*: I demonstrate that 2 is the only even prime by interrelating certain ideas in such a way that I have to assent to that. He could distinguish this compulsion from the one that he says occurs in causal reasoning, by saying that the former comes purely from an engagement with those ideas whereas the latter involves input from past experience. That would echo the tradition, as well as being compatible with Hume's basic views.

Yet what he actually says about demonstration is not that, but this:

With regard to propositions that are proved by intuition or demonstration . . . , the person who assents not only conceives the ideas according to the proposition, but is necessarily determined to conceive them in that particular manner, either immediately or by the interposition of other ideas. Whatever is absurd is unintelligible; nor is it possible for the imagination to conceive anything contrary to a demonstration. (95)

So demonstration involves a compulsion to *conceive* things in a certain manner— namely, 'according to the proposition'. This puzzling idiom occurs in one other place: 'I defy these metaphysicians to conceive the matter [an issue about space] according to their hypothesis' (55). What does it mean?

Well, we are familiar with the locution 'It is inconceivable that P', and we philosophers adapt this to our own purposes, meaning by it that something in our concepts rules out P's being true. This lies in the background of Hume's remarks linking conception with possibility, as here: 'When a demonstration convinces me of any proposition, it not only makes me conceive of the proposition but also makes me sensible that it is impossible to conceive anything contrary. What is demonstratively false implies a contradiction, and what implies a contradiction cannot be conceived' (Abstract 18). Although this is a philosophical commonplace, however, that does not mean that we clearly understand it, or that Hume is entitled to it. I now explain why he is not.

The source of the trouble is that he has no theoretical room for the notion of a pair of propositions P and not-P of which one is the contradictory of the other. This ought to be provided for within a general treatment of propositional structure, which we have seen Hume not to have (§247). Now, in a scheme of things that does not allow for not-P and P as distinct thoughts, one cannot say that P's necessity shows in not-P's being inconceivable. That is why we find Hume trying to steer a different course, saying that when someone assents to P, having demonstrated it, he 'not only conceives the ideas according to the proposition, but is necessarily determined to conceive them in that particular manner' (95), using the 'conceive according to' locution that I have been trying to understand. When he continues that it is not 'possible for the imagination to conceive anything contrary to a demonstration', however, he seems to have recourse to contradictories after all. My grasping the necessity of P shows (or consists) in my being unable to conceive not-P.

So the compulsion involved in demonstration is not a compulsion to believe the conclusion, but rather an inability to conceive its contradictory. That seems to be the best Hume can do. As well as relying on a concept of contradiction which he tries to dispense with, because he has laid no basis for it, this contains a further problem and raises a further question.

The problem is just that Hume here treats a proposition as absolutely impossible on grounds that he uses elsewhere to declare a sentence to be unintelligible or meaningless. 'Whatever is absurd is unintelligible', he writes at 95, and there is the trouble in a nutshell: after arriving at 'absurd' through logical or absolute impossibility, he carries on from 'absurd' into unintelligibility, thus conflating two distinct notions, just as Berkeley did before him (§215).

The question is this. If, having demonstrated P, I cannot conceive not-P, what kind of 'cannot' is that? Hume often implies that it is not a merely psychological impossibility. We have already seen him saying that a demonstrable connection between two items would involve 'the absolute impossibility for the one object . . . to be conceived not to follow upon the other'. He also writes that if it is demonstratively necessary that K_1 events are followed by K_2 ones, then a K_1 event's not being followed by a K_2 one 'implies a formal contradiction; and it is impossible not only that [this sequence of events] can exist, but also that it can be conceived' (111; see also 87). This suggests that the conceiving is impossible in the same way that the state of affairs is. The other passages assert this outright.

If Hume really does mean to accord the same modal status to 'Someone conceives of there being an even prime other than 2' as to 'There is an even prime other than 2', then he faces a difficulty.

How in practice do we discover that it is absolutely necessary that P? Hume's preferred answer seems to be that we discover this by finding that we cannot conceive that not-P. That is a possible epistemic route to conclusions about absolute modality if, but only if, 'inconceivability' does not itself belong to the modal circle. The story goes through if I learn that not-P is inconceivable by trying to conceive it and failing; but it whirls in a circle if what I have to discover is that it is absolutely impossible for me to conceive that not-P.

287. A sceptical attack on reason: preliminaries

In one of many places where Hume separates 'belief that P' into two species, depending on whether P is necessary or contingent, he writes that 'Every kind of opinion or judgment *which amounts not to knowledge* is derived entirely from the force and vivacity of the perception' (*Treatise*, 153; my emphasis).[2] This excludes 'opinions and judgments' which are reached demonstratively, because those all count as knowledge. Indeed, they give us the only knowledge we have, Hume says; his section 'Of Knowledge' is entirely concerned with what can and what cannot be established demonstratively (§257). The tie between knowledge and demonstration is retained throughout the work, with knowledge being presented—in an admitted change of terminology, but not one affecting 'knowledge'—as one of a trio of epistemic states:

[It would be helpful to] distinguish human reason into three kinds, viz. *that from knowledge, from proofs, and from probabilities*. By knowledge, I mean the assurance arising from the comparison of ideas. By proofs, those arguments which are derived from the relation of cause and effect, and which are entirely free from doubt and uncertainty. By probability, that evidence which is still attended with uncertainty. (124)

The firm lines that Hume draws here collapse later. Just because 'knowledge' is a human phenomenon and is therefore 'fallible', it cannot stand secure against the possibilities of error that beset 'proofs and probabilities'; so we find Hume saying: 'All knowledge resolves itself into probability, and becomes at last of the same nature with that evidence which we employ in common life' (181), and that

---

[2] He should say that it *consists in* the force, etc., but that is beside my present point.

'Demonstration is subject to the control of probability' (182). Let us see how this comes about.

It happens in iv.1, entitled 'Of Scepticism with Regard to Reason'. Hume argues there that we ought not to trust anything we reach by demonstrative reasoning. The argument is sound, he holds; he can find no defect that brings it to a halt, and no counter-argument that rolls it back. Yet it does not lead him to doubt the results that he reaches by demonstration, and he is sure that it would equally fail to move anybody who followed it through and saw its soundness. Hume's main purpose in that section is to explain, with help from his theory of belief, why this should be so. The theory is supposed to gain credibility from its role in this explanation.

Hume evidently does not mean to confine this discussion to propositions that we think we know a priori. Although he usually thinks of rigorous a priori demonstration as a quite separate process from probabilistic thinking, in this section of the *Treatise* he seems to assume (rightly, as we now think) that reasoning about probabilities involves the kind of thinking that goes into logic and mathematics. His announced topic in this section is 'the demonstrative sciences [whose] rules are certain and infallible'; and his sceptical undermining of these 'sciences', he says later, threatens us with 'a total extinction of belief and evidence', not merely total scepticism in logic and mathematics. So he must hold that demonstrative reasoning is involved not only in those a priori sciences, but also when we use empirical knowledge to estimate the likelihood that some contingent claim is true, as here:

There is some question proposed to me, and . . . , after revolving over the impressions of my memory and senses, and carrying my thoughts from them to such objects as are commonly conjoined with them, I feel a stronger and more forcible conception on the one side than on the other. This strong conception forms my first decision. (184)

He is poised here to question our inferences from the deliverances of the senses and memory, not to question the latter themselves. I have observed certain things, and I have views about weather in general; from all this I infer demonstratively that it will probably rain tomorrow. Hume will question that inference.

In iv.1 the concept of probability is heavily at work. There are three ways of employing this concept:

(S) subjective probability: I rate his chances of succeeding at about 0.6.
(OR) objective relative probability: On the evidence that he has had only a year in prison, is 25 years old, has an IQ of 105, is physically healthy and not drug-addicted, and has a supportive family, his chances of succeeding are about 0.6.
(OA) objective absolute probability: His chance of succeeding is about 0.6.

In a fully rational person, S is a species of OR: the credence level that such a person will assign to P will match the probability that P has *relative to the totality of that person's other beliefs*. Still, plenty of people are more confident of some proposition than is warranted by the rest of their belief systems; so S is a distinct category. It is a triadic relation, connecting a proposition with a person and a time. In OR a dyadic relation obtains between two propositions; change the second relatum and the truth-value may change. In OA a dyadic relation holds between a proposition and a time: the proposition is accorded an objective chance of truth, this being something it has absolutely, not as estimated by the speaker or relative to stated evidence; but its chance of truth may go up or down as time goes on. In a strictly deterministic world, the only objective absolute probabilities are 0 and 1.

As a determinist, Hume had no use for OA, and nothing in iv.1 indicates a concern with OR. In the *Treatise* as a whole, indeed, I can find nothing that I would interpret in terms of objective probability, whether (OR) relative or (OA) absolute. All through, Humean 'probability' is (S) the subjective variety. That must be what he is operating with when he contrasts 'probability' with 'knowledge' (foot of 181); when he writes that 'probability is founded on the presumption of a resemblance betwixt those objects of which we have had experience and those of which we have had none' (90); when he speaks of 'probability or reasoning from conjecture' (end of 124); and, more generally, when he connects probability with belief and with action both in iv.1 and in the long discussions of probability in iii.11–13.

288. A sceptical attack on reason: the argument

In iv.1 Hume uses a defective argument to bring us to a thesis of his which may be true. The argument purports to use the methods of reason to undermine reason. It starts from a normative thesis, the Actual Evidence Principle:

> One's level of confidence in P's truth—that is, the subjective probability that one assigns to P—ought to be proportioned to how strong one's evidence is for P.

This would be accepted by any defender of reason, as essential to reasonableness; so Hume can fairly use it when trying to turn reason against itself.

Here is the argument that seeks to undermine reason (182–3). Consider some situation where at **stage 1** I engage in reasoning which leads me to conclude that P, giving this a probability of n (some fraction, perhaps close to 1). I know that my reasoning abilities are fallible—the mechanism can malfunction—so at **stage 2** I reflect on my fallibility, and realize that there is a chance that I have mishandled my evidence for P:

Having thus found . . . , beside the original uncertainty inherent in the subject, a new uncertainty derived from the weakness of that faculty which judges, and having adjusted these two together, we are obliged by our reason to add a new doubt, derived from the possibility of error in the estimation we make of the truth and fidelity of our faculties. (182)

So I should modify my subjective probability for P accordingly. Then at **stage 3** I reflect on the fallibility of my proceedings at stage 2, come to realize that there is a chance that I have gone wrong there, and modify my probability for P still further. Then at **stage 4** . . . and so on, *ad infinitum*. 'When I proceed still further, to turn the scrutiny against every successive estimation I make of my faculties, all the rules of logic require a continual diminution, and at last a total extinction of belief and evidence' (183).

The successive adjustments are supposed to lead to—or perhaps to approach asymptotically—the 'total extinction of belief and evidence'. Here, as in some other places, Hume uses 'evidence' to mean 'evidentness', with this understood psychologically: degrees of evidence are degrees of confidence. For many years I thought that by its 'total extinction' Hume meant a lowering of subjective probability to zero; but that credited him with an argument that is too blatantly unsound. Why should a stage 2 consideration of stage 1 lead to a lowering of the initial probability, rather than a raising of it? Also, if the argument were supposed to lead to Prob(P) = 0, that is equivalent to absolute certainty that not-P, and nothing in the tone and atmosphere of iv.1 is friendly to that. Hume says that the argument threatens the total extinction 'of belief', not 'of the belief in P'; and later he speaks of it as enjoining one to 'look upon no opinion even as more probable or likely than another' (268–9).

The badness of my interpretation is something I learned from graduate students at Syracuse University, and Charles Howell showed me what to put in its place. What Hume has in mind, I now see, is not a sinking probability but a widening margin of error. I begin by setting Prob(P) at $n \pm 0.1$; then at stage 2 I alter this to $n \pm 0.1 + k$; then at stage 3 to $n \pm 0.1 + k^*$ for some $k^* > k$; and so on. He thinks that if this is carried on for long enough, it will lead to a result whose margin of error is so wide as to make the probability assignment boring, or even vacuous, the extreme case being Prob(P) = 0.5 ± 0.5, which uninformatively puts Prob(P) in the range from 0 to 1. That is the 'extinction of belief' with which the argument is supposed to threaten us. One might wonder why each stage should further enlarge the margin of error, rather than sometimes shrinking it; but assuming the former is not as gross as assuming that each stage should lower the probability.

I have followed Hume in stating this in terms of what logic requires if I do go on indefinitely making these 'successive estimations'. That is what the Actual Evidence Principle requires; the evidence exists only if we actually reflect and calculate. But none of us will do that; so isn't the problem that Hume purports to be raising negligible? No. He means to be relying also on the normative Available Evidence Principle:

If I believe that *there is some kind K of process of thinking and/or information-gathering such that (1) K is P-unbiased, and (2) if I went through a K process I would acquire beliefs in the light of which my level of confidence in P ought to alter in some manner (perhaps only affecting the margin of error)*, then without going through the process I ought to make that alteration.

By 'P-unbiased' I mean that the kind is not *defined* for me in terms of its tending to favour one side of the question whether P. With that caution built into it, the principle's basic thrust seems right. It would be irrational to say this: 'I think there is only about one chance in a hundred of civil war in Canada in the next decade, but I am pretty sure that if I spent a month in Quebec I would learn things in the light of which I ought to halve the odds against war there.' My present belief that the outcome of further inquiry would be such that it ought to increase my confidence in the war proposition ought to raise that confidence *now*. Similarly with my margin of error. On the strength of the Available Evidence Principle, Hume can argue that even if I do not go beyond stage 1, his argument will get me to believe that if I were to go through many further stages in the process, I would acquire beliefs in the light of which I ought to continue indefinitely expanding my margin of error; from which it follows by the Available Evidence Principle that I ought to subject it to all those enlargements now.

As well as its assumption that the margin of error should always widen, this argument has another defect. Hume is simply wrong here: 'No finite object can subsist under a decrease repeated in infinitum; and even the vastest quantity which can enter into human imagination must in this manner be reduced to nothing.' In fact, an infinite series can have a finite sum. Suppose for instance that the stage 2 reflection increases the margin of error by 0.1, stage 3 by a further 0.01, stage 4 by a further 0.001, and so on *ad infinitum*, the final margin of error does not spread to 1 but merely to 0.11111 . . . A margin of error, in short, may expand for ever without spreading over much of the territory. Hume may be trying to resist this at 30 n.; if so, he fails.

Let us temporarily pretend to think that Hume's argument is sound, and consider what he proposes to do with it.

289. How Hume responds to the attack

In the final paragraph of the section he presents what he takes to be the only possible *argument* for defending reason against his sceptical attack. It points out that his argument uses the methods of reason, so if it succeeds, that shows that reason is good for something after all: 'If the sceptical reasonings be strong, . . . it is a proof that reason may have some force and authority; if weak, they can never be sufficient to invalidate all the conclusions of our understanding' (186). This implies that no argument seeking to discredit reason need be listened to, because any argument is a tribute to the power and authority of reason. Hume rightly says that this is a bad response, and he explains why through a charming metaphor which comes down to this: we start with reason holding unchallenged sway; when a reasonable sceptical argument is brought against it, the immediate effect is to lessen reason's authority; that lessens the power of the sceptical argument, but does not restore reason to its throne.

Here is a sharper way of making the same point. To succeed against reason, an argument does not need methods and assumptions that are true, sound, valid, justified, etc.; all it needs are ones that reason endorses as true, sound, valid, etc. There is nothing suspicious about the claim 'Your faith in reason should lead you to have no faith in reason'. In the background of this is an incontrovertible logical truth: from (if P then not-P) it rigorously follows that not-P.

The sceptical argument concludes that we are not justified in trusting the deliverances of our reason, and Hume accepts this. We need to retain some of our beliefs 'for our purpose in . . . common life' (185), he holds, but he does not offer that as *justifying* our retaining some beliefs, rather than letting them all be swallowed up by an insatiable margin of error. Ignoring justification, he contents himself with a statement of psychological fact, as he takes it to be: namely, that even someone who accepts the sceptical argument as sound will not be led by it to strip himself of beliefs. 'Nature, by an absolute and uncontrollable necessity, has determined us to judge as well as to breathe and feel' (183).

That is a value-free fact about how people behave. Hume raises the normative question in book I's final section (268), asking what our attitude should be to the 'maxim that no refined or elaborate reasoning is ever to be received'. If you accept it, he says, 'you cut off entirely all science and philosophy'. You also 'contradict yourself', because you have been brought to this *rejectionist* maxim by *receiving* the elaborate reasoning of Hume's sceptical argument. Whether this shows Hume misunderstanding the *reductio ad absurdum* form of argument, which he perfectly grasped back in iv.1, I leave to the reader to decide. A third alleged drawback to receiving the maxim is still opaque to me. If, on the other hand, we reject the maxim, Hume says, 'we subvert entirely the human understanding'—an extravagant way of saying that in rejecting the maxim we defy the sceptical argument. Having presented the normative impasse, he declines to look for a way of escape: 'I know not what ought to be done in the present case. I can only observe what is commonly done, which is that this difficulty is seldom or never thought of, and even where it has once been present to the mind is quickly forgot.'

After making the psychological claim back in iv.1, Hume sets out to explain why it is so. He does this neutrally, neither approving nor disapproving the intellectual conduct in question. The explanation depends on his view that belief is a feeling relating to a content. Indeed, it is supposed to support that view:

My intention then in displaying so carefully the arguments [for scepticism about reason] is only to make the reader sensible of the truth of my hypothesis, *that all our reasonings concerning causes and effects are derived from nothing but custom*, and *that belief is more properly an act of the sensitive than of the cogitative part of our natures*. (183)

It is not obvious what the former of those two is doing here. Stroud (1977: 76–7) suggests that in it Hume is urging us to think of human reason in terms of its origins in human nature, rather than of the abstract rules that claim authority over it. I am not much persuaded by this, but I have nothing better to offer.

The other half is more clearly relevant to iv.1. In the paragraph at 183–4 Hume maintains that belief without its 'sensitive' element would be a mere content ('a simple act of the thought'), and that a sound sceptical argument would bring content against content, and there would be nothing to stop it from prevailing in one's mind. That this does not happen is itself proof that 'belief is some sensation or peculiar manner of conception, which it is impossible for mere ideas and reflections to destroy'. Now, it is true that Hume's sceptical argument is supposed to give us *beliefs* about the stage 1 belief; but it does not subvert the latter, he says, because the beliefs delivered by the argument lack vivacity after the first couple of stages. The argument's growing complexity, artificiality, and strangeness drain the ideas of their force or vivacity, so that the conclusions fall ever further short of being full-strength beliefs, and so become increasingly impotent against such sturdily natural beliefs as that the fog will probably lift by noon.

This explanation implies that as we work our way down through the sceptical argument, re-estimating the margin of error at each level, we soon stop believing our results. Hume plausibly depicts the original vivacity as having to run through ever longer and narrower channels, with the result (presumably) that most of it leaks away. But if there is something right in this explanation, it should not be tied to Hume's specific theory of belief. Rather than saying that the longer you follow the sceptical argument, the further you get from believing the results of its individual steps, it would be more plausible to say that the longer the argument, the more reluctant you are to apply transitivity so as to jump from the first premiss to the final conclusion. The reasons for this might be Humean—having to do with nature as a bulwark against elaborate and thus etiolated reason—but they would not suppose that belief involves an exhaustible quantity of a kind of feeling.

290. The real importance of *Treatise* iv.1

The heart of iv.1 is in its first paragraph—Hume's insight that *every* human faculty is a part or aspect of the natural world; its exercise involves the functioning of some mechanism; any mechanism can malfunction; so no human faculty is proof against error. Although the rules of logic are 'infallible', he writes, our faculties are 'fallible and uncertain', from which he infers that the only degree of conviction to which we are entitled is something on the probability scale—perhaps very high on it, but still on that scale. 'Knowledge degenerates into probability' (180), Hume writes, and on the next page: 'All knowledge resolves itself into probability, and becomes at last of the same nature with that evidence which we employ in common life.' The point he is making here (never mind his use of 'knowledge') is right and important: no credence level for any proposition should be quite as high as 1. We have the thought of something shiny and infallible, something that cannot go wrong; but if that thought is legitimate, it cannot concern a faculty of ours that makes *us* infallible about some class of truths. Our confidence in our findings in any intellectual procedure ought—simply because they are *our* findings—to be somewhat imperfect, yielding a subjective probability < 1.

We can apply this moral to a special case of Hume's sceptical argument as follows. Start with stage 1, where you reach a conclusion through nothing but demonstrative reasoning, and give it a subjective probability of 1—no doubts, no margin of error. Then at stage 2 you reflect on the fact that at stage 1 *you* reached a conclusion: this, being an episode in the life of a human being, has some chance of involving error. By the Actual Evidence Principle, therefore, you should lower your credence level a little—it has nowhere to go but down. End of argument; no further steps are necessary. This modest, safe line of thought has a powerful conclusion: namely, that it is wrong to accord a subjective probability of 1 to any proposition, or, as Hume puts it, 'All knowledge resolves itself into probability.'

Some of what is most notoriously awry in Descartes's treatment of scepticism in the *Meditations* comes from his sharing this insight of Hume's while trying to resist its conclusion. He expresses the premiss extravagantly, but the insight is the same: 'Since I sometimes believe that others go astray in cases where they think they have the most perfect knowledge, may I not similarly go wrong every time I add two and three?' (Med 1, CSM 2:14). Having dug this hole and descended into it, Descartes cannot climb out again. He tries to use his theology, and perhaps also his 'truth-rule', to achieve a perfect possession of some truths; but this is a dismal failure (§§147–8). His other project—the search for stability and psychological certainty—is healthier and more Humean.

A final few words on the opening of iv.1, namely: 'In all demonstrative sciences the rules are certain and infallible . . .' Hume is entitled to this in a context in which he is going to turn reason (as traditionally understood) against itself; but he says similar things in other places, where there is not that excuse. For example: 'A demonstration, if just, admits of no opposite difficulty; and if not just, it is a mere sophism, and consequently can never be a difficulty. It is either irresistible or has no manner of force' (31). We might construe the final clause as psychological—perhaps, indeed, as the psychological underlay of the normative judgements implied in the other clauses. But even then, we have Hume saying that any putative demonstration is either overwhelming or trash; he cannot base this stark disjunction on observations of how people think; and the only other possible source for it is an appeal to standard notions of the norms of validity. This is like what he writes about what 'philosophy informs us', and what conforms with 'reasoning and philosophy'. These point to results that are supposedly established a priori, with no inhibiting thoughts about what that could consist in or why it should be trusted.

Hume is not the only philosopher who needs and lacks a decent account of logical norms—the 'infallible rules' that determine what is argumentatively 'just'. But the gap is notable in him because he keeps emphasizing that his thought is grounded in human nature:

It is evident that all the sciences have a relation, greater or less, to human nature; and that, however wide any of them may seem to run from it, they still return back by one passage or another. Even Mathematics, Natural Philosophy, and Natural Religion are in some measure dependent on the science of MAN; since they lie under the cognizance of men, and are judged of by their powers and faculties. . . . The sole end of logic is to explain the principles and operations of our reasoning faculty, and the nature of our ideas . . . There is no question of importance whose decision is not comprised in the science of man. (*Treatise* xix–xx)

Thus, although this part of Hume's work is coloured by a conventional view of demonstrative reason as operating in the light of abstract, non-empirically given rules or standards, this cannot be an integral part of the fabric. The problem of integrating it with his 'science of man' is still a problem for us today. On the one hand, we are thinking animals, whose thoughts supervene causally on events in our brains. On the other, there is logic—clean, abstract, and infallible—and some of our thinking is guided by it. The problem is to couple those two without either adding a mystical element to the human condition or tarnishing the purity of logic. Throughout his post-*Tractatus* career, Wittgenstein wrestled with the problem of 'the hardness of the logical "must"': if something is as hard as the tradition takes absolute necessity to be, how can it relate to animals like us? Hume's fundamental philosophical views committed him to having this problem in as acute a form as Wittgenstein did, and as you and I do; but he did not quite succeed in articulating it and facing it head-on.

Chapter 39

Locke on Diachronic Identity-Judgements

291. Atoms and aggregates of them

Hume's treatment of personal identity will be the topic of my final chapter (40). Wanting to compare and contrast it with Locke's handling of the same subject, I have postponed dealing with the latter until now. The delay has not been harmful, because this part of Locke's work is not intricately connected with the rest of his philosophical thought; unlike Hume's treatment of personal identity in relation to other parts of his thought.

There is good philosophy in *Essay* II.xxvii, Locke's searching chapter about what it is for things of various kinds, especially people, to last through time.[1] That chapter investigates the truth conditions for diachronic identity statements—that is, ones of the form 'The thing that is F at T_1 is the thing that is G at T_2'. In this chapter of mine, unadorned numerical references are to sections of *Essay* II.xxvii.

In I.iv.4 Locke adduces the difficulties about personal identity as evidence that 'our idea of sameness is not . . . settled and clear', but he is wrong about that. If our interest in identity statements about Fs involves us in wrestling, it will be with the concept of F, not with that of identity. The problem about personal identity is chiefly a problem about *person*, as Locke himself says: 'To find wherein *personal Identity* consists, we must consider what *person* stands for' (9; see also 340:23). Compare Frege's offering the truth conditions for 'The number of Fs is the number of Gs', as part of an analysis not of identity, but of number (1884: 74).

Locke announces that his concern is with the persistence through time of God, of minds, and of bodies. After giving reasons (329:2) for not needing to discuss God in this connection, he proceeds to the persistence of bodies. His discussion of this gets off to a poor start in section 1, and has defects further along, but is nevertheless fine. It goes in three stages, of which the first concerns atoms:

Let us suppose an atom, i.e. a continued body under one immutable superficies, existing in a determined time and place: it is evident that, considered in any instant of its existence, it is in that instant the same with itself. For being at that instant what it is, and nothing else, it is the same and so must continue as long as its existence is continued; for so long will it be the same and no other. (3)

This, as it stands, is not helpful. Locke's 'so long as its existence is continued' helps itself to the very thing he is supposed to be clarifying: namely, the concept

---

[1] For helpful comments on this work of Locke's, see Reid 1785, Flew 1951, Allison 1966, and Grice 1941.

of a single thing's staying in existence rather than ending and being replaced by something else. Also (a connected point), the sentence 'it is the same and so must continue as long as its existence is continued' is true of every 'it' whatsoever, and therefore throws no light on the concept of *atom*.

Still, Locke's text indirectly illuminates that. Put together (1) his phrase 'continued body under one immutable superficies', (2) his statement two sections earlier that 'One thing cannot have two beginnings of existence' (328:21), by which he seems to mean that a single thing must have a temporally continuous life span, and (3) the assumption—which Locke does not voice but which he presumably accepted—that a thing cannot get discontinuously from one place to another; and what emerges is the view that the continuing existence of one atom corresponds to the existence of one continuous spatio-temporal track satisfying certain conditions.

Leibniz is sure that there are no atoms (§87), but in *NE* II.xxvii he sets that conviction aside in order to engage with Locke on his own ground. Locke's way of 'distinguishing among things of the same kind', Leibniz remarks, depends on assuming 'that interpenetration is contrary to nature', so that two things of the same kind cannot be in exactly the same place at the same time. 'This is a reasonable assumption,' he writes, 'but experience itself shows that we are not bound to it when it comes to distinguishing things. For instance, we find that . . . two rays of light interpenetrate, and we could devise an imaginary world where bodies did the same. Yet we can still distinguish one ray from the other just by the direction of their paths, even when they intersect' (*NE* 230). Leibniz seems to be right: co-location of portions of matter seems not to be absolutely impossible. Locke could reply that his identity criterion is offered only for worlds at which co-location does not occur, and that at other worlds it may occur, making diachronic questions of identity unanswerable. That is, when at such a world two atoms come to occupy exactly the same region of space at the same time, one moving into it from the north and one from the east, there may be no fact of the matter about which of these two it is that emerges from the 'double' in the southwesterly direction. Or (he could add) the physics of the world in question might offer some basis for identifying that emerging atom with one rather than the other of the two entering ones.

Locke deals next with bodies bigger than atoms. He starts with quantities, or 'parcels', of matter, taking them to be aggregates of atoms and ignoring matter that is infinitely divisible. About aggregates of atoms he asserts mereological (= part/whole) essentialism: 'Whilst they exist united together, the mass consisting of the same atoms must be the same mass, or the same body, let the parts be never so differently jumbled. But if one of these atoms be taken away, or one new one added, it is no longer the same mass or the same body' (3). If the removal of an atom makes a thing no longer 'the same body', and if the thing is (say) a table, must we conclude that the removal of an atom makes it no longer the same table? If so, then strictly speaking no table lasts for more than a second or two. Locke does not mention this threat to the longevity of tables, lakes, mountains, and boulders. Although he is committed to holding that a mountain or lake goes out of existence when one of its atoms peels off, he could say that we have practical reasons for not talking like that. But then he should add some detail about what governs such talk, and, unlike Hume, he does not (§305).

292. Organisms

After masses of matter, Locke turns to organisms. He notes that throughout the history of an oak-tree there is a continuous turnover of constituent matter, which implies that we have 'the same tree' out in the garden, although we do not have 'the same matter'. He deals with this point by distinguishing organisms from masses of matter:

In these two cases of a mass of matter and a living body, identity is not applied to the same thing. We must therefore consider wherein an oak differs from a mass of matter . . . The [latter] is only the cohesion of particles of matter anyhow united, the [former] such a disposition of them as constitutes the parts of an oak, and such an organization of those parts as is fit to receive and distribute nourishment so as to continue and frame the wood, bark, and leaves etc. of an oak, in which consists the vegetable life. (3–4)

We know how to re-identify aggregates of atoms, and we want to know how to re-identify oaks. Locke tells us, a bit sketchily, what an aggregate must be like at a certain time to constitute an oak at that time: an item is an oak *now* if its parts are disposed thus and so *now*. From this synchronic account of oaks, Locke thinks he can infer a diachronic story—that is, the truth about what it is for an oak to last through time. That he means to infer one from the other is indicated by the wording of the sentence starting at 331:3, the word 'consequently' at 332:35, and the conditional clause at 335:6–8.

The inference does not go through. Locke's account of what an oak momentarily is can consistently be conjoined with wildly wrong diachronic accounts, such as this:

The oak which is F at time T_1 is the oak which is G at T_2 just in case a single aggregate of atoms constitutes at T_1 the oak which is then F and constitutes at T_2 the oak which is then G.

That is quite wrong, but Locke's synchronic account of oaks does not rule it out.

His own identity-condition for organisms is better than that, and does not follow from his synchronic account. He continues:

That being then one plant which has such an organization of parts in one coherent body, partaking of one common life, it continues to be the same plant as long as it partakes of the same life, though that life be communicated to new particles of matter vitally united to the living plant, in a like continued organization, conformable to that sort of plants. For this organization being at any one instant in any one collection of matter, is in that particular concrete distinguished from all other, and is that individual life, which existing constantly from that moment both forwards and backwards in the same continuity of insensibly succeeding parts united to the living body of the plant, it has that identity which makes the same plant, and all the parts of it parts of the same plant, during all the time that they exist united in that continued organization which is fit to convey that common life to all the parts so united. (4)

This, I believe, is one of the first concerted attempts to state persistence conditions for organisms in the language of atomism rather than of Aristotelian 'forms'. Boyle tried earlier, but he did not get as far as Locke did. He did see that the problem is tough (1675: 193): 'It is no such easy way as at first it seems, to determine what is absolutely necessary and but sufficient to make a portion of matter, considered at differing times or places, to be fit to be reputed the *same* [human] body.'

Locke's account brings in the notion of continuity, and of turnover of constituent matter (atoms), and makes all this hang together with help from the notion of an 'individual life'; and that is enough to show that the core of the truth is here, even if we could improve its details. Take note also of the elegant restatement in which Locke says that the identity of an animal consists 'in one fitly organized body, taken in any one instant, and from thence continued under one organization of life in several successively fleeting particles of matter, united to it' (6). How neatly that presents first the synchronic and then the diachronic story!

All of that concerns how to tell what counts as the same animal on two occasions. It does not immediately yield an answer to the question 'What is an animal?', and that is 'no such easy' question as one might think. According to Locke, and presumably to you and me, the whole truth about an animal is a truth about particles or masses of matter, which are more basic than animals. That makes it natural to think that 'An animal is . . .' can be helpfully completed in the language of particles or masses. But how? Not by saying 'An animal is a mass of matter which . . .'. There seems to be no way, unless we say with Grandy (1975) that an animal is a function from times to particles or masses of matter. The idea behind this startling proposal is that at each relevant time a certain mass of matter constitutes this rabbit *then*; different masses at different times; and someone who knows which mass constitutes the rabbit at each time—that is, who grasps the function from times to masses—knows the whole lifelong truth about the material composition of the rabbit. But we gag at the suggestion that a rabbit which we can pet or eat is a function.

Locke often takes 'man' to be the name of a kind of animal, and in one place, writing in that vein, he uses the phrase 'the idea of a *man, the same successive body not shifted all at once*' (335:6). The spectacularly awkward, strained, and ingenious phrase which I have italicized shows Locke struggling with the difficulty I have been discussing.

293. Relative identity

The relative-identity thesis says that x may be the same F as y, but not the same G as y, even though Fx and Fy and Gx and Gy. For example, the man now sitting at that desk is the same official as the man who sat there a week ago, but he is not the same man. Or—to get nearer to our Lockean territory—what I now hold in my hand is the same mass of gold as I held last week, but it is not the same coin (because last week's coin was melted down and the gold reminted). The plausibility of such examples has encouraged some philosophers to maintain that the form 'x is identical with y' or 'x is y' is illegitimate unless it is taken as shorthand for something of the form 'x is the same F as y'. Geach and some others have also wanted relative identity to accommodate the doctrine that the three Persons of the Trinity are one substance.

Some adherents of the relative-identity thesis, wanting company, attribute it to Locke. They credit him with holding that 'x is the same oak as y' might be true while 'x is the same mass of matter as y' is false, even though x is a mass and y is a mass, and x is an oak and y is an oak. This misrepresents him. He denies that 'x is a mass and x is an oak' is true for any single value of x. 'In these two cases of a mass of matter and a living body,' he writes, 'identity is not applied to the same thing' (330:30). If I slap a tree and say 'This is what I slapped an hour ago', where the same oak remains but is not constituted by all the same atoms, Locke must say that my remark is referentially ambiguous; it could express any of four propositions—oak-oak, mass-mass, oak-mass, mass-oak—of which only the first is true. In short, the thesis that the oak is one thing and the mass of matter another is a *rival* to the relative-identity thesis, depriving the latter of its best examples. It is good that Locke is not a relative-identity theorist, for that theory is a mere face-saver that does not explain anything.

One aspect of Locke's chapter needs to be explained, and has been thought to support the attribution to him of the relative-identity thesis (Noonan 1978). We have seen that he is a mereological essentialist about masses of matter, and not about organisms, in which 'the variation of great parcels of matter alters not the Identity' (330:22). I now add that he sometimes calls masses of matter 'bodies'— 'If one of these atoms be taken away or a new one added, it is no longer the same mass or the same body' (330:18)—and that he applies the same word to organisms, as when he writes that 'An animal is a living organized body' (332:35). There is a problem. If an animal is a body, and the same body cannot lose or gain any parts, it should follow that an animal cannot gain or lose any parts; but an animal can do just that, and Locke says so. A contradiction threatens.

The relative-identity thesis would make it go away, for it implies that x may be the same animal as y without being the same body as y. I now offer a less drastic and textually better supported resolution. Locke uses 'living body' with a special sense of its own, in which living bodies do not conform to the mereological essentialism that he attributes to bodies *simpliciter*. This special sense is at work in the closing sentence of the very section we have been considering. Locke says there: 'In these two cases of a mass of matter, and a living body, *identity* is not applied to the same thing' (330:30).

On a few occasions he apparently uses 'body' to mean 'living body'—for example, when he speaks of 'our bodies', when he asks 'why the same individual spirit may not be united to different bodies' (332:11), and when he speaks of 'the body of an animal' (331:28). These uses of 'body' are imperfect, I submit, but mildly and understandably so. There are indeed fewer of them than one might expect. Sometimes when Locke explains 'animal' through 'collection of matter' or through 'body' (not 'living body'), the topic is an animal at an instant. There is no problem there, for Locke can say that an animal is at each instant constituted by a mass of matter. (See 331:5, 10, 332:4, 335:5.)

294. 'Same man'

Having finished with 'same animal' at the end of 5, Locke devotes three sections to 'same man'. His account of the concept of *man* is exclusively biological: our ordinary idea of man, he writes, 'is nothing else but [an idea] of an animal of such a certain form' (333:5). He argues that 'x is a rational animal' does not entail 'x is a man', because we have the concept of a rational parrot, which would be a rational animal that was not a man; and there is no entailment the other way either, because we have the concept of 'a dull irrational man'—'a creature of [our] own shape and make [that] had no more reason all its life than a cat or a parrot'.

Given that he confines the meaning of 'man' to biology, we might expect Locke to do likewise with 'same man'. So indeed he does: 'The identity of the same man consists . . . in nothing but a participation of the same continued life, by constantly fleeting particles of matter, in succession vitally united to the same organized body' (6). On this account, the truth conditions for 'same man' are just like those for 'same pig', with nothing mentalistic about them.

Suppose this is wrong, Locke says, and then consider what your basis can be for identifying the embryo with the grown man, or the lunatic with the rational man. He predicts that you will find it hard to secure those identities 'by any supposition that will not make it possible for . . . St Augustine and Cesare Borgia to be the same man' (6). What he is opposing here, it transpires, is the view that what makes the embryo and the adult the same human being ('same man') is not animal continuity, but rather a sameness of 'individual spirit' or of 'soul' or, at the start of 7, of 'substance'. Without explaining these expressions, Locke tries to exclude them from his account of 'same man' by attacking the supposition that 'the identity of the soul alone makes the same man, and there [is] nothing in the nature of matter why the same individual spirit may not be united to different bodies' (6). This goes too fast. It invites us to choose between 'Animal continuity is necessary and sufficient for human identity' and 'Animal continuity has nothing to do with human identity'; but we could reject both, maintaining that what makes x the same man as y is the obtaining of at least one out of several conditions, of which one is animal continuity, another is something else, etc.

Or one might hold that sameness of man requires animal continuity and also something else such as sameness of spirit. Locke could reply that this would still make trouble for identifying the adult with the embryo or the lunatic with the rational man, assuming that embryos and lunatics do not have 'spirits' in the required sense. Yet this two-part view of 'same man' is the one that Locke himself sometimes implies to be his own. Although he affirms that sameness of man consists in 'nothing but' sameness of animal body, he also writes—the italics here are mine—that what goes to 'the making of the same man' is 'the same successive body [etc.] *as well as the same immaterial spirit*' (335:6); and after discussing sameness of 'soul', he insists that 'the body *too* goes to the making the man' (340:14). Evidently Locke did not firmly make up his mind about how the term 'man' is used, let alone how it should be used.

295. Persons

The topic of personal identity is launched in section 9. Locke kicks off with an account of 'what person stands for': he is offering, as he did with atoms, oaks, and animals, a synchronic account on which he will then base his (diachronic) account of what it is for such an item to last through time. Roughly speaking, he says here that a person is a self-conscious item, and he describes the self-consciousness partly in terms of a person's sense of itself as a thing with a history:

[It] is a thinking intelligent being, that has reason and reflection, and can consider itself as itself, the same thinking thing in different times and places; which it does only by that consciousness which is inseparable from thinking, and as it seems to me essential to it; it being impossible for anyone to perceive without perceiving that he does perceive. (9)

Having stressed that thought is essential to personhood and that (self-) consciousness is essential to thought, Locke goes on to imply, rather unclearly, that unity of consciousness is necessary and sufficient for personal identity. Whether that unity of consciousness is carried by 'the same or diverse substances' does not matter, he writes, because:

Since consciousness always accompanies thinking, and it is that that makes everyone to be what he calls self, and thereby distinguishes himself from all other thinking things, in this alone consists personal identity, i.e. the sameness of a rational being; and as far as this consciousness can be extended backwards to any past action or thought, so far reaches the identity of that person.

Here again Locke treats his synchronic account as implying a diachronic one; and the implication still does not hold.

The synchronic account leaves much to be desired. A fully satisfactory one would tell us how to count people synchronically—that is, how to tell when we are dealing with one person at a time and when with two, and how to decide whether the person who is F at T_1 is the person who is H at T_1. Since Locke's section 9 gives us no help with this, it is not a full synchronic account of personhood.

This part of the problem, which Locke avoids, is hard, and I do not know how to solve it. In Grice's powerful attempt (1941) to present a refurbished version of Locke's theory of personal identity, most of the work is devoted to what it is for the person who is F at T_1 to be the person who is G at T_2. This requires him to know what it is for the person who is F at T_1 to be the person who is H at T_1—or, in Grice's terminology, what it is for two personal states to belong to a single 'total temporary state' of a person—and his treatment of this is not convincing. He says that two synchronous states belong to a single person just in case it is possible to know that they occur simultaneously through a single act of memory or introspection. This requires that every real mental state be accessible to introspection, and that we be able to count acts of introspection without yet being able to count persons.

In the remainder of Locke's chapter—sections 10–29—two main things happen. One is negative: a steady drumbeat of argument for the denial that personal identity conceptually involves identity of thinking substance. This will be the topic of my next section. The other is positive: a defence of Locke's view about what is necessary and sufficient for personal identity (§297).

296. Persons and substances

Locke seems to take it for granted that a person at a moment coincides with, or is constituted by, a thinking substance at that moment, but he denies that the substance which constitutes me at one time must be the very substance that does so at another. In this use of 'constitute', I deliberately echo the view that a mass of matter may constitute a coin, and that a mass-stage may constitute an organism-stage. From here on, though, I shall focus on the converse relation, for which I use the verb 'involve': according to Locke a person at each instant involves a thinking substance. He does not use 'involve' in this way, but he does employ the concept that I express through it.

To evaluate Locke's denial that sameness of person requires sameness of involved thinking substance, we need to know what 'substance' means in it. Here we run into a problem. Elsewhere in the *Essay* the word 'substance' figures in two main ways, neither of which fits well here.

(1) Locke mostly uses the term quite untechnically, to mean 'thing'—standing for any item that contrasts suitably with modes and relations. In II.xxvii, however, he denies that persons are substances while asserting that they are things—see, for example, 335:12. It seems, then, that a person is perfectly a 'substance' in

Locke's usual sense of that word, which therefore cannot be at work when he says that one person can involve different substances. This point was raised by Reid (1785: 356), by Shoemaker (1963: 45–6), and probably by others in between.

Equally decisive is a fact about Locke's examples. In our present chapter he declares that to have the same man or the same horse at one time as at another, one need not have the same substance. 'Animal identity is preserved in identity of life, and not of substance' (337:17), he writes, and he explicitly cites *man* (333:4) and *horse* (330:24) as examples of animals. But when he is using 'substance' in his dominant way, men and horses are among his favourite examples of substances. (See *Essay* 296:25; 297:16; 298:19, 27; 317:22.)

One might try to reconcile all this by invoking the relative-identity thesis:

> The item I am now listening to is a man (and thus a substance); it is the same man that I was listening to an hour ago; it is not the same substance that I was listening to an hour ago.

If that were Locke's position, he would not deny that men and horses are substances, but would merely say that they have different identity-conditions *qua* horses/men from what they have *qua* substances. There is, I have noted, little textual support for this reading of Locke. The problem about his use of 'substance' is prima-facie evidence for it, but I shall explain those texts differently, offering a solution devised primarily by Alston, though I helped (Alston and Bennett 1988). It postulates that in the identity chapter Locke uses 'substance' in a different sense from anywhere else in the *Essay*; and that is a drawback, for claims of ambiguity are suspect. This one, however, is well supported, and is preferable to the dark mysteries of relative identity.

(2) Locke's other use of 'substance' connects with the 'idea of substance in general'. He is embarrassed by this 'supposed or confused idea, such as it is', but he thinks he needs it as an ingredient in the complex ideas of specific kinds of substances—men, horses, emeralds, and so on (§203). This ingredient idea of substance is constructed so as to be empty; that is why it troubles Locke, and it is a good reason why it cannot have any role when we re-identify people.

A few parts of the identity chapter seem prima facie to be concerned with this idea of substance in general. When Locke asserts that one substance might be the subject first of one consciousness and then of another, and that a single consciousness might be carried by a sequence of substances, this could be a use of the ingredient or 'substratum' concept. The latter's emptiness enables it to jump through any hoops we choose, as Kant pointed out:

> We can conceive a whole series of substances of which the first transmits its state together with its consciousness to the second, the second its own state with that of the preceding substance to the third, . . . [etc.]. The last substance would then be conscious of all the states of the previously changed substances, as being its own states . . . And yet it would not have been one and the same person in all these states. (*Critique* A 364)

Kant is displaying this as a possibility that you cannot rule out if you tie sameness of person to sameness of substratum.

Alston convinced me that this is not Locke's point in the identity chapter. He emphasized that Locke repeatedly likens 'Same person does not require same substance' with 'Same organism does not require same substance', treating the latter as established, proved, a fixed point in the metaphysical landscape. Locke could not see his doctrine about organisms in that light if he thought it concerned the 'something we know not what' which he sometimes calls 'substratum'. How *that* relates to sameness of organism could not possibly be established and agreed.

To understand how Locke is using 'substance' in the identity chapter, we must start with *material substance* and *atom*. He does not explicitly say that all and only atoms are material substances; his discussion of oaks and horses implies only that any turnover of atoms in an organism involves a turnover of substances; it does not rule out there being a change of substances within an individual atom. His main point is that oaks are not substances, because there are items of a *more* basic kind—items that are *nearer* to being substances—many of which flow through a single oak; and from this it follows also that many material substances flow through a single oak, whether they are atoms or something more fundamental which atoms involve.

Locke discusses atoms as though he took them to be basic; what he says about the integrity of their boundaries may be intended to imply that their constituent matter does not change; so perhaps he equates atoms with material substances. But he does not use 'material substance' to mean *atom*. Rather, he uses it in this chapter to mean *thing that would be listed in a basic ontology of the material world*. By that standard, oaks are not substances, and their relationship to atoms shows this: the basic inventory of the world's contents may mention atoms and will not mention oaks; the truth about oaks can in principle be told through a complex enough story about atoms, whereas the converse does not hold.

In the identity chapter, then, 'thinking substance' means *thing that would be listed in a basic ontology of the mental world*; so a thinking substance is a *basic* subject of thoughts, sensations, and the rest. So for Locke the question 'Same person, same substance?' is the question 'When you have one enduring person, do you have one enduring thing of a basic kind?' His discussion offers a coherent answer to this question, but not to either 'do you have one enduring thing?' or 'do you have one enduring substratum?'

That completes Alston's and my resolution of Reid's puzzle. For Locke, people are 'substances' in the wide sense that they are things, items that have properties and stand in relations. But taking 'substances' to be the basic things out of which all others are composed or constructed, it may be true of people (as it is of oaks) that they are not substances, but are composed of them in such a way that many substances go to the making of one person.[2]

---

[2] For a discussion that agrees with this, and enriches it with much historical detail, see Winkler 1991. But Winkler is wrong in seeing Atherton 1983*b* as anticipating Alston's and my approach. Atherton's account of Locke on personal identity is unlike anyone else's; and, far from sharing our view about how Locke is using 'substance' in the identity chapter, she relies on something like Ayers's interpretation of that part of Locke's thought (§206), supporting it with a startling misrepresentation (1983*b*: 287) of what Locke writes in *Essay* II.xxiii.3.

297. Personal Identity

The negative thesis that a person need not be a single substance follows from Locke's positive theory about personal identity, to which I now turn. In it, the unity of consciousness is crucial, and Locke contends that this emphasis squares with the plain thoughtful person's intuitions on the topic. He evidently expects us to find passages like this one intuitively irresistible:

Consciousness . . . unites existences and actions [which are] very remote in time into the same person, as well as it does the existence and actions of the immediately preceding moment: so that whatever has the consciousness of present and past actions is the same person to whom they both belong. Had I the same consciousness that I saw the Ark and Noah's flood as that I saw an overflowing of the Thames last winter or as that I write now, I could no more doubt that I that write this now, that saw the Thames overflowed last winter, and that viewed the flood at the general deluge, was the same self, place that self in what substance you please, than that I who write this am the same myself now whilst I write . . . that I was yesterday. (16)

This is not obviously right, yet Locke expects us to find it so. I suppose he is working with the thought: I have recollections of such-and-such experiences; and my only grounds for regarding them as mine is the sheer fact that I now recollect them—that is, that a single consciousness takes in both them and my present conscious state. This line of thought is wrong, however. As well as my recollections, I have confirmatory evidence, including the testimony of others about my past—testimony based on assuming that my past is exclusively associated with *this* body.

Anticipating the objection that it must be the same consciousness in the same substance, Locke does not merely say: 'How can we know, when we have no good theory about what the basic reality is underlying personhood?' He argues that the separability of the person from the substance is given 'some kind of evidence' by the separability of bodily parts from a person, once they are no longer tied to the same consciousness (11). His point is that I count my finger as part of me while it relates to the rest of me in such a way that I can feel what happens to it; but if it is amputated, after which its vicissitudes no longer impinge on my consciousness, I no longer own it—it becomes a perfectly external 'it', and in no way part of me. This is supposed to show the power of the unity of consciousness to create unity of person, 'the same immaterial substance without the same consciousness no more making the same person by being united to any body than the same particle of matter without consciousness united to any body makes the same person' (339:36).

298. Locke's analysis is too weak

Locke's concept of 'same consciousness' is that of *memory*. He has committed himself to something like this:

If x has experience E at T_1, and y at T_2 remembers having E at T_1, then x is y.

I shall call this 'the central thesis' of Locke's account of personal identity. What we make of it depends on how we interpret 'y at T_2 remembers having E at T_1'. It could mean that at T_2 y has a veridical recollection of having E at T_1. Then the central thesis is true: y cannot veridically remember having E unless y did in fact have E. But on that reading of it the analysis would be circular: whether y veridically recalls having E at T_1 depends on whether it *was* y who had E at T_1—the very judgement that the analysis is supposed to clarify. Alternatively, the clause might mean that at T_2 y is in a state bearing all the internal marks of being a memory-state and representing an experience just like E. That would rescue the central thesis from circularity, at the price of making it too generous about personal identity to be correct: someone could acquire a memory-like state representing an experience which had previously been had by someone else.

To repair this weakness in his analysis, Locke would have to push further than he actually did. A currently popular way of strengthening the analysans while avoiding circularity is to make it say that y's state at T_2 includes an E-type representation which is caused to occur in y's mind by the occurrence of E at T_1 in x's mind. That is a first step towards a causal theory of memory which, when added to the rest of Locke's account, generates a causal theory of personal identity. (For causal theories of memory and personal identity see, respectively, Deutscher and Martin 1966 and Perry 1976. For a deeper inquiry into the role of causation in personal identity, see Perry 1975.)

To move his analysis in that direction, Locke would have to tackle mental causation—considering how the mind acts upon the mind, for example in memory. That would require him to discuss what kind of item a mind is, which he steadily refuses to do. In one place, for example, he says that memory 'is as it were the storehouse of our ideas', and calls it 'a repository to lay up those ideas which at another time [the mind] might have use of' (II.x.2), without even mentioning the underlying states or structures which dispose a mind to recall experience E if prompted in a certain way. Again, he steadfastly maintains against Descartes that the mind does not always think, meaning that a mind can stay in existence at times when nothing is happening in it; but he does not examine what it is for there to be an inactive mind—the question of what sort of reality this is. Indeed, he explicitly declines to get into that:

I shall not at present meddle [= concern myself] with the physical consideration of the mind, or trouble myself to examine wherein its essence consists, or by what motions of our spirits or alterations of our bodies we come to have any sensation by our organs or any ideas in our understandings; and whether those ideas do in their formations, any or all of them, depend on matter or no. These are speculations which, however curious and entertaining, I shall decline, as lying out of my way in the design I am now upon. (I.i.ii)

In his samples of questions that he will not tackle Locke mentions (animal) spirits, bodies, organs, and matter. These are all 'physical' in our sense; but he is using the term in a broader sense—openly declared at *Essay* IV.xxi.2—that goes back to Aristotle's trichotomy of sorts of knowledge: physics (what is), ethics (what should be), logic (what must be). So he is setting aside all factual questions, whether in psychology or metaphysics, about the nature of the mind.

Still, he has not denied that the mind has an essence or 'physical' constitution which fits it to bear memory-traces and, more generally, to be the locus of causal chains. So he is free to avail himself of the concept of an experience's causing a later mental representation of itself. But he is still in trouble, given that his theory of personal identity is driven by a need to use 'same person' in assigning responsibility, praise, and blame. For that we need to be able to judge personal identity soundly and securely without relying on metaphysical guesswork; and we have no chance of this if personal identity conceptually involves memory, the latter is covertly causal, and the relevant causal propositions depend upon 'physical' matters about which we know nothing.

At 27 Locke acknowledges that if we knew more about 'the nature of that thinking thing that is in us', 'we might see the absurdity of some of those suppositions I have made'. With regard to the thinking thing that is in us, he writes there, we do not know:

what it is,
how it is tied to a certain system of fleeting animal spirits,
whether it could or could not perform its operations of thinking and memory
    out of a body organized as ours is,
whether it has pleased God that no one such spirit shall ever be united to any
    but one such body, upon the right constitution of whose organs its memory
    should depend.

The wording is all Locke's, except for the tense of the first two items. It is a tantalizing list. Had Locke worked on some of these questions, he might have come to realize that they constitute an overdraft on which—as we shall see—he must write several large cheques in his account of personal identity.

299. Locke's analysis is too strong

I have expressed Locke's central thesis as a one-way conditional:

If x has experience E at T_1, and y at T_2 remembers having E at T_1, then x is y.

The converse conditional, offering a necessary condition for personal identity, is also sometimes attributed to him. Whereas the first makes personal-identity statements weaker than they are, implying the truth of many falsehoods, its converse is too strong, implying the falsity of many truths. That is because the converse thesis implies that everyone remembers all his or her past experiences, whereas in fact people often forget.

Locke mentions forgetting as a prima-facie difficulty for his account:

Suppose I wholly lose the memory of some parts of my life beyond a possibility of retrieving them, so that perhaps I shall never be conscious of them again; yet am I not the same person that did those actions, had those thoughts, that I once was conscious of, though I have now forgot them? (20)

He stands by his account in face of this objection, and appeals to us to agree with him. Human laws do not punish 'the mad man for the sober man's actions, nor the sober man for what the mad man did', he writes, because the law judges that in each case there are 'two persons'. In section 22 he admits that this is not true about how the law proceeds; and even if it were, there might be other explanations for it. Notice also that Locke nudges our intuitions his way by speaking of the incurable forgetting of 'parts of my life', rather than the mere forgetting of individual episodes.

The converse thesis is in other trouble too, for it implies that identity is not transitive. This was pointed out by Berkeley, Butler, and Reid, who confidently took Locke to be affirming the converse thesis. (See Berkeley 1732, LJ 3:299.) Adapting an example of Reid's, the converse thesis might imply that the person who is an army general in 1999 was (because he remembers being) a lieutenant who fought in Vietnam in 1965, but was not (because he does not remember being) punished for stealing apples in 1950; yet the lieutenant did in 1965 remember that punishment, and therefore was the boy who was punished; so the general is the lieutenant who is the boy, but the general is not the boy. Since the relations 'remembers' and 'is a memory of' are not transitive, neither can be the whole analytic truth about identity.

The only remedy is to build transitivity into the analysis, which Locke could easily do. With help from Grice's refurbished Lockean analysis (1941), I offer this minimal revision of Locke's account of personal identity:

(1) If x has experience E at T_1, and y at T_2 remembers having E at T_1, then x is y.
(2) If x is y and y is z, then x is z.
(3) No affirmation of personal identity is true unless its being so follows from 1 and 2.

This still puts memory—unity of consciousness, as Locke calls it—at the heart of personal identity, but avoids the absurd denial that identity is transitive.

I doubt that this 'minimal revision' of Locke's account is a revision at all. He does not actually state 1, 2, and 3; indeed, he does not mention transitivity. But he discusses personal identity in terms of sufficient more than of necessary conditions, using the central thesis more than its converse. When the latter does enter the picture, in denials of personal identity such as that in section 19, it is through examples to which transitivity is irrelevant. I suspect that Locke knew what he was doing, intended the transitivity of identity to complete the story, and thought of this as too obvious to need stating. If so, he over-estimated the charity of his critics.

The remedy I have proposed lets us identify the general with the boy, so long as the general recalls the episode of punishment, or recalls some aspect of his state at some earlier time when he recalled the episode, or recalls some aspect of his state at some earlier time when he recalled some aspect of his state at some still earlier time when he recalled the episode, or . . . and so on. If none of these conditions is satisfied, there is a mnemonic brick wall between the general now and the earlier beating: no chain of memories links his present state with that earlier event. If he is as cut off as that from the punishment, it is not so wildly implausible to say that it was not he who was punished. This is certainly less vulnerable than the form of analysis with which Reid and the others credited Locke.

It is still too strong, however, to fit our ordinary ways of thinking about people. We do allow that someone might suffer a memory break so that at no time after it did he ever remember any of his experiences from before. If we believed that at those later times the memories were recoverable by him—because the traces were still there in his brain—then even if he did not in fact ever recover any of them we would still say confidently that he was failing to recall experiences which really had been his. So the analysis should be changed to say that the person who was F at T_1 is the person who is G at T_2 if the latter *can* recall being F at T_1. This sometimes seems to be Locke's actual view, as we recently saw. Here is more evidence:

'. . . have a consciousness that cannot reach beyond this new state' (338:35)

'Consciousness, as far ever as it can be extended, . . . unites existences and actions . . . into the same person' (340:30)

'That with which the consciousness of this present thinking thing can join itself makes the same person' (341:28)

'. . . lose the memory of some parts of my life beyond a possibility of retrieving them' (342:24)

'If there be any part of its existence which I cannot upon recollection join with that present consciousness' (345:17)

'Supposing a man punished now for what he had done in another life, whereof he could be made to have no consciousness at all . . .' (347:2).

Two 'can's, two 'cannot's, a 'could', and a 'possibility'—these modals suggest that the analysis is meant to depend not on actual 'consciousness' or episodic memory, but on the possibility of it. That might enable it to cope with memory-gap examples that made the analysans too strong.

Whether it does so, and how, depends upon what kind of modality is in question. It might be logical, conceptual. But the only basis I can find for that is the meaning of 'recall' in which it is analytically true that if I was not F at T_1, then I *cannot* recall being F at T_1; just as I cannot forgive you a debt for which I am not the creditor. That reading of the analysis, however, again makes it circular. (This is one of several good points made in Flew 1951.) So the modality in question had better be causal. The thesis must be that whether the person who was F at T_1 is the one who is G at T_2 depends upon what it is causally possible for the latter to recall experiencing at T_2.

These days, every philosopher of mind would say that the mind's causal powers are central to all our understanding of it, including what it is for a single mind to last through time. It is significant that causality offers our best chance of remedying both the undue weakness of the central thesis and some of the undue strength of its converse. It is a notion that Locke demonstrably has, with respect not only to what a given mind can do at a certain moment, but also to its more durable capacities and limitations. We have already seen it in his calling memory a storehouse; and it is conspicuous in his polemic against innatism, where he relies on our 'natural faculties', 'inherent faculties', and 'natural tendencies', all of which must be understood in causal terms.

However, he is not well placed to say much about a mind's causal powers, especially about the intrinsic features of a mind which give it these powers. This belongs to the matters that he will not concern himself with; and it raises a question which he says we cannot answer: namely, whether a mind-stage is a stage of an immaterial substance, of a material substance (an atom), or of an animal.

300. People as animals

It is natural to think that Locke went wrong—and made trouble for himself—by supposing that we can re-identify people across time without re-identifying human bodies. That thought rejects his distinction between organism identity ('same man') and personal identity; it says that there is only one concept here: namely, that of a human animal, implying that Locke's mentalism about personal identity was a mistake from the outset.

He has an answer which many people have found persuasive. He argues in section 15 that we can conceive of two people exchanging bodies. It might be that the palace and the cobbler's hut have each been occupied for the past week by just one man (one human animal), but that the person involved in the palace man until yesterday is now involved in the man in the hut, and vice versa. As Locke would express it, the prince and the cobbler have exchanged bodies. We could know this, he thinks, through learning all the facts about what memories are associated with each man today and what were associated with each three days ago.

We can grasp the case conceptually: we can imagine finding that the cobbler wakes up one morning knowing all and only the things that the prince knew last night, and vice versa. What is debatable is Locke's claim, concerning the person who wakes up in the cobbler's bed this morning, that 'everyone sees he would be the same person with the prince'. Some philosophers hold that neither Locke's story nor any embellishment of it could justify us in saying that the prince has come to have the cobbler's body. According to them, there is a conceptual tie between sameness of animal body and sameness of person: the view that people *have* bodies, or that bodies *involve* people, is just a mistake.

To adjudicate this conflict, we need to let Locke take the best example he can, and not saddle him with inessential difficulties. If we land him with a case where the cobbler acquires the prince's interests, likes and dislikes, mental aptitudes, etc., as well as his memories, we may be able to protest that that might be impossible: 'The prince's body might include the sort of face that just *could* not express the cobbler's morose suspiciousness, the cobbler's a face no expression of which could be taken for one of fastidious arrogance' (adapted from Bernard Williams 1956: 12). That shows only that this was an unfair example to use.

Probably nobody today would take Locke's side in the dispute unless it were stipulated that the cobbler's body comes to have memory-states, etc. which are causally descended from the similar states that the prince used to have: the man now sitting at the cobbler's bench has a seeming memory of hunting onagers *because* the prince once hunted onagers. A mere resemblance between this man's present memories and that man's past experiences puts us under no pressure to go Locke's way. He might agree, for he launches his example with what seems to be a causal link: 'Should the soul of a prince, carrying with it the consciousness of the prince's past life, enter and inform the body of a cobbler . . .' Evidently Locke too felt the need for a carrier, something by virtue of which the pre-T mental events in the palace would cause some of the post-T mental events in the hut. A passing reference to a continuing 'soul' is neither a helpful nor an attractive causal story; but Locke might defend it as a stopgap, a place-holder for some 'physical' matter with which he will not 'meddle'.

Even with examples fairly chosen and with causation built into them, some philosophers today find it obvious that Locke is wrong, and that sameness of person must go with sameness of animal body. I do not find it obvious, and I doubt if others would do so if a prince/cobbler kind of story actually came to be true. Still, we need not be reduced to a brawl in which intuitions are traded like punches. There are other ways to get a handle on these issues.

Whatever people *would* say in a prince/cobbler event such as Locke describes, there certainly are prima-facie reasons for holding that in that case two men (human animals) have switched mental contents rather than that two people (minds) have switched bodies. Here is one. It seems natural and true to say that I was once an eight-month foetus; and that requires the Lockean theorist to say that 'I' is ambiguous, and that in this statement it refers not to a person but to a man. One would prefer not to need to resort to such an explanation.

This objection is not fatal. Locke can respond—as indeed he does in section 20—that it owes its seeming power to a certain ambiguity or unclarity in our thinking. I cheerfully assert that I was once a foetus, because I use 'I' to stand both for a certain person and a certain man (= animal); in a given case my judgement may depend on taking 'I' to refer only to the animal; but I may think it applies to the person as well, because in actual fact the two have always coincided:

Suppose I wholly lose the memory of some parts of my life beyond a possibility of retrieving them . . . ; yet am I not the same person that did those actions . . . ? To which I answer that we must here take notice what the word *I* is applied to, which, in this case, is the man only. And the same man being presumed to be the same person, *I* is easily here supposed to stand also for the same person. (20)

That is not the end of the debate. There is more to be said in favour of a purely organic approach to personal identity, and against the psychological approach—see especially Olson 1997. I shall now set that aside, however, and get closer to Locke.

301. 'A forensic concept'

This work of Locke's allows for two ways in which 'same person' might part company with 'same man'—erasures and switches. With switches we have to rely on our thoughts about possible cases, for nothing like the prince/cobbler situation actually occurs. Not so for erasures. Even when understood as involving the causal impossibility that the memories should be recovered, they are a sadly real phenomenon; and when it occurs, we do not think of it in Locke's way. We have seen him trying to explain away this fact, and evincing no worry that his view about it may seem so implausible as to turn people from his theory.

If a switch did occur, a lot might hang on how we handled it conceptually. Is this regal figure the prince or the cobbler? Our answer could have legal, moral, and practical consequences. The decision to be made about an erasure seems to be less weighty: the question is whether the person (involved in the man) who stands before us now existed yesterday; if he did, we know which person he is; there are here no rival claimants to a personal title. Locke might appeal to this fact to explain and partly justify our supposedly slack and inaccurate handling of such cases. If we said that this man involved one person yesterday and a different person today, we would have two people whose lifelines are oddly shaped, one fitting neatly on to the end of the other; we would probably think that the later one should inherit things from the earlier; which would require much trouble, including changes in the law. (I borrow this point from *NE* 237, though Leibniz's use of it is different.) It is simpler, and does no harm and creates no disturbance, if, instead, we treat them as one person who has lost his memory.

That easy way with erasures, however, fails when there is a question about moral accountability and, especially, about reward or punishment. Locke is acutely conscious of this:

Person . . . is a forensic term appropriating actions and their merit; and so belongs only to intelligent agents capable of a law, and happiness and misery. This personality extends itself beyond present existence to what is past only by consciousness, whereby it becomes concerned and accountable, owns and imputes to itself past actions, just upon the same ground and for the same reason that it does the present. . . . And therefore whatever past actions it cannot reconcile or appropriate to that present self by consciousness, it can be no more concerned in than if they had never been done. And to receive pleasure or pain, i.e. reward or punishment, on the account of any such action is all one as to be made happy or miserable in its first being without any demerit at all. For supposing a man punished now for what he had done in another life, whereof he could be made to have no consciousness at all, what difference is there between that punishment and being created miserable? (26; see also I.iv.5)

This presents a confident moral intuition that it could not be right for someone to be punished for something that he could not remember doing.

This is not an argument for Locke's account of 'same person', but is meant to help it in another way. Even someone who agrees with all he says about how our person concept applies to various cases—and especially someone who is still pondering it—might ask why we have such a concept. We have it for 'forensic' purposes, Locke replies. We make judgements and have practices relating to moral accountability; we find it unfair to hold someone accountable for actions that he cannot remember performing; and so we want a concept which collects a person-stage together with everything that that person-stage can remember; this is our concept of person.

In erasure cases, therefore, we are apt to be Lockean in our thinking if moral accountability is at stake—so Locke thinks. He writes:

If it be possible for the same man to have distinct incommunicable consciousness at different times, it is past doubt the same man would at different times make different persons; which we see is the sense of mankind in the solemnest declaration of their opinions, human laws not punishing the mad man for the sober man's actions, nor the sober man for what the mad man did, thereby making them two persons. (20)

When we are thinking carefully in a context of moral accountability, Locke is claiming, our thoughts will conform to his account of personal identity. Leibniz comments that this misunderstands the basis for our judgements relating punishment to sanity. Most of us think it wrong to punish someone for doing some terrible thing—whether or not he can remember it—if he was thoroughly mad when he did it or is mad now.

Leibniz also directly challenges Locke's moral view about accountability and memory. He writes:

I doubt that man's memory will have to be raised up on the day of judgment so that he can remember everything which he had forgotten, and that the knowledge of others, and especially of that just Judge who is never deceived, will not suffice. One could invent the fiction . . . that a man on the day of judgment believed himself to have been wicked and that this also appeared true to all the other created spirits who were in a position to offer a judgment on the matter, even though it was not the truth. Dare one say that the supreme and just Judge, who alone knew differently, could damn this person and judge contrary to his knowledge? Yet this seems to follow from the notion of 'moral person' which you offer. (*NE* 243–4)

Leibniz here treats Locke as saying that I am rightly punishable for *all and only* what I am conscious of having done, and he attacks the 'all' half of that. If I have a false seeming-memory of having sinned, he asks, is it right that I should be punished? Locke has not clearly protected himself against this objection, but he might do so, standing by only the 'only' half of the thesis—namely, that I am rightly punishable for *only* what I am conscious of having done. Later on, though, Leibniz denies that too: 'There are grounds for questioning whether it is absolutely necessary that those who suffer should themselves eventually learn why, and whether it would not quite often be sufficient that those punishments should afford, to other and better informed Spirits, matter for glorifying divine justice' (246). This reveals a basic difference of moral intuition between the two Christian men.

302. Same person, same substance?

Locke has his thesis (1) 'Same person, same consciousness' firmly in hand, though not soundly argued for, when he addresses the question (2) 'Same person, same substance?', which he therefore equates with (3) 'Same consciousness, same substance?'. He sees the truth of 1 as a matter of conceptual analysis, discoverable by attending to our 'ideas'. But because this analysis does not bring in 'same substance', Locke holds that what the right answer is to 2 or 3 is a matter of contingent fact, to which he prudently ventures no answer: he says it can be answered only 'by those who know what kind of substances they are that do think'. This is right. Lacking any theory about what kinds of item will be quantified over at the most basic level in the best theory of mind, we cannot say how many such items could be involved, sequentially or synchronously, in a single person.

This is cautiously agnostic in a way that Locke is not about the identity of oaks. We know, at least down to a certain level, what actually goes on when an oak endures—namely, that there is something more basic which does not stay with the oak. But we have no such knowledge in the case of an enduring person, Locke holds: we have no well-grounded theory about enduring people, analogous to our theory that explains the persistence of oaks in terms of the organization of fleeting particles. So Locke will neither affirm nor deny that an enduring person involves a single enduring substance.

If you are a materialist who holds that the identity of people is just the identity of human animals, he says, you will have to associate a single person with many substances (12). This is plausible, though not quite right. If, on the other hand, you hold that personal thinking is done by immaterial substances, Locke says,

you are not automatically committed to each person's involving just one substance altogether, for it might be that a single person involves a 'change of immaterial substances'. We have seen Kant making this point in connection with the
notion of substance as substratum (§296); but it holds equally for substances in
the more robust sense that is at work in *Essay* II.xxvii. (The 'change of immaterial substances' would not be like the procession of atoms through an oak. An oak-
stage is not an atom-stage, but rather a complex aggregate of many such;
whereas Locke clearly thinks of each person-stage as involving a stage of just one
thinking substance. For him there is no question of a person ingesting and excret-
ing thinking substances as an oak does atoms.)

Although he sees the question as open, Locke has a preferred answer: 'The
more probable opinion is that this [person-making] consciousness is annexed to,
and the affection of, one individual immaterial substance' (25). He is not entitled
to hold that the weight of evidence is on this side; but perhaps he means merely
that this is the simplest and most natural hypothesis.

Or he might have a theological reason for thinking that people correspond,
one for one, to thinking substances. Such a reason surfaced earlier, when Locke
said that in our present ignorance about thinking substances the question of
whether two or more of them could underlie a single consciousness 'will by us
. . . be best resolved into the goodness of God, who as far as the happiness or misery of any of his sensible creatures is concerned in it, will not by a fatal error of
theirs transfer from one to another that consciousness which draws reward or
punishment with it' (13). To understand this dark saying, we must realize that the
'sensible creatures' in question are not people but thinking substances, and that
Locke is here assuming three things.

(1) What sins a person has committed depends upon what sins fall within
the scope of his or her consciousness: that is, what sins are now thought
of by the now-involved thinking substance as ones that it was associated
with.

That follows from his theory of personal identity.

(2) Whether punishment falls on a given person on Judgement Day depends
on what sins that person has committed, not upon what sins have been
committed by or associated with the thinking substance that he or she
involves.

We have met this already, in connection with Locke's view that person is a forensic concept.

(3) When God punishes a person, he thereby hurts the thinking substance
which the person at that time involves.

This is reasonable. You cannot hurt a person except by hurting the thinking substance that he or she involves, just as you cannot magnetize a coin except by mag-
netizing the metal which it involves.

Those three jointly entail that if on Judgement Day the person John involves the thinking substance Subjohn, and Subjohn seems to recollect a sin as one it was associated with, then (by 1) John is the person who committed the sin, even if Subjohn had nothing to do with it; and so (by 2) punishment will fall on John; and so (by 3) hurt will come to Subjohn. A 'fatal error' indeed! This gives Locke a sober basis for thinking that God in his goodness is not likely to let different thinking substances take turns in being involved in (constituting, etc.) a single person: that would be unfair to some of the substances.

Locke, we have seen, holds that we have the Lockean concept of person because we need it if we are to be fair in our judgements of moral accountability. Now it turns out that those will bring serious unfairness unless people correspond one to one with thinking substances, which we cannot know that they do. Faced with this, he might say: 'We do indeed risk unfairness, and we must hope that God so arranges things that it does not occur. But we cannot avoid that risk by basing our judgements of accountability directly on facts about sameness of thinking substance, because we cannot know any of those.'

Chapter 40

Hume and Leibniz on Personal Identity

303. Diachronic identity statements: Hume's approach and Locke's

In *Treatise* iv.6, entitled 'Of Personal Identity', Hume examines diachronic identity statements about various kinds of item. He structures this section on the model of Locke's identity chapter. The latter sets out conditions for the truth of 'The . . . which was F at T_1 is the . . . which was G at T_2', where the blank is filled successively by

'mass of matter'
'artefact' or 'organism'
'person'

Hume covers the territory in that order, with those divisions. With respect to the first category he agrees with Locke entirely, for the second partly, for the third hardly at all.

He pretty much follows Locke also in helping himself to a material world. Although near the start of iv.6 Hume may be thinking primarily in terms of perceptions, rather than of an objective realm, he soon starts to assume that there is real matter, and does not fret over continuity or mind-independence. The concerns in iv.2 about whether something can remain in existence when nobody perceives it have no place here. Their slight appearance in the paragraph on 253–5 is an intrusion; they do not lie on the path that Hume has marked out for himself in iv.6.

In discussing what it is for a mass of matter to last through time, Hume avails himself of the unexplained notion of an enduring and re-identifiable 'part' of such a mass. Locke does better than that. Because he does not hold that things are constructs out of perceptions, or out of tropes, he is fairly well placed to help himself to the concept of an enduring particle of matter: if this is not a construct, it has no need for rules of construction. Yet he starts his identity chapter by working to entitle himself to the notion of a re-identifiable atom, before proceeding to treat masses as collections of them. Hume, by contrast, is committed to an ontologically grudging attitude to atoms or particles or parts of material masses, because of one challenge from perceptions and another from tropes. Yet in iv.6 he takes particles of matter on board as though they were unproblematic.

Unlike Locke, Hume confines himself in iv.6 to questions about what it is for an F thing to last through time; he does not preface this with an account of what it is for something to be an F thing at a moment, or to be an F-stage.

Here is a deeper difference between the two. Locke's chapter is an exercise in analysis through thought-experiments: it investigates what an intelligent person would think about various cases, aiming for an account of the relevant concept that will make true/false all the things that plain careful folk would regard as true/false. Hume's investigation, on the other hand, is not driven by facts about what it would be normally acceptable to say and think. Rather, he has a highly general theory about what will incline people to say or think 'The thing that was F at T_1 was G at T_2'; on the basis of this he *predicts* how the language of identity will operate on masses of matter, organisms, and people; and when the predicted results fit the intuitive data, he claims to have explained the latter.

This theory of Hume's embodies a further difference between him and Locke. Whereas Locke sees himself as inquiring into the truth conditions of various diachronic identity statements, Hume holds that all or most such statements are false. His topic in iv.6 is the conditions under which we accept these falsehoods, mistaking them for truths. So the pursuit of truth conditions yields place to the pursuit of conditions for acceptability.

304. Optimal diachronic identity statements

Here is Hume on the concept of identity: 'We have a distinct idea of an object that remains invariable and uninterrupted through a supposed variation of time; and this idea we call that of identity or sameness' (*Treatise* 253). We can understand 'interrupted' well enough: our common conceptual scheme probably does imply that if something goes out of existence, it cannot come into existence again, though a duplicate might do so. But 'invariable'? Hume means 'unchanging' rather than 'incapable of change' (§7), but that gives us enough of a problem. He seems to imply that things can endure only if they do not alter, and that is indeed his position in iv.6. He implies it often—for instance, here: 'However at one instant we may consider the related succession as variable or interrupted, we are sure the next to ascribe to it a perfect identity, and regard it as invariable and uninterrupted' (254). This implies that a thing can last through time only if it is unchanging as well as uninterrupted. The humanly acceptable falsehoods that Hume will explore in iv.6 are propositions implying that certain items last through time while altering.

Hume does not defend his view that strict identity is inconsistent with alteration, apparently expecting that careful reflection will lead us to accept it. In fact, he is wrong—things do last through time, and alter—and we should consider why he thought otherwise.

Well, doesn't dissimilarity defeat identity? Does not the statement 'The thing that is F at T_1 is the thing that is not F at T_2' identify an item with an item which is *unlike* it and therefore distinct from it? If so, then the statement is false. Hume may have thought along these lines; but if he did, he was mistaken. Consider the proposition *The log that was hot at T_1 was cool at T_2*. This implies something about dissimilarity: namely, that the log's state at T_1 is unlike its state at T_2; so these are two states, distinct from one another; but it is not implied that the log is unlike itself. What rescues us from that conclusion is a beautiful truth which has been known at least since Aristotle: a logical *contradiction*, when properly combined with the concept of time, turns into a report of an *alteration*: 'x is F and x is not F' turns into 'x is F and then x is not F'.

Hume might say: 'You purport to talk about a log that lasts while altering; but our question is whether there can be such a thing. What *is* clear is that we are confronted by a log-at-T_1 and by a log-at-T_2, and *these* are dissimilar and therefore diverse.' That would bring back the concept of a log-stage—an item that is like an enduring log except that it exists only at an instant or through a tiny interval of time. If there are enduring logs, there may also be log-stages, each of which would be a temporal part of a log. I whipped through this topic in §282, but I shall deal with it here more patiently.

The concept of a temporal part of a material thing does not belong to our everyday intellectual kit. Whereas it is natural to say that only a part of Route 81 lies within the confines of Syracuse today, the rest of it being *elsewhere*, it would seem peculiar to say that only a part of Bowen Island is in Howe Sound today, the rest of it being *elsewhen*. If you think that our ordinary statements about how things are at times plainly commit us to such entities as things-at-times or thing-stages, you may be making a mistake against which Peter van Inwagen (2000) has warned us—namely, that of construing 'The log was hot at T_1' as 'The log-at-T_1 was hot' rather than as 'The log was hot-at-T_1' or 'At T_1: the log was hot'. Still, many of us find the concept of a thing-stage useful in philosophical analysis, and we need it here because Locke and Hume tacitly employ it.

Let us then grant that

The log that was hot at T_1 is the log that was cool at T_2

can be expressed as a proposition about two stages. Still, the proposition does not identify the two with one another. Rather, it says:

The hot T_1-log-stage was a stage of the same log as the cool T_2-log-stage,

in which the key relation is not identity, but being-a-stage-of-the-same-thing-as, which obviously can interrelate distinct stages.

This has an exact analogy with spatial parts. Let 'Pac' name the mile-long stretch of the Panama Canal that is closest to the Pacific Ocean, and 'At' the mile-long stretch at the other end. Pac has an average depth of 90 feet, while At has an average depth of 100 feet (I'm making this up); these depths are different, which proves that Pac is not At. Yet they are parts of a single canal.

Forget about depths. Pac would not be At even if they were perfectly alike: their distinctness is secured by where they severally are. Similarly with a log that does not alter between T_1 and T_2: if Hume is impressed by the difference between a hot log-stage and a cool one, why is he not equally impressed by the difference between a cool earlier stage and a cool later one? Well, much of the time he is. In iv.2 he committed himself to there being no true diachronic identity statements, even about things that do not alter during the relevant interval (§282); and that ought to be his view in iv.6 as well. To allow that two intrinsically alike items can be stages of a single unaltering log is to distinguish enduring things from their stages; and if Hume does that, he has no basis for denying that two intrinsically *unalike* items can be stages of a single cooling log.

If we hold Hume to the denial of all diachronic identity statements, we can still make sense of his strategy in iv.6. For he can still hold that such statements divide into the *optimal*, the *respectable*, and the *non-starters*. Optimal ones assert the identity through time of a supposed object which does not alter; they are still false, but they are as near to true as the concept of identity allows; and everyone regards them as true. Respectable ones pertain to supposed objects which do alter, but which it is natural and humanly permissible to accept as true. Non-starters are ones which only an idiot would think to be true. Within this framework, we can see Hume as offering to explain what marks off the merely respectable from the optimal on one side and from the non-starters on the other, while holding that no member of any of the three categories is strictly true.

We *can* take iv.6 in this way, but Hume himself not infrequently implies there that the statements I have called merely 'optimal' are true. He does so, for instance, in one statement of his Similarity Theory (as I shall call it):

That action of the imagination by which we consider the uninterrupted and invariable object, and that by which we reflect on the succession of related objects, are almost the same to the feeling . . . The relation facilitates the transition of the mind from one object to another and renders its passage as smooth as if it contemplated one continued object. This resemblance is the cause of the confusion and mistake, and makes us substitute the notion of identity instead of that of related objects. (*Treatise* 253–4)

In short: (1) if some items are R-related, contemplating them is like contemplating a single object; and (2) if two contemplations are sufficiently alike, a concept that is involved in one will seem to us to be involved in the other. Find the values of R that satisfy 1, and you have the relations that ordinary folk will mistake for identity. The above formulation, as I have said, implies that an object can last through time if it does not alter, so some diachronic identity statements are true after all. I shall go along with this pretence; everything I say about the line between acceptable and true can be routinely translated into a discourse about the line between respectable and optimal.

305. Hume tries to explain some of Locke's results

For sameness of a mass of matter, Hume says, we need only sameness of parts; so the same mass might be successively kneaded into different shapes. He goes on to say—agreeing with Locke—that if any particle is added to the mass or removed from it, 'this absolutely destroys the identity of the whole, strictly speaking' (255–6). He continues:

yet as we seldom think so accurately, we scruple not to pronounce a mass of matter the same where we find so trivial an alteration. The passage of the thought from the object before the change to the object after it is so smooth and easy that we scarce perceive the transition, and are apt to imagine that it is nothing but a continued survey of the same object.

Hume here attributes to us not merely slack speech, but error of thought: 'we scruple not' to say that the same mass endures because we 'are apt to imagine' that it really is so. Locke had no reason to disagree with this, but he does not say anything like it in *Essay* II.xxvii.

What Hume says about our tolerance of 'same heap of sand' even after a turnover of a few grains rests on his Similarity Theory; its crux is the likeness between two kinds of mental event. That could result from a resemblance between the items that are contemplated—for example, two masses that share nearly all their parts—but it could have other sources:

The objects which are variable or interrupted and yet are supposed to continue the same are such only as consist of a succession of parts connected together by resemblance, contiguity, or causation. . . . The relation of parts which leads us into this mistake [of assenting to an identity] is really nothing but a quality which produces an association of ideas and an easy transition of the imagination from one to another. (255)

Hume seems to imply that we are most apt to identify one item with another if they are related by one or more of our old trio—resemblance, contiguity, and causation. (There is no point here, as there was in §252, in insisting that it is really a quartet.) He employs each of these when deploying the Similarity Theory, but their roles are somewhat jumbled, and this use of them owes little to his theory about the association of ideas.

In two paragraphs on 256–7 Hume says that we sometimes think that a single body has undergone great changes in its constituent matter; we may be seduced into this when the changes are gradual. This, he contends, can be explained only on his principles. When we contemplate (what we would call) a body slowly undergoing a turnover in its constituent matter, the 'easy passage' of the mind is not blocked or bumped at any point in the journey. When the overall changes have become 'considerable', however, we jib at attributing identity unless we are encouraged by a further factor: namely, an enduring common 'end or purpose' which we have for the particles of matter in question. If a ship has had many of its planks replaced, we still think of it as the same ship because 'The common end in which the parts conspire is the same under all their variations, and affords an easy transition of the imagination from one situation of the body to another' (257).

The identity of organisms through time involves all this and more: namely, 'a sympathy of parts to their common end'. The parts of a plant or animal 'bear to each other the reciprocal relations of cause and effect in all their actions and operations' (257). Hume does not explain how this facilitates the 'easy transition' of the mind, contenting himself with this: 'The effect of so strong a relation is that . . . we still attribute identity to them.' This unexplained use of 'strong relation' sounds like theoretical whistling in the dark. I cannot link it with the doctrine of the association of ideas. Hume, I suggest, has adopted Locke's account of organisms because he can see that it is true, and merely hopes that it is predicted and explained by his Similarity Theory.

The conditions that Locke and Hume both lay down for the continuing existence of a mass of matter do not secure it for any organism; they agree about that. Hume concludes that since the rabbit that I saw at T_1 was a mass of matter, and the rabbit that I saw at T_2 was a different mass, it is not strictly true that I saw a single rabbit twice—though I may think I did. Locke, by contrast, holds that I did see one rabbit twice: it is just a fact about the rabbit-concept that a single instance of it can be composed of different masses at different times. Hume would declare this to be incoherent: no *one* thing can be made up first of one portion of stuff and then of another. Locke might reply: 'For one kind of thing, that can be the case: it is the kind *organism*. The evidence that organisms are as I describe is given by our agreed strong intuitions about what does and what does not count as the same organism.' Hume could respond: 'Of course you will get people to agree with you; when outside my study, I agree too. But people's beliefs cannot conjure absurd things into existence. You need to explain how there can be such a thing as an organism—and I'll bet that you cannot.' This face-off is worth thinking about.

Most of us will side with Locke against Hume: we are sure that we can see a rabbit and then see *it* again after it has eaten and excreted. Very well, but let us not be complacent about this. The question 'What is a rabbit?' is not easy to answer, and its difficulty shows in Locke's peculiar phrase 'the same successive body not shifted all at once' (§292).

306. Hume on personal identity: negative

The thesis that nothing alters implies that there are no enduring people; Hume's refusal to distinguish objects from their stages leaves him with no way out of this. When it comes to the concept of person, however, he complicates the discussion. Without relating it to his thoughts about the distinctness of stages and so on, he now confronts the hypothesis of an enduring thinking substance or self of which distinct perceptions are states. If this were legitimate, he seems to concede, that would secure some true diachronic identity statements about changing things, after all. But it is not legitimate, Hume says.

In the background of this are his attacks on the notion of substance in i.6 and iv.3; and we should look at these. The long attack on immaterial thinking substance, to which iv.5 is devoted, is full of interesting things; but they do not contribute to our present topic.

In the tiny section i.6 Hume attacks the Lockean 'idea of substance in general' (understanding it, of course, as Leibniz, Berkeley, and nearly everyone else always has). There is no impression from which such an idea could be copied, Hume says, because our impressions represent only qualities. Thus, 'We have . . . no idea of substance distinct from that of a collection of particular qualities, nor have we any other meaning when we either talk or reason concerning it' (16).

He returns to the topic early in iv.3, remarking that philosophers have used this 'fiction' to help make acceptable some false statements of identity, both synchronic and diachronic. Synchronically, we override something's 'compound' nature by supposing it to be 'one thing' and to exhibit 'simplicity'. We naturally think of this pebble I am holding out to you as being, at least at this one moment, a single simple thing, rather than an aggregate or composite which is made up of parts. I here ignore the sub-pebbles of which it is composed: Hume was sympathetic to the Leibnizian view, which he seems to have learned from Malezieu, that they too stop the pebble from being a genuinely single thing;[1] but his present concern is with the pebble's being an aggregate not of bits of stone but rather of tropes. He sees it as being, at a given moment, a collection of instances of sphericalness, greyness, hardness, coldness, and so on. These tropes, he holds, are parts of the pebble; but we dodge the thought of its having such parts by treating them rather as qualities *of* a single simple thing, an underlying substance, which *has* them, and which is the pebble. In short, we replace the genuine part/whole relation by a spurious quality/possessor one:

The imagination conceives [a] simple object at once, with facility, by a single effort of thought, without change or variation. The connexion of parts in [a] compound object [such as a body] has almost the same effect, and so unites the object within itself that the fancy feels not the transition in passing from one part to another. Hence the colour, taste, figure, solidity and other qualities combined in a peach or melon are conceived to form one thing; and that on account of their close relation, which makes them affect the thought in the same manner as if perfectly uncompounded. (221)

Hume here presents a metaphysical picture in which we do not have things with qualities, but only bundles of tropes, with so-called 'things' being a mere *façon de parler*, a way of verbalizing facts about tropes.

Diachronically, we override something's 'alteration' by supposing it to be 'the same' thing and to exhibit 'identity'. I need not quote any more passages relating to this.

Given that Hume has an ontology, one might expect him to have views about what things there are—not 'things' that he can explain away as fictions or collections, but real, basic *things*. And so he has:

---

[1] See *Treatise* 30. The relevant part of Nicolas de Malezieu's *Elemens de Geometrie* is reproduced in Kemp Smith 1949: 340–2.

If . . . anyone should [say] that the definition of a substance is *something which may exist by itself*, . . . I should observe that this definition agrees to every thing that can possibly be conceived, and never will serve to distinguish substance from accident or the soul from its perceptions. . . . Since all our perceptions are different from each other and from everything else in the universe, they are also distinct and separable, and may be considered as separately existent, and may exist separately, and have no need of anything else to support their existence. They are therefore substances, as far as this definition explains a substance. (233; see also 244)

Hume holds also that tropes can exist by themselves: 'Every quality . . . may be conceived to exist apart, and may exist apart, not only from every other quality but from that unintelligible chimera of a substance' (222). So they are also 'substances' in this sense. This notion of substance, therefore, 'never will serve to distinguish substance from accident', because according to it, accidents are substances (§36).

When Hume gets to iv.6, he seems to suggest that substantial selves might be rescued by empirical evidence for their existence, should there be any:

For my part, when I enter most intimately into what I call myself I always stumble on some particular perception or other, of heat or cold, light or shade, love or hatred, pain or pleasure. I never can catch myself at any time without a perception, and never can observe any thing but the perception. (252)

He is confident that you and I will give similar reports. His suggestion that 'some metaphysicians' might not do so is mere sarcasm; he does not really think that his doctrine on personal identity is vulnerable from that quarter. Pears contends that in this passage Hume is implicitly arguing that 'we could not possibly have an internal impression of such a self' (Pears 1990: 123; see also 126–7). Bearing in mind Hume's earlier case against the idea of substance, that message can reasonably be read between the lines of iv.6.

For more on Hume's rejection of a unitary self, read his report in the Appendix on 'the arguments . . . that induced me to deny the strict and proper identity and simplicity of a self or thinking being' (633). He gives seven of these, starting:

'When we talk of *self* . . .'
'Whatever is distinct . . .'
'When I turn my reflexion . . .'
'We can conceive . . .'
'The annihilation . . .'
'Is *self* the same . . .'
'Philosophers begin to be . . .'

Also relevant at this point is the next paragraph down to '. . . a promising aspect'.

From his denial that there are thinking substances in addition to perceptions, Hume immediately infers that there are no continuant minds or persons. He does not consider the possibility that a person might be real, yet composed of perceptions in the elusive way in which an organism is composed of particles. But then he does not think that organisms are real either.

307. Hume on personal identity: positive

Whereas Locke reaches the threshold of his treatment of personal identity with no prior commitments, Hume has already espoused some principles which imply that there are no people who last through time, and that the contrary illusion can be explained by the Similarity Theory. That explanation leads him to a treatment of personal identity that differs considerably from Locke's—not only through the difference between acceptability- and truth-conditions, but also in what the conditions are.

Locke ties personal identity to sameness of 'consciousness', by which (we gather) he means something about memory-overlaps; and he defends this tie through intuitions about cases. Hume brings memory into the picture less directly, and through theory rather than intuition. Memory has a large role in the story of personal identity, he maintains, not in its own right, but because memory involves resemblance. 'What is the memory but a faculty by which we raise up the images [= resemblances] of past perceptions?' (260). 'In this particular, then, the memory not only discovers the identity, but also contributes to its production, by producing the relation of resemblance among the perceptions' (261).

This is ingenious. It tries to get much of Locke's result without appealing to intuitions about cases. We can see Locke as proceeding thus: 'We have a concept of an enduring person; let us consider what we are inclined to think about cases, in order to discover the nature of that concept. . . . Aha! we find that memory links play a crucial role.' Hume's procedure is rather like this: 'We slip into thinking that there are enduring people, which must result from our mistaking non-identity relations for identity. We shall do this when the movement of the mind from one thing to another is smooth and easy; that happens when the two items are alike; such alikeness obtains between the ideas of memory and what they are memories of; so in cases where we think that differently dated perceptions belong to a single person, the odds are that some will be memories of others of them.' Ingenious, but hardly credible, if only because of its false assumption that memory represents through resemblance.

Memory is not the whole story, Hume rightly says, because our ordinary thinking about personal identity allows that something may have been the case about me even though I do not now remember it. He is better placed than Locke was to allow for forgetting, because he is working with two relations—resemblance (which brings in memory) and causation. He makes the latter carry most of the burden:

The true idea of the human mind is to consider it as a system of different perceptions . . . which are linked together by the relation of cause and effect, and mutually produce,

destroy, influence, and modify each other. Our impressions give rise to their correspondent ideas, and these ideas in their turn produce other impressions. One thought chases
another and draws after it a third by which it is expelled in its turn. (261)

This resembles Hume's Lockean account of organisms; only here it is perceptions, rather than particles of matter that are ingested and excreted, drawn in and
chased out.

Having brought in memory as a producer of resemblance, Hume now rein-
troduces it in a different role. If I am to have evidence that my present perceptions are causally connected with such-and-such past ones, he says, I must be
informed about the latter, and for that I need memory. In these cases 'memory
does not so much *produce* as *discover* personal identity, by showing us the relation
of cause and effect among our different perceptions' (262).

In fact, memory connects with causation in a stronger manner: a present perception can be a memory of a past one only if the latter kicked off a causal chain
leading to the present one (§112). There is no hint of this in Hume.

Our agreement that the concept of an enduring person is shot through with
causal notions should not deter us from asking what justifies Hume in saying
this. He writes as though his positive account of personal identity follows from
his own general theories; the resemblance part of it does, but the causal part does
not. Back in i.4 he implied that the association of ideas was going to do the job,
comparing it to Newtonian gravity: 'These are . . . the principles of union or
cohesion among our simple ideas . . . Here is a kind of attraction, which in the
mental world will be found to have as extraordinary effects as in the natural, and
to show itself in as many and as various forms' (12–13). This is echoed in iv.6: 'It
is therefore on some of these three relations of resemblance, contiguity and causation that identity depends'; 'These are the uniting principles in the ideal world'
(260). A detailed scrutiny of Hume's text shows that really causation does all the
work; and that it functions not as one of the three relations that produces association, but rather as the one relation that is involved in every instance of association (§254). Hume's view that individual pseudo-minds owe most of their unity
to causation owes nothing to his doctrine about the association of ideas.

His reliance on causation can be traced back to i.6, where he says that we permit ourselves a fictional thing thought when confronted by a number of tropes
that are 'supposed to be closely and inseparably connected by the relations of
contiguity and causation'. Locke had brought in contiguity, associating the thing
thought with ideas or qualities which 'go together'; but he had made no room
for causation in this story. Why did Hume do so?

The bundle theory of substances certainly needs contiguity: this pewter ring has
a certain colour, shape, size, texture, etc., none of which is a cause or effect of any
of the others. Locke and Hume would say that those tropes count as qualities of a
single thing because of their spatial contiguity. (For Hume some *ideas* are not spatially related to others, but our present topic is not ideas, but 'qualities' = tropes.)
Now, suppose I know that about the ring, and then discover another of its properties, and include that in the collection. Although I did not initially include it, says

Hume, I admit it now because of its causal links with the collection's original members. But why? Why not admit it simply on grounds of contiguity? This causal emphasis of Hume's seems to be idle, yet he insists upon it.

That is because he has slid from our present question to a different one about the meanings of certain general words. According to Locke, what people meant by 'gold' at a certain time was 'stuff that is yellow, heavy, malleable, ductile and fusible'; if they later came to believe that whatever is like that is also soluble in aqua regia, this could not be added to their 'idea of gold' without thereby changing the meaning of the word. That seems wrong; and in §200 I sketched the better account that Leibniz first proposed. Hume seeks to improve on Locke in a different way, implying that 'gold' means 'stuff that is yellow, heavy, etc. and has whatever other properties are causally bound to those':

The particular qualities which form a substance are . . . supposed to be closely and inseparably connected by the relations of contiguity and causation. The effect of this is that whatever new simple quality we discover to have the same connexion with the rest, we immediately comprehend it among them, even though it did not enter into the first conception of the substance. Thus our idea of gold may at first be a yellow colour, weight, malleableness, fusibility; but upon the discovery of its dissolubility in aqua regia we join that to the other qualities and suppose it to belong to the substance as much as if its idea had from the beginning made a part of the compound one. (16)

That is inferior to Leibniz's solution, because it stays on the surface; but at least it makes the meaning of 'gold' more stable, by letting it quantify over properties that we are not, at a given time, in a position to list by name.

However, it does not concern what leads us to identify a collection of tropes as a particular bit of gold, but rather what leads us to identify a collection of universal qualities as the essence of gold or as determining the meaning of 'gold'. It concerns the meaning of 'gold', 'water', etc., not the meaning of 'thing' or the nature of things.

Hume concludes that issues about personal identity are purely verbal: 'All the nice and subtle questions concerning personal identity can never possibly be decided, and are to be regarded rather as grammatical [= verbal] than as philosophical difficulties' (262). His explanation of this involves two elements. (1) 'Identity depends on the relations of ideas, and these relations produce identity by means of that easy transition they occasion. But as the relations and the easiness of the transition may diminish by insensible degrees, we have no just standard by which we can decide any dispute concerning the time when they acquire or lose a title to the name of identity.' So, Hume thinks, there is bound to be something arbitrary about how we dispose of the hard cases, the 'nice and subtle' disputes about personal identity—using 'nice' in *OED*'s sense 8: requiring or involving great precision, accuracy, or minuteness. Such cases all lie in border territory where determinately right answers cannot be found. (2) Anyway, these questions all concern the conditions under which something deserves 'the name of identity', and that is plainly verbal. Neither 1 nor 2 justifies what Hume says about 'grammatical difficulties', but they are his only basis for it.

308. Pears on omitting the body

It is sometimes thought that a full account of mental identity will have to connect minds with bodies; that may be right, but I do not find it as obvious as Pears
seems to. I agree that in the world as we know it, 'only the brain is capable of carrying the required causal link' (Pears 1990: 131); but that does not oblige Hume
to bring bodies into his analytical examination of our thoughts about personal
identity.

Pears also holds that bodies must enter the story if we are to have a coherent
story about what separates one mind from another at a single time: this work of
Hume's was bound to come to grief, because it tries to say what it is for a mind
to last through time without first saying what it is to be a mind-stage (ibid. 140),
and this requires bodies. I shall discuss the latter claim.

Hume's account implies that if your mental history is fairly like mine, all that
keeps our minds apart is that each is a sequence of perceptions that is internally
bound together by causation, with little or no direct causal connection between
the members of one sequence and those of another (though there may be indirect connections, mediated by testimony and other bodily events). Pears sees this
as fatal: 'Causation does not keep within the confines of a single mind, and so,
though the internal structure of each mind owes much to the causal processes
that go on within it, the lines of demarcation between one mind and another cannot possibly be determined by causation alone (ibid. 137).' I submit that 'cannot
possibly' is too strong. Pears writes later: 'Even if telepathy never in fact occurs,
that can hardly be what enables us to draw a line between one mind and another'
(ibid. 142). I reply that if there were enough telepathy, minds might well start to
coalesce.

Pears is certainly right that by leaving out bodies Hume debars us from using
his account of personal identity in a criterial manner—that is, as an aid to deciding, for a given pair of perceptions, whether it is acceptable to say that they have
occurred in a single mind. He thinks that Hume may not have been (I am sure he
was not) trying to do that: 'It almost looks as if he was not really concerned with
the criteria for answering questions of personal identity spanning periods of
time. Certainly, his main interest was in the question how much unity or inte-
gration is achieved by a sequence of impressions and ideas which are already
known to belong to a single person' (ibid. 132). If Hume tackled the criterial
question, he would fail, Pears says. 'Nobody starts by identifying an array of
impressions and ideas and then has to face the task of sorting them into bundles,
one of which will be himself, while the rest will be other people' (ibid. 134). That
is right. For me to have, now, a serious diachronic question about my own identity, I must now know that someone had (say) an experience as of viewing the
Watts Towers in 1996, but not be sure whether it was I. The only way for me to
have such knowledge is through bodies: for example, I find a record of such a perception's being had, or someone tells me that it was had, or I remember some-

one shouting about having such a perception. Hume's disembodied treatment of mental identity allows me no recourse to anything like that, and throws me back on unaided memory. That can indeed inform me that someone had a Watts Towers visual experience, but not in such a way as to leave me wondering who the lucky person was.

309. Hume's recantation

Book III of the *Treatise* was published about a year after book I, and in the interim Hume had second thoughts, most notably about personal identity. On 633–6 he sketches again his case for his view about this, giving seven arguments for it, and then says that it is wrong and that he does not know how to correct it. The turning-point is dramatic: 'The present philosophy, therefore, has so far a promising aspect. But all my hopes vanish when I come to explain the principles that unite our successive perceptions in our thought or consciousness' (635–6). Here is Hume's account of the difficulty:

There are two principles which I cannot render consistent, nor is it in my power to renounce either of them, viz. [1] that *all our distinct perceptions are distinct existences*, and [2] that *the mind never perceives any real connexion among distinct existences*. Did our perceptions either inhere in something simple and individual, or did the mind perceive some real connexion among them, there would be no difficulty in the case. For my part, I must plead the privilege of a sceptic, and confess that this difficulty is too hard for my understanding. (636)

Hume really meant it. He did not return to personal identity in later writings; indeed, the word 'identity' does not occur in his philosophical works outside the *Treatise*.

The overall shape of his trouble is as follows. He sees 1 as ruling out a continuing-substance account of persons, according to which 'our perceptions inhere in something simple and individual'. This requires his rival theory, according to which persons are constructs out of perceptions; but that is ruled out by 2, Hume thinks, leaving him with nothing he can think about personal identity.

Here is how 2 disturbs Hume's account of what a (pseudo-)person is. The rest of this paragraph is to be thought of as written by Hume. Even if there are no enduring minds, there seem to be. There are facts which we can acceptably state in the diachronic language of mind- or person-identity, and we need a decent account of them. What must some perceptions be like for them to count, by everyday standards, as differently dated states of a single mind? My answer rests primarily on causation: two perceptions count informally as co-owned if they are causally linked in the right way. But what can I mean by 'causally linked'? This cannot stand for a real connection between them: I could make sense of such a connection only if it were given to me in experience, but it is not; and that was the burden of my long discussion of causation in I.iii. So the mere fact that (2) 'the mind never perceives any real connexion among distinct existences' deprives me of any simple, straightforward appeal to causation in my account of what a (pseudo-)person is. On the other hand, the treatment of causation which I have espoused will not serve either. It starts with the thought of a unified mind whose causal thinking is to be explained, and my explanation depended on regularities that have previously been exhibited among the perceptions *in that mind*. Thus, my account of causation can be given only with help from the concept of a unified mind, and my account of mental unity can be given only with help from the concept of causation. There is no starting-point, chronological or analytic. Neither account can get going until the other has been completed.

I suppose that is what underlies Hume's recantation. It fits the skimpy text well enough, and the point it makes is plausible. Being sympathetic to the main outlines of Hume's accounts of causation and of personal identity, I regard this as a philosophical problem that needs to be solved. One might try to solve it by contending that one can legitimately construct the two accounts in parallel, rather than in sequence, explaining both concepts—causation and mind—at the same time. This sometimes works, as for instance with the concepts of belief and desire (§§77, 248); but the prospects for such a success with our present problem look bleak.

310. Coda: Hume and Berkeley on the passage of time

We have seen that iv.6 is dominated by the thesis that diachronic identity statements cannot be true of items that alter: nothing that persists alters. Yet, back in ii.3–6, Hume argued that only through fallacy and fiction can one apply the concept of time to an unchanging object: whatever persists alters. These two are compatible, and jointly entail that nothing persists, so that no diachronic identity statement is true; but Hume is not proposing anything as neat as that.

Rather, in iv.6 he discusses objects against the unexamined background of the passage of time, whereas in ii.3–6 he discusses the passage of time against the unexamined background of enduring objects. I shall not try to reconcile these two approaches, or comment on the tension they create.

We know why Hume holds that alteration rules out persistence; but why should he think that non-alteration does so? Well, if we have an idea of time, he says, it must be copied from some impressions:

From the succession of ideas and impressions we form the idea of time . . . Time cannot make its appearance to the mind, either alone or attended with a steady unchangeable object, but is always discovered by some perceivable succession of changeable objects. (*Treatise* 35)

Because our idea of time *comes entirely from* our experiences of diachronic variety, Hume continues, it *is applicable only to* items that are diachronically various.

Concerning objects that are 'unchangeable' (= unchanging), he writes: 'Since the idea of duration cannot be derived from such an object, it can never in any propriety or exactness be applied to it, nor can anything unchangeable be ever said to have duration' (37). Thus, nothing can last without altering.

This echoes Berkeley's treatment of time in *PHK* 98. Time 'abstracted from the succession of ideas in our minds' is 'nothing', Berkeley writes, inferring that 'the duration of any finite spirit must be estimated by the number of ideas or actions succeeding each other in that spirit or mind'. He takes this to entail that whether time passes at all for a given person depends upon whether ideas are processing through her mind. He agrees with Descartes that 'the soul always thinks', but not for his reasons. Descartes assumes the time through which a soul lasts, and asserts that during that time the soul never shuts down. Berkeley assumes nothing about time's passing, and says that, for as long as the soul operates, time passes, and if the soul shuts down, the passage of time does likewise. That no time passes while a soul does not think is for Descartes a thesis about the soul, for Berkeley a thesis about time.

In Berkeley's solipsistic view of the passage of time, each soul has its own time, which passes only while that soul changes; and the notion of a single objective time in which all souls participate is silently snubbed. He was challenged about this in correspondence. He had slapped his all-purpose term of abuse, 'abstract idea', on to the supposed concept of a thing's enduring while not altering, and a friend commented:

> When I suppose the existence of spirit while it does not actually think, it does not appear to me that I do it by supposing an abstract idea of existence, and another of absolute time. The existence of John asleep by me, without so much as a dream, is not an abstract idea, nor is time passing the while an abstract idea. (LJ 2:289)

Berkeley's response to this sensible remark is at once lordly and evasive. We are led into trouble by 'supposing that the time in one mind is to be measured by the succession of ideas in another', he asserts, but he does not say why (ibid. 293).

Hume takes a similar line about 'objects' of any kind. Each 'object' has its own time, and must sustain it by constantly altering. He thus joins Berkeley in rejecting any objective, all-encompassing time in which things can participate even while not changing.

Hume knows that we do in fact 'apply the idea of time to what is unchangeable', and he promises to explain later 'by what fiction' we do this. He makes good on his promise at 65, with an account of the 'fiction' which depends on three propositions which all defeat me. Hume refers back to this baffling passage in iv.2, alluding to 'a fiction of the imagination by which the unchangeable object is supposed to participate of the changes of the coexisting objects' (200–1). What are 'the coexisting objects' if not the objects that exist throughout the same period of time?

However, we can get some sense of what pushed Hume along this rocky path if we return to his statement that 'since the idea of duration cannot be derived from [an unchanging] object, it can never in any propriety or exactness be applied to' such an object. He is here applying the general thesis that no idea is properly *applicable to* something that could not have been *a source for* the idea. Details apart, we can agree with Hume that our experiences of objects can play some part in our getting concepts; seeing horses may play some part in one's getting the concept of *horse*. So we can come to terms with the general thesis, and can even find it plausible. According to it, what makes this concept of ours applicable to those animals also makes them suitable as helps towards getting the concept in the first place. But this plausible thesis, when applied to the concept of time and unchanging objects, turns out to be preposterous. What has gone wrong?

One answer is that the concept of time is special, and that no experiences—even of alterations—could help one to acquire it, because the only way to make any sense of our experience is by taking it as temporally organized, and thus by applying the concept of time to it. I am sympathetic to that Kantian point, but even without it, we can find a weak spot in Hume's line of thought.

Encounters with triangles might help me to get a concept of *triangle*. What concept will it be? Will it apply to a closed plane figure with three straight sides of which two are a billion times longer than the third? A figure with that shape could not help anyone to acquire the concept of *triangle*, because no one could take in its being a triangle. How, then, do we come by a concept of triangle that covers such long thin ones? It could be as follows. Items that we recognize as triangles help us to get a concept of triangle*, which applies to all and only triangles whose lengths of side are not too disparate. We then think about this concept we have acquired, start to develop some general theory to put starch into it, and find that the best theory removes the limits on length difference. Thus we stretch our concept to cover triangles which would in practice never be recognized as such.

Something analogous could hold for the concept of time. Set aside Kantian and other doubts, and suppose with Hume that our experiences of changes in ourselves and the rest of the world help us to get a concept of the passage of time. As we think about this, and try to apply it to our world and our experience in more refined and useful ways, we find that we are helped by moving from the-time-of-x and the-time-of-y to the absolute concept of *time*, the public time through which everything lasts. Then it dawns on us that our newly acquired concept of inter-object, or public, time allows that an object might endure without altering. This thought could not have been directly prompted by our experiences of the passage of time, which all involve alteration; but it could come from a salutary development of thoughts that were prompted in that manner.

311. Leibniz on what a substance is

Leibniz's responses to Locke's discussion of personal identity are coloured by his evident assumption that God can be trusted to ensure that each Lockean person is associated through time with just one substance. Being untouched by concept-empiricism, he does not share Locke's worries about the idea of substance, let alone Hume's rejection of it; he is happy to classify the concept of substance as innate (§179). Also, in so far as Hume's negative view about continuant objects of any kind comes from a mixing-up of objects and object-stages, Leibniz is free of that too.

All this could easily suggest that for Leibniz the concept of an enduring substance is basic, primitive, not subject to further analysis; and it seems that for much of his life that was so. In some of his later writings, however, he does dig into the substance concept in a manner that somewhat resembles Hume's account of personal identity.

It is adumbrated in a letter to Arnauld in which Leibniz asks what makes it the case that two events are episodes in the history of a single substance:

Suppose a straight line ABC representing a certain length of time. And suppose an individual substance, for example myself, enduring or subsisting during that time. Let us first take myself subsisting during time AB, and then myself subsisting during time BC. Then, since we are supposing that it is the same individual substance that endures throughout, or that it is I who subsist in time AB, being then in Paris, and that it is still I who subsist in time BC, being then in Germany, there must necessarily be a reason for the true statement that we endure, i.e. that I who was in Paris am now in Germany. For if there is no such reason, we would have as much right to say that it is someone else. It is true that my internal experience convinces me *a posteriori* of this identity; but there must also be an *a priori* reason. (AG 73*)

Leibniz is here using '*a posteriori*' and '*a priori*' in the senses I explained in §107, to contrast *evidence* that P with *what makes it the case* that P. He seems poised to offer an analysis of the concept of substance, a metaphysical account of what a substance is; but he does not do so. Here, as often in that middle period, the complete-concept concept seduces him into triviality:

The only reason that can be found is the fact that my attributes in the preceding time and state and my attributes in the succeeding time and state are all predicates of a single subject ... Now, what is it to say that the predicate is in the subject, except that the notion of the predicate is in some way included in the notion of the subject? And since, once I began existing, it could truly be said of me that this or that would happen to me, it must be admitted that these predicates were laws included in the subject or in my complete notion, which constitutes what is called *I*, which is the foundation of the connection of all my different states and which God has known perfectly from all eternity. (ibid.*)

According to this, two differently dated personal states count as states of a single substance, *me*, because the concepts of them are included in my total individual concept.

This is disappointing. God's mind contains a great store of conceptual material: what splits it up into complete concepts of individual substances? To answer that is to explain what an individual substance is. Leibniz writes as though the question

> What makes it the case that being-F and being-G belong to a single complete concept-of-a-substance?

needs no answer. So he uninhibitedly uses the notion of co-occurrence in a single complete concept in answering this:

> What makes it the case that the being-F and being-G episodes belong to a single substance?

I submit that if the latter needs an answer, then so does the former. The two hardly differ; and if there is enough space between them for one to help explain the other, it would be in the reverse of Leibniz's direction.

In that passage, however, Leibniz hints in passing at a different answer to our question. In speaking of what is contained in my complete concept, he says that it contains 'laws' that govern the unfolding of my successive states. At an early stage in my history, he says, it could be truly said of me that I was going to be F at T_1 and G at T_2; he seems to mean that it was then settled that I was going to be F at T_1 and G at T_2. People sometimes say such things in the spirit of fatalism: if I was G at T_2, then it follows by logic that from all eternity it was *true that I would* be G at T_2, and in that sense my being G at T_2 was settled in advance. Leibniz's 'complete concept' doctrine sometimes drew him in that direction, but not here. In this context he is writing about genuine settledness, resulting from the laws governing the substance. That I should be G at T_2 was settled at T_1 because it followed deterministically from my state at the earlier time.

There is no news for us in Leibniz's view that each substance unfolds in accordance with deterministic laws of immanent causation that God lays upon it (§94). But here he says this when discussing what makes it the case that two episodes belong to a single substance; and that is noteworthy. If the laws of immanent causation enter into such a 'reason', that can only be because the obtaining of such laws is analytically involved in the concept of *same substance*. Leibniz is working towards the thesis that *Two perceptions count as being had by the same substance if one causes the other.* The causation may be indirect, running through intermediaries. If two synchronous perceptions have a common cause P, then—because identity is transitive—each belongs to the same substance as P, and thus to the same substance as one another. The same result follows by similar reasoning if they are both (partial) causes of a single later perception.

That now gives a plausible necessary condition for two perceptions to belong to a single substance. If neither causes the other, and there is no third perception which they both cause or are caused by, it is reasonable to suppose that they do not belong to a single substance. So:

(1) If one perception is a cause of another, the two belong to a single substance;

(2) No two perceptions belong to a single substance unless their being so follows from 1 together with the transitivity of identity.

That is in the spirit of the position that Loeb (1981: 319) has attributed to Leibniz:

The simple Leibnizian causal theory of persistence does not in any way appeal to the existence of substances or substrata in which perceptions inhere. Further, substances or substrata are not needed to account for the 'unity' of a set of perceptions at a time. Distinct perceptions at a given time are perceptions of the same monad just in case there is some perception such that they are both partial causes of that perception. At this point, Leibniz was in a position to dispense with substances or substrata, at least insofar as they might seem to provide accounts of persistence and unity.

I have modified Loeb's view in a couple of ways, but it was he who first led me to realize that Leibniz had such a view about the concept of substance. If I had read Beck's fine 1969 book more alertly, I would have been put on to it by that: 'Every created monad is a law of its manifestations. It is not a bit of matter or substance which falls under its own individual law' (Beck 1969: 222). 'An existing thing is not one thing and the laws of nature something different, but the former is only an actualization of the latter in the real dynamic relation among its own states' (ibid. 231).

There is plenty of textual evidence for this, but I am not alone in having been awoken to it by Loeb. Here are some relevant fragments:

'This law of order . . . constitutes the individuality of each particular substance' (L 493).

'"I do not see", you [De Volder] say, "how any succession can follow from the nature of a thing, viewed in itself. . . . Unless", you add, "the thing itself is successive." But all individual things are successive or are subject to succession, and so your view coincides with mine. For me nothing is permanent in things except the law itself, which involves a continuous succession and which corresponds, in individual things, to that [law] which is of the whole universe' (L 534*).

'The fact that a certain law persists, which involves the future states of what we conceive to be the same—this is the very fact, I say, that constitutes the same substance' (L 535).

'Every simple substance has perception, and . . . its individuality consists in the perpetual law which brings about the sequence of perceptions that are assigned to it' (1710: 291, G 6:289).

The same general idea shows up also in the *New Essays*, when Leibniz alludes in passing to 'this continuity and interconnection of perceptions that makes someone really the same individual' (*NE* 239). We find it again when he writes to Des Bosses: 'The causal connections between perceptions, according to which subsequent ones are derived from preceding ones, makes up the unity of the percipient' (L 599). Notice that all this concerns differently dated perceptions. I have not found Leibniz applying this line of thought to synchronous ones, perhaps because he saw that he had no need to: the doctrine about them follows from the other together with transitivity of identity.

Sleigh (1990: 126–32) agrees with Loeb's interpretation of Leibniz's views on substantial unity, and has built upon it. He points out that the doctrine of immanent causation within the individual substance 'is a consequence of Leibniz's extraordinarily rigorous conception of what is involved in being an individual substance' (ibid. 130). That is right. From the causal analysis of substantial unity, it follows that a causally driven unfolding goes on within any substance, and that this is all the causation there is. The causal analysis will not allow a perception in one substance to cause a perception in another, because, according to it, the obtaining of a causal link between two perceptions entails that they belong to a single substance. There is no circularity here: the causal analysis is stated in terms of causation, not of immanent causation; that all causation is immanent is a consequence of it.

There can be weaker, yet similar, theories about what it takes for distinct states to pertain to a single thing. David Armstrong (1980: 75) has proposed a partial analysis of the concept of an individual thing: namely, the conditional that two thing-stages are stages of a single thing only if one is at least a *partial* cause of the other. There are various ways of strengthening that while still falling short of the biconditional causal analysis—for example, by saying that S_1 and S_2 are stages of a single thing only if S_1 causally contributes *more* to S_2 than does any other part of the world at T_1.

Leibniz, however, accepted the causal analysis, rather than any such weakened version. We might conjecture that this is the outcome of his liking for the general idea that is common to the strong theory and weaker versions of it such as Armstrong's, together with his independently grounded dislike of transeunt causation as involving trope transfer.

Although the strong theory keeps all causation within the monad, it does not entail that everything is caused (or, what comes to the same thing in the seventeenth century, it does not entail determinism). A fragment of monad M's history might include a perception P_1 that is not caused but belongs to M because it collaborates with others of M's perceptions to cause P_2. For his strict determinism, then, Leibniz has to look elsewhere—specifically to the principle of sufficient reason.

Nor does the causal analysis yield his doctrine of traces, the temporal dual of determinism, which says that a monad's entire past can in principle be read off from its present (§112). In the passages I have quoted, the analysis is stated, or alluded to, in terms of a 'law' that governs how monadic states 'succeed' others, or 'bring about' states, and in terms of how 'future states' are involved in present ones, and how 'subsequent states are derived from preceding ones'. The texts are intensely and exclusively forward-looking. Leibniz could beef up his theory of substantial identity so that it did entail the doctrine of traces, but this would be arbitrary and opportunistic.

312. Leibniz and Hume compared

Compare Leibniz's account of the concept of an individual substance with what Hume writes about personal identity: 'The true idea of the human mind is to consider it as a system of different perceptions . . . which are linked together by the relation of cause and effect' (*Treatise* 261). The two treatments are similar; yet Leibniz took himself to be explaining what a substance is, while Hume denied that there are any qualitatively complex substances, and thought he was laying bare what the facts are that we wrongly report in the language of 'thinking thing'. What basis is there for this difference?

According to Hume, your perceptions are parts of your mind, and they count as belonging to a single mind because of a certain relation amongst them. He tended to agree with Leibniz that no substance properly so-called has parts (§306), and his account of the pseudo-unity of minds led him to hold that minds are not substances. Leibniz would not have agreed, but why not?

(1) Hume's causally related items do not differ from Leibniz's. For each philosopher, they are tropes; Hume calls them 'perceptions', and sometimes Leibniz does so as well. Sameness of label sometimes veils a deep metaphysical difference, but not in this case.

(2) The causal relation that Hume thinks to hold amongst perceptions differs from the one that Leibniz postulates: for Leibniz it is a real making or compelling, an intrinsic relation between one state and another; Hume rejects that as incoherent, and holds that the causal relatedness of perceptions is just their obedience to a certain pattern (§270). This difference, however, does not answer my question. We still seem to have Leibniz and Hume both saying that a mind is a suitably interrelated set of perceptions or tropes; and just that—whatever the relation is—seems to commit them both to minds' not being genuine substances.

(3) Hume regards perceptions as in principle able to exist outside any mind: 'Perceptions . . . may exist separately, and have no need of anything else to support their existence' (*Treatise* 233). Leibniz does not say anything like this, and his usual objection to transeunt causation implies the contrary: if a given perception or trope cannot be owned first by one substance and then by another, presumably it cannot exist when not owned by any. But this difference between the two philosophers does not answer my question. It may show why Leibniz cannot agree with Hume that perceptions are substances, but it does not protect him from Hume's view that minds or monads are not substances. Anyway, how could Leibniz justify his view that perceptions must be owned, if that consists only in their being suitably related to other perceptions?

(4) To save Leibniz's metaphysic of substance from coalescing with Hume's, we must not take it as saying:

A substance is an aggregate of momentary states that are law-related in a certain manner, with this understood as similar in form to:

A staircase is an aggregate of steps that are spatially related in a certain way.

The boldest and sharpest way of separating Leibniz from that is by taking his view to be that:

A substance is a law whereby momentary states follow from one another.

Identify the substance with the law, and its unity is assured, unchallenged by the multiplicity of states that fall under it. That is how Cover and O'Leary-Hawthorne (1999) understand Leibniz (§132). They explain that these 'laws' are not occupants of a third realm, or Platonic heaven, but rather are 'immanent', or in the world. The main textual support for this is in Leibniz's letters to De Volder: 'For me nothing is permanent in things except the law itself' (L 534); what 'constitutes the enduring substance' is 'the fact that a certain law persists' (L 535). There are texts that go the other way, as when Leibniz writes that God 'gives' a law to each monad (NS, FW 151; to Clarke, AG 344). Still, the interpretation by Cover and O'Leary-Hawthorne does good explanatory work, especially in solving our present problem, which I cannot otherwise solve.

We ordinarily think of a law as reapplicable: the very same law might lead to one monadic history given one initial state, and to a different one given another starting-point. The interpretation of Leibniz we are now considering cannot understand laws in this manner, however; for then a single substance (= single law) could be associated with several distinct monadic histories, which is absurd. Cover and O'Leary-Hawthorne avoid this by supposing that the laws which (they say) Leibniz identifies with monads are of a special kind which are not reapplicable; thus, when you have the law, you have the history, with no need to specify a starting-point in addition to the law. Whereas our ordinary view of laws takes them to be analogous to *add one, then add one, then add one, . . . ,* Cover and O'Leary-Hawthorne take the laws that Leibniz identifies with monads to be analogous to *start with zero, then add one, then add one, then add one . . .* , the point being that the latter of these does, as the former does not, specify the whole series of natural numbers. There is no direct textual support for this, but it is a reasonable guess as to what Leibniz believed.

Bibliography

Aaron, R. I. (1970). *John Locke*, 3rd edn. Oxford University Press.

Adams, Robert Merrihew (1975). 'Where Do Our Ideas Come From? Descartes vs. Locke', in S. P. Stich (ed.), *Innate Ideas*. Berkeley: University of California Press, 71–87.

Alanen, Lilli (1988). 'Descartes, Omnipotence, and Kinds of Modality', in P. H. Hare (ed.), *Doing Philosophy Historically*. Buffalo: Prometheus Books: 182–96.

Alexander, Peter (1974). 'Boyle and Locke on Primary and Secondary Qualities', repr. in Tipton 1977: 62–76.

Alexander, Samuel (1908). *Locke*. London: Constable.

Allison, Henry (1966). 'Locke's Theory of Personal Identity: A Re-Examination', repr. in Tipton 1977: 105–22.

Alston, William P. (1954). 'Particulars—Bare and Qualified'. *Philosophy and Phenomenological Research*, 15: 253–8.

——(1993). *The Reliability of Sense Perception*. Ithaca, NY: Cornell University Press.

——and Bennett, Jonathan (1984). 'Identity and Cardinality: Geach and Frege'. *Philosophical Review*, 93: 553–67.

————(1988). 'Locke on People and Substances'. *Philosophical Review*, 97: 25–46.

Anscombe, G. E. M. (1981). 'Substance', in her *Metaphysics and the Philosophy of Mind*. Minneapolis: University of Minnesota Press, 37–43.

Aquinas, Thomas. *Summa Theologica*.

Aristotle. *Categories*.

Armstrong, David M. (1980). 'Identity through Time', in P. van Inwagen (ed.), *Time and Cause*. Dordrecht: Reidel, 67–78.

Atherton, Margaret (1983a). 'Locke and the Issue over Innateness', repr. in Chappell 1998: 48–59.

——(1983b). 'Locke's Theory of Personal Identity'. *Midwest Studies in Philosophy*, 8: 273–93.

——(1984). 'The Inessentiality of Locke's Essences', repr. in Chappell 1998, 199–213.

Augustine, Bishop of Hippo. *Confessions*.

Austin, J. L. (1962). *Sense and Sensibilia*. Oxford University Press.

Ayer, A. J. (1946). *Language, Truth and Logic*, 2nd edn. London: Gollancz.

Ayers, M. R. (1975). 'The Ideas of Power and Substance in Locke Philosophy', repr. in Tipton 1977: 77–104.

——(1981). 'Mechanism, Superaddition, and the Proof of God's Existence in Locke's *Essay*'. *Philosophical Review*, 90: 210–51.

——(1991). *Locke*. London: Routledge.

Beck, Lewis White (1969). *Early German Philosophy*. Cambridge, Mass.: Harvard University Press.

Bennett, Jonathan (1960–1). 'A Myth about Logical Necessity'. *Analysis*, 21: 59–63.

——(1961). 'On Being Forced to a Conclusion'. *Proceedings of the Aristotelian Society*, suppl. vol. 35: 15–34.

——(1964). *Rationality*, reissued Indianapolis: Hackett, 1989.

Bennett, Jonathan (1965a). 'Berkeley and God'. *Philosophy*, 40: 207–21.

——(1965b). 'Substance, Reality and Primary Qualities'. *American Philosophical Quarterly*, 2: 1–17.

——(1966). *Kant's Analytic*. Cambridge University Press.

——(1976). *Linguistic Behaviour*, reissued Indianapolis: Hackett, 1990.

——(1979). 'Analytic Transcendental Arguments', in P. Bieri *et al.* (eds.), *Transcendental Arguments and Science*. Dordrecht: Reidel, 45–64.

——(1987). 'Substratum'. *History of Philosophy Quarterly*, 4: 197–215.

——(1994). 'Descartes's Theory of Modality'. *Philosophical Review*, 103: 639–67.

——(1995). *The Act Itself*. Oxford University Press.

——(1996). 'Ideas and Qualities in Locke's *Essay*'. *History of Philosophy Quarterly*, 13: 73–88.

Berkeley, George (1708). *Philosophical Commentaries*, in LJ 1:9–104.

——(1709). *An Essay Towards a New Theory of Vision*, in LJ 1:171–279.

——(1710). *A Treatise Concerning the Principles of Human Knowledge*, in LJ 2:21–145.

——(1713). *Three Dialogues between Hylas and Philonous*, in LJ 2:163–263.

——(1732). *Alciphron, or the Minute Philosopher*, in LJ 3.

Blackburn, Simon (1990). 'Hume and Thick Connexions'. *Philosophy and Phenomenological Research*, 50 suppl.: 237–50.

Bolton, Martha Brandt (1976). 'Substances, Substrata, and Names of Substances', repr. in Chappell 1998: 106–26.

Boyle, Robert (1675). 'Some Physico-Theological Considerations about the Possibility of the Resurrection', repr. in Chappell 1998, 192–200.

Broad, C. D. (1923). *Scientific Thought*. London: Routledge.

Chappell, Vere (1994). 'Locke's Theory of Ideas', in V. Chappell (ed.), *The Cambridge Companion to Locke*. Cambridge University Press, 26–55.

——(1998) (ed.). *Locke*. Oxford University Press.

Copleston, Frederick (1950). *A History of Philosophy*, vol. 2. London: Burns Oates & Washbourne.

Cover, J. A., and O'Leary-Hawthorne, John (1999). *Substance and Individuation in Leibniz*. Cambridge University Press.

Craig, Edward (1987). *The Mind of God and the Works of Man*. Oxford University Press.

Curley, Edwin M. (1972). 'Locke, Boyle, and the Distinction Between Primary and Secondary Qualities'. *Philosophical Review*, 81: 438–64.

——(1984). 'Descartes on the Creation of the Eternal Truths'. *Philosophical Review*, 93: 569–97.

Davidson, Donald. (1963). 'Actions, Reasons, and Causes', repr. in his *Essays on Actions and Events*. Oxford University Press, 3–19.

Day, J. P. de C. (1952–3). 'George Berkeley'. *Review of Metaphysics*, 6: 83–113, 265–86, 447–69, 583–96.

Descartes, René (1633). *The World* and *Treatise on Man*, excerpts in CSM 1:81–108, complete in AT 11:1–202.

——(1641). *Meditations on First Philosophy* and *Replies to Objections*, in CSM 2:3–385.

——(1644). *Principles of Philosophy*, mostly in CSM 1:179–404, complete in MM.

Deutscher, Max, and Martin, C. B. (1966). 'Remembering'. *Philosophical Review*, 75: 161–96.

Drake, S. (1963). 'Galileo Galilei', in Edwards 1963.

Dummett, Michael (1956). 'Nominalism'. *Philosophical Review*, 65: 491–505.

——(1964). 'Bringing about the Past', repr. in his *Truth and Other Enigmas*. Cambridge, Mass.: Harvard University Press, 1978, 333–50.

——(1973). *Frege: Philosophy of Language*. London: Duckworth.

Edwards, Paul (1963) (ed.). *Encyclopedia of Philosophy*. New York: Macmillan.

Falkenstein, Lorne (1990). 'Berkeley's Argument for Other Minds'. *History of Philosophy Quarterly*, 7: 431–40.

Fleming, Noel (1985). 'The Tree in the Quad'. *American Philosophical Quarterly*, 22: 25–36.

Flew, Antony (1951). 'Locke and the Problem of Personal Identity'. *Philosophy*, 26: 53–68.

——(1961). *Hume's Philosophy of Belief*. London: Routledge.

Frege, Gottlob (1884). *Die Grundlagen der Arithmetik*, reissued as *The Foundations of Arithmetic*, ed. J. L. Austin. Oxford: Blackwell, 1950.

——(1892). 'On Sense and Reference', repr. in P. Geach and M. Black (eds.), *Translations from the Philosophical Writings of Gottlob Frege*. Oxford: Blackwell, 1952, 56–78.

——(1918). 'The Thought', repr. P. F. Strawson (ed.), *Philosophical Logic*. Oxford University Press, 1967, 1–38.

Galileo Galilei (1623). *The Assayer*, partly repr. in S. Drake (ed.), *Discoveries and Opinions of Galileo*. Garden City, NY: Doubleday, 1957, 231–80.

Garrett, Don (1997). *Cognition and Commitment in Hume's Philosophy*. New York: Oxford University Press.

Gaukroger, Stephen (1995). *Descartes: An Intellectual Biography*. Oxford University Press.

Geach, P. T. (1957). *Mental Acts*. London: Routledge.

——(1965). 'Assertion'. *Philosophical Review*, 74: 449–65.

——(1973). 'Omnipotence'. *Philosophy*, 48: 7–20.

Gennaro, Rocco J. (1999). 'Leibniz on Consciousness and Self-Consciousness', in GH 353–71.

Gibson, James (1917). *Locke's Theory of Knowledge and its Historical Relations*. Cambridge University Press.

Goodin, Susanna (1999). 'Locke and Leibniz and the Debate over Species', in GH 163–76.

Grandy, Richard (1975). 'Stuff and Things', repr. in F. J. Pelletier (ed.), *Mass Terms: Some Philosophical Problems*. Dordrecht: Reidel, 1979, 219–25.

Greig, J. Y. T. (1932) (ed.). *The Letters of David Hume*, vol. 1. Oxford University Press.

Grey, D. (1952). 'The Solipsism of Bishop Berkeley'. *Philosophical Quarterly*, 2: 338–49.

Grice, H. P. (1941). 'Personal Identity', repr. in John Perry (ed.), *Personal Identity*. Berkeley: University of California Press, 1975, 73–95.

Gueroult, Martial (1953). *Descartes selon l'ordre des raisons*. Paris: Aubier.

Hacking, Ian (1975). *Why Does Language Matter to Philosophy?* Cambridge University Press.

——(1976). 'Individual Substance', in Harry G. Frankfurt (ed.), *Leibniz: A Collection of Critical Essays*. University of Notre Dame Press, 137–53.

Hall, A. R. (1954). *The Scientific Revolution 1500–1800: The Formation of the Modern Scientific Attitude*. London: Longmans.

Hardin, C. L. (1988). *Color for Philosophers: Unweaving the Rainbow*. Indianapolis: Hackett.

Heller, Mark (1990). *The Ontology of Physical Objects: Four-Dimensional Hunks of Matter*. Cambridge University Press.

Hobbes, Thomas (1640). Objections to Descartes's *Meditations*, in CSM 2:121–37.

Hume, David (1739). *A Treatise of Human Nature*, ed. L. A. Selby-Bigge. Oxford University Press, 1964.

——(1748). *An Enquiry Concerning Human Understanding*, ed. L. A. Selby-Bigge. Oxford University Press, 1955.

Ishiguro, Hidé (1986). 'The Status of Necessity and Impossibility', in A. O. Rorty (ed.), *Essays on Descartes's Meditations*. Berkeley: University of California Press.

Jackson, Frank (1975). 'On the Adverbial Analysis of Visual Experience'. *Metaphilosophy*, 6: 127–35.

Jackson, Reginald (1929). 'Locke's Distinction between Primary and Secondary Qualities', repr. in Martin and Armstrong 1968: 53–77.

Jolley, Nicholas (1978). 'Leibniz and Locke on Essences', in Michael Hooker (ed.), *Leibniz: Critical and Interpretive Essays*. Baltimore: Johns Hopkins University Press, 196–208.

——(1984). *Locke and Leibniz: A Study of the New Essays on Human Understanding*. Oxford University Press.

——(1990). *The Light of the Soul: Theories of Ideas in Leibniz, Malebranche, and Descartes*. Oxford University Press.

Kemp Smith, Norman (1949). *The Philosophy of David Hume*. London: Macmillan.

Kripke, Saul (1972). 'Naming and Necessity', in D. Davidson and G. Harman (eds.), *Semantics of Natural Language*. Dordrecht: Reidel, 253–355.

Leibniz, G. W. (1678). 'What is an Idea?', in G 7:263–4, and in L.

——(1686a). *Discourse on Metaphysics*, in G 4:427–63, and in FW, AG, PM, and L.

——(1686b). 'A Specimen of Discoveries', in G 7:309–18, and in PM.

——(1690). Correspondence with Arnauld, in G 2:11–138, and in Mason, excerpts in FW, AG, PM, and L.

——(1695). 'New System of the Nature of Substances and their Communication', in G 4:477–87, and in FW, AG, PM, and L.

——(1697). 'On the Ultimate Origin of Things', in G 7:302–8, and in AG, PM, and L.

——(1699–1706). Corrrespondence with De Volder, in G 2:148–283, excerpts in L and AG.

——(1705). *New Essays on Human Understanding*, ed. P. Remnant and J. Bennett. Cambridge University Press, 1981.

——(1709–15). Correspondence with Des Bosses, in G 2:291–521, excerpts in AG and L.

——(1710). *Theodicy*, in G 6.

——(1714a). 'Monadology', in G 6:608–23, and in FW, AG, PM, and L.

——(1714b). 'Principles of Nature and Grace, Based on Reason', in G 6:598–606, and in FW, AG, PM, and L.

——(1716). Correspondence with Clarke, in G 7:352–440, and in Alexander, excerpts in AG, PM, and L.

Lewis, David (1973). *Counterfactuals*. Cambridge, Mass.: Harvard University Press.

——(1980). 'Veridical Hallucination and Prosthetic Vision', repr. in his *Philosophical Papers*, vol. 2. New York: Oxford University Press, 1986, 273–90.

Locke, John (1690). *An Essay Concerning Human Understanding*, ed. P. Nidditch. Oxford University Press, 1975.

——(1706). 'An Examination of P. Malebranche's Opinion of Seeing all Things in God', in *The Works of John Locke in Ten Volumes*. London: Johnson, 1801, 9: 211–55.

Loeb, Louis E. (1981). *From Descartes to Hume*. Ithaca, NY: Cornell University Press.

McCann, Edwin (1985). 'Lockean Mechanism', repr. in Chappell 1998: 242–60.

McCracken, Charles J. (1979). 'What Does Berkeley's God See in the Quad?' *Archiv für Geschichte der Philosophie*, 61: 280–92.

McFetridge, I. G. (1990). 'Descartes on Modality', in his *Logical Necessity and Other Essays*. London: Aristotelian Society.

MacIntosh, John J. (1976). 'Primary and Secondary Qualities'. *Studia Leibnitiana*, 8: 88–104.

MacKenzie, Nollaig (1978). 'Analysing with Subjunctives'. *Dialogue*, 17: 131–4.

Mackie, J. L. (1976). *Problems from Locke*. Oxford University Press.

Mandelbaum, Maurice (1964). 'Locke's Realism', in his *Philosophy, Science, and Sense Perception*. Baltimore: Johns Hopkins University Press, 1–60.

Martin, C. B., and Armstrong, D. M. (1968) (eds.). *Locke and Berkeley*. Garden City, NY: Doubleday.

Moore, G. E. (1903). *Principia Ethica*. Cambridge University Press.

——(1922). *Philosophical Studies*. London: Allen and Unwin.

——(1953). *Some Main Problems of Philosophy*. London: Allen and Unwin.

——(1962). *Commonplace Book*. London: Allen and Unwin.

Newman, Lex (1999). 'The Fourth Meditation'. *Philosophy and Phenomenological Research*, 59: 559–91.

Noonan, Harold (1978). 'Locke on Personal Identity'. *Philosophy*, 53: 343–51.

Olson, Eric (1997). *The Human Animal: Personal Identity without Psychology*. New York: Oxford University Press.

Parkinson, G. H. R. (1981). 'Kant as a Critic of Leibniz'. *Revue internationale de philosophie*, 136–7: 302–14.

Passmore, John (1952). *Hume's Intentions*. Cambridge University Press.

Pears, David (1990). *Hume's System*. Oxford University Press.

Peirce, Charles Sanders (1903). 'The Reality of Thirdness', in *Collected Papers of Charles Sanders Peirce*, vol. 5, ed. C. Hartshorne and P. Weiss. Cambridge, Mass.: Harvard University Press, 1934, 64–76.

Perry, John (1975). 'Personal Identity, Memory, and the Problem of Circularity', in J. Perry (ed.), *Personal Identity*. Berkeley: University of California Press, 135–55.

——(1976). 'The Importance of Being Identical', in A. O. Rorty (ed.), *The Identities of Persons*. Berkeley: University of California Press, 67–90.

Pitcher, George (1977). *Berkeley*. London: Routledge.

Price, H. H. (1935). 'Some Considerations about Belief', repr. in A. P. Griffiths (ed.), *Knowledge and Belief*. Oxford University Press, 1967, 41–59.

——(1953). *Thinking and Experience*. Cambridge, Mass.: Harvard University Press.

Putnam, Hilary (1975). 'The Meaning of "Meaning"', repr. in his *Mind, Language and Reality*. Cambridge University Press, 1975, 215–71.

Quine, W. V. (1950). 'Identity, Ostension, and Hypostasis', repr. in his *From a Logical Point of View*. Cambridge, Mass.: Harvard University Press, 1953, 65–79.

Quinton, A. M. (1963). 'Knowledge and Belief', in Edwards 1963.

Reid, Thomas (1764). *An Enquiry into the Human Mind*, reissued Indianapolis: Bobbs Merrill, ed. K. Lehrer and R. E. Beanblossom, 1975.

——(1785). 'On Mr. Locke's Account of Personal Identity', in his *Essays on the Intellectual Powers of Man*, reissued New York: Garland, 1971, 356–62.

——(1788). *Essays on the Active Powers of the Human Mind*, repr. Cambridge, Mass.: MIT Press, 1969.

Ryle, Gilbert (1933). 'John Locke on Human Understanding', repr. in Martin and Armstrong 1968: 14–39.

——(1938–9). 'Categories', repr. in A. Flew (ed.), *Logic and Language*, 2nd ser. Oxford: Blackwell, 1953, 65–81.

Savile, Anthony (1972). 'Leibniz's Contribution to the Theory of Innate Ideas'. *Philosophy*, 47: 113–24.

Shoemaker, Sydney S. (1963). *Self-Knowledge and Self-Identity*. Ithaca, NY: Cornell University Press.

——(1980). 'Causality and Properties', repr. in his *Identity, Cause and Mind: Philosophical Essays*. Cambridge University Press, 1984, 206–33.

Sleigh, Robert C., Jr. (1990). *Leibniz and Arnauld: A Commentary on their Correspondence*. New Haven: Yale University Press.

Spinoza, Benedict (1675?). *Ethics Demonstrated in Geometrical Order*, in CS 408–617.

Strawson, Galen (1989). *The Secret Connexion: Causation, Realism, and David Hume*. Oxford University Press.

Strawson, P. F. (1959). *Individuals: An Essay in Descriptive Metaphysics*. London: Methuen.

——(1985). 'Causation and Explanation', in B. Vermazen and M. B. Hintikka (eds.), *Essays on Davidson: Actions and Events*. Oxford University Press, 115–35.

Stroud, Barry (1977). *Hume*. London: Routledge.

Tipton, Ian C. (1974). *Berkeley: The Philosophy of Immaterialism*. London: Methuen.

——(1977) (ed.). *Locke on Human Understanding*. Oxford University Press.

van Inwagen, Peter (2000). 'Temporal Parts and Identity across Time'. *Monist*, 83: 437–59.

Warnock, G. J. (1953). *Berkeley*. Harmondsworth: Penguin.

White, Morton (1956). *Toward Reunion in Philosophy*. Cambridge, Mass.: Harvard University Press.

Williams, Bernard (1956). 'Personal Identity and Individuation', repr. in his *Problems of the Self*. Cambridge University Press, 1–18.

——(1972). 'Deciding to Believe', in his *Problems of the Self*. Cambridge University Press, 136–51.

Williams, Donald C. (1953). 'The Elements of Being', repr. in his *Principles of Empirical Realism*. Springfield, Ill.: C. C. Thomas, 1966, 109–74.

Wilson, Margaret D. (1978). *Descartes*. London: Routledge.

——(1992). 'History of Philosophy in Philosophy Today; and the Case of the Sensible Qualities'. *Philosophical Review*, 101: 101–243.

Winkler, Kenneth (1989). *Berkeley: An Interpretation*. Oxford University Press.

——(1991). 'Locke on Personal Identity'. *Journal of the History of Philosophy*, 29: 201–26.

Wittgenstein, Ludwig (1958). *The Blue and Brown Books*. Oxford: Blackwell.

Wolff, Robert Paul (1960). 'Hume's Theory of Mental Activity', in V. C. Chappell (ed.), *Hume: A Collection of Critical Essays*. University of Notre Dame Press, 99–128.

Yolton, John (1970). *John Locke and the Compass of Human Understanding*. Cambridge University Press.

Index of Persons

Index of Subjects